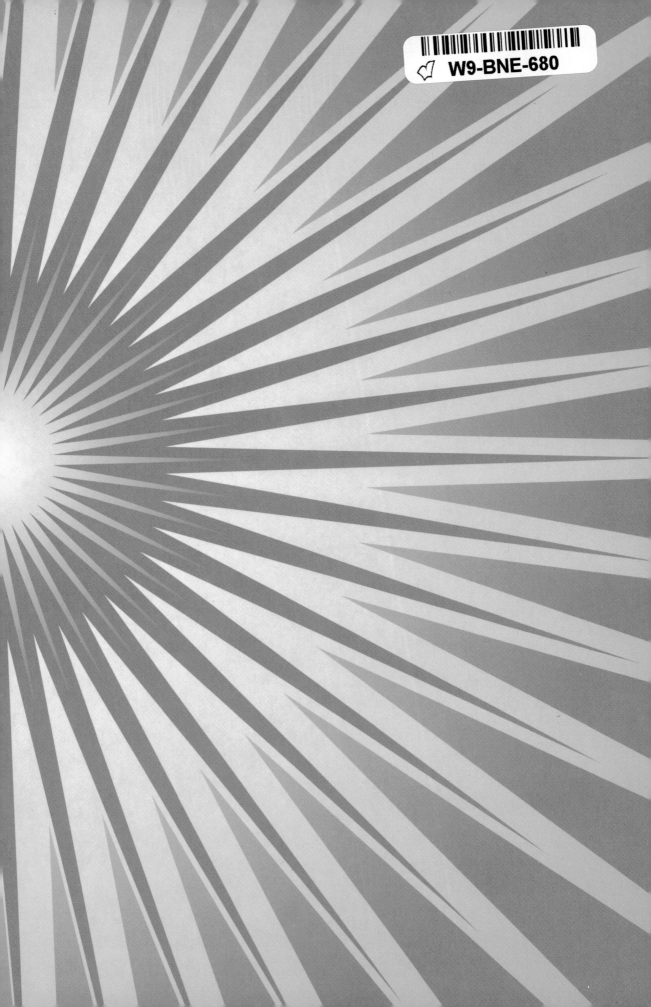

A CENTURY OF SERVICE

THE STORY OF ROTARY INTERNATIONAL

David C. Forward

ISBN 0-915062-22-4

Large front cover photo: Jean-Marc Giboux
Cover and interior design: Amanda Mansk-Perryman
Typography: ITC New Baskerville, Centaur, and Frutiger

CONTENTS

OBJECT OF ROTARY

The Object of Rotary is to encourage and foster the ideal of service as a basis of worthy enterprise and, in particular, to encourage and foster:

FIRST.
The development of acquaintance as an opportunity for service;

SECOND.
High ethical standards in business and professions; the recognition of the worthiness of all useful occupations; and the dignifying of each Rotarian's occupation as an opportunity to serve society;

THIRD.
The application of the ideal of service in each Rotarian's personal, business, and community life;

FOURTH.
The advancement of international understanding, goodwill, and peace through a world fellowship of business and professional persons united in the ideal of service.

Acknowledgments and Thanks

For the three years that I have been researching and writing this book, I have felt a growing sense of concern, and perhaps this is the best place for me to attempt to discharge those feelings. Rotarians the world over were so excited and supportive at the idea of a book that would tell the story of Rotary's first century that they literally threw open their doors to welcome me. Some, like Bill and Sandra Sturgeon in San Francisco, insisted I stay in their homes while on research trips. Others, in places like Singapore, Kuala Lumpur, and Istanbul, arranged for entire panels of longtime Rotarians to brief me on the history of Rotary in their part of the world. Nearly every living past president of Rotary International shared his time and wisdom with me.

So why should I feel concerned?

Because Rotarians would give me entire books commemorating Rotary's history in their region, and I would take pages and pages of notes of their amazing accomplishments. But I realized there was no practical way to include all those stories in the book that Rotary International had commissioned me to write. For as Past RI President Charles Keller said at the project's beginning, Rotary could be compared to a river. Although the tributaries that feed the river are themselves interesting, it would require thousands of pages to tell the story of all the tributaries as well as the river itself. This is, after all, a book about the river, not about each contributing stream. It would take an encyclopedia, not a single book, to accomplish that. So please understand, dear Rotarians, why your club, city, or favorite service project may not be covered in great detail—or perhaps at all—in the pages to follow.

The first person I talked to with reference to this book project five years ago was Willmon L. White, former editor in chief of THE ROTARIAN magazine, who established the first formal archives of RI in 1998. Less than halfway through the three-year process of writing the book, Will retired from RI after 30 years of service to the organization. Yet he continued to serve as a volunteer and my most valued adviser until the last word was typed. Will was a mighty fortress of knowledge, a free-flowing river of ideas, and his experience and contacts in Rotary were so extensive that there was no door he could not open. I would write each chapter and submit it to him only after considering it exactly right. Then he would make a suggestion here, an editorial comment there, a point of historical interest I had not uncovered somewhere else—and only then did I realize that now the chapter was good enough. If you find this book readable and interesting, it is Will White who deserves the credit, and I am lost for words as to how I can adequately thank him for his expertise and friendship.

Six months into the research, Cynthia M. Beck joined RI's newly established archives department. From that moment on, she was my right arm. Cyndi's professional expertise and abiding love for her work made it easier to research long-hidden facts, and the historical accuracy of this book is a tribute to her can-do attitude.

In January 2001, after nearly 27 years of service on THE ROTARIAN, Charles Pratt retired as editor and manager of the RI Communications Division, having decided to become a high school English teacher. That October, Charles agreed to edit the finished book manuscript as a special assignment. I appreciate his professional eye and his ability to recognize what could be cut and what should be emphasized.

There were many other staffers at RI World Headquarters—such as Cary Silver, executive editor of THE ROTARIAN, and Vince Aversano, Communications Division manager—who could not do enough to help. Never once did they say "I'm too busy" or "You're being a pest!" as any normal person would have responded. Beyond Evanston were the staff in Zurich, Switzerland, and RIBI Headquarters in Alcester, England, who opened their archives to me.

The Centennial History of Rotary Book Committee, appointed in 1997 by RI President Luis Vicente Giay, was composed of 18 members from around the world, and they too were helpful and constructive in their comments on the evolving manuscript. They were Past RI President Charles C. Keller (California, Pennsylvania, USA), Willmon L. White (Evanston, Illinois, USA), Mario de Oliveira Antonino (Recife, Brazil), Asbjorn Austvik (Trondheim, Norway), Richard E. Burnett (Kansas City, Missouri, USA), Jamil Dunia (Antimano, Venezuela), José Maria Ferrer (Rosario, Argentina), H. Paul Henningham (Glenbrook, New South Wales, Australia), Harry D. Hester (Birmingham, Alabama, USA), Tario Kanno (Miyagi, Japan), Umberto Laffi (Pisa, Italy), Jo Nugent (Spearfish, South Dakota, USA), Herbert A. Pigman (Boswell, Indiana, USA), Geoffrey H. Pike (Swanage, Dorset, England), Sabino S. Santos (Bulacan, Philippines), M.K. Panduranga Setty (Bangalore, India), C.P. Jorge Villanueva R. (Mexico City, Mexico), and Jean Ann Ziegler (Plano, Texas, USA). I also owe thanks to all liaison members of the RI Board of Directors and The Rotary Foundation Trustees who worked with the committee over the years.

I must single out for special thanks the committee's chairman, Charles Keller. Chuck is an experienced and dedicated Rotarian with a passion for both Rotary and the written word. His insights and suggestions made every chapter stronger. I began this endeavor knowing Chuck as simply a past RI president; I finished it thinking of him as a mentor and friend.

And finally, with the forbearance of those of you who did not acquire this book to read about the author, I ask you to let me thank some people who have helped shape my life to one of service to mankind through Rotary. To my beloved wife, Chris, and son, David, who endured my absences while traveling for three years to research and write the book: "Thank you" is simply not enough! And I dedicate this book to Ernie Bareuther, the first person to invite me into Rotary, back in 1978, to past district governors Don Yeager and Harold Smick, who showed me the difference between being a member of a Rotary club and being a Rotarian, and to my fellow members of the Rotary Club of Marlton, New Jersey, who keep the home fires of service burning in our community and make Tuesday evenings a real joy. To these and all the people I simply did not have space to mention by name—THANK YOU, and may we forever travel together on the path to peace and service that we call Rotary.

David C. Forward
Medford, New Jersey, USA

Introduction

Even the world's mightiest rivers have humble beginnings. They start as tiny springs, bubbling to the surface, or as a single, melting snowdrop. As the rivulet trickles down, it brings new life to everything it touches. Soon, other tiny streams join its path and together they unite as a river, ever more confident and forceful.

One hundred years ago, the river called Rotary was born. A lonely lawyer named Paul P. Harris called together three business associates for an evening meeting. They shared similar backgrounds and missed the friendliness and trustworthiness of dealing with people they knew. Compared to the small communities of their boyhood, the frantic pace of life in America's second-largest city was depressing and lonesome. That night, they decided to form a club where they could meet and deal with one another in friendship and trust. It was the spring that started a mighty river.

The United States had many clubs in 1905. There were trade and labor groups as well as associations of people who shared common ethnic backgrounds, religious beliefs, and political persuasions. But Paul Harris, Silvester Schiele, Gustavus Loehr, and Hiram Shorey wanted their new Rotary club to be unlike any other. Instead of having numerous lawyers or bankers or accountants, they wanted only one man to represent each profession. They soon attracted other members, people from diverse backgrounds who found respite from the strains of big city business at the meetings where fellowship and jocularity took them back to their boyhood days.

One of the early objectives was for members to exchange business with each other. But just as streams sometimes change direction, so did the Rotary club, and it did so by discovering the joys of service. Soon, service—to their community, their customers, their employees, children—gathered such momentum that Rotary became known as the first "service club." The Rotary Club of Chicago grew to 200 members in three years, and many of them were so proud of what they had created that they wrote to friends in other cities and invited business associates to the meetings when they visited Chicago.

When Chicago Rotarian Manuel Muñoz told Paul he planned to visit San Francisco in 1908, Paul asked him to tell businessmen there about Rotary. On the day after he arrived, Muñoz met a young lawyer named Homer Wood; and Wood was so interested in Muñoz's story that he immediately wrote to Paul Harris for details on how he could start a San Francisco club. Within weeks, Rotary had its second club. But Wood went beyond the confines of his adopted city, traveling to Oakland to persuade his friends to start a club there. His fellow San Francisco charter member Arthur Holman did the same in Seattle, and then Holman and Wood took the word to Los Angeles; within two years there were Rotary clubs from coast to coast and from the northern to the southern borders. The movement spread to Canada and Ireland, England and Scotland, and soon Rotary clubs were being formed around the world.

The following chapters will tell the story of how these small streams contributed to the journey of the mighty Rotary River. They will trace the evolution of the organization from an American institution with foreign outposts to a truly global movement. You will learn the origin of many of the practices and procedures that today's Rotarian takes for granted. This book is both a word picture of the founder of Rotary and an introduction to some of the unsung heroes who have contributed to the river's flow. For as with many famous waterways, whose names are universally recognized, the tributaries that feed them often go unknown.

Some of those men and women are small rivers in their own right; others were but a few raindrops. They contributed their time, talents, and thoughts not for personal recognition or financial gain, but because they became swept up in the torrent of service, Service Above Self. As Mother Teresa wrote in *Words to Love By:* "The whole work is only a drop in the ocean. But if I didn't put the drop in, the ocean would be one drop less."[1]

Rotary had barely been established in Europe when "the war to end all wars" broke out in 1914. Further challenges to the organization's very existence came along in the Great Depression of the early 1930s and the Second World War a decade later. Yet the Rotary River flowed on, and the narrative will tell uplifting stories of how individual Rotarians tried to calm those troubled waters by applying the principles of service.

During the worst days of World War II, Rotarians in England convened a conference on education and cultural exchange, and that meeting subsequently led to the formation of UNESCO, one of the agencies of the United Nations. When the UN charter was signed, Rotarians were serving as ambassadors and ministers, captains of industry, and religious leaders of all faiths. The Rotary organization that the UN invited to observe and consult on matters of world peace in 1948 was far stronger and more influential than that first meeting back in 1905.

Yet some characteristics continued to be the organization's hallmark. Tolerance, high ethical standards, fellowship among members, commitment to community service—especially toward children—and world peace have engaged the time and efforts of Rotary volunteers since the first club was founded. And they continue to do so today.

As Rotary attracted members from many countries, those people of differing ethnicities, cultures, and faiths came together at conventions and conferences to discover they shared many common interests. As they broke bread together in gatherings far from home, they shared their dreams for a peaceful world, ethical business practices, safe and healthy environments for

INTRODUCTION

---

1   Mother Teresa, *Words to Love By* (Notre Dame, Indiana: Ave Maria Press, 1983), 79.

their families, service to their communities—with Rotary providing the bond to help them realize those dreams.

So Rotarians, realizing that even greater needs often existed beyond their own communities, added international service to their commitment to club, community, and vocational service. Soon, clubs in Rhodesia were sending African students on university scholarships to Canada, Norwegian Rotarians were digging wells to provide safe drinking water for villages in India, and clubs in Japan and Peru were sponsoring cultural exchanges. Within hours of natural disasters, Rotary clubs around the world responded with financial help, donated supplies, and sent teams of volunteers.

This book cannot possibly tell of every contribution that clubs, or even countries, have made and does not pretend to be a compendium of projects. As Rotary, the pioneer of all service organizations, celebrates its centennial, it has over 1.2 million men and women members in more than 31,000 clubs in over 165 countries around the globe. They comprise a dedicated army of humanitarian volunteers the likes of which the world has never seen, often accomplishing beneficial deeds that otherwise might never have been done. It is a force for world peace and arguably the most effective nongovernmental agency ever to bring relief from human suffering and eradicate disease on a global scale. The following pages tell the stories that prove how one person can make a difference in the world. It is a story that could be told and retold thousands of times each year for 100 years.

Paul Harris deserves the credit for the original idea, but without Manuel Muñoz and Homer Wood, would this have been a one-club story? Without Chesley R. Perry there would probably be no Rotary International today, for he picked up the mantle just as Paul Harris fell into poor health and managed the association for 32 years. The book will show how Rotarians with vision and determination can accomplish great things. It will tell of compassionate Rotarians whose love for crippled children led to the formation of the Easter Seals Society, and of adventurous Rotarians who explored both poles and the limits of outer space, then returned to serve as ordinary members of their local clubs. The book tells of brave Rotarians in France, Germany, Holland, China, and Japan who courageously continued their pursuit of Rotary's ideals even when their lives were at risk—and sometimes sacrificed. It will take you behind the scenes of the PolioPlus Campaign and show the phenomenal organizational effort that resulted in "Rotary's finest hour," in which Rotarians raised more than US$219 million toward the goal of the total eradication of polio from every country on earth.

People have admired and paid tribute to Rotary since its inception, although it was customary for members to do their good deeds while shunning publicity. Because of its work, many kings, princes, and political leaders have chosen to be patrons—and in some countries, members—of Rotary. That is an honor and confers an element of prestige on the organization. But Rotary has never been about princes and potentates. It has always been about making our community—the local and global village in which we live—a better place through honorable action and voluntary service.

Rotary has sometimes been a lightning rod in society, attracting the barbs and derision of social commentators. Although the positive values and unrelenting optimism of Rotarians often rankle professional naysayers, Rotarians go about their business of doing good in the world, undeterred by uninformed criticism or ridicule, for they do not perform their service activities for public adulation. Ultimately, even those who poke fun at Rotary, in the tradition of such celebrated critics as Sinclair Lewis, H.L. Mencken, Clarence Darrow, and George Bernard Shaw, eventually recognize Rotary's contribution to the community.

The following pages will show the birth and evolution of the Rotary idea and, since it has been said that the whole idea of citizen volunteerism was born in Rotary, examine such questions as what has made the idea work (and be successfully emulated in subsequent service organizations such as Kiwanis and Lions) and why the idea is important in today's world.

This book will help you know more about some of the people whose names you have heard before, yet it is dedicated to those whose names do not appear. It will demonstrate how time and again Rotary has given well-intentioned individuals the forum to do things that no person could have accomplished alone. The pages introduce you to those people who meet each week at the local Rotary meeting and discover why they feel compelled to give so generously and enthusiastically of their time. They will take you into inner city job training centers and remote villages for polio immunization days—all to see the Rotary service ideal in action. This book will tell of lives saved, lives changed, and life given by small groups of Rotarians who still come together as Paul Harris convened that first meeting in 1905.

The Rotary River is wide and runs deep. No one can know where its journey will take it, but all who gaze on these waters can be proud of its source. It grows ever stronger because it offers men and women something they yearn for: the desire to help others, the determination to make a difference.

CHAPTER I

THE MAN BEHIND THE MOVEMENT

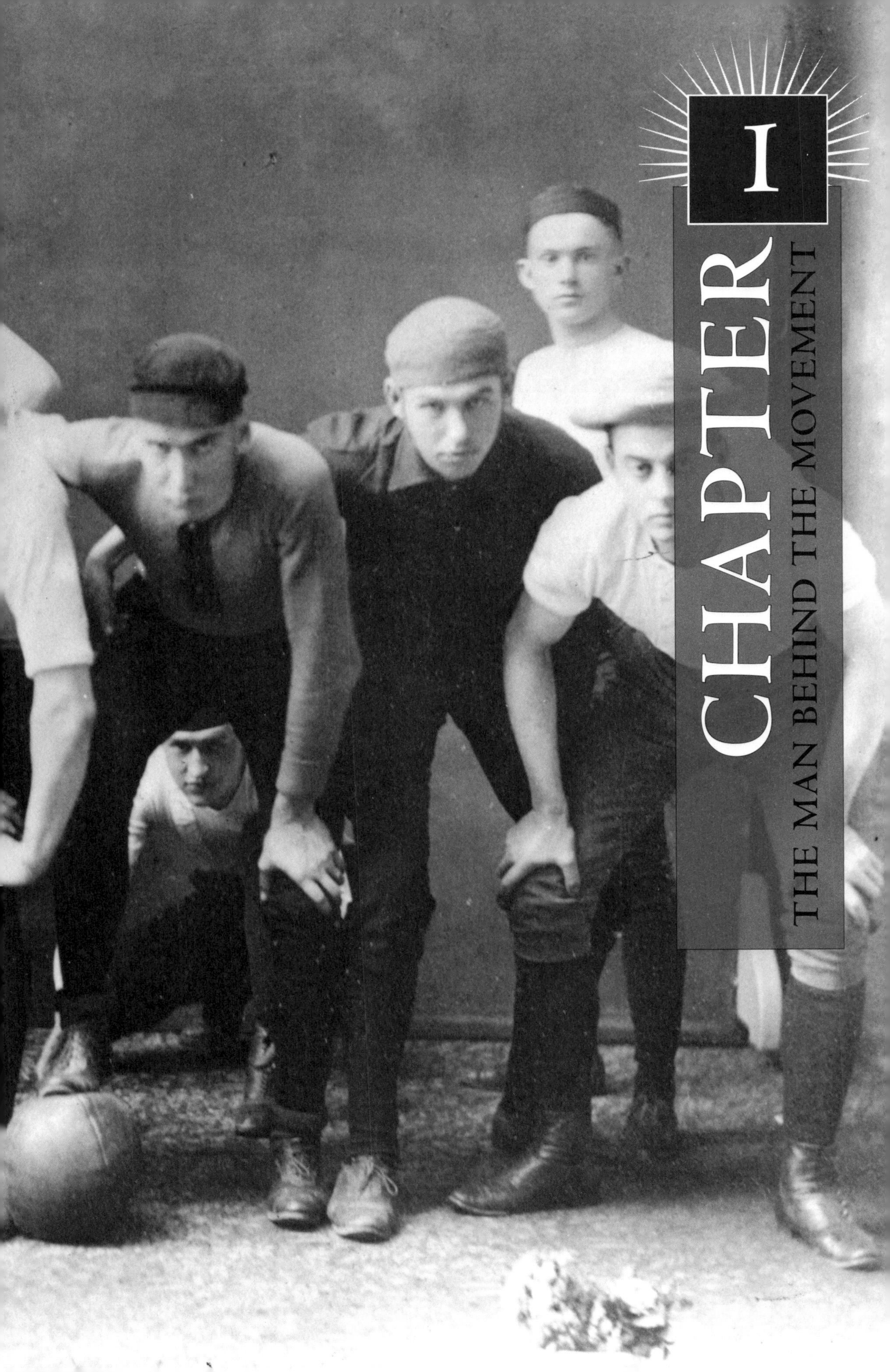

Chapter 1 – The Man behind the Movement

The terse telegram message Western Union delivered to Rotary district and international officers caused business and professional men around the world to pause in their busy activities:

PAUL HARRIS DIED TODAY STOP AM NOTIFYING ALL GOVERNORS AND REGIONAL OFFICERS OF DEATH AND PAUL'S SPECIFIC REQUEST TO OMIT FLOWERS AND INSTEAD MAKE CONTRIBUTIONS TO ROTARY FOUNDATION FOR PAUL HARRIS MEMORIAL STOP FUNERAL THURSDAY STOP
PHIL LOVEJOY.

The announcement of Rotary's founder's death, like the life he lived, emphasized not the individual but his desire to make a difference. The date was 27 January 1947, and the frail 78-year-old Paul Harris had slipped away peacefully at Comely Bank, his beloved home in south Chicago, after a lengthy illness. He left behind his wife, brother, a host of friends, and Rotarians in 6,000 clubs around the world.

The mourners who filled the Morgan Park Congregational Church on 30 January 1947 were sad indeed. They had lost their leader, Paul P. Harris, the founder of the organization now known as Rotary International.

"But Paul Harris is not dead," 1945-46 Rotary International President Tom A. Warren of England told the congregation. "His spirit lives on. It abides everywhere. It is woven into the very fiber of men's lives. As we take leave of his mortal self, we rededicate ourselves to the never-ending task he has inspired and bequeathed to those who will assuredly follow his paths down the years to come."

Panoramic view of Wallingford, Vermont, USA

Overleaf: The 1889 freshman football team of the University of Vermont. Paul Harris, foot planted firmly on the ball, is fourth from the right.

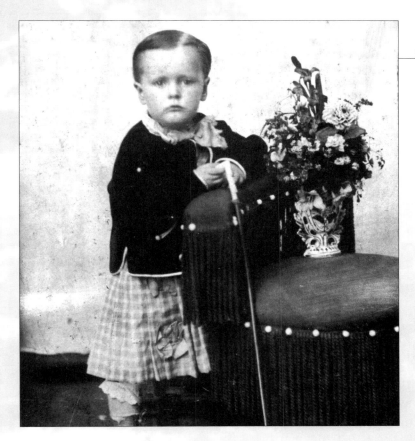

And follow him they did. The mourners filed out into the bitter Chicago afternoon, following the casket, which was borne by the president and all past presidents of the Rotary Club of Chicago. Through the swirling snowstorm they walked, every Rotary International president and all directors who had been able to get to Chicago in time. At Mt. Hope Cemetery, two miles from the church, they offered words of comfort to his widow, Jean, and then solemnly watched as the Rev. Hugh S. MacKenzie ordered the body lowered into a simple gravesite. Paul's final resting place was close by that of Silvester Schiele, his dearest friend of 45 years—the man who had been the first president of the first Rotary club.

Twelve days later, half a world away, 300 people braved bad weather, petrol rationing, and an electricity blackout to attend a memorial service for Paul Harris in London's St. Paul's Cathedral. Similar religious and secular services and newspaper and radio tributes were made around the world.

Yet like many other great apostles of peace—Mohandas K. Gandhi, Martin Luther King Jr., Mother Teresa, Nelson Mandela—Paul P. Harris was not a person of wealthy, aristocratic roots, but of humble and meager beginnings. Paul's mother, Cornelia Bryan, was born in Racine, Wisconsin, and grew up in a comfortable middle-class family. Her father, a lawyer, was the city's second mayor. Cornelia married George H. Harris in 1864 in a double

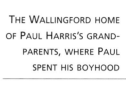

wedding with her sister. The couple soon had their first child, Cecil, followed on 19 April 1868 by a second, whom they named Paul Percy Harris.

But this was not a perfect family. George was a gregarious type whose financial planning and business acumen fell far short of his ideas and dreams. He had drifted from job to job, finally settling in to run a Racine drug store, which his thrifty Vermont father had paid for. The young family was under tremendous pressure. Cornelia's family was well-known and respected. George, a stranger in their midst, must have felt the strain of needing to provide for his family in his wife's hometown while going home each night having seen his business slip a little lower. "The affairs of my father's family were always at boiling point," Paul later recalled.

After George's father refused any further bailouts, the business failed. In 1871, unable to provide for his family any longer, George took five-year-old Cecil and three-year-old Paul on the long train journey back to his home village of Wallingford, Vermont (population 2,052), leaving Cornelia and their infant daughter, Nina May, in Racine.

One of Paul's most vivid memories was of that cold night when he stepped off the train at Wallingford and met his paternal grandparents for the first time. Of grandfather Howard, Paul wrote: "The tall man took my clenched fist in his warm, strong hand, which was ever so much larger than father's, with enormous thumbs which made excellent handles for little boys to hold on to." After walking the short distance from the railway station in near silence, the foursome arrived at the Harris home, and there the two children first saw their grandmother, Pamela Harris, "a dark-eyed elderly lady, who weighed precisely 89 pounds, never more, never less."

George Harris stayed in Wallingford for a while and then moved on, but for the rest of his childhood, Paul called Wallingford home. It was an education that proved to him that life is not measured by what you have but what you are inside, that integrity, frugality, tolerance, and friendship are core values.

Of his grandmother, Paul later wrote: "It is said that fine goods come wrapped in small packages, and grandmother was certainly fine goods." In her home he found wholesomeness, orderliness, cleanliness, kindliness, and thoughtfulness.

Grandfather Howard Harris taught Paul the work ethic and the need for tolerance. Paul described the older man as an ambassador of goodwill who "never spoke evil of any man's religion or politics." He saw how his grandfather worked six days a week, 52 weeks a year, to provide for the household. He noticed how he wore the same work clothes, repairing them when necessary, instead of buying new ones. Although others in the village referred to the sole Jewish and Roman Catholic residents as if they were oddities, Howard Harris treated them with the same friendship and respect that he showed all people. The boy learned from his grandmother, too. She was the one into whose loving arms he could run when he was scared. She was a wonderful listener, a faithful churchgoer, and always the first to prepare hot meals or baked goods for a sick or needy neighbor, which Paul would gladly deliver.

Paul Harris reminisced throughout his life about "my New England Valley," and there was very little of it he did not explore in his boyhood years. He disappeared for hours at a time, hiking to the top of a mountain, following a river's meandering course, or fishing in its clear, cool ponds. He made many friends in the village, and all shared a deep love for the outdoors.

Yet the fine lessons of his grandparents did not deter him from being a boy. He developed—and proudly protected—a reputation for pranks and practical jokes. He once arrived at church early, placing bent pins on the pews. Then he and his cohorts sat in the back row and watched the people plop their posteriors onto the hard pews, only to shoot skyward with anguished looks on their faces. His grandmother believed all the sins of the universe were committed at night, and in keeping with their simple farm lifestyle, she strictly enforced Paul's nine o'clock bedtime. However, he later admitted, just because he was in bed at nine o'clock did not necessarily mean he was still in bed at ten o'clock! On one occasion, he and his friends—they called themselves the Rapscallions—escaped after bedtime and met at the railway station where they waited for the late-night train to Manchester. They climbed aboard the steel cowcatcher in front of the engine

PAUL HARRIS IN 1891, A RECENT GRADUATE OF THE UNIVERSITY OF IOWA'S LAW SCHOOL

and, risking certain death if they fell (or encountered a cow on the tracks), had a thrill ride to Manchester and back.

Grandfather Harris could hardly have been more different. He was a man with little patience for foolishness and pranks. Yet he had great hopes for Paul. "One day," Paul overheard him tell a kitchen worker, "that boy will make his mark in the world." Perhaps all the hope he had invested in grandson Paul helped compensate for the deep disappointment he felt over his own son's failings.

The records suggest that Paul's parents did not live together as a family in the ensuing years. George Harris reappeared from time to time, often taking his sons on long walks and berry-picking expeditions. Sometimes they went fishing for trout—one of Paul's favorite activities. But the encounters were too brief and rare to establish much of a paternal bond.

A three-year-old's memories quickly fade, and so must have Paul's recollections of his mother. There is no mention in his own writings of any letters

PAUL HARRIS AS A CADET AT THE
VERMONT MILITARY ACADEMY

or contact between Racine and Wallingford. Then one day he noticed "the most beautiful lady I had ever seen" walking with a little girl up Wallingford's Main Street a few minutes after the train had arrived. She noticed him immediately and asked, "Are you little Paul Harris?" It was his mother and sister, arriving for a surprise visit and attempted reconciliation.

George and Cornelia did reunite and moved with Cecil, Paul, and Nina May to Fair Haven, about 25 miles from Wallingford. George tried his best to be a good provider for the family, working briefly in various jobs. His mother gave piano lessons in people's homes, so both parents were absent from their own children much of the time. After a few months of diminishing income and increasing marital tension, the family broke up for the last time. Paul and Cecil returned to Wallingford and the comfort, happiness, and solid predictability of life with their grandparents.

The whole family never lived together again. Three more sons came along: Guy, who died at the age of 11; Claude, who died in service to his country in the Philippines at the turn of the century; and Reginald, who outlived Paul. Both parents spent their final years in Denver, Colorado, and despite Paul's embarrassment and frustration with his father's shortcomings, his actions expiated all those earlier failings. "Mother was sadly broken, totally blind and helpless and then came the transformation of your life," he wrote to his father. "You waited on mother so tenderly all of those latter years, lifting her from her bed and placing her in her wheelchair. I remember so well

Paul Harris is buried in Mt. Hope Cemetery on the South Side of Chicago in the Morgan Park community. His headstone is beside that of Silvester Schiele, his close friend, one of the first four Rotarians and the first president of the Rotary Club of Chicago. Twenty-seven months after Paul's burial, in April 1949, his casket was dug up and moved from one side of his tombstone to the other. The reason is not known.

how patiently you fed her with a spoon, how you hung on her every word and became her abject slave." Cornelia Harris passed away in her Denver home on 22 July 1919; George died in 1926. Both are buried in Mt. Greenwood Cemetery on Chicago's South Side.

Having seen his only son fail to succeed in his business and family life, Howard Harris was determined not to let Paul follow the same path. He saw education as the key to a good career, yet school was, to his teenage grandson, an annoyance that interfered with fishing and other boyhood pleasures. Paul was, at best, an average student academically. He would have been stunned to know that one day the Wallingford Schoolhouse would be dedicated in his name.

As Howard Harris grew older, he felt an abiding duty to provide Paul with a good education. He realized that the child's own parents were incapable of preparing him for the world, that it was up to him to provide Paul with the skills needed to build a successful career. He sent the teenaged Paul to Black River Academy in Ludlow, Vermont, but he soon discovered that Paul's penchant for pranks was not welcomed there. Within weeks, "the President of the Academy took an inventory of the good and the bad in me, and concluded that there was insufficient of the good to justify any attempt at salvage," Paul wrote in 1925. And so, to the obvious despair of his grandparents, he was expelled.

They sent Paul to another private school, Vermont Military Academy, and this time he did well in both his studies and his behavior. He earned admission to the University of Vermont in 1886, but 18 months later was wrongly accused of misconduct and was expelled. Many years later, the university apologized, absolved him, and conferred a B.A. in physical culture, in 1919, and an honorary Ph.D., in 1933. Paul was admitted to prestigious Princeton University in New Jersey and, despite being far from his friends and beloved Vermont valley, enjoyed the university and did well academically.

Then, one winter day in 1889, he received a telegram from his Uncle George, a doctor in Rutland, Vermont, which read: COME HOME AT ONCE IF YOU WANT TO SEE GRANDPA ALIVE. Paul rushed to the station and took the first train north, but he was too late. The only positive male role model in his life had not made it through the night. It was Paul whom his grandmother asked to sit beside her at the funeral, and it was Paul who felt the need, after returning to Princeton, to complete the year and then go back to be with her in Wallingford. His life suddenly had no direction. He took a menial job sweeping floors and cleaning furnaces at Sheldon Marble Company in nearby Rutland, and the work ethic he had inherited from his grandfather caused his boss to quickly promote him to more important duties. It was a year for mourning, reminiscing, and thinking about his future.

He remembered the times he had sat at the dinner table while Howard talked effusively about a local attorney called Lawyer Lawrence. Lawrence had been nominated for judge, and although politics were rarely discussed in the Harris home, Howard—who had never used an attorney in his life—said he knew all he needed to know about Lawyer Lawrence: He had integrity, was always interested in justice, and had the respect of judges and juries wherever he appeared. Long before Paul made a conscious career choice, that conversation suggested to him that the law would be a worthy profession.

One day after Paul returned from Sheldon Marble Company, his grandmother, now frail and elderly, asked him to come sit with her. She reminisced about the 60 years she had been married to Howard and the three children they had lost. Then the subject changed to Paul, whom she had raised from a frightened toddler to a tall, handsome teenager. "Paul, I wonder at times if you realize how much you meant to Pa," she said. "At times, it used to seem to him that his life had been a failure. He had high hopes for your father. He spent money freely for his education, and his disappointment almost broke his heart. And then you came to us quite providentially, and Pa fastened all his hopes on you. Paul, you must not fail him. Work hard and live honorably for your grandfather's sake."

If ever Paul Harris heard a motivational speech, this was it. His grandmother urged him to pursue his dream of studying law. Thirteen months later, his beloved grandmother passed away quietly in her sleep.

Paul chose to start law school in 1889 at the University of Iowa in Des Moines, and to reach that city he had to change trains in Chicago. He was so mesmerized by the huge, bustling city that he spent a week there. Chicago was still very much a frontier town. Muddy streets carried fancy carriages with elegantly dressed ladies on the way to shopping emporiums; open carts moved construction materials to the building boom that was underway since the great Chicago Fire. That cataclysmic 1871 event had destroyed four square miles of the city, including the central business district, leaving 90,000 residents homeless. With office space in such short supply, land values had skyrocketed. Since it was too expensive to build in the traditional—horizontal—dimension, Chicago architect William L. Jenney had in 1884 erected the world's first skyscraper on the corner of La Salle and Adams streets. It was an idea others quickly copied, and soon Jenney's 12-story Home Insurance Building was surpassed by ever higher structures. In 1893, the 16-story Monadnock Building became the world's tallest office building with load-bearing walls.

The young man turned one way and saw windows filled with imported goods, then turned the other to hear barkers yelling invitations to the bars and brothels on every street. It was a melting pot of immigrants with rich, exotic accents from around the world. It was, to this sheltered youth, like one big circus, a veritable adventure, which he was now free to explore at will.

After his Chicago stopover, he continued to Iowa where for the first year he read law at the University of Iowa and clerked for the law firm of St. John, Stevenson, and Whisenand in Des Moines. He then transferred to the Iowa City campus where he earned his law degree in June 1891. He had been a good, but not outstanding, student, saying years later that the greatest benefit he derived from his educational experiences was the contact he had with other students. He would call on those acquaintances time and again later in life as he sought to spread Rotary.

Paul Harris heard a keynote speaker who lectured the graduating class. The speaker, an accomplished lawyer who had graduated from the university a decade earlier, urged each young lawyer-to-be not to rush out and hitch up with a big law firm right away but to first go into a small town and make a fool of himself for five years, after which he could settle down in the city, find the practice of his choice, and forge a career. The esteemed lecturer was telling them all to go out and have fun! There was only one change in Paul's own plan: Instead of living in another small town, he would embark on a world-class adventure. Thus began one of the most exciting, and transforming, periods of Paul Harris's life.

THE SCHOOL PAUL HARRIS ATTENDED IN WALLINGFORD HAS NOW BEEN CONVERTED INTO THE PAUL HARRIS MEMORIAL. PAUL'S GRANDFATHER BUILT THE SCHOOL.

Setting off to discover the world, Paul followed the trail of American explorers on a hunting and fishing foray to the northwestern United States. His money soon ran out, so he headed for San Francisco and got a job as a newspaper reporter for the *Chronicle*. When his pockets were full again, he set out across California's verdant farm country, picking fruit as a day laborer. In Los Angeles, he held a teaching post at Los Angeles Business College; nine months later, he moved to Colorado, working first as an actor at the Old Fifteenth Street Theater, then again as a newspaper reporter, and next as a cowboy on the range.

Tiring of mountain country, he made his way to Jacksonville, Florida, where he found work as a night clerk in the Hotel St. James. It was there that he met George W. Clark, a marble and granite dealer, and the two became close friends. Clark soon persuaded Harris—who had previous experience with Sheldon Marble Company in Vermont—to work for him as a salesman. But despite the friendship, Paul wanted to continue on his grand adventure; he wanted no ties. On he moved to Washington, D.C., Kentucky, Pennsylvania, doing whatever jobs came his way for the sheer experience of discovering people and places and the purpose in life.

While in Philadelphia, he saw a newspaper advertisement seeking crewmen for a cattle boat about to sail for England. England! The land of his childhood dreams! The home of Dickens and Shakespeare. He applied to the shipping company, and before dawn the next day he was hired and underway.

It was a dreadful experience. The ship was filthy, the seas rough. Sanitary conditions and food were no better for the crew than for the cattle. Worse yet, when the ship arrived in Liverpool 14 days later, Paul had but a few hours ashore in the grimy docklands before having to set sail for the return voyage. Yet despite the conditions—the boat had no mattresses or eating utensils—Paul saw the experience as part of his adventure. "Travel is a good corrective for mental near-sightedness—if the traveler sets aside his prejudices," he wrote. "People will see what they want to look for, the ugly or the beautiful. If they seek things to condemn, they will find them in plenty and return home more prejudiced and arrogant than ever."

No sooner had he returned home than he searched for another ship. He soon found one with much better conditions and which was destined for London. He finally got to see the British capital, and the few days he spent there were some of the happiest of his life.

The day Paul Harris arrived back in the United States in 1893, he immediately took a train to Chicago to see the World's Fair. The Windy City had outbid all other cities for the honor of hosting the World's Columbian Exposition, which celebrated the 400th anniversary (albeit off by a year) of Christopher Columbus's arrival in the Americas. Much had changed since Paul's first visit to the city, and there was an added excitement and civic pride for a town brimming with tourists from every state and many foreign countries. Posters advertising the exposition were even placed in railway stations across Europe, and visitors—a total of 27 million people attended between May and September—were fascinated by the latest inventions such as moving sidewalks, the world's first elevated electric railway, the Ferris wheel, and exhibits or pavilions from 52 countries. It was during this brief visit that he decided Chicago would be the place for him to launch his law career once his vagabond years ended.

Then he was off again, first to New Orleans, which he described as America's most fascinating city. He worked for a while picking oranges in Plaquemine Parish and was in the fields on 1 October 1893 when a sudden storm hit the region. At seven o'clock a tidal wave struck the low-lying plantation, destroying buildings and sweeping away people. Paul and his crew carried several women and children through rising snake-infested waters to safety. When daybreak came, authorities said this "storm of the century" had claimed 1,200 to 1,500 lives. "Although years have elapsed," he wrote decades later, "the suffering and horror of that night still remain in my memory."

He was halfway through his five-year adventure and realized it was time to start saving money in preparation for his move to Chicago. Paul returned to Jacksonville where his friend George Clark welcomed him with a job selling marble and granite. It was the perfect position for Paul: He enjoyed the friendship of his employer and mentor, the money was good, and the job involved considerable travel. He covered the southern states, the Bahamas, and Cuba. A year later, mindful of Paul's memories of, and affection for, London, Clark sent Paul on a long buying trip that extended from Scotland to Italy. For two and a half years, their relationship continued to deepen.

George was so pleased with the revenue Paul had brought his firm that he offered him a partnership. But Paul had already given notice that his five years were up. It was time to go. George pleaded with him to stay, promising him he would earn far more money if they continued to work together, but Paul replied, "I am not going to Chicago for the purpose of making money; I am going for the purpose of making a life." After doing George a final favor of moving to New York to resolve some problems in his office there, Paul P. Harris, now almost 28 years old, headed for Chicago on 27 February 1896.

In his five vagabond years he had known what it felt like to be hungry, cold, and alone. He had learned to survive based only on his own resources. He had needed to use his sense of humor, his intellect, and his raw hands to get by. He had seen strangers perform extraordinary acts of human kindness and others cheat and steal to gain the upper hand. In the midst of evil he had found goodness; he had learned that one gets no more out of life than one puts in. He had gained vision and a better understanding of his fellow man. He now saw the world as a place of many cultures, a place that needed more understanding, not to be viewed from the isolationist's perch. It had been quite a ride, but now it was time to get serious.

On the morning he arrived, the *Chicago Tribune* was responding to the *New York Sun*'s attacks on the city's rampant political corruption. The London Lyceum Company, starring Henry Irving and Miss Helen Terry, was at the Columbia Theater; there was "continuous vaudeville at the Olympic, with seats at 10, 20, and 30 cents," and the Hub Store was advertising spring overcoats at US$5, $6.25, and $8.

PAUL HARRIS, AGE 28, AROUND
THE TIME HE STARTED PRACTICING
LAW IN CHICAGO

Paul rented a small office near Lake and Dearborn streets and obtained his license to practice law in Illinois. He soon found that being a lawyer and earning a living at it were not necessarily synonymous. As he later put it himself, "To hang up my shingle was a simple matter, and while I had not expected it to attract many, on the other hand I had not thought it would be completely ignored." Chicago had plunged into a recession following the overbuilding that led up to the World's Fair and the exodus of business that followed its closing. It still had a pioneer-town mentality, with "survival of the fittest" and caveat emptor the rules of the day. There were few consumer protection regulations, and Paul gradually built up a practice representing victims of fraud, bankruptcy, and embezzlement. This laissez-faire business attitude probably contributed to his campaign for ethical conduct a few years later.

Paul was active in the Chicago Association of Commerce and the bar association and took on a number of different partners. One of them was Fred Reinhardt, who said of his 28-year association with Paul Harris: "Never in those many years was there ever a word spoken in anger to anyone in our office family." Harris made known his belief that no person had the right to practice law unless he was prepared to give conscientious preparation to every case he accepted. He was a very patient but also a most exacting senior partner.

Yet while he was successful in developing his professional life, he found the big city a barren place in which to find many personal friends. He saw people obsessed with greed, selfishness, and competition. He felt increasingly isolated, desperately lonely, a village boy dropped in the midst of an impersonal metropolis. He frequented Chicago's Bohemian eateries, dining each night in a different ethnic restaurant. In his inquiring way, this allowed him to escape from the Chicago rat race and learn more about the cultures of India, Hungary, Italy, Germany, Greece, and China. His favorite dining room was Madame Galli's Italian Restaurant on Illinois Street. Madame Galli's was not the favorite of Paul Harris alone; it was also a choice of world-famous tenor Enrico Caruso. One night, the proprietor had told the famous star, "Signore, I would give the whole world if I could sing like you." To which Caruso replied, "Madame, I would give the whole world if I could cook spaghetti like you."

On Sundays Paul would attend church—any church, since he felt no allegiance toward any one faith or denomination. One week he worshiped in a Presbyterian church, the next in a Jewish synagogue, then a Quaker meeting hall and a Muslim mosque. It was typical behavior for the Paul Harris who was yearning to learn more about his fellow man. He frequently took walks in the parks, or long country hikes, returning late in the evening to his lonely rented room. Several years later, reflecting on those days, he wrote: "I was dreadfully lonesome. I pondered the question of increasing my acquaintance with young men who had come to Chicago from farms and villages, who knew the joys of friendliness and neighborliness.... Oh [how I missed] the green fields of my New England Valley and the voice of a kindly old friend." He had made acquaintances, but not true friends. This made all the more poignant the plaque he kept on his office wall, which quoted Ralph Waldo Emerson, his favorite poet: "He who has a thousand friends has not a friend to spare."

"I had neither the thousand nor the one," he admitted, sadly.

A seminal moment in Paul Harris's life came one afternoon in the autumn of 1900. Another attorney, Bob Frank, invited Paul to dinner at his home in the Rogers Park neighborhood, north of downtown. After the meal, Frank suggested a neighborhood walk, and as they strolled, they stopped at several shops. In contrast to the rudeness and indifference typical of merchants he saw downtown, Paul noticed how these storeowners greeted Frank with a smile, a handshake. At the grocery, the soda fountain, the newsstand, the proprietors and Bob Frank greeted one another by their first names. It was obvious they exchanged business with each other because of a genuine mutual trust and friendliness.

That simple afternoon constitutional came back to Paul Harris's mind a thousand times over the next five years. He had finally found an oasis where strangers could be united in commerce and friendship, where Wallingford and Chicago came together. A seed had been sown in the fertile mind of Paul Percy Harris.

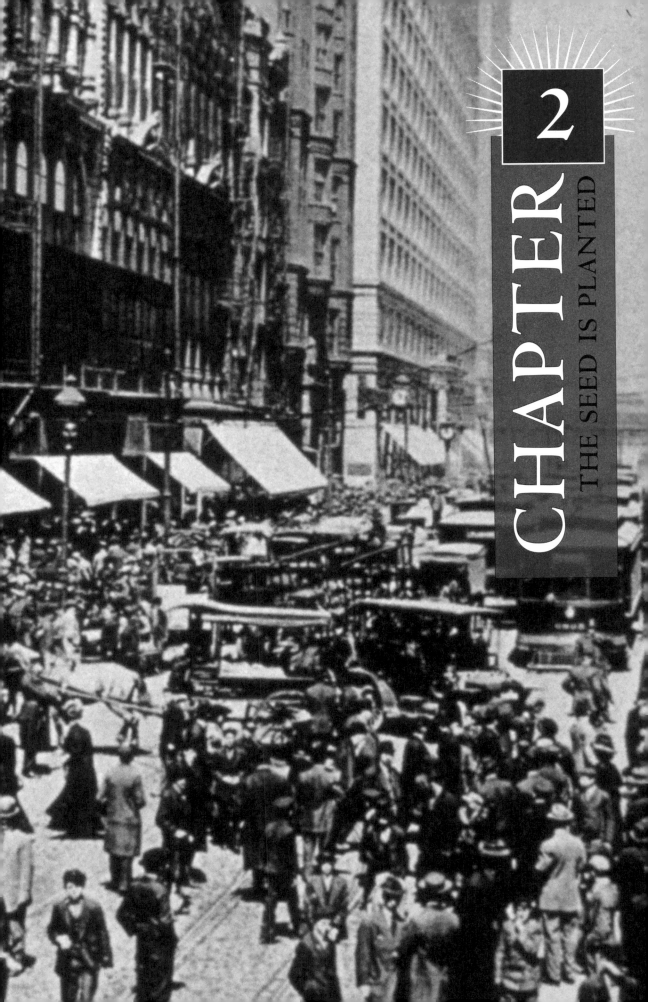

CHAPTER 2

THE SEED IS PLANTED

Chapter 2 – The Seed Is Planted

By 1905, Paul Harris had developed his Chicago law practice where it provided a steady stream of clients. He was certainly not making a fortune, but the financial concerns of nine years earlier had dissipated. For a while, he occupied an office in the same building as Clarence Darrow, one of the nation's most famous attorneys who was at the vanguard of the social consciousness movement.

Less than two years earlier, the Wright brothers had created aviation history by flying an airplane under its own power for the first time. Japan had established itself as a mighty naval power, and its ships defeated Russia in a war. Norway seceded from Sweden. Russia's Czar Nicholas II was coming under increasing pressure for reforms, and sensing an opportunity, Lenin chose 1905 as the time to return to his homeland from his self-imposed European exile. In Austria, a physician named Sigmund Freud was making startling claims that would remain controversial a century later. Roald Amundsen of Norway discovered the magnetic North Pole. Picasso moved from Spain to Paris and began his Rose Period. In Britain, Parliament denied women voting rights, and Albert Einstein, a young physicist in Switzerland, published a brief thesis on his special theory of relativity, which suggested, for the first time, that man could create energy from matter.

In the United States, Theodore Roosevelt was in the White House; the first pizzeria had just opened, in New York City. The words *smog* and *depression* had entered the vernacular. New York City had opened the United States' first subway system, and Henry Ford had just broken the world land-speed record

The first Rotary club project, a "comfort station" in downtown Chicago

Overleaf: A bustling Chicago street around the turn of the 20th century

when he raced a car across frozen Lake St. Clair, near Detroit, Michigan, at 91 mph (146 km/h).

Chicago was a maelstrom of commercial exploitation, social unrest, political corruption, and religious fundamentalism—all brought together in one giant melting pot. In just 70 years, it had grown from a settlement consisting of log cabins and a frontier fort to a sprawling metropolis of 1.6 million and a skyline punctuated by skyscrapers. In his book *Fabulous Chicago,* author Emmett Dedmon quotes French poet Paul Bourget describing Chicago's high-rise architecture as "a new kind of art."[1] But not all visitors were so complimentary. Rudyard Kipling wrote, after his visit: "I have struck a city—a real city—and they call it Chicago. The other places don't count. Having seen it, I urgently desire never to see it again. It is inhabited by savages."[2] Another Englishman, William T. Stead, had gone to Chicago to cover the 1893 World's Fair and then stayed on to write a book, *If Christ Came to Chicago,* which attacked the city's sleaze, greed, and corruption.

Chicago's bars and brothels continued to pander to the desires of the flesh. Crime, from street muggings to murder, was rampant. And if you survived your walk through the streets, you probably did so gagging from the stench. Chicago was the Midwest's great stockyard capital, and millions of cattle were brought to the city's slaughterhouses. Nauseating hydrogen sulfide gas from burning bones filled the air, and the effluents—fats, blood, gristle, guts—were dumped into the rivers that crisscrossed the city, creating lagoons of waste as they flowed into Lake Michigan. Those oily wastes often caught fire, further contributing to the stench and air pollution. As a result of the outrage caused by Stead's book, a reform movement called the Civic Federation was started, with the goal of cleaning up the city. Slowly, very slowly, social consciousness awakened and civic and business leaders launched the first attack on vice and crime.

Chicago was, at this dawning of the new century, a city of contrasts. New-found conscience was pitted against corruption; abject poverty and ostentatious high living rubbed shoulders. It was where gangsters and God, alcohol and prohibitionists, towering skyscrapers and teeming tenements all met. In 1905 it was both the city of progress and the place where a motorist was arrested outside the Unity Building after his Haynes automobile scared some horses.[3] If ever there was an ideal crucible for the birth of a movement that advocated social change, business ethics, and honest friendliness, it was Chicago.

In the days before television, radio, and movies, people socialized by joining clubs, and there was no shortage of clubs in the city. But they were clubs organized for narrow special interests: sporting associations, religious clubs, trade or union affiliations, ethnic groups, and political parties. It was considered unacceptable to use the club forum to promote one's business interests. For more than four years, Paul Harris had been mulling over in his mind that evening he witnessed the genuine friendship between merchants during his stroll through Rogers Park. He had, by 1905, developed

1   Emmett Dedmon, *Fabulous Chicago* (New York: Random House, 1953).
2   Rudyard Kipling, *American Notes* (Freeport, New York: Books for Libraries Press, 1972).
3   Rotary International, *Rotary: Fifty Years of Service* (Evanston, Illinois, 1954), 13.

several cordial business connections, but no true personal friends. His closest acquaintance was Silvester Schiele, a coal dealer and client who from time to time told Paul interesting anecdotes of his rural Indiana boyhood. It was Schiele to whom Harris first told his idea: a club where businessmen could share friendship with one another, at the same time using this trusted circle of friends to exchange trade. Neither man was prone to impulsive decisions, so the idea lay dormant for several months.

Thursday, 23 February 1905, is the most significant date in the history of Rotary—perhaps in the history of volunteerism. As the day broke, there was little evidence of its significance, however. The Chicago newspapers led with headlines announcing President Theodore Roosevelt's initiative to broker a peace between Russia and Japan. The carpenters' and bricklayers' unions in Chicago were threatening to strike unless their members were granted a half-day off on Saturdays.

Late that afternoon, Paul and Silvester met at Madame Galli's for dinner and discussed the idea of the fellowship and business booster club. A few days earlier they had talked about it with a mutual customer, a mining engineer named Gustavus Loehr, and he was so enthusiastic about it that he offered to host the organizational meeting in his office. After dinner, Paul and Silvester walked over to Gus's office on the seventh floor of the Unity Building at 127 Dearborn Street. It was a small room, not well lighted, with a desk and three or four uncomfortable chairs, a coat rack in the corner, and an engineering

> The first Rotary meeting was held in Room 711 of the Unity Building on Dearborn Street in downtown Chicago. The room, the office of mining engineer Gus Loehr, was restored to its original condition for RI's 75th anniversary in 1980. When the building was demolished in 1989, Rotarian members of the Paul Harris 711 Club removed and preserved the room's flooring, wood trim, office equipment, and furnishings. In 1994, the room was re-created at RI World Headquarters in Evanston. Hundreds of Rotarians visit the office each year.

chart on the wall.[4] Gus was waiting with his friend Hiram Shorey, a merchant tailor he had invited to the meeting. Loehr did not have a conference room, so the four men pulled up chairs and sat around the desk in his office.

They each introduced themselves, telling the others about their vocations and sketching out their backgrounds that led them by remarkably similar paths to Chicago. Silvester told of his German heritage and of his life growing up on an Indiana farm. He showed them pictures of his family around the fireplace in their log cabin; of the hardships they endured, with snow that often blew so heavily through the broken roof that he would awaken to find a

The first Rotarians, from left: Silvester Schiele,
Paul Harris (pointing to book), Hiram E. Shorey,
and Gustavus H. Loehr

THE SEED IS PLANTED

drift on the floor beside his bed. He went on to serve his country in Cuba during the Spanish-American War and was active in church and charitable work.[5] Gus Loehr, according to Harris, was "a stormy petrel, vehement, impetuous, domineering in one breath, then calm, docile, lovable in the next." He was prone to rapid-fire speech, yet his words invariably compelled thought. His business caused him to travel extensively, and while he was loyal to the club, he was not able to contribute much after the first few meetings. Hiram was a quiet, likeable fellow who had grown up in Maine and whose heart remained there. He had the most difficult time of them all in adjusting to life in the big city and, in fact, never did so.

Then Paul Harris shared with them his sense of emptiness at having no true friends in the city, his indignation at the dog-eat-dog business attitudes and the uncertainty of knowing whom he could trust in his personal and commercial dealings. He proposed they form a club different from any other, one which he described as "a very simple plan of mutual cooperation and informal friendship such as all of us had once known in our villages."

One member would be invited from each profession or line of business, and only those for whose integrity the other members could vouch would be invited. It would thus be a natural "booster club," where reciprocal trade could be practiced, but also a group of men with whom they could all enjoy fellowship. Since it would be limited to one representative per profession, they could truly select the best men in town, and who would not want to join a club, which could potentially refer so much business to him? Paul would buy his suits from Hiram, Hiram would purchase coal from Silvester, Gus would use Paul for legal work, and so on. The foursome were enthusiastic about the idea, and each of them agreed to meet again in two weeks and pledged to recruit potential new members and bring them to the next meeting.

The day after the meeting, an enthusiastic Paul Harris visited Harry Ruggles, a young printer he had used for his law firm's stationery. Harry was another farm boy, raised in Michigan by a deeply religious family; he worked his way through Northwestern University as an apprentice in a printing company. He had developed a reputation for solid business ethics and was deeply troubled by the poverty and despair he saw in Chicago. Harry became member number five of the yet-unnamed club and went on to serve Rotary for 55 years, becoming the only original member to outlive Paul Harris.

The second meeting was held in Paul's law office in the Wolff Building, and the original foursome were joined by Harry Ruggles, real estate broker Bill Jensen, and organ manufacturer A.L. "Al" White.

Silvester Schiele hosted the third meeting of the group at his coal-yard office on 23 March 1905. There were 15 men present, and the occasion was significant in that it was the first real business meeting at which decisions were made, some of which the organization still honors 100 years later. The first question addressed was what they should call themselves. There was no shortage of suggestions. Some members felt the club should reflect their community: Windy City Roundup, Chicago Fellowship, Chicago Circle, the Lake Club, and the Chicago Civic Club were proposed. Others argued the name should have a business ring to it, such as the Booster Club, Friends in Business, Men with Friends, the FFF [Food-Fun-Fellowship] Club, and the Trade and Talk Club.

None of these names generated much enthusiasm, although all were apt descriptions of the group's purpose. Other proposals included the Blue Boys and the Conspirators. The Round Table earned several votes, but not a majority. Then Paul Harris quietly made a new suggestion. They had already agreed to rotate meetings between members' places of business, with the leadership of each meeting also rotating to the man hosting that meeting. Why not call themselves the Rotation Club? They knew they were on to something,

PIONEER ROTARIAN HARRY RUGGLES, THE PRINTER WHO INTRODUCED SINGING TO ROTARY CLUB MEETINGS

The "trophy" office of Paul Harris is located on the 16th floor of RI World Headquarters. Furnishings, photos, and memorabilia are arranged almost exactly as they were in the founder's original office. His desk, with inlaid wood of different kinds, was a gift from Australian Rotarians. You can also see a chessboard made of butterfly wings, a Rotary flag flown by Admiral Byrd over the South Pole, medals of honor from various nations, and Paul's favorite quotation: "He who has a thousand friends has not a friend to spare."

but that name sounded a little clumsy. "How about Rotary Club then?" suggested Paul. The name was unanimously approved.

The fledgling organization decided there would be no dues—all club expenses would be paid from 50-cent fines collected from miscreant members for such misdeeds as missing meetings. Membership would last for one year, with each member needing to requalify annually. A single "nay" vote from existing members would prevent anyone from joining, and a three-fourths vote would be required to stay in the club at each anniversary. To promote fellowship, members would greet one another using only first names; any salutation beginning with "Mister" would surely incur a fine, as would risqué jokes and religious or political discussions. A board of directors was elected at that third meeting, and although Paul Harris was the obvious choice for president, he declined the position, nominating Silvester Schiele instead. Thus Silvester became president number one of club number one by acclamation, with Paul preferring to work behind the scenes to attract new members and shape the club's early character.

Hiram Shorey only attended two more meetings,[6] although he did return for a short time in 1906 before dropping out. Gus Loehr's health deteriorated and he subsequently left the club. (Both men were always supportive of the club and voiced pride at their early association with it.) But far more men joined. By October 1905, when Harry Ruggles printed the first roster, the Rotary Club had 30 members. A little more than a year later, the number had grown to 80.

By the fifth meeting, it was clear that the membership was too large to fit into any member's office. Al White suggested to President Schiele that they meet in a hotel. White approached the manager of the Palmer House hotel and persuaded him to let the club use a meeting room on the balcony at no charge. It was such a success that President Schiele asked White to make similar arrangements for the next meeting. This time, the club met at the Brevoort Hotel which served them dinner.[7] This marked the beginning of another tradition: that of having the meeting over lunch or dinner, usually every two weeks, except during July and August.

6   Rufe Chapin, "An Outline of Rotary's Beginnings."
7   A.L. White, "Questionnaire to the Members of the 1905 Group Now Still Living and Still Holding Membership," [1929], RC Chicago, Historical Club Files, RI Archives.

For many months thereafter, they rotated between hotels and restaurants throughout the Loop—Chicago's central business district. For a while, they ate dinner in the dining room of the Sherman Hotel and then retired to a guest room to conduct the club meeting. "The members would not only occupy all the chairs that could be crowded in, but perch on the window sills, bureaus, radiators, and even fill up the beds," recalled Rufus Chapin, a 1905 member. Increasing membership soon rendered such a venue impractical. Following a complete renovation of the Sherman Hotel, the Rotary Club of Chicago elected to make this its permanent meeting place in January 1911.

The reciprocal exchange of business was a central theme of early Rotary. Indeed, one of the most important club officers was the statistician. Whenever a member gave business to, or received an order from, another member, he wrote the details on a postcard and mailed it to the statistician. Detailed records were maintained and the results reported regularly at club meetings. One did not have to belong to the club for very long before realizing that patronizing other members had obvious advantages. Yes, it would help each

member's business. Yes, it made sense to trade with people of integrity whom one knew personally. But the best reason was that these were people who enjoyed each other's company.

Many members were assigned nicknames. The youthful florist Charlie Schneider was "Boy Orator," Rufus Chapin the banker became "Rufe," and undertaker Barney Arntzen was "Cupid." They joined "Doc" Hawley, who remained a faithful and much loved member for 26 years, John the decorator, Judson the artist, "Max" the furniture dealer, and "Freddie" Tweed, about whom Paul Harris said, "His cup runneth over with brotherly love," and who went on to help found the New York City club.

Harry Ruggles, who served as the club's first treasurer, was as enthusiastic a contributor to Rotary as any man. He was the club's fourth president, provided all the printing gratis, served on the first board of directors of the International Association of Rotary Clubs in 1912, and lived long enough to serve on the nominating committee for 1956-57 RI President Gian Paolo Lang of Italy.

But Ruggles will forever be remembered for a spontaneous act that went on to become a century-long tradition. There was a lull in the meeting one autumn night in 1905. The buzz of conversation had inexplicably ended. Without warning, and at his own initiative, Harry Ruggles sprang to his feet and called out, "Hell, fellows, let's sing!" He led them in several popular songs of the day, and singing at Rotary meetings thereafter became a tradition. Harry printed the first of many editions of a Rotary songbook in 1910. For decades afterward, whether during a boisterous dinner at Ireland's Restaurant following a club bowling event or at the more formal regular meetings, Harry would bring the group together in song.

Even today, longtime members of the Rotary Club of Chicago tell how the president would call the meeting to order, and then the Sherman Hotel's Grand Ballroom would go dark. A solitary spotlight would pierce the black-

Even though Paul Harris wrote in 1911 that "Rotary is entirely without precedent in the history of clubdom," he later learned that his idea was not entirely original. A social club based on a similar vocational classification system had been organized in London, England, 200 years before Rotary's founding in 1905. It was also similar to the classification-based Junto, established in 18th-century Philadelphia by U.S. scientist-philosopher Benjamin Franklin.

ness to highlight a slight man on the west balcony. With the room in hushed anticipation, Harry Ruggles would raise his arms and cry, "Come on, fellows, let's sing!" And sing they did. Harry led the singing at his club, at district conferences around the country, even at international conventions. On 23 October 1959, while on the way to speak at the Rotary Club of Cathedral City, California, Harry had a heart attack and the voice, which had brought song and sunshine to Rotary for 54 years, was silenced.

The club continued to grow, but while its members joined for the objectives outlined in 1905—business reciprocity and friendship—others began to wonder if they should do more. It is noteworthy to remember that many members hailed from rural villages and farms, where helping a neighbor in need was considered a natural, unquestioned act of service. Paul Harris later stated that in his mind, the club was never intended solely to promote business between members: "Whether a member was selfish or unselfish depended, of course, upon where he found his happiness." He added that many of those 1905 members had designated their days at the dawning of Rotary as "the sweetest and most selfless of their lives."

Long before the club adopted "service" as an objective, individual members gave freely of their time, talent, and treasure to those in need. In 1907, Paul Harris agreed to assume the Rotary Club's presidency, and he used his bully pulpit to move the club toward the vision that was evolving in his mind.

Back in 1905, he had realized that the club needed a formal structure, so he had drafted its first constitution and bylaws, which the club adopted in January 1906. They contained only two Objects:

1. The promotion of the business interests of its members.

2. The promotion of good fellowship and other desiderata ordinarily incident to social clubs.

Both these goals were clearly being met. The statistician regularly reported impressive amounts of business that members were referring to one another. And with the singing, friendly meetings, frequent ladies' nights, summer outings and trips to sporting events, fellowship was certainly a signature theme of the club.

But several members wanted the club to reach for higher, altruistic goals. This was due, in part, to scattered press reports criticizing Rotarians for selfish motives, but largely because the members wanted to give something back to their community, to make it a better place. Frederick H. Tweed, a glass sign manufacturer who had joined the club in December 1905, used Donald M. Carter as a patent attorney. In April 1906, he made a visit to Carter to acquaint him with Rotary. Since the classification "patent attorney" was unfilled, he seemed a good candidate for membership. Carter was both flattered and interested, and he inquired as to the club's objectives. When Tweed explained that it had two—to boost everyone's business and promote friendship—Carter was not satisfied. "What about the purpose of the Rotary Club?" he asked. Tweed pulled out the new constitution and bylaws and proudly showed them to the attorney. "The way it looks," Carter said, after reviewing the documents, "such a club has great possibilities if it could do something of some benefit to people besides its own members. I believe it should do civic service of some kind." Tweed responded with an offhand suggestion that would have ramifications both immediately and for 100 years to follow: "Why don't you join the club, and perhaps we could amend the constitution the way you think it should be done?"

Donald Carter joined the club in May 1906 and drafted a third Object, which was added in 1907:

3. The advancement of the best interests of Chicago and the spreading of the spirit of civic pride and loyalty among its citizens.

This was a pivotal moment in Rotary's history. With Don Carter—who became known as the Father of Community Service—as the driving force, Rotary One enthusiastically embraced civic service as an ideal. Men who ran banks, law firms, and insurance companies were soon building comfort stations, helping disadvantaged children, and packing food baskets and delivering them to impoverished tenement dwellers.

Paul Harris served as club president for nearly two years; his unfinished second term was completed by Harry Ruggles. The Rotary Club was now a registered nonprofit corporation with more than 140 members.

Although Rotary's early focus was on fellowship and business networking, members soon incorporated the elements of service. In 1906, Donald M. Carter proposed an amendment to the club bylaws: "An organization that is wholly selfish cannot last long. If we, as a Rotary Club, expect to survive and grow, we must do some things to justify our existence. We must perform a civic service."

Harris wasn't satisfied, though. He thought: If the Rotary Club has been this well received, if it made such a difference in Chicago, why not replicate it in other large cities? He had written to business contacts and former college friends in other cities, but none of them had shown any interest in picking up the mantle. Even his dear friend George W. Clark in Florida had not responded favorably. Then there was his own club, which would have to commit manpower, money, and effort to extend the club to other cities.

When he proposed the idea to Chicago members, he found considerable opposition. After all, they argued, they had formed and joined the Rotary Club to make friends, increase their business from other local merchants, and later, to improve the city of Chicago. What benefits would they gain by devoting time and effort into starting a club in New York City or Jacksonville? Paul Harris empathized with their rationale, saying: "Rotary in Chicago was something definite, understandable; Rotary in San Francisco and New York was vague, shadowy, visionary, probably quite impossible. These men had never known failure; they were not speculators."

Paul knew he would lose if he insisted that the club officially embrace his expansion ideas. It was therefore only in a casual way that he talked with Manuel Muñoz in June 1908. Sperry & Hutchinson Company had transferred its young salesman from Cranford, New Jersey, to Chicago, and for a while he and Paul Harris had been roommates at the Del Prado Hotel. When Muñoz told Harris that his company was sending him on a business trip to San Francisco, Paul said, "Maybe you could get someone interested in starting a Rotary club out there." This almost offhand suggestion changed forever the shape of the Rotary movement.

CHAPTER 3

THE EXPANSION ACROSS AMERICA

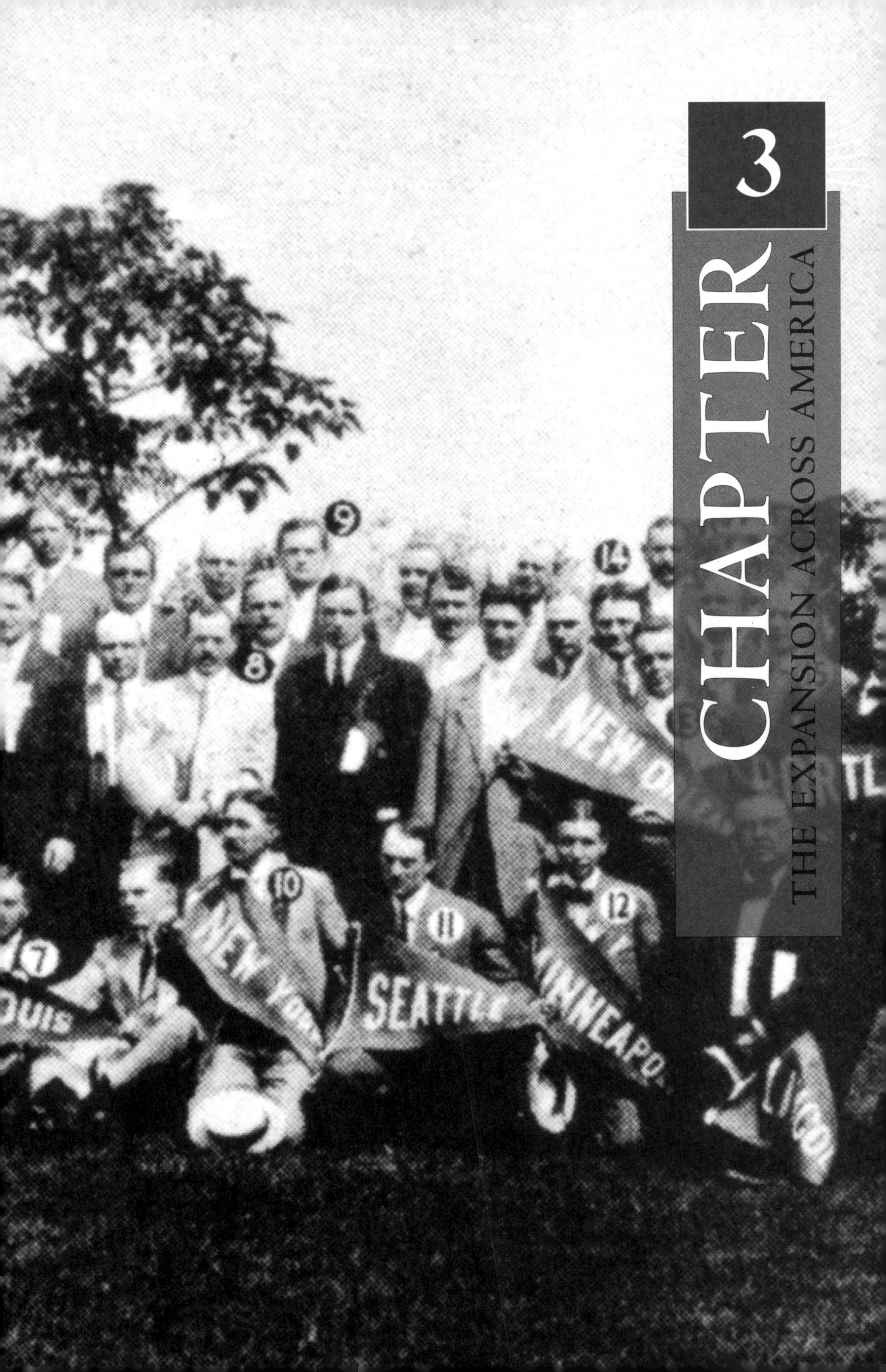

Chapter 3 – The Expansion across America

For half a century, on the other side of the United States, hundreds of thousands of ambitious adventurers had been heeding the call to "Go west, young man!" The gold rush of the mid-19th century had spawned tales of incredible fortunes made overnight, and the stories that came east—of majestic mountains, verdant agricultural land, and the magnificent Pacific coast—were magnets for those seeking a better life.

Homer W. Wood was one of 10 children born to a Methodist minister and his wife. In addition to his pastoral duties, Homer's father, Jesse, was a successful businessman and politician. He owned and published newspapers in Oroville and Chico, California, and served as Butte County's supervisor of schools. Homer had two older brothers who became lawyers—a profession his father expected him to follow. But his application to law school was denied, and at the age of 19, with eyesight problems and financial worries, he had to find a job. Homer went to the scruffy, ramshackle boomtown of Bodie, California, to work in the gold mine run by his brother-in-law. Later, Homer became a newspaper publisher, and then an attorney, serving as clerk to the Court of Appeals in Sacramento. He moved to San Francisco and opened a law practice shortly after the great earthquake of April 1906.

In June 1908, the young salesman Manuel Muñoz arrived in San Francisco from Chicago and registered at the Cadillac Hotel. The next evening he was seated at a table in the lobby, working on his appointment schedule for the following day. Not being familiar with the city, which was still rebuilding after the disastrous earthquake of two years before, he introduced himself to

Chicago at the turn of the century

Overleaf: Attendees at the first Rotary Convention in Chicago, 1910

the man sitting across the table from him and asked for directions. Manuel Muñoz had just met attorney Homer Wood, then living at the hotel. As they talked, the conversation drifted far beyond where certain streets were located. They discussed one another's vocations, hometowns, the differences between Chicago and San Francisco. Then Manuel remembered Paul Harris's request of him, and he told Homer about the Rotary Club. "It occurred to me that here was a man to cultivate and a fertile field in which to plant the Rotary seed," Muñoz recalled later.[1] The young attorney found this to be an intriguing idea: He was a joiner and could benefit from both increased business and more friends, and this Rotary Club was unlike any other club in the city. At the end of the meeting, Muñoz suggested that Wood write to Paul Harris in Chicago. Paul Harris was ecstatic when Homer's letter arrived from San Francisco, the city where he had worked as a cub reporter during his early vagabond years. He had always imagined New York, Boston, Detroit—even Jacksonville—would be the next cities, but San Francisco would be just fine. He immediately responded, enclosing copies of the Chicago club's constitution and bylaws. As soon as the documents arrived from Chicago, Homer took them to his dear friend Dr. Chester H. Woolsey and asked him for his opinions of the potential for such a club in San Francisco.

Over the next few months, barely a week passed without a couple of letters being exchanged between Wood and Harris. When Homer anticipated a problem, Paul would reply with a solution. Paul sent copies of club documents, which prompted further questions from Homer. One thing was clear, however: Paul's encouraging words and Homer's enthusiasm and vision were moving them closer to the world's second Rotary club.

Homer called five friends together for a meeting at his law office in the First National Bank Building; and when he told them of his idea, showing them the file from Paul Harris, they unanimously embraced his proposal to start a similar club. Thus John Fraser, Dr. Chester Woolsey, Roy R. Rogers, Arthur S. Holman, and Frank Turner joined Homer Wood as the nucleus of the Rotary Club of San Francisco. Four men were added to this exploratory committee and 12 November 1908 was selected for the inaugural meeting.

The 10-member group compiled a list of almost 100 of the top business and professional leaders in the city. Then they set out to invite them; but instead of using heavy-handed recruitment tactics, they agreed that each prospect would only once be given the opportunity to join. If he declined, their invitation would be made to the next person on the list in that vocation.

The banquet on 12 November was a grand affair. Held at the opulent St. Francis Hotel, it was attended by many luminaries, including General M. H. DeYoung, publisher of the *San Francisco Chronicle*, and John Britten, vice president of Pacific Gas & Electric Company. As the meeting started, Homer learned that Charles M. Schwab, America's most prominent steel magnate, was dining in another restaurant within the same hotel. He left the meeting, found Schwab, introduced himself and explained what was happening with the new club, and persuaded the famous industrialist to join them a little later and make an inspiring and supportive speech. The evening ended with

---

1 Manuel Muñoz to Chesley R. Perry, 25 July 1930.

Homer Wood's election as president, and the next day's newspapers promi-
nently featured the story of the city's new Rotary club and its renowned speaker. Wood ordered 1,000 reprints of the *Chronicle* article on the new club and
mailed them to Paul Harris, for distribution to other cities he was targeting
for Rotary expansion.[2]

Many people would have considered their work completed, having
launched the San Francisco club, but not Homer Wood and Arthur Holman.
Within two weeks of San Francisco's inaugural banquet, they had persuaded
25 business leaders, friends, and clients to start a club across the bay in Oakland. On 4 December 1908, the provisional club elected Frank W. Bilger, president of Harbor Bank and past president of the chamber of commerce, as
club president with Oakland's Mayor Mott and Homer Wood made honorary
members. Since club number three had attracted members from the three
adjacent cities of Alameda, Berkeley, and Oakland, they called it the Tri-City
Rotary Club. Tri-City had the distinction of being the first club to hold regular
weekly meetings; Chicago and San Francisco were still meeting fortnightly at
the time. It also ruled that since it served three cities, it would allow one person from a classification from each city. In August 1911, the club name was
changed from Tri-City to Oakland.

Holman and Wood, flush with their second success, attacked extension
with missionary zeal. Arthur Holman was the San Francisco agency manager
for Traveler's Insurance Company. Early in 1909, he made a business trip to
Seattle, where he was friends with his counterpart Roy R. Denny. When Arthur spoke about the Rotary clubs in Chicago, San Francisco, and Oakland,
Roy Denny immediately recognized the advantages of forming a similar club
in Seattle.

Before Holman left town, Denny arranged a lunch meeting with an associate, Earl J. McLaughlin, and by the end of the day, Roy and Earl had assembled an organizing committee. For three weeks this group met daily, adding

2   Rotary Club of San Francisco, *Bulletin*, December 1908.

potential members to their prospect list and planning the inaugural dinner at the Olympus Cafe. Once again, the Chicago club's constitution and bylaws were adopted, almost verbatim.

June 1909 was a significant month for Seattle. On 1 June, the Alaska-Yukon-Pacific Exposition—unique as a World's Fair—opened, and on 15 June the Rotary Club of Seattle was officially founded. The club elected Roy R. Denny as founder-president and E.L. Skeel, who later would serve the National Association of Rotary Clubs, as its first secretary.

Shortly after he had helped form the San Francisco club, Homer wrote to his brother Walton, an attorney in Los Angeles, asking if he would help start a club in that city. Walton, two years older than Homer, had only recently opened his practice and did not seem enthused about acting on his brother's request. In May 1909, Arthur Holman hosted a visit to San Francisco by Irwin J. "Jerry" Muma, the Los Angeles branch manager for Traveler's Insurance. Once again, Holman's anecdotes of the Rotary clubs inspired his guest, and Muma returned to Los Angeles eager to form a similar club. Before Muma left, Homer Wood met him and told him of the correspondence with his brother. By coincidence, Jerry Muma and Walton Wood had attended university together and were old acquaintances.

Once back in Los Angeles, Muma wasted no time in talking with his friend, and the two of them followed the organizational blueprint that had worked so well in the other cities. They mailed 50 invitations to a targeted list of prospects, and 31 of them attended the first meeting, held at the Hollenbeck Hotel on 25 June 1909. Muma and Wood were declared co-founders of the club with Muma accepting the position of president. After nearly four years as a movement with a single club, Rotary had grown, within seven months, to five clubs, including a presence in the West Coast's four largest cities.

There is an interesting footnote to the Los Angeles story. Walton Wood and Irwin Muma admitted they lacked the time and contacts to launch a membership drive. But they were introduced to Herbert C. Quick, a professional organizer and promoter whose most recent assignment had just ended. He knew every prominent manager and professional in the city and had proven success in recruiting people to causes. They offered him the position of club secretary with the promise that he would earn a portion of the membership dues from each person who joined. It was Quick who followed up on every inquiry; when he ran out of those, he used sales calls, business lists, even the telephone directory to solicit members. Less than a year after Muma and Wood had hired Quick, the board fired him, for reasons now unclear. But Quick had seen opportunities in the Rotary movement for personal gain, so he formed his own corporation, which he called the National Rotary Club.

Now Los Angeles had two competing clubs, but Herbert Quick stood to gain when the club's coffers swelled with membership dues. He recognized the profit potential from franchising clubs across the country, and when he incorporated in February 1910, he discovered that the Rotary Club of Los Angeles had never done so. Thus, in the annals of the California Secretary of

State, the National Rotary Club is recorded as being the first club in that city, whereas "Rotary Club of Los Angeles" was not incorporated and registered until April 1910—10 months after it was actually formed. Homer Wood, already alarmed by the news that some who had been turned down for membership in the Rotary Club of San Francisco had threatened to start their own "Rotary" club, acted quickly to incorporate the San Francisco club and register the name "Rotary" as a trademark.[3]

Herbert Quick decided to expand next to Seattle, and he quickly submitted registration papers to the State of Washington. But word of his efforts had leaked out, and Los Angeles club members immediately warned Rotarians in Seattle. They rushed their own paperwork through just in time to beat Quick's rival registration. He could go no further, and shortly thereafter, the board of his own club became so outraged at his motives and financial dealings that they removed him from office. Herbert Quick was never heard of in Rotary circles again.

Although the two Los Angeles clubs had become bitter rivals, they buried their animosity with Quick's departure. In November 1912, the clubs agreed to merge into the Rotary Club of Los Angeles. To cement the reality that it was now a single, unified club, the board passed a rule in which any member who referred to either the National or Los Angeles as "the other club" would be fined. Soon the Los Angeles club, with 300 members, was the largest in the country.

Paul Harris and Homer Wood came to like one another immensely, despite not having met. They regularly corresponded and agreed to each send encouraging letters to anyone with the potential for starting a new club. Having failed to win over his dear friend George Clark in Florida, Harris asked Wood to write him with inspiring news from the West Coast. Homer heard of a prospect in Denver and not only wrote to him but also quickly passed on the lead to Paul. A few days later, Harris wrote to Wood, asking him to send "the Rotary letter" to somebody in Washington, D.C. Skeptics have argued that selfish interests were behind the person who organized a business-boosting club in his own city, but that charge cannot be leveled against a person who helps the movement grow in distant towns where he has no interests. In 1938, Arthur Holman described Homer Wood as "the secret ingredient" in Rotary, adding, "In those early days, the original Rotary idea hit Homer Wood harder than anyone else, for here was the first real missionary of Rotary."

Immensely satisfied, Paul Harris shared the news of the westward expansion with his fellow club members in Chicago. He had proven, while avoiding a confrontation with the doubters, that Rotary was as inspiring a concept in other cities as it was in their own town. Nevertheless, there were still hurdles to clear. While many Chicago Rotarians were ambivalent toward extension, a small but vigorous minority was vocal in their resistance. "My Chicago associates in office seem to me a little phlegmatic, some of them, somewhat subject to a feeling of jealousy," Paul wrote to a friend in New York. "The vote in favor of extension went through...although the enthusiasm is not so pronounced as my more enthusiastic nature craves."[4]

3   Homer Wood to Paul Harris, 9 August 1930.
4   Paul Harris to Daniel L. Cady, 22 October 1909.

"Their opposition caused me deep concern at a time when my burdens were many and heavy," Paul later admitted. To ease those burdens in managing a fast-growing club, he appointed an executive committee, and those officers generally felt that the success on the West Coast could motivate some in Rotary One to help develop the movement in the East.

New York was the obvious first city targeted, and Paul Harris wrote to Daniel L. Cady, an old University of Vermont friend who was now practicing law in Manhattan. Cady was interested; a client whose head office was in San Francisco had mentioned that his president was a member of that city's new Rotary club. That was Paul's motivation to immediately ask Homer Wood to write an encouraging letter.

Cady provided a list of potential club organizers and asked Harris to write to them. During this exchange of letters, one of the 1905 members of the Chicago club, Frederick H. Tweed, told Paul of his impending business trip to New York. Harris knew of no better man to plant the seed in the country's largest city. "Fred's manifest geniality impresses even the passing stranger," he wrote. "Men stop in the street, take a second look at him, smile broadly and pass on. He never learned how to be a gentleman. He didn't need to. He was born that way."

On 18 August 1909, Daniel Cady hosted a meeting in his office for local businessmen Elmer De Peu and Arthur Bullock. Fred Tweed soon joined them. The visitor spoke enthusiastically for an hour on the Rotary concept, the benefits to all concerned, and its evolving focus on civic service. After a lengthy question and answer session, they continued the discussion over lunch at a nearby restaurant. They finished their meal but still wanted more information, so they moved into Bullock's office for most of the afternoon. By the time the meeting ended, it was their unanimous decision to bring Rotary to New York.

Fred Tweed invited the group to a dinner a few days thence and suggested they each bring three prospective members with them. And so it was that on 24 August 1909, 26 men gathered for dinner at the Café Martin on Fifth Avenue and 26th Street and decided to charter the Rotary Club of New York. They elected Arthur Bullock as founder-president, and within a few weeks club number six had grown to more than 100 members. Bullock became the engine that helped drive the movement into other cities, too. He printed an eight-page brochure titled "Rotary Is One Kind of Thing and Every Other Club Is Something Else" and mailed it to friends and business contacts in cities where he thought there should be a club.

At almost the same moment the New York club was being formed, similar discussions were taking place in Boston. On 7 October 1909, office furniture dealer John C. Fennelly wrote to Paul Harris advising him of his actions; on 27 December the club was officially inaugurated. Barely a week passed during which Paul Harris did not receive an inquiry about establishing Rotary in a new city—or the good news that a club had been formed. The Rotary Club of Tacoma, Washington, just south of Seattle, was formed in January 1910.

Dan Cady of New York wrote to another University of Vermont friend, Frank H. Waterman of Minneapolis, which resulted in Waterman and his acquaintance Frank Thresher inviting 125 prominent local businessmen to an organizing banquet on 18 February 1910. Since Minneapolis is only 408 miles (656 km) from Chicago, Waterman and Thresher invited Paul Harris to attend. Paul headed a delegation of nine Chicago Rotarians, including Fred Tweed, Harry Ruggles, and incumbent club president A.M. "Red" Ramsay by train to Minneapolis. This was the first occasion when organizers encountered serious opposition to their plans for a club, and Paul Harris and several other Chicago Rotarians appeared before the chamber of commerce, successfully fielding questions from those who believed Rotary would be antagonistic to their own objectives. The inaugural banquet was a total success, and 63 men signed up to join the new club. By the end of the week, membership had grown to 80, and within a year the new club in Minneapolis had 163 members.

42

A RE-CREATION OF ROOM 711, GUS LOEHR'S OFFICE IN THE UNITY BUILDING, IS NOW ON DISPLAY AT ONE ROTARY CENTER IN EVANSTON, ILLINOIS.

But before the evening was over, Frank Thresher told Paul Harris of his conversations with Edward Randall, a friend in neighboring St. Paul. Randall had been so interested in starting a St. Paul club that he had arranged for a group of men to meet for lunch the following day. The Chicagoans immediately decided to extend their visit by a day; and by the time they boarded their train home, even though the temperature was a bone-chilling 10 degrees Fahrenheit below zero (minus 23 Celsius), they were warmed by having witnessed the formation of two Rotary clubs within 24 hours.

From west to east and across the central states, the movement was spreading faster than even the most optimistic Rotarian imagined. Bruno Batt, a St. Louis piano dealer, organized that city's Rotary club on 22 February 1910, and within six months it had 280 members. The next day, following a business trip to New Orleans by Charles A. Newton, one of the Chicago club's earliest members, 24 men officially formed the Rotary Club of New Orleans. Thus five years to the day after the organization of the very first club, New Orleans became club number 12 in a movement that extended across the country.

While steering his new St. Louis club through phenomenal growth, Bruno Batt worked tirelessly to extend Rotary to other cities. Through his efforts, the Kansas City, Missouri, club was formed on 15 May; Lincoln, Nebraska, spawned a club on 10 June, and Detroit, Michigan, was organized on 25 July.

While Batt was working his magic in the Midwest, Rotarians on the West Coast sent word to their friends and business associates in Portland, Oregon, urging them to start a club in that city.

President Phil Grossmeyer of the Portland club had barely been elected when he received a telegram from members of the Seattle and Tacoma clubs informing him that they had recruited a delegation of 184 people, chartered a train, and would be arriving in a couple of days to help the new club celebrate their membership in the Rotary family. By the time the train arrived, the Portland members had arranged accommodations and hired a band. The entire group marched in their own parade through the streets. "I will tell you, the Portland Rotary Club was organized with a vengeance," Grossmeyer wrote.

There were now 16 Rotary clubs with 1,800 members across the United States. While nearly every club had adopted almost verbatim versions of the Chicago club's constitution and bylaws, there was no requirement to do so. Indeed, as the National Rotary Club had demonstrated, anyone could start a club, name it "Rotary" if there was not already one in that city, and could then allow all kinds of undesirable activities in the name of Rotary.

Even before the San Francisco club had been chartered, Paul Harris wrote to Manuel Muñoz on 2 October 1908 suggesting "a national body with legislative capacities of its own" that could also assist local clubs and coordinate policy and programs. By the time there were clubs on both coasts, several Chicago members had become strong proponents of Paul's idea for a national body. There was still opposition to the idea of extension within the Chicago club. They did not resist the idea of additional clubs so much as they disliked having to fund the costs of national expansion from their own pockets. The two sides compromised with the idea of forming a federation of clubs that would share both the financial and administrative burdens of extension.[5]

Clubs around the country agreed to support a national convention at which an association could be formed after democratic discussion of its objectives and rules. Chicago seemed the obvious location, and they agreed it should begin on 15 August 1910. In May, the clubs nominated a board of commissioners to plan the convention and set the agenda that would lead to the formation of the National Association of Rotary Clubs of America.

Proud and excited, the delegates converged on Chicago that sweltering August week. Fourteen of the 16 clubs were represented, and voting delegates, observers, and guests arrived with the conviction that for all they had witnessed of Rotary pioneering at a local level, they were about to become a part of a new chapter in the organization's history—and perhaps America's history as well.

5   Rufe Chapin, "An Outline of Rotary's Beginnings," RC Chicago, Historical Club Files, RI Archives.

NATIONAL ROT
CHICAGO Aug.

ROTARY CHICAGO

ROTARY DELEGATES

CHAPTER 4

THE ARCHITECT AND THE BUILDERS

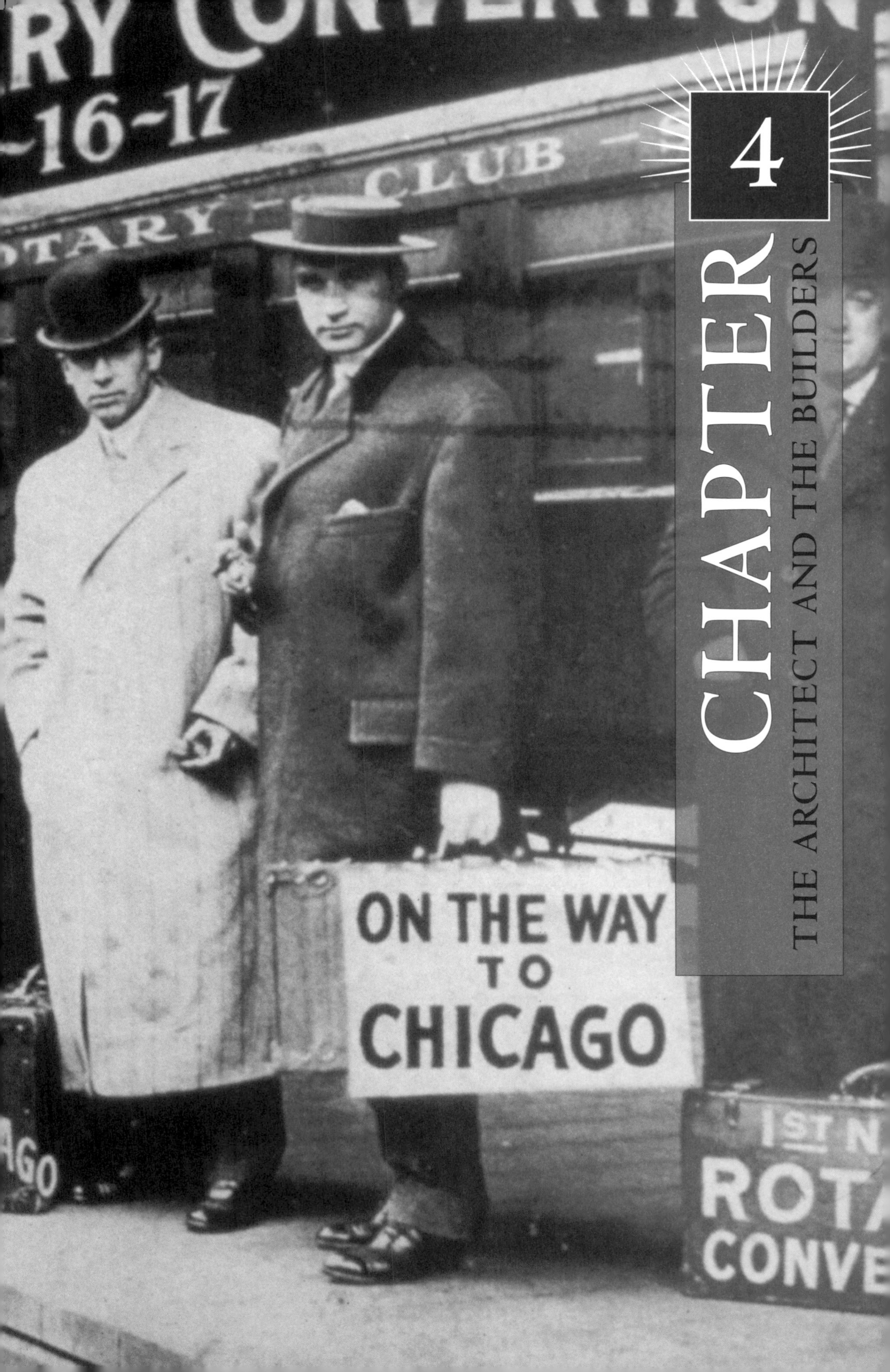

Chapter 4 – The Architect and the Builders

Organizing a convention for an as-yet-unnamed association, and hosting delegates from around the country, was no easy task. This was even more difficult in an age when telegrams and letters were the main form of communication.

In perhaps one of the most profound moves in Rotary's history, Chicago Rotary club president "Red" Ramsay appointed Chesley R. Perry chairman of the extension committee in late fall of 1909. Paul Harris later recalled how Ches, after a full day's work at his own business, came to Paul's law office and "worked every day late into the night." Hundreds of letters arrived from around the country inquiring about new clubs, and the two men spent countless more hours planning the convention and proposed national association.

It was also the beginning of the transition from a Paul Harris–driven organization to a more democratically governed one. Paul admitted this when, in 1925, he said: "That was the first time I had ever had the initiative taken away from me in Rotary. Ches did not want to be told what to do; he did it. He did more work than I in the calling of the first convention, a great deal more work. I certainly needed Ches. I was about tired out."

Chesley R. Perry and Paul Harris were cut from different cloth. While Harris never stopped yearning for his rural upbringing, Perry was a city boy. He was born on the West Side of Chicago on 12 September 1872, the year after the city's great fire. His father, Captain Charles A. Perry, was a Civil War veteran who named his son after his friend George Chesley, who had helped stranded gold seekers during the 1849 gold rush.

Paul and Jean Harris, with their dog, in 1917

Overleaf: Members of the Rotary Club of Chicago, including Paul Harris (third from left), on a train platform

The Perrys home-schooled their son until age 15, when he entered high school, where he passed through five grades in two years. He planned to attend the University of Chicago and took a temporary job at the Chicago Public Library until classes began. But his cultural upbringing and love for literature persuaded Ches to pursue a career at the library for the next nine years. During that time, he also managed amateur football and baseball teams and taught night school.

When the Spanish-American War erupted, Perry volunteered with the Illinois National Guard and was sent to the front lines in Cuba. He became a war correspondent and sent daily dispatches and weekly features to the *Chicago Times-Herald,* and by the time he was discharged, attained the rank of captain.[1] His experiences in Cuba had a lasting effect on Ches: He learned Spanish and was later a driving force to make Rotary's extension into Latin America a priority.

Having spent his early career years in both literary and military circles, Ches Perry elected to work in the business world. He made several profitable investments in Mexico and was a principal in a sugar company, insurance firm, and several other interests. It was while working for Parmelee-Perry-Parmelee, a cement-brick machinery manufacturer, that Ches met Harry Ruggles, who introduced him to Rotary. He joined the Rotary Club of Chicago on 28 June 1908—the same night as Arthur Frederick Sheldon, who later gave Rotary its early slogan "He profits most who serves best."

Although Perry was hardly an effusive, outgoing man, his organizational skills were evident to all who met him. It quickly became Ches Perry to whom the club turned when it needed something done properly. And few projects seemed more important than the need for a national association, an organized extension plan, and a convention to chart the future.

Those who attended the 1910 Rotary Convention never forgot the experience. The Chicago club enlisted many of its members to help with the arrangements. They were intent on being great hosts and even formed an automobile committee, where club members met arriving delegates at Union Station in a car bedecked with Rotary pennants, then chauffeured them to their hotel.

Sixty Rotarians registered, along with an equal number of wives and guests. Fourteen of the 16 clubs sent delegates, the remaining two having designated proxies to represent them. Every club was allowed one delegate for each 50 members, and they came together at the convention as equal partners. They were committed to the common purpose of building a national association and understood that a framework for future growth should include an idea exchange to learn about different clubs' programs and policies.

Paul Harris called the meeting to order in the Congress Hotel, and delegates quickly tackled the agenda. First, they elected convention officers. Chesley R. Perry was resoundingly voted chairman. He took the podium and announced: "Rotary is already a wonderful force, and no one can attempt to foretell its future growth. You have important work to do in establishing the fundamental laws of this association."

---

1   Chesley Perry, Biographical Files, RI Archives.

Silvester Schiele
1905-1906

Albert L. White
1906-1907

Paul P. Harris
FOUNDER
1907-1908

H. L. Ruggles
1909-1910

A. M. Ramsay
1910-1911

W. S. Miller
1911-1912

H. A. Crofts
1912-1913

1905   1920

ROTARY LEADERS PROUDLY CELEBRATE THE 15TH ANNIVERSARY
OF THE ROTARY CLUB OF CHICAGO IN 1920.

The delegates worked diligently; one meeting of the Constitution and Bylaws Committee did not end until four in the morning. Some delegates, accustomed to doing things their own way in their home clubs, objected to proposed new rules; but even when heated, their debates were conducted with civility and respect. They discussed such topics as:

- Social activities
- Membership qualification and growth
- Dues
- Business reciprocity between members
- An emblem
- Compensation for officers (many clubs paid their secretaries or treasurers a percentage of the membership dues)
- Population of cities eligible for a Rotary club
- The number of clubs that a city may support

The delegates were in Chicago for serious business, but the atmosphere was more like a pep rally. Here were people from all around the country, whose scant experience with Rotary was the few months their home club had existed. Now they were meeting others who shared the same ideals and excitement. It was a time for sharing, fellowship, and fun.

"We want you to feel that Chicago is yours," host club president Red Ramsay told the audience in the opening session. "We have thrown the key into the lake long ago." A year earlier, the Chicago club had held a contest to elect their officers. The two slates ran as the red team and the blue team; the reds won, and their leader, who assumed the presidency, was known forever after as "Red" Ramsay. Red was a senior executive of the telephone company and chaired the Convention Entertainment Committee. He involved many other club members as they took the visiting Rotarians and their guests to dinner parties, swimming at Wilson Avenue Beach, and to a baseball game between the Chicago White Sox and New York Highlanders at the new Comiskey Park.

On Tuesday, the delegates joined the Rotary Club of Chicago at their regular weekly luncheon, then toured the city's broad avenues, lush parks, and towering skyscrapers. That evening they dined al fresco at the famous Bismarck Beer Garden. The after-dinner keynote speaker, Daniel L. Cady of the Rotary Club of New York, told the exuberant audience, "Within 80 years, Rotary will encircle the earth, and by that time the Rotary wheel will contain a thousand spokes."[2] He was 69 years off in his predictions: the 1,000th Rotary club was added in 1921.

At the closing banquet, Chicago Rotarian Arthur Frederick Sheldon addressed the crowd. In the middle of his speech, he said: "[Man] comes to see that the science of business is the science of service. He comes to see that he profits most who serves his fellows best."[3]

In the end, delegates adopted the constitution and bylaws and the formation of the National Association of Rotary Clubs of America. They unanimously elected its first slate of officers, naming Paul Harris as president. By Wednesday afternoon, their mission fulfilled, they adjourned the convention and returned home.

But the newly elected Board of Directors remained and had its first meeting the next day. Their first order of business was to approve reimbursement to the Rotary Club of Chicago of the almost US$360 it had spent to organize the convention. It then turned to finding a secretary to run the association. To the directors it seemed there was one obvious choice: Chesley R. Perry. No sooner had Ches returned to his workplace than he received a message asking him to go to Paul Harris's office where the Board was meeting. They asked him to accept the position temporarily until they could find a suitable candidate, and he agreed.

His "temporary" post lasted 32 years. Ches Perry was reelected as secretary "against my wishes" at the 1911 Rotary Convention, again at the 1912 convention, and every year thereafter until he insisted on retiring in 1942, at age 65.

When he first agreed to the position in 1910, Ches conducted all Rotary work from his own office at 189 La Salle Street. What started with a card box and correspondence file atop his desk soon became filing cabinets and cartons of paperwork. Ches reported that in his first year as secretary he had handled 2,500 incoming—and written more than 6,000 outgoing—letters, all on a single typewriter.

"While the first five issues (of *The National Rotarian*) each showed a loss, the sixth issue showed a profit of US$63 and the last two issues showed a profit of $777...made possible (in part) by the very generous advertising support given by the members of the Philadelphia and Duluth Rotary Clubs.... Our magazine, however, is still in a more or less experimental stage."

Annual report of Secretary Chesley R. Perry, 1912

2   THE ROTARIAN, June 1930, 48.
3   Rotary Clubs of America, *First National Convention* (Chicago, 1910), 98.

CHESLEY R. PERRY, THE FIRST
GENERAL SECRETARY OF ROTARY
INTERNATIONAL, SERVED FOR
32 YEARS.

50

Much of the correspondence was repetitive, and before long, Ches realized the need for a more effective way of communicating with the clubs, a way that in a single writing, could send them all important news about Rotary. One delegate to the 1910 convention had proposed that the association publish a magazine, but the idea was rejected for fear that such a centralized voice might usurp the autonomy of local clubs. They worried that "he who had control of the publication would have control of the Association," Perry recalled later.[4] So the convention had modified the proposal to permit the secretary to "distribute literature."

Thus Paul Harris began what was to become an unbroken tradition. Halfway through his first term as National Association president, Paul wrote a 6,000-word tome titled "Rational Rotarianism," in which he analyzed the appeal of Rotary to different business and professional categories. It was pure Paul Harris.

"If by the interposition of Providence I some day were to find myself standing on a platform in some great Coliseum looking into the eyes of every living Rotarian, and were to be told that I could have but one word to say, without an instant's hesitation and at the top of my voice, I would shout: Toleration!" it began.

Paul asked Ches to mimeograph the essay and mail it to all 2,000 Rotarians in the 23 clubs nationwide. Perry pointed out that he had no funds, but then he had an idea. Why not reproduce the essay in a pamphlet, like a newspaper, for which paid advertisements could be sought for the unused space? He quickly produced a mock-up and showed it to members of his own club, several of whom committed to buying advertising space. One retailer offered ostrich plumes for sale.

The first issue of *The National Rotarian* newsletter was mailed to every Rotarian in January 1911. Perry's idea had allowed for the entire project to be completed for a net cost of only $25.44. He thought this would be a one-time assignment, as he had neither the time, budget, nor staff to repeat the effort. But he was inundated with requests for more magazines—he subsequently printed an additional 2,000 copies—and for new editions. The Board saw this as an ideal organ with which to promote attendance at the August 1911 Rotary Convention at Portland, Oregon. So in July of that year, Perry mailed out issue number two. This edition also contained his editorial, along with tidbits of news from numerous clubs—and 20 paid advertisements.[5]

4   THE ROTARIAN, January 1961, 28.
5   THE ROTARIAN, February 1995, 7-A.

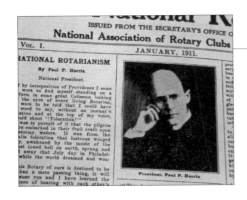

When the delegates convened in Portland in August 1911, they unanimously endorsed the idea of a regular national magazine. Despite their enthusiasm, they only approved a 25-cent levy on each Rotarian's dues to fund *The National Rotarian*. Ches Perry was left to produce a magazine of ever-increasing size and quantity on a mere $65 per month in budgeted funds. It is no small credit to the man that in addition to all his other duties as National Association secretary, he was editor, chief advertising salesman, and publisher of the magazine for many years.

In September 1912, following Rotary's growth into an international organization, the word *National* was dropped from the magazine's title and THE ROTARIAN became a monthly publication. RI President Glenn Mead of Philadelphia, who succeeded Paul Harris in 1912, called for the magazine to include features of general interest—not just Rotary stories. It was a call heard—and heeded—ever since. THE ROTARIAN has featured articles written by some of the most famous personalities, scientists, humanitarians, authors, and business and political leaders of the 20th century. Ches, perhaps influenced by his affinity for Latin America, was the driving force behind *Revista Rotaria*, the Spanish-language edition of the official magazine, which he launched in 1933 for distribution to members in Spanish-speaking countries.

The early years were not easy for the National Association of Rotary Clubs. The member clubs often displayed hostility at what they saw as centralized control where they previously enjoyed independence. From Perry and Harris's standpoint, many clubs were being petty and isolationist when they fought the association's drive for unity of purpose and procedures. Then there was the frugal budget approved by convention delegates. Elmer Rich, the first National Association treasurer, reported the association finished its 1910-11 year with $44.38 in the bank. What he did not reveal—or perhaps did not know—was that Ches Perry had found it impossible to run the office on the $25 monthly allowance the Board

DEPARTMENT HEADS (FROM LEFT) HILKERT, STRUTHERS, AND POTTER (RIGHT) MEET WITH SECRETARY CHES PERRY (CENTER) IN ROTARY'S CHICAGO OFFICES.

had given him. So he had paid $816.75 from his own pocket, just to keep the office open.[6] The National Association began its first year with 16 U.S. clubs; it ended the year with 36 clubs in the United States, Canada, Ireland, and Britain.

On 8 August 1912, delegates to the third annual Rotary Convention in Duluth, Minnesota, adopted the motion made by Rotarian C.E. Fletcher of Winnipeg and voted unanimously to change the association's name to the International Association of Rotary Clubs. Paul Harris had been president of the National Association for two years and stepped down at the end of the Duluth convention. The convention adjourned after conferring on Paul the title "president emeritus," and so he was for the rest of his life.

Romance had never ranked high in Paul Harris's life. But a few months prior to the first Rotary Convention in 1910, at age 42, he had joined a Saturday afternoon hike organized by the Chicago Prairie Club. As he climbed over a barbed-wire fence, Paul ripped his Harris-tweed jacket, an accident that was noticed by another hiker, a young Scottish woman named Jean Thomson.

"The sight of that rip seemed to call up my Scottish instincts," Jean later recalled, "and I offered to mend the tear for the dismayed young man." Three months later they were married, and two years later they built themselves a fine house in the very woods where they had met. There, Jean would sew clothing for the fatherless babes of the county hospital, plan her church projects, and listen to Paul read Burns and Dickens.

PORTRAIT OF JEAN THOMSON HARRIS

Paul was not a well man by the time his second term as National Association president ended. His exhaustion was obvious. His law practice had suffered, and his new marriage had taken second place to his Rotary activities. He had spent hundreds of days on the road, addressing Rotary groups and planning future development. Although he did practice the tolerance he preached, he had, on frequent occasions, showed his frustration at the toll his duties as Rotary standard-bearer had taken on his personal life and professional practice.

And so began a transition period for Rotary. The ensuing years saw a succession of energetic, dedicated leaders at the International Association of Rotary Clubs, always guided behind the scenes by the man whose name became synonymous with wisdom and continuity—Chesley R. Perry.

52

6   Rotary Clubs of America, *Second National Convention*.
7   International Association of Rotary Clubs, *Proceedings of the Ninth Annual Convention*.

When Paul Harris passed the president's gavel to Glenn Mead of Philadelphia on 9 August 1912, he dropped almost from sight for a decade. He seldom attended conventions, although he always sent warm written greetings. In his address to the 1918 convention, President E. Leslie Pidgeon referred to this when he told the audience: "I thought at one time I might have the privilege of introducing the President-Emeritus, Paul P. Harris, even though my predecessors did not. But we haven't got Paul here yet. His address is here and will be read to you by our esteemed Secretary."[7] Paul answered mail—although much of his correspondence was handled through Rotary headquarters—and made occasional visits to clubs of personal interest. "I am neither happy nor successful in the playing of a central part," he wrote in 1923. But even his fellow members in the Rotary Club of Chicago noticed his prolonged absences.

Paul Harris was unquestionably Rotary's father. He had the profound effect of creating and shaping its very existence and early years. But then he stepped back, and during his hiatus years the long-term philosophy of the organization—almost all of which remains today—was influenced by other men of vision and action.

In the 1920s, Harris returned to serve the rest of his lifelong term as president emeritus. In 1929 he suffered a heart attack. Thereafter, he became Rotary's roving ambassador, traveling around the world, usually with Jean at his side, to conferences, conventions, and club assemblies. He rekindled the spirit of his vagabond days. Paul memorialized many of those trips by writing articles for THE ROTARIAN and three books of "Peregrinations," recounting his visits to the exotic ports of the Rotary world.

When they were not traveling, Paul and Jean often hosted visiting Rotarians to their home, just outside of Chicago. The official address was 10856 Longwood Drive, Morgan Park, but Paul and Jean called it Comely Bank, after the Edinburgh neighborhood in which Jean grew up. It was in the garden of Comely Bank that they began the practice of planting trees of friendship in honor of their visitors from distant lands. Many of those trees are still standing in the garden today. Paul watched as two world wars ripped apart nations in which Rotary clubs had been planted, yet he never despaired of his dream for tolerance. Until his last breath, he believed that Rotary could be an instrument for peace in the world.

His health deteriorated, and there were several periods in the 1930s and 1940s when he was forced to take long periods of convalescence. When he died, on 27 January 1947, the Rotary world mourned.

JEAN AND PAUL HARRIS BOARD A BOAT
AFTER A ROTARY VISIT TO BERMUDA.

Paul's and Ches's lives had been intertwined for 40 years. They were so different and yet so similar in purpose and vision. Their differences strengthened Rotary because each was able to bring strength where the other was weak, but their passion for the ideal of service, their single-minded determination that tolerance and ethics and fellowship were Rotary's driving forces far outweighed their personality differences.

Paul was gone, but Ches was there to help organize the funeral. The future of Rotary had not dimmed. "The grandeur of Rotarianism is in its future, not in its past," Paul had said in his farewell address to the 1912 convention, as he bade farewell after two years of leading the association.

Ches Perry married Jessie Booth, a Chicago socialite.[8] Ches was a workaholic, inevitably the first person to arrive at the office and the last to leave. "Saturdays, Sundays, nights and holidays meant nothing to him," Paul had once said. "He was always there. He only took one vacation in 25 years."[9] The marriage failed, and for the rest of his career, Ches was married to his work.

In a club survey sent to all Chicago Rotarians in 1919, Ches answered the questions as follows:

Question: What is your favorite game?
Answer: Baseball.
Question: What is your particular hobby?
Answer: My work.
Question: What is your foremost accomplishment?
Answer: My work.[10]

Indeed it was.

"It has been said that no man is indispensable. I don't believe it. I know

PAUL AND JEAN HARRIS BID GOODBYE TO BERNARD ARNTZEN, MONTAGUE BEAR, RUFUS CHAPIN, ROBERT FLETCHER, HARRY RUGGLES, AND SILVESTER SCHIELE ON THE FRONT STEPS OF COMELY BANK AFTER A REUNION OF THE EARLIEST MEMBERS OF THE ROTARY CLUB OF CHICAGO.

such a man," 1914-15 RI President Frank Mulholland said of Perry.[11] Although he seldom laughed, never joked, and was a strict administrator, Ches Perry was the keyway that made the Rotary wheel work. He and Paul, their personalities so different, did not always see eye to eye. In 1923, a piqued Ches resigned after writing to Paul Harris: "You abused and mistreated me so during my first year of service as secretary when I was doing my very best to help you. For 13 years I have tried to convince myself that the influence of Rotary could make me get along even with you. However, your letter of 28 March 1923 convinces me that it is impossible. Good-bye, Paul. I am sorry."

Luckily for all concerned, they reconciled, and Paul went out of his way thereafter to redirect some of the spotlight from himself to Ches. "If there are Rotarians who think Ches cold and unemotional, I, after more than a quarter-century of intimate contact with him, am prepared to testify to the contrary," he wrote.[12]

Albert I, king of Belgium, knighted Perry in 1927 in recognition of his services to Rotary.[13] When he retired on 30 June 1942, the organization, which had numbered one club when he joined, had grown to more than 5,000 clubs around the globe. Despite an avalanche of requests that he run for president of Rotary International, he declined. Ches returned to his home club, ultimately serving it as president.

He had one surprise for everyone, though. As he retired, he announced that he and his secretary, Peggy, were engaged. They married shortly thereafter and lived in Evanston until his death on 21 February 1960. At the time of his passing, the organization he had helped form had 10,400 clubs from 115 countries in its membership.[14]

Rotary is not an organization of heroes. It is composed of men and women who choose to serve for the privilege of doing so rather than for personal accolades. Nearly every one of the 1.2 million Rotarians can name the founder, and some can recall the names of the four original members. Yet few have ever heard of Chesley R. Perry or know of his contributions to the movement. It is clear that, without Ches Perry, there might be no Rotary today.

It was the founder himself who wrote: "If in truth I can be called the architect, Ches can with equal truth be called the builder of Rotary International."

8 Perry, Biographical Files, RI Archives.
9 THE ROTARIAN, February 1975, 16.
10 Perry, Biographical Files, RI Archives.
11 THE ROTARIAN, August 1942, 8.
12 Paul P. Harris, *This Rotarian Age* (Chicago: Rotary International, 1935), 102.
13 Perry, Biographical Files, RI Archives.
14 THE ROTARIAN, April 1960, 49.

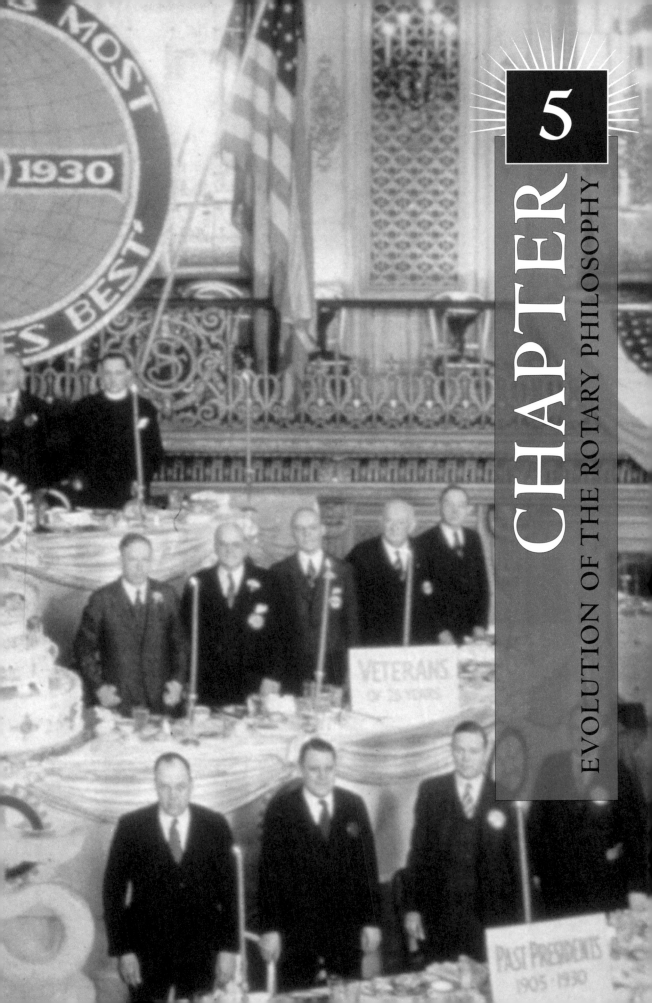

CHAPTER **5**

EVOLUTION OF THE ROTARY PHILOSOPHY

Chapter 5 ~ Evolution of the Rotary Philosophy

P ast RI Director Sabino Santos of the Philippines describes Rotary as "a philosophy that seeks to reconcile the need to provide for oneself with the constant obligation to share what one has with another." Many would agree with that pithy analysis, built upon a century of service and reflection by Rotarians.

Most of the Rotary philosophy known today around the world was etched into the cornerstone of the organization during its formative years between 1910 and 1922. These were the times when men became imbued with the idea of Rotary and were evangelistic in their efforts to spread the good news. But not every Rotarian had joined for the same reasons, and in the early days not every Rotary club emphasized the same programs or practices. As the organization—first as the National Association, then the International Association of Rotary Clubs—began setting standardized policies for all clubs to follow, it did not always meet with wholehearted approval. Most Rotarians enjoyed their independence and wanted to continue exercising it.

Clubs in Small Towns

One debate that lasted for years was whether Rotary clubs could thrive in small towns. The organization's genesis had been in large cities, ostensibly to bring small-town friendship to big-city businessmen. Ches Perry, now firmly in charge at headquarters, argued against granting charters to new clubs in towns of fewer than 100,000 people. He claimed they would fail financially

Paul Harris and Ches Perry with the Objects of Rotary

Overleaf: Rotarians at a 25th anniversary celebration salute the motto "He profits most who serves best."

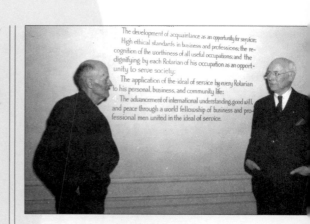

The development of acquaintance as an opportunity for service;
High ethical standards in business and professions; the recognition of the worthiness of all useful occupations; and the dignifying by each Rotarian of his occupation as an opportunity to serve society;
The application of the ideal of service by every Rotarian to his personal, business, and community life;
The advancement of international understanding, good will, and peace through a world fellowship of business and professional men united in the ideal of service.

and said that "Rotary, with its 'representatives' of hundreds of business 'classifications' was really better suited to the economic life of a big city."[1] Besides which, people in small towns already had the camaraderie among local businessmen.

But for all these attempts to control Rotary's growth, there were soon exceptions. H.W. Stanley, Rotary vice president for the Western Division of the United States, toured towns with and without Rotary clubs in Texas in 1913 and wrote to headquarters that he believed Rotary could succeed just as well in towns of 20,000 as in cities of 100,000.[2]

In 1916, THE ROTARIAN magazine published a debate on the subject of lowering the minimum population requirement to below 25,000; as a result, many members came to believe that the "large city" restriction should be lifted. Frank L. Rawson of the Rotary Club of Portland, Maine, wrote a paper that was read to delegates at the 1916 convention in Cincinnati, Ohio. "The 37 Rotary clubs now chartered in cities under 25,000...have something they are proud of," he argued, adding that many more small-town clubs were awaiting their charter approval. "Shall we let them come in? Can they be treated as sub-units of Rotary? We are sitting in judgment...but are we doing anything to help them? Surely we do not believe that the statistician with a U.S. Census Report and a slide rule can numerically determine for us where a new Rotary club shall be chartered. Rotary is based on quality and not quantity."[3]

By 1917, the size of a city was generally not considered to be as important as the number and composition of the prospective members in chartering a new club. In 1917, RI President Arch Klumph of Cleveland, Ohio, wrote: "Each year we have set the population mark lower, until now cities are considered eligible with a population of 10,000 or even less. Personally, I feel that if a delegation of citizens from a town of 1,000 were to apply...with the positive assurance that they would be able to sustain [such a club], I would welcome the signing of their charter equally as much as though it were for a city of a million."[4]

Constitution and Bylaws

In the early years, there were no bylaws or constitutional documents in Rotary. Charles A. Newton, a 1905 Chicago Rotarian, wrote in 1927: "We worked on a gentleman's agreement with a complete understanding of our rules. Members were elected by a *viva voce* vote in open meetings, and one negative vote was sufficient to keep a man out." He told the story of an event that caused the Chicago club to draw up written laws of conduct. "One day a speaker was addressing the club on the wisdom of using lumber versus brick for building. An enthusiastic member jumped to his feet and moved a resolution that the club get behind that statement. They voted to adopt his resolution. Within a week, we had all the brick men on our backs, and we very wisely passed a rule not to pass resolutions in the future until referred to the board of directors."

---

1   Jeffrey A. Charles, Service Clubs in American Society (Champaign, IL: University of Illinois Press, 1993), 64.
2   THE ROTARIAN III, no. 8 (April 1913): 16.
3   THE ROTARIAN IX, no. 4 (October 1916): 353.
4   THE ROTARIAN XI, no. 2 (August 1917): 119.

In 1976, the RI Board of Directors was interested in creating a concise definition of the fundamental aspects of Rotary. They turned to Rotary's Public Relations Committee, which prepared a one-sentence summary that is still used today: "Rotary is an organization of business and professional persons united worldwide who provide humanitarian service, encourage high ethical standards in all vocations, and help build goodwill and peace in the world."

The first 16 clubs, not governed by any national board, generally copied the constitution and bylaws of the Chicago club. They did this for expediency's sake rather than any legal obligation. From the earliest meetings of the National Association Board, the officers realized there needed to be a standard constitution by which all clubs would be bound. The matter gained urgency when, by the time of the second convention in Portland, Oregon, in 1911, Rotary had grown to 36 clubs in three countries—each with its own constitution and bylaws.

James Pinkham of Seattle, chairman of the Resolutions Committee, reported to the delegates at Portland that his committee recommended clubs adopt a model constitution and bylaws. National Association President Paul Harris then appointed a committee to prepare those documents.[5] Headed by Seattle's Ernest L. Skeel, the committee worked on the model constitution and bylaws for a year; when Skeel presented them to the 1912 Rotary Convention in Duluth, Minnesota, they were adopted by an overwhelming majority of the delegates. Over the next few years, these governing documents were revised and, in some places, rewritten, but their central theme remains at the heart of what guides Rotary today.

Yet having the constitution did not mean each club started using it. Rotarians were business leaders, decision makers accustomed to setting their own rules. In 1915, the International Association found its clubs had 300 constitutions and, therefore, 300 sets of objectives. Rotary was never intended to be 200 different organizations with differing objectives and principles, but rather one, unified movement.

Allen D. Albert of Minneapolis, Rotary's president for 1915-16, appointed Arch Klumph chairman of a committee to draft a constitution and bylaws for the International Association of Rotary Clubs. Klumph presented his committee's report to the 1915 San Francisco convention, and the delegates unanimously adopted it. During the next year, the committee prepared another set of documents, one that would serve as a model constitution and bylaws for each Rotary club. It standardized such important issues as the name of the club, its objects, conditions for and categories of membership, territorial limits, and the prohibition against political endorsements. Delegates at the 1916 Cincinnati convention adopted the model constitution and bylaws, requiring that all new clubs adopt them. "Existing clubs will be grandfathered [permitted to remain], but any subsequent changes to their local constitutions must have the written consent of the International Association Board," Ches Perry wrote in the *Weekly Letter*.

The most radical change with the new International Association of Rotary Clubs' Constitution was the division of Rotary into 10 geographic units called districts. It created the new title "district governor" to further the objects of the association, organize new clubs, and promote the interests of existing clubs, and to do so under the general supervision of the International Association's Board. Ninety years later, the district governor remains the link between the Rotary International Board and local Rotarians. Over the years, there have been several revisions to the RI Constitution, but other than alterations to accommodate cultural or geographic changes, the amendments have been minor.

The Rotary Platform and the Object of Rotary

The constitution and bylaws established rules and procedures for the association and its clubs to follow. But it did not answer the basic questions: *What is Rotary? What do Rotarians believe in?* Those core values were outlined in a speech originally called "The Rotary Platform" and later, "The Object of Rotary."

The Rotary Club of Seattle had composed a platform defining its beliefs almost from the day it began. Three of its members, James Pinkham, Ernest Skeel, and Roy Denny, adapted the club position paper and presented it as a

suggested "Rotary platform" at the second annual convention in Portland in 1911. The five-paragraph statement set out the classification system of membership, the commitment to fair and honest dealings, and the idea that service is the basis of all business. The platform ended with the words "He profits most who serves best."

On the same day in August 1912 as the delegates adopted the Rotary platform, they approved the Objects of the association. The original Chicago Rotary club constitution in 1906 had two objects:

1. The promotion of the business interests of its members.
2. The promotion of good fellowship and other desiderata ordinarily incidental to social clubs.

A CHINESE TRANSLATION OF THE ROTARY CODE OF ETHICS

---

5   Rotary Clubs of America, *Second National Convention* (Chicago, 1911), 4.

Later that same year, the club added a third Object:

3. The advancement of the best interests of Chicago and the spreading of the spirit of civic pride and loyalty among its citizens.

Delegates to the first National Association of Rotary Clubs convention in 1910 set five Objectives for the fledgling organization:

1. To organize new clubs.
2. To promote the common good of all clubs.
3. To encourage civic pride and loyalty.
4. To promote honorable business methods.
5. To advance the business interests of the individual members.

As interest in service took root, Rotarians became more involved in helping others; and in 1915 the delegates to the San Francisco convention amplified the fifth Object and added a sixth:

5. To quicken the interest of each member in the public welfare of his community and to cooperate with others in civic, social, commercial and industrial development.
6. To stimulate the desire of each member to be of service to his fellow-man and society in general.

In 1918, the International Association approved another revision, and the Objects were restated as four points. However, the rapid growth of both clubs and projects soon made these untenable, and they again became six Objects. Over the years, Rotary has repeatedly tweaked its definition of itself, with the last significant change coming in 1951. It was then decided that Rotary really had but a single Object: "To encourage and foster the ideal of service as a basis of worthy enterprise." With that noble aim firmly planted, the credo goes on to describe four areas in which Rotarians accomplish the Object:

First. The development of acquaintance as an opportunity for service;

Second. High ethical standards in business and professions; the recognition of the worthiness of all useful occupations; and the dignifying of each Rotarian's occupation as an opportunity to serve society;

A COMMITTEE MEETING IN SESSION AT THE 1912 ROTARY CONVENTION IN DULUTH, MINNESOTA, USA

"If we had nothing but the great political associations...we would have hardly any hope of coming through the great adventure in which we now find ourselves—and I have lived through this great concern for the future of humanity with my friend, Einstein...and know that he, too, was waiting for a great movement. And now this movement has come in your association, Rotary, and in others, and we shall fight on while remaining profoundly human."

Albert Schweitzer, Rotarian and Nobel Peace Prize laureate

Colmar, France, 1960

Third. The application of the ideal of service in each Rotarian's personal, business, and community life;

Fourth. The advancement of international understanding, goodwill, and peace through a world fellowship of business and professional persons united in the ideal of service.

The Shift toward Service

One main reason for the many changes in the early Objects was the evolutionary shift in attitudes away from "self" toward "service." Rotary had begun as a group of men who enjoyed the fellowship of one another's company. It was only natural that this had elements of a business-boosting club. Early Rotary Club of Chicago rosters carried this advice: "Cultivate your fellow members and use them to get business from them; they in turn [should] do the same with you....Influence all the business of your friends and acquaintances that you can for the benefit of your fellow members. The spirit of reciprocity is strong in Rotary."[6] But before long, some members resisted the pressure to only trade with fellow members; and in 1911, Paul Harris, following a spate of unfavorable press articles citing Rotary's insularity, urged clubs to drop the business exchange practice.[7] As one of his last acts as National Association president, he struck the statistician, who kept records of business exchanged between members, off the list of club officers.[8]

Even before there was a national Rotary association and corporate shift toward service, members of the earliest clubs had started reaching out beyond their own ranks and personal interests to help those in need in their communities. Paul Harris wrote: "The question of business advantage to me was entirely lost sight of. In common with my fellow members, I had learned to place emphasis on the giving rather than the getting."

What began as a ripple in the Chicago club in 1907 became a tidal wave a decade later. Hundreds of clubs embraced thousands of projects, which propelled the movement toward two objectives: community service and ethical business practices.

---

6   University of Chicago, Social Science Committee, *Rotary? A University Group Looks at the Rotary Club of Chicago* (Chicago, IL: The University of Chicago Press, 1934), 8.

7   Charles, 10.

8   THE ROTARIAN IV, no. 1 (September 1913): 30.

When *The National Rotarian* became a monthly magazine in 1912, it fueled the fire even more. Perry let clubs use its columns as a "brag sheet" for their successful programs while other clubs used those very stories as a springboard for projects in their own communities. Some examples include:

- The Los Angeles club in 1912 donated US$4,000 toward a proposed coast-to-coast highway; a year later, they gave Christmas gifts to 15,000 needy people.
- The Portland, Oregon, club exposed and publicized local corruption schemes in 1913.
- The Lincoln, Nebraska, club sponsored the movement to build a paved highway from Lincoln to Omaha in 1914-15. In another project, they financed a local hospital.
- Many clubs purchased sacks of flour for Belgian World War I relief in 1914-15.
- The Boston club trained office boys in business ethics in 1916-17.
- Detroit Rotarians maintained a "fresh-air" camp for crippled children in 1916-17.
- The Oakland club sent thousands of pairs of shoes to war refugees in 1917-18.
- New York Rotarians established an employment bureau for discharged soldiers and sailors in 1917-18.

The idea that Rotarians should promote ethical business conduct also stemmed from the days when Paul Harris yearned to do business with trustworthy tradesmen, just like those he had known in the Vermont village of his boyhood. Paul wrote in 1912: "It is the Rotarian idea that a man's business is the best and truest expression of the man; that if the man's business life is clean, his social life is likely to be. The character of the membership of Rotary clubs must be kept high because from the membership of Rotary clubs come your friends and mine."[9]

> "In the Rotary club, men of all tongues and of all climes have united, men who know well the eternal values in the sphere of the individual, in the sphere of art and culture, men who are determined to defend it against the accusation of materialism; men, however, who are equally determined that they will permit no false romanticism to interfere with their will to serve and work for a better human organization."
>
> *Thomas Mann, Rotarian and Nobel Prize laureate in literature*
> *Munich, Germany, 1930*

PARTICIPANTS AT THE 1915 ROTARY CONVENTION IN
SAN FRANCISCO, CALIFORNIA, USA

Rotarians, clubs, and the International Association soon clamored for ethics to become a part of Rotary's manifesto. Glenn Mead of Philadelphia, who succeeded Paul Harris to become the International Association's second president, called Rotary "a solid and substantial bridge from the old order of the business world to the new," and he called for his successor to appoint a committee of Rotarians to formulate a code of ethics. The delegates to the 1913 Buffalo, New York, convention passed the resolution without a dissenting vote.

In less than a decade, Paul Harris's original dream had substance. By 1912, those early Rotarians not only sensed that they had an organization in which they could enjoy fun and fellowship but also were beginning to believe they could make the world a better place.

The loosely defined early movement now had structure: a uniform constitution, bylaws, objects, a code of ethics, and three of what today are called the four Avenues of Service: Club Service, Vocational Service, and Community Service.

Chapter 6 – Origins of Rotary Traditions

The Rotary gearwheel is one of the most familiar symbols in the world today. In some countries it is displayed at the city limits of every town with a Rotary club. But for many years, there was no standard emblem. Rotary clubs designed their own.

The Rotary Club of Chicago first used a wagon wheel, an idea attributed to Paul Harris, who reasoned that it symbolized civilization and movement. The appearance changed from time to time, depending on the engravings the club printer, Harry Ruggles, had in stock. Then Montague M. Bear, an engraver, joined the club and offered to design a permanent emblem. Members rejected his first idea—a plain buggy wheel—as looking "lifeless and meaningless." To give the appearance of action, Monty added clouds of dust ahead of and behind the wheel. He also placed the words "Rotary Club" above it. Rotarians used this design for a time until one observant member pointed out that a wheel would not generate clouds of dust in front of it! Monty removed the offending cloud and that design remained the emblem for Chicago—and many other Rotary clubs—until about 1912, the only difference being that some clubs added local landmark designs along with their own city name on a banner over the wheel.[1]

Ches Perry, secretary of the National Association of Rotary Clubs, had suggested to delegates at the 1911 Portland convention that they should adopt a standard emblem, based around the wheel, which he said "has become the

The evolution of the Rotary gearwheel emblem

Overleaf: RI President Snedecor (center), other Rotarians, and spouses at the 1921 Edinburgh convention

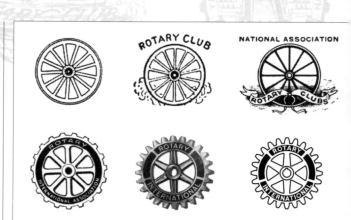

> "If we really want to love, if we really want to live, we must love until it hurts. . . . No Rotarian whose motto is Service Above Self, I think, should call himself a Rotarian if he does not make time to serve. . . . If we love, we begin to serve. And this is where that beautiful motto begins that the Rotarians have made this year, Take Time to Serve."
>
> *Mother Teresa of Calcutta, India*
> *1981 RI Convention, São Paulo, Brazil*

generally adopted emblem of Rotary clubs." At the 1912 convention, the Board of Directors appointed an executive committee to do just that. The chairman was George W. Clark of Jacksonville, Paul Harris's one-time employer, closest friend, and mentor.

Some were amazed at how quickly Clark's committee acted; they were appointed in August and had the emblem ready a month later. But it is now clear they did not start with a clean sheet of paper—they simply copied the emblem of the Rotary Club of Philadelphia.

Philadelphia's club was chartered on 30 November 1910, and the National Association assigned it club number 19. Club president Glenn Mead asked Weston Boyd the printer, George Fry the engraver, and Jack Berlet the jeweler to design an emblem. They argued that none of the wagon-wheel designs the other clubs were using conveyed the Rotary idea, submitting that adding cogs would create a working wheel, symbolic of the members working together—literally interlocked with one another to achieve the organization's objectives. They added a banner proclaiming "Trade Follows the Flag" and, for a patriotic finishing touch, an eagle.

Mead approved their design and then told Berlet of his idea of a metal lapel pin that Rotarians could wear on their coats. George Fry created a wheel with 19 cogs, emblematic of club number 19, and Berlet started making them. Thus the millions of Rotary pins men and women around the world have worn on their jackets ever since had their genesis in the mind of a club president and a jeweler in Philadelphia.

The 1912 convention appointed the design committee of George Clark, J. Filiatrault of Duluth, Mac Olson of Des Moines, and Philadelphia's Weston Boyd, who served as secretary. When Boyd showed the committee the emblem he had helped design for his own club, they accepted it. The only modifications were the removal of the eagle and the "Trade Follows the Flag" streamer. To assure uniformity, the club name was replaced by the association's name. They used the same design for the lapel pin, but because it was impossible to fit "International Association of Rotary Clubs" on such a tiny object, they abbreviated it to "Rotary International"—nine years before the 1922 Los Angeles

---

1   Rufe Chapin, "An Outline of Rotary's Beginnings," RC Chicago, Historical Club Files, RI Archives.

PAUL HARRIS (SEATED, SECOND FROM RIGHT) WITH MEMBERS OF THE
ROTARY CLUB OF LONDON AND RIBI OFFICERS IN 1932. SYDNEY
PASCALL SITS AT PAUL'S RIGHT.

convention officially made that change. The Board accepted the committee's design. It probably helped their cause that Glenn Mead had just succeeded Paul Harris and was now president of the International Association of Rotary Clubs, but Ches Perry could not resist sending Mead a letter asking, "Glenn, is it possible that Boyd came to Duluth with the design in his pocket?"

Yet despite Mead's acceptance of the committee's design and its subsequent publication in THE ROTARIAN, there was an astonishing divergence of artistic expression in the local clubs' emblems. Almost every Rotary club had its own wheel. Even within one district, some clubs designed wheels with eight spokes, others with 10, others with none at all. Some had 16 gear cogs, some 20, some none. Amazingly, the wheel on the cover of THE ROTARIAN in April 1919 had 19 cogs, yet the May cover had a wheel with 20. In June, the wheel sported 27!

The gearwheel remained an object of some contention. In 1918, Charles Henry Mackintosh started a campaign to amend the standard design. Citing objections from Oscar Bjorge, a distinguished engineer and fellow member of the Rotary Club of Duluth, he wrote to Ches Perry: "A cogwheel with 19 cogs is an anachronism to engineers." The two men, along with Rotarian George Berringer of Camden, New Jersey, lobbied Rotary International for six years to correct the emblem. They argued it had square-cornered teeth of disproportionate size, that the cogs were irregularly spaced, and that it was "an insult to engineering…that only the brain of an artist could conceive."

2   THE ROTARIAN, January 1920, 15.
3   THE ROTARIAN VII, no. 2 (August 1915): 126.
4   THE ROTARIAN VI, no. 2 (February 1915): 24.

From his hospital bed, where he was recovering from an appendectomy, Bjorge sketched out a new wheel with six spokes (some say emblematic of the six Objects of Rotary at that time) and 24 teeth.[2] Finally, he added a keyway, which locks a wheel to a hub, thus making it a "worker and not an idler." In 1928, Bjorge's exact specifications were written into the *Manual of Procedure*, and approved by the 1929 Dallas convention. Rotary's emblem has remained unchanged ever since.

The geared Rotary wheel appears throughout the world on millions of lapel pins, flags, men's ties, and jewelry. It has been pasted on huge highway billboards and on postage stamps in more than 100 nations. From its casual origins through its varied early manifestations, the Rotary wheel ultimately exceeded the aims of its designers: It symbolized action and a million members working together to make the world a better place. It also allowed fellow Rotarians to identify each other and silently informed the general public "I am a Rotarian."

The Rotary Flag

In September 1914, National Association President Frank Mulholland of Toledo, Ohio, in compliance with the instructions of the 1914 Houston convention, appointed a committee to design a flag for all Rotary clubs. Committee chairman Russell F. Greiner of Kansas City, Missouri, the third president of the International Association of Rotary Clubs, sketched an acceptable design. Greiner described it this way: "The main portion to be white which is the banner of internationalism and is looked upon as the lily white banner of international amity and goodwill. It stands for advancement among men and nations and is the flag of humanity. In the center of the flag should appear the official emblem of the organization worked out in gold and blue and containing the words 'Rotary International.' The blue stands for constancy of purpose, and the gold for the pure standard upon which rotates the wheel of eternal progress."[3] The honor of flying the Rotary flag for the first time was

Observance of the first Rotary months began in July 1983 when special weeks were designated as special months. The Rotary calendar today: July, Literacy Month; August, Membership and Extension Month; September, New Generations Month; October, Vocational Service Month; November, The Rotary Foundation Month; December, Family Month; January, Rotary Awareness Month; February, World Understanding Month (and Rotary's anniversary, 23 February); April, Magazine Month; and June, Rotary Fellowships Month. Rotary weeks include World Interact Week in November and World Rotaract Week in March.

> One of the colorful traditions of many Rotary clubs is the exchange of small banners, flags, or pennants. Rotarians traveling to distant locations take banners to exchange at make-up meetings as a token of friendship. Clubs use the decorative banners for displays at meetings and district events. The exchange is a meaningful gesture that serves as a tangible symbol of international fellowship.

accorded to Russell Greiner, and he did so before a large crowd of Rotary and civic dignitaries when he raised it on the flagstaff of the Baltimore Hotel in Kansas City at 11 a.m. on 4 January 1915.[4]

Rotarian Admiral Richard Byrd flew the Rotary flag over the South Pole in 1929 and the North Pole four years later. In 1932, Professor Auguste Piccard carried a Rotary flag given to him by the Rotary Club of Zurich on his record-setting balloon ascent to 55,577 feet (18,526 m). A year later, the flag headed in the opposite direction when the Rotary Club of Houghton, Michigan, carried it 6,254 feet (2,085 m) beneath the earth's surface for a meeting at the bottom of the Quincy Copper Mine.[5] The first Rotary club banner flew in outer space when astronaut Frank Borman, a Rotarian from Space Center, Houston, Texas, took it on his orbit around the Moon.[6]

The Four Avenues of Service

As Rotary grew, so did the complexity of its practices, making it difficult for Rotary International to succinctly and clearly answer the question, "What is Rotary?"

In 1923, RI President Guy Gundaker of Philadelphia wrote a booklet titled "A Talking Knowledge of Rotary." It was an excellent resource for club officers and new members, but it hardly summarized the organization's universal objectives into a memorable definition.

One Sunday morning in 1926, Sydney Pascall and Vivian Carter went for a walk in the woods not far from London. Pascall was then president of Rotary International in Britain & Ireland (RIBI), and Carter was RIBI secretary. The woods were so dense that the two had to walk in single file, so conversation was difficult. Pascall told Carter that he felt few Rotarians really understood what the organization's objects were. "We should be able to consolidate all Rotary activities onto a half-sheet of paper," he reasoned.

The two arrived at the conclusion that Rotary was like a three-lane highway: one lane where a Rotarian could serve his club, one to serve his vocation, and one to serve his community. They named it the Aims and Objects Plan, and clubs in Britain and Ireland adopted it and found it very helpful. A year later, Rotary International invited Vivian Carter to Chicago to explain the A & O Plan to the Board of Directors, and that body was impressed at how he

72

5   Rotary International, *Rotary: Fifty Years of Service* (Evanston, Illinois, 1954), 33.
6   Clifford L. Dochterman, *The ABCs of Rotary* (Evanston, Illinois: Rotary International, 2000), 9.
7   THE ROTARIAN, February 1949, 7.

DISTRICT 65 GOVERNOR HARRY CUMMINS, 1931-32 RI PRESIDENT
SYDNEY PASCALL, AND CLUB PRESIDENT SPENCER NALL AT A DISTRICT 65
CONFERENCE IN GEELONG, AUSTRALIA

could explain the entire Rotary philosophy on a blackboard.[7] When the plan
was proposed to the 1927 Ostend convention in Belgium, the delegates overwhelmingly approved its worldwide usage.

Yet while these three lanes were adopted, others within the movement
were urging Rotary to embrace international peace and goodwill as an added
emphasis. In 1924, Rotarians in Kansas City, Missouri—about as far from an
international border as any city in America—petitioned Rotary International to devote a year's program to emphasize international service. Although
their suggestion was not accepted, over time Rotarians became imbued with
the idea of committing themselves to improving international relations. The
1928 Minneapolis convention unanimously adopted International Service as

The Rotary emblem was first printed on six postage stamps to commemorate the 1931 RI Convention in Vienna, Austria. The stamp set
sold for about US$2 at the time and is worth more than $300 today.
More than 100 nations have honored Rotary with commemorative postage—several of them more than once. Many Rotarians collect Rotary
stamps along with special envelopes, cards, cancellations, and other phil-
atelic items.

JIM DAVIDSON DELIVERED THE KEYNOTE ADDRESS AT THE 1930
CHARTER DINNER OF THE ROTARY CLUB OF SINGAPORE.

the final track of what has forever since been known as Rotary's four Avenues of Service:[8]

- Club Service, where members are educated about Rotary, where fellowship is encouraged, and where committees handle club administration.
- Vocational Service, where members connect the ideals of the organization—ethics, service, the drive for leadership excellence—with their trade or profession.
- Community Service, the very heart of service, where every Rotary club on earth acts as the good neighbor in its local community.
- International Service, the Object added at the 1921 Edinburgh convention, where Rotarians reach far beyond their own communities to advocate peace among nations, understanding among peoples, and the elimination of hunger, suffering, and disease.

Other Avenues Advocated

Many Rotarians still felt strongly drawn toward working with children and repeatedly called for Youth Service to be a fifth Avenue. Others argued that service to the handicapped should become another Avenue. But succes-

---

8   THE ROTARIAN, August 1928, 11.

sive RI Boards and Councils on Legislation felt that the reason the four Avenues worked was that they were simple, easy to remember and repeat. The Boards countered that if "youth" became an avenue, there would soon be an argument for "the elderly" to become one; if "handicapped" were added, how long would it be before "poverty" or "environment" was demanded?

Over the years, some programs were introduced that transcended any one Avenue. RYLA, the Rotary Youth Leadership Awards, involves community and vocational service when Rotarians teach local teenagers leadership skills, ethics, and serving others. Rotaplast, a program initiated by the Rotary Club of San Francisco, has Rotarian surgeons recruiting other medical practitioners, who are not necessarily Rotarians, to go at their own expense to Latin America where they operate on injured and deformed patients in impoverished areas. Here Vocational Service and International Service combine to accomplish Rotary's mission.

The four Avenues of Service helped define Rotary's programs, added organization to its mission, and for 80 years thereafter have made it a simple and proud task for Rotarians to answer the question "What is Rotary?"

The annual Rose Parade on New Year's Day in Pasadena, California, USA, is arguably the largest public relations project of Rotary clubs in the United States and Canada. Since 1924, a Rotary float has been entered 25 times, including every year since 1981. North American Rotarians fund the entry, which highlights a program or service theme. The festive parade is seen by more than 250 million television viewers worldwide.

Images of Rotary

Founder Paul P. Harris enjoys sukiyaki in Tokyo during a 1936 Pacific goodwill tour.

Paul Harris plants a "friendship tree" in Tokyo in 1935.

1982-83 RI President Hiroji Mukasa of Japan.

1992-93 Ambassadorial Scholar Jennifer Amyx of North Carolina, USA, makes rice cakes in Japan.

Past RI President Paulo V.C. Costa and 1995-96 RI President Herbert G. Brown present Sadako Ogata, UN high commissioner for refugees and former Ambassadorial Scholar from Japan, with the Rotary Award for World Understanding and Peace at the 1996 convention in Calgary, Alberta, Canada.

Youth Exchange students from Australia and the United States participate in a Shinto shrine festival in 1997 in Japan.

The 1961 Tokyo convention broke an attendance record, with 23,366 Rotarians and guests.

Rotarians plant a tree as part of Rotary's Preserve Planet Earth program.

RI General Secretary George Means, 1952-53 RI President H.J. Brunnier, and Francis Kettaneh at the 1953 convention in Paris, France.

French Rotarian Guy Blancheton takes a break with a young transplant patient during a 560-mile (900-kilometer) cycling rally in 1999 to promote awareness of organ donation.

Rotarians from Belgium and the Netherlands visit a Health, Hunger and Humanity project in Zaire (now Democratic Republic of the Congo). The ongoing effort is helping to develop orchards of *Treculia africana* trees, which produce a nutritious fruit and edible seeds to fortify the local diet.

Jean-Paul Moroval of Thionville, France—the one millionth member of Rotary, in 1986. He and his wife, Danielle, celebrated at the RI Convention in Las Vegas, Nevada, USA.

1927-28 District 25 Governor Joaquin Anorga, Paul and Jean Harris, and 1926-27 Governor Urbano Trista meet in Cuba in 1927.

World Community Service projects help fund the construction of water wells in Haiti.

A Rotarian physician in Chile provides instructions to a young mother before discharging her son, who had cleft-lip surgery. Rotaplast International, a World Community Service project supported by Rotary clubs in North and South America, provides free reconstructive facial surgery to children in need.

The Rotary Club of Torrelavega Cantabria, Spain, provided its community with the gift of a bronze statue, "Monument to Human Values," which depicts helping hands supporting the globe. The artist is club member Mercedes Rodriguez Elvira.

Megan Morris, an Interactor from California, USA, demonstrates the correct way to brush teeth in a personal hygiene program sponsored by Project Amigo in Mexico.

Rotary volunteers help construct the Hospital of Hope in the Dominican Republic, a project sponsored by districts 7070 (Canada) and 4060 (Dominican Republic).

Tomas Muñoz, 17, celebrates his new mobility with local children in Honduras. Rotarians have provided thousands of wheelchairs by teaming up with the nonprofit Wheelchair Foundation.

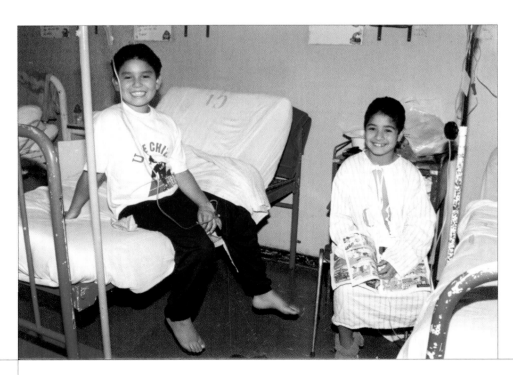

District 4340 (Chile) received a Children's Opportunities Grant that provided surgery for these two patients.

These boys learn shoemaking skills at an orphanage in Lima, Peru. The vocational service project was funded through a Rotary Foundation Matching Grant and supported by Rotarians in the United States and Peru.

Dong-Kurn Lee, 1995-96 governor of District 3650 in Korea, celebrates with his wife, Young-Ja, and RI President Herbert Brown at the 1996 Calgary convention. RI District 3650 was the top international winner of the Calgary Challenge, a major membership drive. Under Lee's leadership, the district chartered 32 clubs and inducted 1,783 new members.

1998-99 Ambassadorial Scholar Hea Kyung Park from Korea puts his studies into practice at a laboratory in New Haven, Connecticut, USA.

Korean Rotarians sponsor a walk-a-thon as a fundraiser for people with disabilities.

Rotarians of Gangreung-Jungang, Korea, assist local farmers with a rice harvest in 1996.

To commemorate the first anniversary of the Rotary Club of Jeonju-Hanbyeok, Korea, in 1996, Rotarians present students with scholarships.

Children play at a fellowship event sponsored by Rotaractors in Korea.

Rotarians of Kyoto-Southwest, Japan, host six students from their sister club in Korea.

Renato Figueiredo (right), 1998-99 president of the Rotary Club of São Paulo-Memorial da America Latina, Brazil, presents keys to a van for a local cancer center for children. A Matching Grant allocated to districts 4610 (Brazil) and 3090 (India) funded the vehicle, which transports children to the facility for treatment.

Rotary Volunteer Dr. Otto Austel (right) trains a health-care worker as part of a Health, Hunger and Humanity project to promote medical care in Brazil. The project has funded medical clinics and a clean-water system and provided fruit trees.

Paulo V.C. Costa welcomes Mother Teresa of Calcutta, India, at the 1981 RI Convention in São Paulo, Brazil. Costa served as RI president in 1990-91.

In this 1936 ceremony, Brazil's Foreign Minister Macedo Soares presents Paul Harris with the Order do Cruzeiro do Sul in recognition of Rotary's humanitarian efforts.

More than 8,000 young people participate in Rotary's Youth Exchange program each year, including these students in Brazil.

To commemorate Brazil's 500th anniversary in April 2000, schoolchildren plant trees as part of a special event sponsored by the Rotary Club of Arcos.

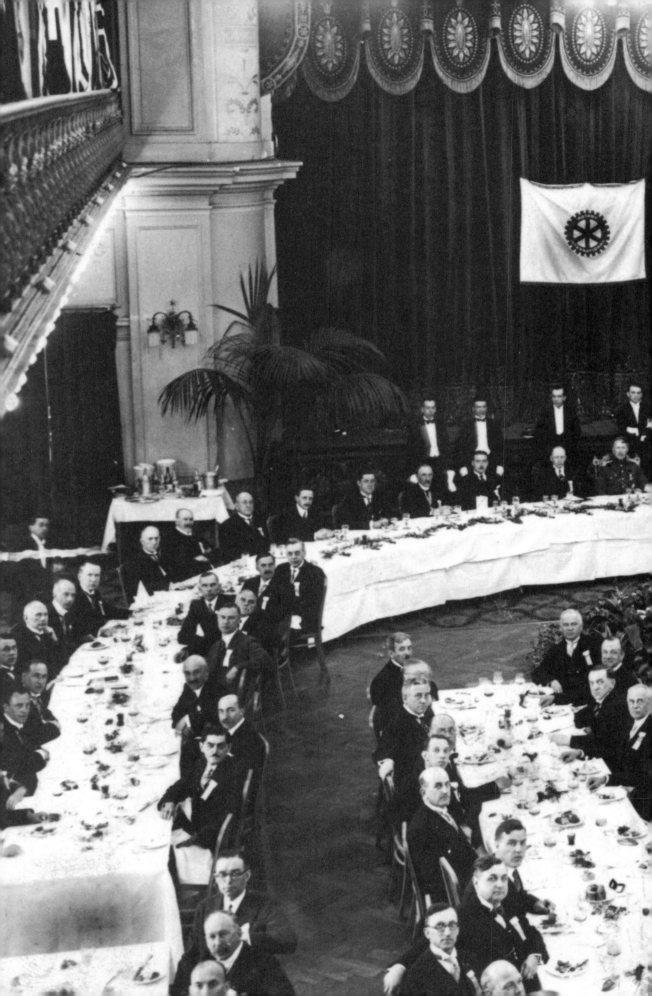

Chapter 7 — Rotary Goes International

In November 1910, just three months after the National Association of Rotary Clubs' formation and convention, fellow Chicago Rotarian Arthur Frederick Sheldon provided Ches Perry with a startling revelation. Sheldon had just returned from Winnipeg, Manitoba, Canada, where he had met a Mr. McIntyre, who learned about Rotary while living in Chicago. McIntyre told Sheldon that he, too, was a Rotarian, one of the 30-plus members of the new club in Winnipeg. The local businessmen had started a Rotary club but never bothered to inform anyone about it in the United States.

Ches Perry immediately wrote to McIntyre, extolling the virtues of the club becoming a member of the National Association. After much debate within the club, Winnipeg applied for affiliation in February 1912 and was admitted on 1 March. Winnipeg Rotarian C.E. Fletcher attended the 1912 Rotary Convention in Duluth, Minnesota. "I move that we change our name from the National Association of Rotary Clubs to the International Association of Rotary Clubs," he told the crowd. The delegates unanimously adopted his motion.[1]

Paul Harris was delighted to see his movement become international, one of his early dreams. "Were I now to tell you what plans and thoughts I

Rotarians assemble at the sprawling Kursaal for the Ostend convention.

Overleaf: Luncheon for the king of Belgium during the 1927 RI Convention in Ostend

have for the future of Rotary, you would consider me a vagarist," he remarked at the closing session of the inaugural 1910 Chicago convention. A year later, he confided to the Portland convention, "I have thought this Rotary idea so great it might be permitted to extend beyond the confines of this country." He then confessed, "Without authority of the Board of Directors, I have taken up the matter of a club in London, also [clubs] in Paris, Glasgow, Melbourne, and Sydney."[2]

Britain—and Ireland!

Harris had discovered that a Boston Rotarian, Harvey Wheeler, made frequent trips to London, and in 1911 he wrote to Wheeler, asking him to help start a club there. Arthur Sheldon told Paul he, too, was to visit London at the same time as Wheeler. Paul knew the timing was perfect. The two men met in the British capital and arranged a dinner with their business associates. The result was the formation of the Rotary Club of London, in August 1911. Wheeler cabled Paul Harris on 4 August, and the exciting news arrived as Paul was about to give the opening address to the 1911 Portland convention. Yet for all Paul's plans to make London Rotary's first foothold in Europe, a man he later called "the Runaway Irishman" outdid him.

Stuart Morrow had migrated to America in 1885 at the age of 20. He joined the

Rotary Club of San Francisco a few months after it began in 1909 under the classification "collection agency." But he failed in business and by early 1911 had returned to Ireland. Morrow had enjoyed Rotary, and he soon approached business and professional leaders in Dublin with the idea of starting a club there. His first convert was his brother-in-law, Bill McConnell, an insurance agent. Morrow was a persuasive talker and effective organizer—all the more through his scheme to keep as a finder's fee half of each member's initiation dues. The first meeting of the Rotary Club of Dublin was on 22 February 1911; the club was officially organized on 21 March—more than four months before the London club—but they failed to advise headquarters.

By the time Chicago Rotarians heard of the Dublin club, Morrow was already establishing a club in Belfast. Ches Perry congratulated him and asked

---

1   THE ROTARIAN III, no. 1 (September 1912): 5.
2   Rotary Clubs of America, *Second National Convention* (Chicago, 1911), 42.

him to move on to Scotland and England as Rotary's roving ambassador. Paul Harris's Runaway Irishman went on to start clubs in Glasgow, Edinburgh, Birmingham, and Liverpool and then was sent to open new clubs in the London area. The association planned to send him to do extension work in Australia and New Zealand; but several British Rotarians wrote to headquarters complaining about his recruiting tactics—and profiteering by keeping the initiation dues—and the name Stuart Morrow soon faded like a fallen star.[3] A decade later, London Rotarians were amazed when they heard that Morrow had just arrived back in their city from the United States where he had founded a female equivalent of Rotary, which he called Soroptomist Clubs of America. He was in their city once again, this time to present the charter to the Greater London Soroptomist Club.[4]

In 1912, delegates to the Duluth convention heard that men in Germany, Switzerland, and France had already taken preliminary steps toward establishing Rotary clubs in those countries. But World War I intervened, and although many new clubs were started in Britain, not a single club was to be established in continental Europe until after the war ended.

Over the Seas and Far Away

In March 1916, with Europe embroiled in "the war to end all wars," the International Association Board appointed a committee of 16 Rotarians to explore extension in Latin America. Each man had interests and experience in that region, and many spoke Spanish or Portuguese. Three members of

DISTRICT GOVERNOR THOMAS LIST (LEFT) AND 1932-33 RI PRESIDENT CLINTON P. ANDERSON HOLD THE ROTARY FLAG CARRIED OVER THE SOUTH POLE BY ADMIRAL BYRD.

LOCAL ROTARIANS FLANK (FROM LEFT) PAST RI PRESIDENT
FRANK MULHOLLAND, RIBI PRESIDENT FRANK EASTMAN,
RI PRESIDENT GUY GUNDAKER, AND VIVIAN CARTER
ABOARD SHIP IN ENGLAND IN 1924.

the committee—John Turner, Ernest Berger, and Angel Cuestra—belonged
to the Tampa, Florida, club. Through their efforts, in April 1916 they chartered the Rotary Club of Havana, Cuba—the first in Latin America and the
first non-English-speaking club.[5]

Businessmen in Montevideo, Uruguay, started the first Rotary club
in South America two years later. When Rotary finally entered continental
Europe, in Madrid in October 1920, it came about through the efforts of
Tampa-Havana Rotarian Angel Cuestra, a noted cigar maker and a native of
the Spanish capital, who donated a substantial amount of his own money to
help the new club's community service programs.[6]

Although never officially recognized as a club, Rotarians in Paris had
been meeting since August 1918. By then, the United States had entered the
war, and the many U.S. military officers, diplomats, and humanitarian agency
workers based in France who in civilian life had been Rotarians started the
Allied Rotary Club in France. Ancil T. Brown from the Indianapolis club became its first president, and such notable Rotarians as General John J. "Black
Jack" Pershing, U.S. Ambassador William Sharp, and Major James Perkins,
Red Cross commissioner for Europe, were regular attendees.[7]

As World War I ended, Rotary began to spread rapidly around the world.
The first club in Asia—Manila—was launched in July 1919; Rotary was also

3   University of Chicago, Social Science Committee, *Rotary? A University Group Looks at the Rotary Club
    of Chicago* (Chicago, IL: The University of Chicago Press, 1934), 37.
4   James P. Walsh, *The First Rotarian: The Life and Times of Paul Percy Harris, Founder of Rotary* (West
    Sussex, Great Britain: Scan Books, 1979), 103.
5   THE ROTARIAN VIII, no. 4 (April 1916): 274.
6   Walsh, *The First Rotarian*, 114.
7   THE ROTARIAN XIII, no. 5 (November 1918): 222.

introduced to China with the Shanghai club in July 1919 and to Japan with the charter of the Rotary Club of Tokyo in October 1920. Africa established its first Rotary club when Johannesburg, South Africa, was organized in April 1921.

The "real" Rotary Club of Paris was started in April 1921. Rotary then spread to Oslo, Copenhagen, Amsterdam, Ostend, Milan, Zurich, and Prague. It was not by coincidence that each of these clubs was launched in former Allied and neutral countries. There was still a strong sense of hostility between the two sides of the Great War. But it was that very antagonism that gave Rotary the opportunity to advance its now-renamed sixth Object: the aim to create peace and goodwill among all people. It was therefore a historic turning point when, in 1923, the Rotary Club of Milan introduced Rotary to Italy. In 1925, a

Scandinavia has produced many prominent Rotarians. Swedish King Gustaf VI walked from his castle to the Grand Hotel to enjoy pancakes with Stockholm Rotarians. Norway's Thor Heyerdahl was a scientist, oceanographer, and Rotarian who in 1947 sailed 4,300 miles (6,920 km) on a raft from Peru to Polynesia. Lennart Nilsson was a Stockholm Rotarian and master in microphotography, taking images inside the human body. Finnish composer Jean Sibelius was a Helsinki Rotarian.

club was chartered in Vienna, Austria, and on 8 October 1927, the first Rotary club was established in Germany, in Hamburg. Danish Rotarian T.C. Thomsen organized the Hamburg club, and its first president was former German Chancellor Wilhelm Cuno, who later became Rotary's first district governor in Germany.

In March 1921, the International Association Board asked two prominent Canadian Rotarians to introduce Rotary to Australia and New Zealand. The two men, Colonel J. Layton Ralston, president of the Halifax club, and Colonel James "Big Jim" Davidson of Calgary, gave four months of their time and a considerable financial contribution to attain that goal. They traveled by train to San Francisco and then embarked on a 21-day voyage.

"I had started off lightheartedly for a trip and more or less incidentally to tell our friends Down Under about Rotary," Ralston recalls. "But he [Jim Davidson] was going to carry to them something new and fine, and he was going to see that they understood what it was and valued it and lived it as he did. There was no 'take it or leave it' in the approach he planned for us. It was 'take it and keep it and use it.' I learned more about Rotary in that three-week voyage with him than in my previous eight years of membership."[8] By the time they returned, they had established Rotary clubs in the four largest cities of Australia and New Zealand,[9] and Rotary was planted on all six continents.

The Canadians' success was so remarkable that the Board asked them to do more "missionary work"; but shortly after his return from Australia, Ralston entered politics. He went on to become one of Canada's most renowned statesmen, serving as minister of national defense and minister of finance. Without hesitation, the Board turned to Jim Davidson, often called the "Marco Polo of Rotary."

"Big Jim" Davidson

Colonel James Wheeler Davidson was a consummate adventurer. Born in Austin, Minnesota, in 1872, he excelled at only one subject in school: geography. He dreamed of visiting faraway lands. At age 18, an uncle introduced him to Admiral Robert E. Peary, whom young Jim persuaded to take him along on his historic expedition to the North Pole in 1909. He returned from the epic journey and landed a job as a reporter for the *New York Herald*, which promptly dispatched him to Asia to cover the war between China and Japan.

Davidson was so fascinated with Japanese culture that he joined the Imperial Army, learned the language, and wrote an acclaimed book, *Formosa, Past and Present.* The emperor of Japan awarded him the Order of the Rising Sun for saving a community from marauding Chinese pirates. Davidson then joined the U.S. Foreign Service. As consul-general in Shanghai, he won praise from U.S. presidents William McKinley and Theodore Roosevelt. Roosevelt sent him to map out Manchuria. Even the Russian government employed him as a special commissioner to report on the economic potential of its proposed Trans-Siberian Railroad.[10]

The only thing that stopped him was typhoid. When he contracted the disease in 1906, the 34-year-old Davidson, lingering near death, was sent to San Francisco. Lillian Dow, whom he had met in Shanghai, accompanied him home and tended to him during his long recuperation. They later married and settled in Calgary, where he joined the Rotary club in 1914.

JIM, LILLIAN, AND MARJORY DAVIDSON
TRAVELING IN ASIA

8 Layton Ralston to Lillian Dow Davidson, July 1933, *Making New Friends*, copy 1, RI Archives.
9 N.T. Joseph, *James Wheeler Davidson: Profile of a Rotarian* (Cochin, India: Rotary Club of Cochin, 1987), 14-20.
10 Joseph, 8.

Davidson had established a reputation at Rotary International after his successful South Pacific expedition with Ralston. For several years he served on international extension committees, but remained, at heart, a "doer" rather than a "discusser." In 1928, the RI Board appointed Davidson honorary general commissioner, with the mandate to add the missing links in the chain of Rotary clubs between Europe and Asia.

Armed with a portfolio of glowing testimonials—including letters of introduction from ambassadors, two kings, three presidents, and five prime ministers—66-year-old Jim, Lillian, and their young daughter, Marjory, set sail from Montreal on the *Duchess of Athol* on 23 August 1928.[11] He had spent months laying the groundwork and had planned meetings with local civic and business leaders at every stop. In many cases, he even arranged audiences with the head of state.

Davidson's work began in Turkey, and the family traveled there on the Simplon-Orient-Express from Paris. Ironically, this first stop was one of the only places where Jim could not organize a Rotary club right away. Then he moved on to Greece, which had been embroiled in a civil war. Davidson met with Prime Minister Venizelos and pointed out that Rotary was an ideal vehicle for bringing people from different religious and political sides together. He later wrote of the satisfaction he felt when, at the organizational meeting of the Rotary Club of Athens on 14 December 1928, traditional sworn enemies sat side by side and shook hands.

Rotary headquarters had for years vainly tried to start a club in Cairo, Egypt. Within two weeks of arriving from Athens, Davidson had convened an organizational meeting, and the Rotary Club of Cairo, with 22 charter members, became official on 2 January 1929. The Cairo club quickly set about establishing a Rotary presence in six other Egyptian cities. Davidson's fruitful journey took him next to Palestine, Syria, across the desert to Iraq, and then, by steamer, to Bombay, India.

He followed the same successful formula at every stop: first, meet with the highest-ranking official in town and "sell" him on what a Rotary club could do for the community. Then, meet individually

JAMES WHEELER DAVIDSON, WHO TRAVELED NEARLY 150,000 MILES IN HIS QUEST TO ESTABLISH ROTARY CLUBS IN EUROPE AND ASIA

"In my blur of memories is a garden party in New Delhi...[with] 3,000 or so men and women from around the globe [having] come together under the Rotary banner. There were silken saris and white jackets and non-alcoholic drinks and good spirits. Suddenly heads turned toward someone arriving at the edge of the party...being surrounded and hugged. It was Pandit Nehru himself."

Karl Krueger

Editor, THE ROTARIAN, *1952-74*

with as many civic, business, and professional men as he could, many of whose names he had obtained from his first meeting. A few days later, he would bring them all together for an organizational dinner; and with Davidson as the eloquent and informed keynote speaker, those present usually signed up on the spot. After completing his report to headquarters and charging the new club's officers with their duties and responsibilities, Davidson and his family would move on to the next city.

Jim, Lillian, and Marjory Davidson journeyed around the world on every form of transport known at the time, from steam train to canoe to elephant. While Jim met incessantly with prospective Rotarians, Lillian tutored their daughter, exposing Marjory to sights and cultures that few children before or since have experienced. At night, Lillian wrote colorful travelogues for THE ROTARIAN, so that members around the world could follow their exploits. Lillian later put these all together into a book, *Making New Friends.*

From India they sailed south to Ceylon, then on to Burma, Malaya, and Singapore. It was an exhausting journey through some very inhospitable terrain. In Malacca, their speeding driver crashed the car, trapping them beneath the vehicle. Luckily, local villagers rushed to rescue them. As soon as they were released from the hospital, they resumed their mission. Marjory contracted a fever from an insect bite, Lillian caught malaria, and Jim fell victim to dengue. Yet he arose from his sick bed in Singapore and met 200 prospective Rotarians in groups of one and two, his reward being the formation of the Rotary Club of Singapore on 6 June 1930 with 71 charter members.

Occasionally, they would arrive in a town that already had a Rotary club. The Rotary Club of Calcutta, India, had started 10 years earlier, organized by R.J. Coombes, an Englishman who had been introduced to Rotary by A.C. Terrell while on a business trip to Grand Rapids, Michigan, in 1918. Coombes had organized the club in September 1919, receiving its charter in January 1920. But it did not induct its first Indian member until 1921. Jim Davidson was the first Rotary official they had ever seen. Jim insisted that the clubs he formed include among their members the local leaders and not be "expatriate

---

11 Lillian Dow Davidson, *Making New Friends from Near to Far East for Rotary* (Chicago: Rotary International, 1934), ix.

clubs." Nitish Laharry, the first Indian secretary of the Calcutta club, in 1926, went on to become president of Rotary International in 1962-63.

The Djokjakarta Rotary club, founded in 1927 by Dutchman G. Jh. West-enenk, was effusive in welcoming the Davidsons. "Please do not call me Your Highness," Prince Pakoe Alam told Lillian. "I want to be known here simply as Rotarian Pakoe."[12]

By meeting with the local men of influence, Davidson learned of suit-able locations for clubs, often extending Rotary to towns that strategists back in Chicago would have ignored. In the Dutch East Indies (now Indonesia), such advice led to the formation of the Rotary Club of Batavia (later Jakarta), with 70 charter members, and Bandoeng with 45. The Malang club began with 30 Rotarians and Medan with 47.

Rotary attracted men of high standing—kings, princes, ambassadors, sultans, and government ministers—and this further added to the cachet of the organization. When Jim established the Rotary Club of Bangkok on 17 September 1930, five princes were among its 70 charter members. The char-ter president was His Royal Highness Prince Purachatra.[13]

In Hong Kong, 80 members joined the club at its inaugural dinner, and similar successes followed in the Philippines, Japan, and Korea. Jim then took his family to the territory he had once covered as a young reporter 30 years earlier. The Rotary Club of Shanghai, now 12 years old, had 175 members, and he urged them to sponsor new clubs, which they did, in Hangchow and Canton. After a stopover in Jim's beloved Formosa (now Taiwan), the family sailed for home.

In March 1931, two-and-a-half years after they had departed for an "eight-month" trip, the Davidsons arrived back in Vancouver to a tumultu-ous welcome. Ches Perry came from Chicago to greet them, and Rotary clubs from miles around convened a multicity meeting in their honor. During his keynote speech, Jim entranced the audience with colorful anecdotes. He had traveled almost 150,000 miles (240,000 km), had made his two-hour Rotary recruiting speech to 2,000 men, and fewer than a dozen had declined his in-vitation. Solely as a result of his persuasive efforts, 23 Rotary clubs were now operating in every major city between Europe and Asia.

When Davidson made his report to the RI Board a month later, Paul Harris showed up to congratulate and thank him. Jim admitted that the trip had its high points, but that there were also times when he wanted to give up. One such instance was in Rangoon, Burma (now Yangon, Myanmar), when the core group Jim had assembled all changed their minds. He was deter-mined to move on, but Lillian and Marjory convinced him to try again. A few weeks later, Jim presided over the inauguration of the 80-member Rotary Club of Rangoon.[14]

Jim had come home just in time. He was not a well man, and over the next year his health worsened. When he was unable to speak at the 1932 Seattle convention, Lillian took his place. She told the audience of all the oc-casions when people told Jim that he could not possibly start a club that al-lowed people from different races, religions, castes, and cultures to mix. "But

MARJORY, LILLIAN, AND JAMES DAVIDSON ON A BEACH IN SINGAPORE

the only word Jim knows in extension is 'can,'" she said, adding that although Kipling wrote "East is East, and West is West, and never the twain shall meet," among Rotarians "there is neither East nor West, nor border, nor breed, nor birth, when two strong men stand face to face, though they came from the ends of the earth."

Jim Davidson died a year later, on 18 July 1933. Tributes poured in from royalty, government leaders, and ordinary men and women he had met around the world. The 1920s was the greatest decade in international expansion in Rotary's history; the movement had spread to 50 new countries on six continents in less than 10 years. For all the tributes from palaces and potentates, the real tribute to Jim Davidson lives on to this day in the work done by those Rotarians along that long, winding trail he trekked as Rotary's "missionary extraordinaire."

12 Davidson, 99.
13 Davidson, 113.
14 Joseph, 61.

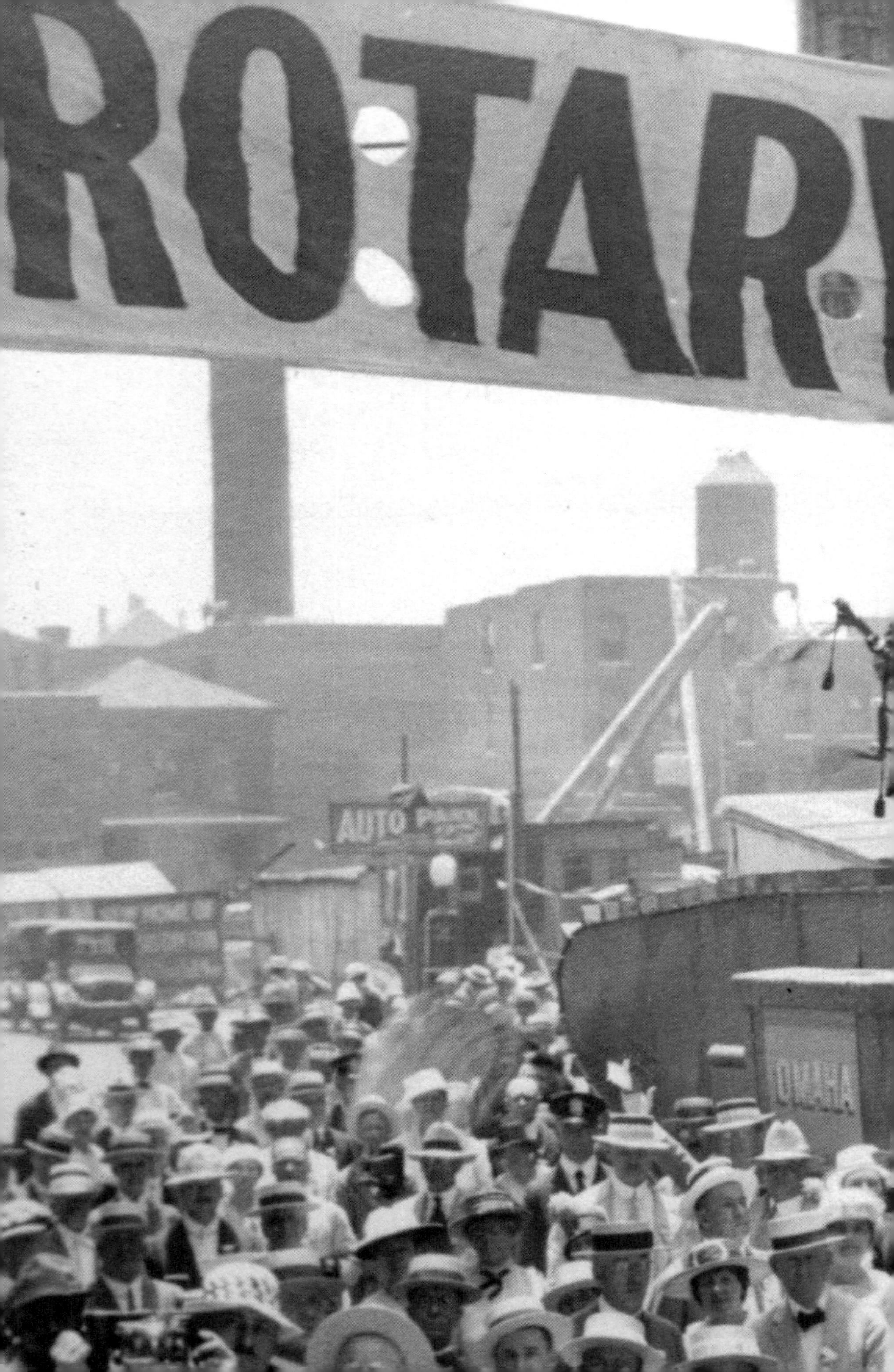
ROTAR
AUTO
OMAHA

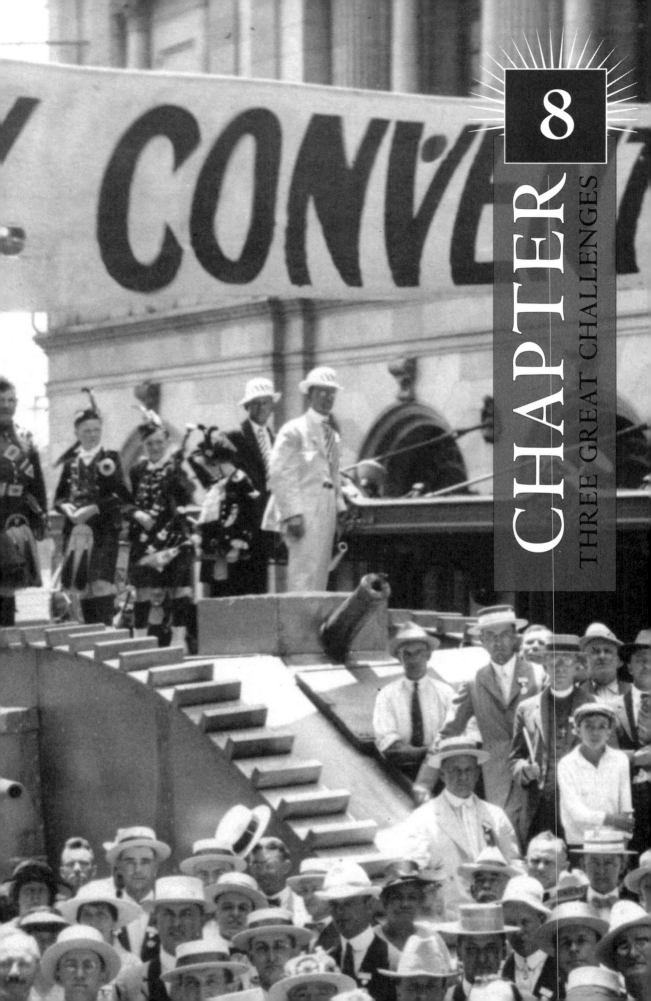

CHAPTER 8

THREE GREAT CHALLENGES

Chapter 8 – Three Great Challenges

Every river can present troubled waters, and Rotary's first century has encountered turbulence. But three events were especially threatening: the First World War, the Great Depression, and World War II.

The first flicker of war appeared in the forgotten southeast corner of Europe. At the time, the only European Rotary presence was in Britain and Ireland, and Rotarians there took little notice of the assassination of an obscure Austrian archduke named Ferdinand, in Sarajevo, Serbia. But within weeks that faraway spark had become a firestorm that engulfed Europe. By the autumn of 1914, every major world power except one—the United States—was at war.

Many Rotarians went to the front. Those at home worried about their loved ones in the armed forces and restrictions imposed on their daily lives. "Well, I suppose our Rotary lunches will now be suspended *sine die*," one member surmised to British Rotary Secretary Thomas Stephenson. "Absolutely not!" Stephenson declared. "Rotary means SERVICE, not only with a capital S, but all capitals, and if ever there was a time for SERVICE, it is now."[1]

As the ashes of war replaced the flame of hope, British Rotary rallied its members and communities into patriotic service. Clubs across Britain appointed war service committees, which in turn had subcommittees charged with international trade, encouraging enlistment, war relief, unemployment problems, and maintenance and development of local industries. In Ireland, the Rotary Club of Belfast formed the Ulster Motor Ambulance Division,

Paul Harris placing a wreath at the Tomb of the Unknowns in Washington, D.C., in 1940.

Overleaf: Rotarians gather around a tank at the 1918 RI Convention in Kansas City, Missouri, USA.

which prepared and delivered vehicles for wounded soldiers in France. Rotarians in Glasgow, Scotland, who were ineligible to join the fighting forces formed a special constable unit, filling the shortfall created when so many Scottish policemen were sent to war.[2] The club went on to form a volunteer battalion, which earned several commendations for valor at the front. The Rotary Club of Edinburgh entertained 25,000 children while their fathers were fighting overseas. The club also raised a battalion of the Royal Scots Regiment and sponsored two wards at the Bangour Military Hospital.[3] London Rotarians helped care for injured soldiers scattered in hospitals throughout the city.

"Our advice to any of our American brethren who want to see these islands and our national life at its best is to come along now," wrote London Rotarian Charles Dewey in THE ROTARIAN of December 1914.[4] Canada, a British Commonwealth country, had been in the war since the start, and its Rotary clubs had provided incalculable help. Toronto Rotarians alone had donated US$22,000 to the Red Cross for war relief. As the war dragged on, many Rotary clubs in the United States followed Canada's lead in donating money and material goods to help refugees, the sick, and the fighting forces.

For three years, the United States refused to enter the war. U.S. President Woodrow Wilson was an honorary member of the Rotary Club of Birmingham, Alabama,[5] and while the political stance was for neutrality, many Rotarians were deeply distressed by the press reports of the widespread carnage.

"Let this war go on if must needs be, but let us give thought now to the horrors of war and the blessings of peace," wrote Ches Perry in THE ROTARIAN for September 1914.[6] "Let Rotary make International Peace and Goodwill its mission as an international organization. Let us draw into the fellowship all the great fraternal orders, the press, the church, the institutions of learning… and create a public sentiment that will by its seriousness and its extent cause rulers to pause and hesitate long before attempting again to declare war after the present trouble has been settled." Rotary at the time had no plank of international peace in its platform, and Perry's editorial was prescient in that it started a movement toward adopting peace as an organization objective.

In April 1917, the United States entered the fray; now every country where there was a Rotary club was aligned on the same side of the bloodiest war in human history. Hundreds of clubs across the United States now put their backs behind the war effort. Los Angeles Rotarians supplied 20 field ambulances; Akron, Ohio, Rotarians sent their own ambulance to France.

Government officials already recognized Rotary as a powerful force for good. When the United States entered the war, it needed people to arrange entertainment and hospitality programs for soldiers in camps awaiting shipment to Europe; but officials were concerned that enemy sympathizers or spies might enroll. The government quietly brought Rotary leaders to Washington one weekend, and within 24 hours they had the entire project organized and over 100 Rotarians across the country committed to running it.[7] U.S. Rotarians subsequently raised $4 million for the War Camp Community Recreation Fund and provided hot meals and hometown hospitality to

---

1   THE ROTARIAN V, no. 6 (December 1914): 71.

2   THE ROTARIAN V, no. 6 (December 1914): 72.

3   THE ROTARIAN XI, no. 2 (August 1917): 188.

4   THE ROTARIAN V, no. 6 (December 1914): 73.

5   THE ROTARIAN VI, no. 3 (March 1915): 76.

6   THE ROTARIAN V, no. 3 (September 1914): 23.

7   Chesley R. Perry, "Rotary and the Day After," speech to RC of New York, 1 March 1923.

soldiers and sailors far away from their loved ones.[8] The Rotary Club of Philadelphia's Rotary Army and Navy Club served troops hot meals daily—as many as 500 would show up for Sunday lunch—and provided free sleeping accommodation for 188 men.

Clubs sponsored Rotarians at the front and sent them gift packages; many of the men sought to replicate the fellowship they had left behind. Rotarian Ernest W. Tickle of Liverpool, a gunner in the British Army, wrote in a letter home from France: "On Thursdays, my mind at 1 o'clock is transmitted to the Bear's Paw and over my Dixie can of army stew my gastronomic mind dwells on the Rotary luncheon. Please send me three copies of the 'Ethics of Rotary'—I want to show my companions exactly what the Rotary ideal is. Amidst the devastation of places where the great guns roar, I would almost sell my soul for the congenial company of that table. Our English 'Service—not Self' is really a truism of thousands of men out here."[9]

Rotarians serving in the war in Paris started the Allied Rotary Club in France. U.S. General John J. "Black Jack" Pershing was a Rotarian. In April 1919, another U.S. Rotarian, serving with the army of occupation in Germany, wrote to Rotary headquarters asking for the names of other members posted to that country. Ches Perry sent him a list of Rotarians serving in the Third Army, along with program suggestions; thus, long before there was an official Rotary club in Germany, Rotarians were meeting there.[10]

So many farm workers in the United States joined the fighting forces that there arose a serious threat to the nation's food supply. Again, the government turned to Rotary. Chicago Rotarian Howard Gross formed the Boys to the Farm committee, which recruited 680 unemployed urban teenagers and sent them to work on rural farms. The project was so effective that it was replicated across the country and by mid-1918 had 200,000 young men at work.[11] The War Department showed its appreciation of Rotary's support by inviting representatives of Rotary International to participate in the burial of the Unknown Soldier at Arlington National Cemetery in November 1921.

The British government also asked Rotary for help. When the war ended, hundreds of thousands of troops returned, needing jobs and housing. Rotary clubs were able to organize housing, and Rotarians—most of whom owned businesses or had influential positions—provided employment.

ROTARIANS OF 1905 GATHER AT THE 25TH ANNIVERSARY CHICAGO CONVENTION. FRONT ROW, FROM LEFT: RUFUS CHAPIN, ALBERT L. WHITE, SILVESTER SCHIELE, PAUL HARRIS, HARRY RUGGLES, CHARLES A. NEWTON, HARRY A. CROFTS. BACK ROW: WILLIAM JENSEN, JOHN P. SULLIVAN, L.G. LAWRENCE, FRED H. TWEED, BERNARD E. ARNTZEN, ROBERT C. FLETCHER, CLARK W. HAWLEY, CHARLES SCHNEIDER, MAX GOLDENBERG, WILL R. NEFF.

Despite the hardships and restrictions of the conflict, Rotary grew during the war years on both sides of the Atlantic, from 15,000 to 33,000 Rotarians and from 123 to 311 clubs. New clubs were formed in Cuba, and then-independent Hawaii and Puerto Rico. With the signing of the armistice on 11 November 1918, there was a sense among Rotarians that, having survived the Great War, they were better equipped than ever before to chart their future course and to handle whatever rough waters might be around the next bend.

They embarked on the greatest decade of growth in Rotary's history. In the two years following the ceasefire in 1918, the number of Rotarians grew by 16,346, almost doubling the number of clubs, from 415 to 758, and expanding into Latin America and Asia. Rotary not only had survived the worst conflict in human history, but had thrived, both in membership growth and the service of its members to humankind.

The Great Depression

The 1920s were as much a boom decade for Rotary as for the economies of the developed world. As 1930 approached, there was plenty to celebrate during Rotary's Silver Anniversary year. Then the stock market crashed. Rotarian Herbert Hoover had predicted in 1919 that the harsh conditions of the Versailles Treaty would cause "inevitable economic collapse"—and his prediction came true on his watch as president of the United States. Gaiety and free-wheeling optimism gave way to soup lines and bank failures. It was not just a national or regional downturn; it was a global economic depression.

8 THE ROTARIAN XII, no. 1 (January 1918): 20.
9 THE ROTARIAN XII, no. 4 (April 1918): 142.
10 Chesley R. Perry, "A Rotary Luncheon in Germany," The Weekly Letter, 21 April 1919, 2.
11 THE ROTARIAN XIV, no. 3 (March 1919): 113.

How could Rotary, an organization whose membership was the business community, survive when business was essentially bankrupt? Many clubs reduced attendance costs by allowing members to bring their own sandwiches to meetings, and many men ate no food because they were "on a diet." The 1939 Council on Legislation in Cleveland adopted a "senior active" membership category, which opened new opportunities for younger, more vigorous men to join. And many clubs changed their meeting places from fancy restaurants to church basements or community centers, where the ladies' auxiliary cooked frugal meals. Most clubs stopped paying outside speakers for their programs, thus beginning the tradition continued today of having vocational talks and other speaking assignments by the Rotarians themselves.[12]

Once the shock of the collapse had subsided, Rotarians sought ways to both bolster the morale of their fellow members in distress and to help their communities survive. THE ROTARIAN became the voice of calm, with articles by distinguished authors each month espousing reasoned optimism. "No nation becomes great by becoming rich," wrote clergyman Roy L. Smith in September 1931. "Neither does a man find enduring satisfaction in life by owning something—only by becoming something. This Depression has cost us some of the things we created, but it has robbed us of none of our power to create."[13]

Other writers prompted employers to shorten the workweek so that more employees could have a job. Yet others urged Rotarian business leaders to assure their workers that their jobs were safe, reasoning that this feeling of security would then cause them to feel freer to spend more, thus stimulating economic growth.[14]

In times of crisis, people often rush to remedy the wrong things. One delegate to the 1933 Boston convention asked Ches Perry if the current conditions meant Rotary should temporarily soften some of its ideals. Such a notion did not go over well with Perry, who had helped frame many of those ideals. "Today the world suffers—not because of an abundance of ideals, but because of a lack of ideals in those years when anything was all right that seemed to

1933-34 RI PRESIDENT JOHN NELSON RIDES A CAMEL IN EGYPT DURING A VISIT TO THE PYRAMIDS IN 1934.

1939-40 RI PRESIDENT WALTER D. HEAD AND 1940-41 RI PRESIDENT ARMANDO DE ARRUDA PEREIRA OF BRAZIL SHARE THE STAGE AT THE 1940 HAVANA CONVENTION.

yield profit," he replied. "We can do without brownstone mansions, expensive cars, and even bank accounts. These are not essential ingredients to happiness. But one thing we must not lose is our vision. And one thing we must not do is permit a moratorium on that ideal of serving others."[15]

Rotary clubs around the world launched projects to help the most desperate in their communities, despite the financial plight of many of their own members. The Rotary Club of Bahia Blanca, Argentina, founded a food kitchen that fed hundreds of impoverished people every day. In Jackson, Tennessee, USA, Rotarians replaced their weekly luncheon with soup and crackers— then used the $85 they saved each week to feed hungry schoolchildren. In Poland, the Rotary Club of Warsaw took care of feeding, clothing, and providing school supplies for the children of unemployed workers. Rotarians in Britain, Canada, and Singapore initiated hundreds of projects for young people on the dole; fully 23 percent of the world's unemployed were juveniles aged 14 to 25.

In Muncie, Indiana, USA, the Rotary club helped launch what became known as the Muncie Plan. It started when one man realized that he had time on his hands to repair his home. The paint, wood, nails, and other supplies he needed were a valuable sale to the struggling local hardware store, so then he wondered, "What if hundreds of people followed my example?" The Muncie Rotary club helped promote his idea, and soon so many people were busy buying materials that the hardware stores had to hire more help and the 80 percent unemployment rate among local construction workers was eliminated. Workers from out of town rented rooms and bought meals, lifting the economy of the entire city.[16]

"Thinking of Rotary, I visualize a series of concentric circles which, starting with the smallest and going to the largest, I denominate as the community, national, and international influence. I see Rotary International as a generating force of incalculable value."

Franklin D. Roosevelt
U.S. president and honorary Rotarian

12 THE ROTARIAN, January 1933, 33.
13 THE ROTARIAN, September 1931, 5.
14 THE ROTARIAN, December 1931, 6.
15 THE ROTARIAN, May 1933, 36.
16 THE ROTARIAN, April 1932, 8.

Rotary International President Clinton P. Anderson wrote in 1933:

"[The writer] Roger Babson, who warned of the collapse in the stock market, gives this note to merchants now: 'Next to recklessness at the top of the boom, the most foolish thing in the world is discouragement at the bottom of a slump.' I suggest Rotary clubs need again to resume their study of vocational service, not alone from the standpoint of better relationships between employer and employee or between competitors, but equally from the standpoint of doing a service to the individual himself."[17]

By 1935, the recovery had started, and soon the global economy was growing again. During the Depression there had been two years when Rotary experienced the first membership decline in its 25-year history. Yet for all the clubs in the industrialized world that surrendered their charters, there were more that joined in developing nations. On 30 June 1930, there were 3,177 clubs with a membership of 144,000. Six years later that had risen to 170,000 Rotarians in 4,004 clubs.

The Second World War

While the economic tide was turning, a new, more ominous wave began sweeping across Europe. The repressive fascist government of Premier Benito Mussolini had tolerated Rotary in Italy, but when Adolf Hitler's National Socialist (Nazi) Party assumed power in Germany in 1933, it threatened the end of Rotary in that part of the world.

Rotary International President John Nelson visited Berlin in 1933, accompanied by Vice President Herbert Schofield, General Secretary Ches Perry, and European Secretary Dr. Alex O. Potter. They met with German government officials to explain Rotary's work and principles, and Nelson delivered a speech to the Berlin Rotary club in which he said: "Rotary as an organization does not interfere in forms of government nor with political systems or schools of thought. These are things for the people of every country to decide for themselves. [A Rotarian] must apply Rotary principles to national and international problems as he has learned to apply them in his club, in his vocation, and in his community. Rotary is not a place in which we bring the affairs of

ARMANDO DE ARRUDA PEREIRA, R. COOMBES, T.A. WARREN, AND C. WARREN-BOLTON READ WAR NEWS FROM EUROPE DURING THE HAVANA CONVENTION.

RI OBSERVER SYDNEY PASCALL, CANADIAN DELEGATE DR. W. RIDDELL, AND RI EUROPEAN SECRETARY ALEX O. POTTER AT THE LEAGUE OF NATIONS, GENEVA, 1932

the world for solution, but a place in which we prepare men to accept life's duties and stimulate them to do so."[18]

Following his return to the United States, President Nelson penned an article in THE ROTARIAN titled "Rotary Carries On in Germany." In addition to printing the text of his Berlin speech, he wrote:

"Representatives of the Hitler party in some sections had difficulty for a time in reconciling Rotary principles with what they regarded as governmental policy, and, in the situation which temporarily followed, some of our Jewish Rotarians terminated their membership under varying conditions."[19]

After Hitler became German chancellor in 1933, the Nazis declared that Germans of Jewish descent or faith were second-class citizens who were forbidden to hold important jobs or own businesses. As a result, many lost their classifications and had to resign their membership in their Rotary club.

Whatever grace the Rotary delegation believed they had earned for the movement was short-lived. By 1935, articles began appearing in Nazi media accusing Rotary of numerous transgressions but especially of being linked with Freemasonry and sympathetic to Jews. One of the more incredible claims was that some of the letters in the name Rotary, if rearranged, spelled "tora," for Torah, the Jewish law, which "proved" that Rotary was a Jewish organization. On 23 August 1937, German Supreme Party Judge Walter Buch issued a decree banning Nazi Party members from membership in Rotary. His edict read:

"The Rotarian is not anti-Semitic...for him the Jew occupies a similar position in relation to his host nations as the German. The Rotarian therefore does not as a matter of principle refuse him in his society. He considers personal relations with Jews possible. National Socialism does not." He went on to repeat that Rotary and Freemasonry were connected and concluded: "He who wishes to lead in Germany may no longer belong to a society with any kind of international affiliation."[20]

Rotary's European Secretary, Alex O. Potter, and his successor, Leslie B. Struthers, made several visits to Germany, but it was clear to all that being a Rotarian was increasingly dangerous. German Rotarians floated a range of ideas designed to save their organization. Those having contacts with senior Nazi Party officials Himmler, Goering, and Ribbentrop tried personal intervention.

17 THE ROTARIAN, April 1933, 27.
18 THE ROTARIAN, November 1933, 57.
19 THE ROTARIAN, November 1933, 21.
20 Walter Buch, "Dual Membership National Socialist Party-Rotary Club Not Permissible," Munich, Germany, 23 August 1937.

PAUL HARRIS (RIGHT) AND ROTARIANS FROM COLOMBIA, CUBA, ENGLAND, GERMANY, AND SPAIN AT THE 1933 RI CONVENTION IN BOSTON

Another Rotarian attempted to arrange a meeting between the Rotary International president and Hitler. The district governor for Germany convened a meeting of club leaders from which came the suggestion that Rotary offer to exclude Masons and non-Aryans and have a Nazi official as its patron. Judge Buch spurned even that desperate idea, and it certainly would have been rejected had the proposal reached Rotary International. Rather than compromise their ideals, the club leaders sadly voted to disband all Rotary clubs in Germany effective 15 October 1937, returning their charters to Rotary International.

"It was a soul-stirring moment when our senior Rotarian Vogel stated with deep emotion what he is to be deprived of by dissolution," reported the secretary of the Rotary Club of Chemnitz. "In all his long life he had found no other circle of men where he had spent so many delightful, inspiring hours as with Rotary. He is prepared to sacrifice much for them. He asked to postpone as long as possible the parting day."[21]

In 1936, Spain, embroiled in civil war, had banned Rotary and shut down its 36 clubs. Now Germany's 42 clubs (including that in the free city of Danzig) dissolved within a year, so did those in Austria and Italy, both countries having formed closer ties with Germany. Meanwhile, on the other side of the world, the news was just as bad. The Japanese invaded China, and Rotary clubs in six cities were forced to close. As war erupted and entire countries fell

21 Rotary Club of Chemnitz, *Weekly Bulletin* 10/IX-382 (7 September 1937).
22 THE ROTARIAN, May 1940, 12.
23 Ray Lamont-Brown to Geoffrey Pike, 11 June 1998.
24 Lester B. Struthers to Chesley Perry, 8 August 1939.
25 Lester B. Struthers to Chesley Perry, 11 April 1939.
26 Lester B. Struthers to Chesley Perry, 1 November 1939.
27 Lester B. Struthers to RI Board of Directors, 16 August 1938.

> "We sincerely regret that the Rotarians of Germany and Austria, in the face of circumstances, felt that the only decision they could take was to disband their Rotary clubs. . . . But even if the members of Rotary clubs in Germany are no longer Rotarians, they are still our friends."
>
> *Maurice Duperrey, Paris, France*
> *RI president, 1937-38*
> *1938 RI Convention in San*
> *Francisco, California, USA*

to invading armies, 484 clubs and 16,700 Rotarians were wiped off the rolls of Rotary. As influential men in their communities, many Rotarians paid a heavy price when the Gestapo found membership records of the local clubs; 12 members of the Warsaw club were executed when the Germans captured that Polish city.[22] Japan's feared *kempeitai* (military police) also put Rotary and Rotarians on their "subversive" list; yet almost every Rotary club in that country, when closed down by the government, continued to meet under the name of the day of the week on which they met, such as the Tuesday Club.[23]

In many occupied countries, Rotarians continued to meet clandestinely. After the Germans took over Bohemia and Moravia (the Sudetenland), home to 39 clubs, Leslie Struthers notified Ches Perry of his concern lest the Gestapo discover that Rotarians there were holding meetings in one another's homes.[24] The Gestapo raided the home of District Governor Frantisek Kral, pointing guns at him while demanding "everything he had pertaining to Rotary." Struthers explained that just the previous day Kral had anticipated such an incursion and had burned everything he considered incriminating.[25]

In Vienna, several members of the disbanded Rotary club continued to meet each Tuesday, not as Rotarians but as "golfers."[26] Bernard Goldschmidt of the disbanded Kiel Rotary club in Germany formed an underground club called Freitagsgesellschaft (Friday Company) with trusted former Rotarians. In 1951, when Rotary returned to Germany, Goldschmidt was elected district governor. Word reached Struthers via the underground that similar groups of former Rotarians met frequently in as many as 25 German and Austrian cities,[27] often disguising themselves as singing societies. Harry Ruggles, Rotary's original song leader, would have been proud.

French Rotarians also continued to meet surreptitiously long after Germany had occupied their country and banned Rotary. "One day we were having [our club] lunch when a German officer,

RI PRESIDENT T.A. WARREN PRESENTS A NEWSPAPER CLIPPING ABOUT THE END OF WORLD WAR II TO ROTARY CLUB OF HARTFORD, CONNECTICUT, USA, PRESIDENT LEO GOLDEN.

General Schippert, came into the private dining room where we were sitting," recalls the Paris Rotary club's Henri Tard. "The last mouthful stuck in our mouths as we thought he was coming to arrest us. But he was a Rotarian and past governor from Germany and said he had come to pay his respects to past International President Maurice Duperrey. Weren't we relieved!"

Just 21 years after the armistice, the world was again caught up in the slaughter of humankind, with Rotarians on both sides of the conflict. Many Rotary clubs scaled back their activities to focus on war relief. Swiss Rotarians helped Belgian and French refugees. In Finland, Rotary clubs initiated projects to aid children orphaned by the war, while the Rotary Club of Liverpool, England, arranged for overseas Rotarians (and their sons) fighting in Europe to spend their leave in the comfort of their own members' homes.

A significant event in Rotary history occurred in 1940. Delegates to the 31st annual convention in Havana, Cuba, voted to establish the Rotary Relief Fund to help war victims. They contributed from surplus funds $50,000 to the Red Cross for direct war relief—then they adopted a resolution calling for "respect for human rights." It was the first time Rotary had issued such a declaration about human dignity. The expression, even some of the language from the resolution, later found its way into the Universal Declaration of Human Rights, authored largely by Eleanor Roosevelt, wife of the U.S. president.

PAUL AND JEAN HARRIS ENTERTAIN SCOTTISH AVIATION CADETS TRAINING IN FLORIDA DURING WORLD WAR II. ROTARIAN SAM SMITH OF LAKELAND, FLORIDA, USA, IS AT LOWER RIGHT.

London became the epicenter for refugees, many of them Rotarians. In November 1940, Casimir Zienkiewicz, past president of the Rotary Club of Katowice, Poland, escaped to London where he established the Inter-Allied Rotary club. It became a haven of good fellowship, local community service, and internal fellowship for visiting and refugee Rotarians and met regularly until 1946.[28]

In Singapore, Japanese troops invaded on 15 February 1942. Members of the Singapore Rotary club were imprisoned; others continued to meet secretly and provided comfort and moral support to the most needy victims of that terrible time. "It was community service at the most basic but necessary level," Philbert S.S. Chin, past district governor and club historian, recalled many years later.

AN ARMISTICE DAY
DISPLAY BY THE
ROTARY CLUB OF
INDEPENDENCE, IOWA,
USA, COMMEMORATES
THE END OF WORLD
WAR I.

By the early 1940s, many senior Rotarians began discussing how the organization could help once the fighting stopped. Twenty years had passed since Rotary had added International Service to its Object, and it was desperately needed now. Rotary was no longer considered "an American organization"; it was now clearly one with a global membership and diverse international leadership. "Rotary has no tanks, no army, no way to force people to stop fighting; but when the fighting stops—and it always does—that's when Rotary can shine," said William C. Carter of Windsor, England, 1973-74 RI president, years later.

Paul Harris was an elderly man by the time the guns of World War II fell silent. He had seen his idea spread around the globe; in 1945, there were 5,441 Rotary clubs with a membership of 247,212 men. Paul, the tireless advocate of friendship, tolerance, and high ethics, had grieved as he saw those basic tenets of human decency shredded by war, bloody brutality, and hateful propaganda. But in 1947, as he approached the end of his 78 years, Paul must have also rejoiced. Rotary had not only survived; it had grown. The three greatest challenges to its existence had caused Rotarians to examine what they stood for. Had their Rotary organization been worth suffering, fighting, and dying for? Paul Harris—and many other brave Rotarians—went to their graves convinced that the answer was a resounding "Yes!"

28 General Secretary report to RI Board of Directors, January 1941.

Chapter 9 – Navigating through Turbulence

As the Rotary movement spread through continental Europe in the 1920s, especially those countries where the Roman Catholic Church was influential, rumors surfaced about Rotary's connection to Freemasonry. In some countries, the local Masonic lodge is considered a meeting place for fraternal fellowship, while in others, it's suspected as a dark and secret society.

Although some Rotarians were Freemasons, Paul Harris argued forcefully that the movement had no special connection with Masonry. "I will answer by unequivocally stating that I have never been a Freemason, nor have I either directly or indirectly had any dealings or relationship with them," he wrote in a letter to Romanian district governor Agripa Popescu in 1937.[1] "I can say that Rotary has never been in any manner associated with Masonry, and I have never heard of Masonry's having influenced or attempted to influence Rotary."

In the late 1920s, certain Catholic Church officials embarked on a campaign against Rotary. The authoritative Vatican journal *Civilta Cattolica* leveled severe criticism at the organization, based on the alleged link between Freemasonry and the Rotary Code of Ethics. This moralizing and philosophical teaching, the church leaders claimed, indicated that Rotary was promoting itself as a universal religion, in opposition to the church's view that the pope is the leader of the one true church. "By presenting itself as a guide to good living, in complete independence of any denominational creed or moral authority, Rotary encourages the all too common view that man is his own sufficient guide in interpreting the moral law," explained the pamphlet "Forbidden and Suspect Societies."[2]

Past RI President Rolf J. Klärich speaks at a 1989 meeting in Tallinn, Estonia.

Overleaf: Cuba's President Federico Laredo Bru receives RI President Walter D. Head (center) and other distinguished Rotarians during the 1940 RI Convention in Havana.

RI PRESIDENT FERNANDO CARBAJAL (THIRD FROM LEFT) WITH A
LOCAL CATHOLIC PRIEST AND ROTARIANS DURING A 1943 VISIT
TO CARACAS, VENEZUELA

The Vatican banned priests from Rotary club membership—despite the affirmation by the many Rotarian priests that they had never witnessed any Masonic connection or promotion of a universal religion in Rotary's manifesto. "Many of our leading Catholic priests are enthusiastic Rotarians, and I believe that all our Catholic bishops admire the spirit and the work of Rotary," attested Father John Cavanaugh, CSC, of Notre Dame University in Indiana, USA.[3]

RI President Tom Sutton of Mexico—a Catholic—traveled to Rome and Madrid in 1929 to explain Rotary to bishops, cardinals, and the pope. Much of the antagonism had begun in Spain where, in 1928, the bishop of Palencia issued a bulletin titled "Good Catholics Cannot Belong to Rotary Clubs." The edict was widely publicized, and in 1929 the church issued a Resolution of the Holy Congregational Consistory that led to similar warnings from bishops in Spain, the Netherlands, and Quebec, Canada.[4]

That same year, the RI Board drafted a statement declaring that Rotary had no connection with Freemasonry, that religious discussions were "positively forbidden in Rotary," and that it had no secret political connections of any kind. *La Civilta Cattolica* published the eight-point statement and the Board considered eliminating the Code of Ethics but realized that would create dissent in its ranks, especially if it were suspected that it was done to appease the

---

1   Paul Harris to Agripa Popescu, 19 September 1937, Catholic Church and Rotary, Subject Files, RI Archives.
2   Lawrence I. McReavy, "Forbidden and Suspect Societies," 15.
3   John Cavanaugh to RI Board of Directors, 27 May 1927, Catholic Church and Rotary, Subject Files, RI Archives.
4   Catholic Church and Rotary 1928-29, Subject Files, RI Archives.

pope. So they chose a more passive approach. New members who had traditionally been issued a framed placard of the Rotary Code of Ethics would now receive the Object of Rotary, while references to the code would be downplayed in speeches and printed articles.

This seemed to satisfy the Vatican, and for a while the relationship improved noticeably. Count Franco Ratti, a nephew of the pope, even joined the Rotary Club of Milan, having first obtained permission from his uncle. But for many years there was an uneasy feeling about Rotary among senior Catholic clerics, especially those in Spain and Italy.

In 1935, *La Osservatore Romano*, the official Vatican newspaper, printed a story headlined "Beware of Rotary," the root of which was the choice of Mexico City for the annual Rotary International Convention. The article claimed this selection showed Rotary's support for Mexico's atheistic government "and its persecution of the Catholics and of all honest people" and that "Rotary was siding decidedly with the enemies of religion."[5]

It took time to heal these wounds. As more Catholics—including priests—joined the organization, they attested to its value to society, and the Vatican tacitly accepted that Rotary did not represent a threat to its moral teachings. The relationship was sealed in 1979 when a smiling Pope John Paul II officially welcomed a delegation of Rotarians and their leaders attending the RI Convention in Rome. Two years later, RI President Stanley E. McCaffrey presented the pontiff with the Rotary Award for World Understanding and Peace.[6]

Claims about a link with Freemasonry still inhibit Rotary's extension in several Muslim countries, although the movement is very strong in others, notably Bahrain, Indonesia, Malaysia, Nigeria, Pakistan, and the band of countries that stretches from Mauritania across North Africa to Turkey.

Race

Rotary clubs in the United States were composed almost exclusively of white men until the 1960s. There was rarely any overt discrimination; its roster simply reflected the economic reality then that few African Americans owned large businesses or occupied upper-level positions in the corporate world.

The issue had been addressed as early as the 1920s, when Will Manier Jr. of Nashville, Tennessee, who became RI president in 1936, answered a letter from James Carmichael of Cape Town, South Africa:

SEATED, FROM LEFT: PAST RI PRESIDENT ROLF J. KLÄRICH, RI PRESIDENT HUGH ARCHER, AND ROTARIAN ALEXANDER TARNAVSKI AT A 1990 MEETING OF THE PROVISIONAL ROTARY CLUB OF MOSCOW

RI President Clifford L. Dochterman presents an award to South African President F.W. de Klerk at the 1992 President's Conference on Goodwill and Development in Johannesburg.

"Though in theory Rotary would belie the principles which it professes, in particular its universality, if Negroes were proscribed...the thing to do is to sidestep the issue."[7]

Eventually, of course, the issue could not be sidestepped. Although by the 1980s there were thousands of non-Caucasian members in Rotary clubs across the United States—and internationally—the Rotary Club of Birmingham, Alabama, continued to enforce the "White males only" membership clause it had written into its constitution in 1915. In 1982, club member Angus McEachan asked the club to remove that restriction; when it refused, he resigned. The club's charter predated the 1922 date after which all new Rotary clubs had to adopt the standard club constitution. The RI Board considered the matter, voting overwhelmingly to remove any membership restrictions based on race, color, or creed, and referred it to the 1982 annual convention in Dallas. The Birmingham club then reconsidered and in a near-unanimous vote, amicably solved the problem by adopting the standard club constitution.

Rotary had been a strong organization in South Africa since the 1920s, and that country's apartheid policy drew occasional criticism of Rotary for maintaining clubs there. But as then-International President John Nelson pointed out in Berlin in 1933, Rotary has no mandate to countermand government policies; that is the right of each nation's citizens. The majority of South African Rotary clubs organized community and vocational service projects to help the people against whom their government discriminated. Some Rotarians in other countries wanted to ban youth exchanges and Group Study

NAVIGATING THROUGH TURBULENCE

"We in Europe...want to contribute to Rotary.... We want to contribute something not pseudo-American, for our North American friends are better Americans than we can ever hope.... We want to contribute something European, something compact of our heart, our better traditions, our culture, our national character."

Sydney W. Pascall, London, England
RI president, 1931-32

5   Luigi Piccione to RI Board of Directors, 18 April 1935, Catholic Church and Rotary, Subject Files, RI Archives.

6   Rotary International, *1982 Proceedings Seventy-third Annual Convention* (Evanston, Illinois, 1982), 34.

7   Jeffrey A. Charles, *Service Clubs in American Society* (Champaign, IL: University of Illinois Press, 1993), 30.

The novel *Babbit*, written by Sinclair Lewis and published in 1922, caused some to poke fun at Rotary. (The book's character, George Babbit, was a member of the Zenith Booster Club.) During a tour of England in 1928, Lewis stated to the press: "I have been accused of saying some nasty things about Rotary, but I assert that the growth of Rotary in Great Britain…is more important for world tranquility than all the campaigns of the reformers put together."

SINGING CHILDREN GREET RI PRESIDENT A.Z. BAKER AT A NURSERY IN BLOEMFONTEIN, SOUTH AFRICA, IN 1955.

Exchange teams to and from South Africa, but others argued that it was precisely such programs that would shine light on the injustice of racism and help bring about change when students and GSE team members returned home.

The Cold War

During the 1930s, some of Rotary's most vital and valued clubs were in Eastern Europe. Members there suffered during World War II; just as they saw a glimmer of hope at the end of the war, Soviet Communism intruded. For the next 44 years, former Rotarians peeked out from behind the iron curtain, forbidden to enjoy the Rotary of their distant memories.

Rotarian Jan Masaryk, Czechoslovakia's foreign minister and son of the country's first president, was a member of the Prague Rotary club like his renowned father. "Czechoslovakia, which stands in the cockpit of war-devastated Europe, is looking forward into the future," he wrote in THE ROTARIAN in August 1947. "Although she was one of the first victims of Hitlerism—a sacrifice upon the altar of appeasement—she is not wasting her time in vain regret." Six months later he was dead, having mysteriously "fallen" from an office window after the Communist coup.

And so for half a century, Czechoslovakia joined Poland, Hungary, Bulgaria, Romania, the Baltic and Balkan states, East Germany, Cuba, and China as countries where Rotary was blocked along with basic human rights like freedom of speech and assembly.

When democracy finally emerged in the former Eastern Bloc countries in 1989, and the Berlin Wall toppled, no group played a greater leadership role in reintroducing Rotary than German Rotarians, who made numerous visits to help establish 80 new clubs in the east. They continue to cooperate on joint projects and friendship exchanges.

"Babbitt" and Critics

As the Rotary movement spread across America and Britain, it became a favorite target for cynical writers and social critics. One newspaper editorial opined: "The Rotary club is composed of business men. The functions of a Rotary club are summed up in one word—talk. That is about all the members of the club do. The Rotary club never takes any action. Its members simply talk, or listen while others talk."

"Where is Rotary going? It is going to lunch," sneered British playwright George Bernard Shaw.

Rotary's most outspoken critics in the 1920s and 1930s included Shaw, author Sinclair Lewis, attorney Clarence Darrow, editor H.L. Mencken, and writer G.K. Chesterton. Mencken, the acerbic editor of the *American Mercury,* wrote of his contempt for Rotary's "commercial civilization." He also derided Rotarians for their habit of greeting one another by their first names or nicknames: "The first Rotarian was the first man to call John the Baptist, 'Jack,'" he scoffed.[8]

Sinclair Lewis touched on the same point in his 1920 novel, *Main Street.* But it was his 1922 novel, *Babbitt,* that raised howls of protest from Rotarians.

POPE JOHN PAUL II GREETS RI VICE PRESIDENT PAULO V.C. COSTA AND RITA COSTA AT A ROTARY AUDIENCE FOLLOWING THE 1979 RI CONVENTION IN ROME.

RI PRESIDENT HERBERT G. BROWN WITH SOUTH AFRICAN PRESIDENT NELSON MANDELA

WITH A SPRAY-PAINTED DECLARATION OF "ROTARY '89" AS A
BACKDROP, A ROTARY GROUP VISITS A STILL-STANDING SECTION OF
THE BERLIN WALL IN 1989.

In it, the title character is a bumbling, middle-class, small-town businessman,
a follower, not a leader, whose weekly highlight is the backslapping, singing
camaraderie of like-minded men at his booster club.

Taking their lead from such famous authors, other writers joined in the
parody parade with potshots of their own. They were rarely scathing attacks,
but *Babbitt*, especially, was such a bestseller that the criticism endured for decades. By then, the word *Babbitt* had even entered the official national vernacular. Dictionaries included it, with the
definition in Webster's New Collegiate:
"A business or professional man who
conforms unthinkingly to prevailing
middle class standards."

PAST RI PRESIDENT FRANK L. MULHOLLAND
(LEFT) WITH AUTHOR AND FORMER ROTARY
CRITIC SINCLAIR LEWIS

When in 1934 another dictionary
leaked that it was considering equating
its own definition of *Babbitt* with
Rotarian, Editor Leland D. Case of THE
ROTARIAN took action. One August
morning he paid an unannounced visit
to Sinclair Lewis's summer home in
Vermont.

"Who the hell're you, and what do
you want?" growled the sleepy cynic as
he opened the door in his blue pajamas.

Case explained that he edited Rotary's magazine in Chicago and had come to find out why Lewis disliked Rotarians.

"Sit down," Lewis commanded. "First, we'll have breakfast. Then we'll talk."

When they finally talked, Lewis offered his first objection: "I don't like their singing!"

"Neither do I," Case concurred. "What else?"

"Calling strangers by their first names," Lewis continued. "I visited a Rotary club near here and right away they were calling me 'Sinclair,' something I hadn't heard since I last saw my mother." Case knew that Lewis hailed from the tiny town of Sauk Center, Minnesota. He told him the story of Rotary's founder, Paul Harris, another young man from a small village who felt lonely in the big city, and explained that Harris discovered that using the nicknames and first names of his new friends enhanced their camaraderie with one another. It was, Case noted, a Rotary tradition.

The amicable meeting lasted all morning. When Case arrived back at his Chicago office, he was greeted by a telegram from Lewis saying that their chat had "made me approve of Rotary."[9] Eventually, Case persuaded Lewis, Darrow, Mencken, and Shaw to write for THE ROTARIAN, and no one ever heard a sarcastic remark about Rotary from any of them again.

9 THE ROTARIAN, April 1980, 23.

CHAPTER 10

FOUNDATION OF HOPE

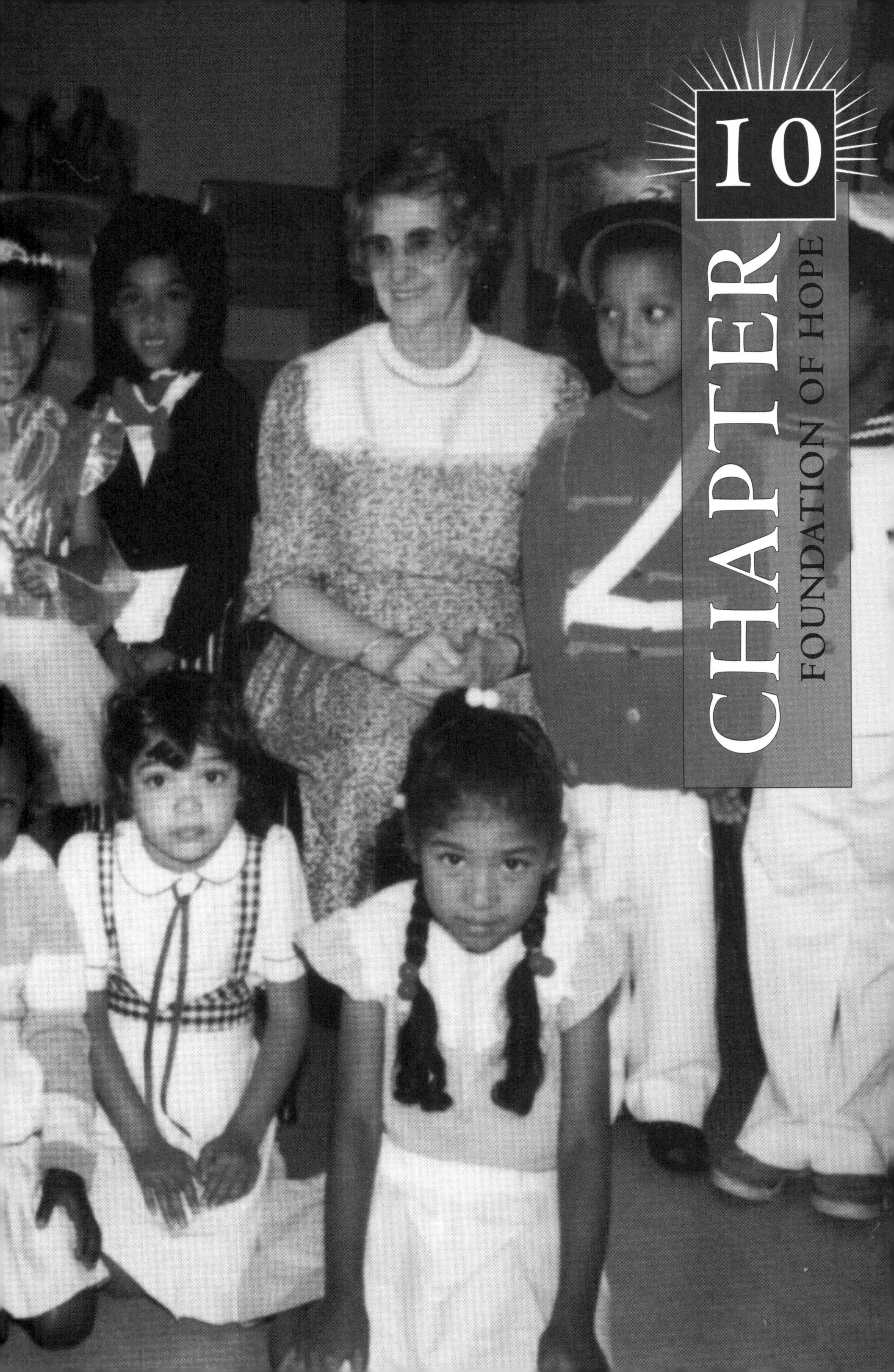

Chapter 10 ~ Foundation of Hope

It was all Arch Klumph's idea. As RI president in 1917, he told delegates to the Atlanta convention, "Carrying on as we are, a miscellaneous community service, it seems eminently proper that we should accept endowments for the purpose of doing good in the world."[1] It was hardly a stirring call to action or a motivational moment for those present. But it was the first pebble in what would later become a landslide of support that would improve millions of lives. And as happened so many times before in Rotary, it began in the mind of one man.

That man—Arch Klumph—was a remarkable fellow. Born into a poor family in Conneautville, Pennsylvania, USA, in 1869, Klumph moved with his parents and two brothers to Cleveland, Ohio, while he was a child. To supplement the family's income, he left school at age 12 and went to work. At 16, he became office boy for the Cuyahoga Lumber Company. At his own initiative, he enrolled in night school; after a hard day's work, he would walk four miles each way to school to save the tram fare.

When the business began to fail, Cuyahoga Lumber made Klumph manager. He turned the company around and made it one of the most profitable firms of its type in the Midwest. He subsequently bought the company. Even-

114

Paul Harris with some of the founders of the International Society for Crippled Children, in February 1922

Overleaf: 1988-89 RI President Royce Abbey and Jean Abbey with children at a school built by the Rotary Club of Claremont, South Africa

tually, the self-educated former office boy became president or vice president of several other business enterprises, including a bank and a steamship line.

When he was 18, Klumph taught himself the flute and three years later had so mastered the instrument that he became a flutist with the Cleveland Symphony Orchestra. He continued to play for the symphony for 14 years.

In 1911, Klumph became a charter member of the Rotary Club of Cleveland with the classification of "lumber—wholesale and retail." His Rotary path followed his brilliant business and

PAST RI PRESIDENT ARCH KLUMPH AND A PAIR OF BOY SCOUTS LOOK OVER A TOY BOAT THE YOUNG MEN MADE (CIRCA 1930).

personal record of accomplishments. Arch became club president in 1912 and president of the International Association of Rotary Clubs for 1916-17.

In his final address as club president, Klumph suggested "an emergency fund should be built up which will enable the club in future years to do many things."[2] He went on to become chairman of the committee that wrote the new constitution for Rotary International, and it was his idea to divide Rotary into districts, create the office of district governor, and establish the annual district conference. But he never forgot his concept of a fund to expand the good works of Rotary.

The Rotary Endowment Fund, as it was called at first, came to Klumph as "a vision, a little inspiration all of a sudden one day that the organization was peculiarly adapted to the purpose of accepting endowments to do great things." The RI Board approved his idea but did not provide a mechanism to fund it. Indeed, for the next decade, Rotary's leaders went along with Klumph's proposal, but without any tangible action or enthusiasm.

As Klumph's presidential term wound down, the Rotary Club of Kansas City, Missouri, collected contributions for a gift for the retiring association president. When the club closed out that account, they discovered a surplus of $26.50 and decided to donate that money to start the Rotary Endowment Fund.[3] The first seeds had been sown for the fund known today as The Rotary Foundation of RI.

Over the next several years, Klumph pressed the association to activate the endowment fund to help develop new Rotary clubs and provide humanitarian relief. But after six years, the fund balance stagnated at a paltry $700.

1   THE ROTARIAN XI, no. 2 (August 1917): 117.
2   Rotary Foundation of Rotary International, *The Rotary Foundation: 75 Years of Service* (Evanston, Illinois, 1992), 2.
3   International Association of Rotary Clubs, Board minutes, Item 11, 25-26 July 1917.

In 1928, delegates to the Minneapolis convention changed the fund's name to The Rotary Foundation. This change in the RI Constitution stipulated that a board of five trustees—all past RI presidents—should govern the new Foundation and that funds should be kept separately from the parent organization. Contributions started to come in; four years later, there was $50,000 in the bank.

After the stock market crash of 1929, donations to good causes dried up. It was then that Paul Harris asked The Rotary Foundation to make its first donation; and it sent a $500 check to the International Society for Crippled Children, whose own work had begun in 1919 as the inspiration of Rotarian Edgar F. "Daddy" Allen of Elyria, Ohio, USA.[4]

The 1937 RI Board announced plans for a $2 million fundraising goal for The Rotary Foundation, and it looked as if Arch Klumph's vision would finally be realized. The outbreak of World War II dashed those hopes again, but the tragedy of war made Rotarians reflect more seriously on the Foundation's potential for peacemaking. Ches Perry, who had retired as general secretary in 1942, used the pseudonym Perry Reynolds to pen an April 1944 article in THE ROTARIAN urging members to donate to the Foundation in addition to their normal Rotary dues. "An additional contribution of $5 a year by each Rotarian for the next two years would give Rotary International an endowment of two million dollars and make its Foundation an instrument of great good in the postwar period," he reasoned.

When the war ended in 1945, Rotary rewrote its objectives for The Rotary Foundation:

RI GENERAL SECRETARY GEORGE R. MEANS DISPLAYS CHECKS TO THE ROTARY FOUNDATION FROM DISTRICT 638'S "MILLION DOLLAR MEALS" PROGRAM.

"1. The promotion of Rotary Foundation Fellowships for advanced study;

2. The fostering of any tangible and effective projects which have as their purpose the furthering of better understanding and friendly relations between the peoples of different nations; and

3. The providing of emergency relief for Rotarians and their families wherever war or other disaster has brought general destruction and suffering."[5]

In 1947, when Paul Harris died, RI asked that individuals and clubs wishing to honor the founder make gifts in his name to The Rotary Foundation, suggesting $10 per member.[6]

Money poured in from all over the world. Thus, in the first year after Harris's death, the Foundation granted 18 Rotary Foundation Fellowships—later called Ambassadorial Scholarships—for one year's university study abroad.

By 1948, contributions had exceeded $1,775,000; in addition to granting study fellowships to 37 students from 12 countries, The Rotary Foundation allocated $15,000 for war-relief assistance to 150 families. By 1954, the Foundation had collected $3.5 million—and new contributions reached $500,000 in a single year. In 1955, Rotary's 50th anniversary year, it awarded scholarships to 494 young men and women from 57 countries.

AMBASSADOR OTTO BORCH, ROTARY FOUNDATION SCHOLAR FROM DENMARK, STUDIED AT COLUMBIA UNIVERSITY.

The Rotary Foundation had quickly become the successful program that Arch Klumph had long predicted. In 1956, the RI Board urged clubs to give further emphasis to the Foundation during The Rotary Foundation Week, which they decreed be held in mid-November each year. The Secretariat suggested that clubs and districts plan programs publicizing the Foundation during that week, and their efforts were so successful that in 1982 the Trustees changed it to The Rotary Foundation Month, still observed every November.

This ongoing desire to honor Rotary's founder by making gifts to the Foundation spurred one of the most significant ideas in its history. By 1957, a decade after Paul's death, donations had begun to decline. The Trustees announced that anyone who contributed $1,000 to The Rotary Foundation would become a Paul Harris Fellow. Paul Harris Fellows were presented with a plaque, medallion, and lapel pin, all bearing the founder's likeness. In 1968, the Trustees added a category called Sustaining Member for those who could not give the entire $1,000 at one time but pledged to give $100 annually. When they attained the $1,000, they became Paul Harris Fellows.

Allison G. Brush, a past RI director from Laurel, Mississippi, USA, was the first Paul Harris Fellow. The second was Rufus F. Chapin, one of the 1905 Chicago members who became the longtime treasurer of Rotary International. By 1984 there were 100,000 Paul Harris Fellows, a number that swelled to 250,000 in 1989 and 500,000 by 1995.

Ambassadorial Scholarships

The Rotary Foundation's Ambassadorial Scholarships program is the world's largest privately funded international scholarship program for university studies. Its purpose is to promote further international understanding and friendly relations between people of all nations—the first step to a peaceful world. The graduate- and undergraduate-level scholars are proposed by local Rotary clubs and selected by their district. Ambassadorial Scholars have two priorities: first, to be ambassadors for Rotary between their home and

4   *The Rotary Foundation*, 7.
5   Rotary International, *Rotary: Fifty Years of Service* (Evanston, Illinois, 1954), 33.
6   Rotary International, Board minutes, Item 252, May 1947.

SADAKO OGATA (RIGHT), ROTARY FOUNDATION SCHOLAR, 1996 ROTARY
AWARD FOR WORLD UNDERSTANDING AND PEACE RECIPIENT, AND FORMER
UNITED NATIONS HIGH COMMISSIONER FOR REFUGEES

study countries by sharing with others the culture in their host country, and
second, to successfully complete their academic course of study.

Some of the world's most distinguished leaders are alumni of the Rotary
scholarship program, including: Ambassador Otto Borch of Denmark; the
late Carlos Alberto da Mota Pinto, prime minister of Portugal; Sadako Ogata,
the former UN high commissioner for refugees; Bill Moyers, prominent television journalist and former deputy director of the U.S. Peace Corps; Paul
A. Volcker, professor, economist, and former chairman of the U.S. Federal
Reserve Bank; Sir William Dean, last governor of the Commonwealth of Australia; Philip Lader, former U.S. ambassador to Great Britain; and renowned
pianist Van Cliburn, winner of the first Tchaikovsky International Piano Competition in Moscow.

In 1971, the Trustees enhanced the Ambassadorial Scholarships program by adding a special program to fund teachers of the mentally, physically, and educationally impaired. Since 1994, The Rotary Foundation has
included three new types of awards: a Multi-Year Ambassadorial Scholarship
for two years of study abroad; the Cultural Ambassadorial Scholarship, which
provides for intensive language or cultural study in another country for three
to six months; and the Japan Ambassadorial Scholarship, which provides for
intensive Japanese language study and an internship in Japan for 12 months.

Over the years, Rotarians have been justifiably proud of their Ambassadorial Scholarships program but also puzzled why it is often eclipsed by other
foundations that send fewer students abroad and spend much less money.

The Rotary Foundation invests about $20,000 in each scholar. In 1991, Rotary commissioned a study by the Institute of International Education (IIE) to evaluate the effectiveness of The Rotary Foundation's scholarship program. Some findings were:

- "The Rotary program compares favorably to its peers in the international scholarship community." IIE compared it to the scholarships offered by the Rhodes, Fulbright, Marshall, Luce, American Association of University Women, and American Scandinavian foundations.
- "It is far too little known in the field…considering Rotary's size, years of existence, and general level of excellence."
- "There is enormous gratitude to Rotary [by scholars] for what most believe to be the most significant experience of their lives."
- "The Rotary program as it now exists achieves rather well what it set out to do."

Group Study Exchange (GSE)

The first Group Study Exchange (GSE) teams were organized in 1965 between districts in California and Japan. The program was such a success that it quickly spread around the world. A district selects a Rotarian as team leader and then four to six men and women aged 25-40 who are not Rotarians but who would make excellent goodwill ambassadors. The Rotary Foundation then matches that team with a district in another country and pays all the travel expenses. For four to six weeks, the host district takes the visiting team to points of interest and arranges for them to visit schools, courts, civic leaders, businesses—and Rotary clubs. They live in Rotarians' homes, dine together, exchange family photographs, and visit those in the same trade or profession as their own. The role reversal, where the host district sends its own team out, has occurred at various times, either in the same or succeeding year. There are some 46,000 GSE alumni.

The precursor and model for GSE may well have sprouted in New Zealand. The New Zealand ROTA (Rotary Overseas Travel Award) Program was operating from 1955 with two-month study tours by teams of six young professional and business men and a Rotarian leader. Visits (in odd-numbered years) were to the United Kingdom, United States,

"The Rotary Foundation is not to build monuments of brick and stone. If we work upon marble, it will perish; if we work on brass, time will efface it; if we rear temples they will crumble into dust; but if we work upon immortal minds, if we imbue them with the full meaning of the spirit of Rotary…we are engraving on those tablets something that will brighten all eternity."

Arch C. Klumph
Cleveland, Ohio, USA
RI president, 1916-17

MEMBERS OF A GROUP STUDY EXCHANGE TEAM FROM FRANCE VISIT A FARM OUTSIDE AMANA, IOWA, USA.

Ceylon (Sri Lanka), India, Japan, Indonesia, Malaysia, and Singapore. In even-numbered years, reciprocal visits were to New Zealand. The program continued until GSE became an activity of The Rotary Foundation.

GSE has sent specialized teams, such as all-women or same-vocation teams. One such example was an exchange between Boulder County, Colorado, USA, and Melbourne, Victoria, Australia. At that time, Boulder had the highest teen suicide rate in the country, and Melbourne was the world's suicide capital. The teams were composed exclusively of youth workers who explored new approaches to the problem of teen suicide. "We returned home energized with new perspectives and new ideas," said Stuart Williams, the team leader and past president of the Rotary Club of Forest Hill, Victoria, Australia.[7]

Group Study Exchange has become one of the Foundation's most popular and successful programs. It helps people from different countries better understand one another and realize the dreams and aspirations they share. In this way, GSE is a vital instrument in Rotary's commitment to world understanding and peace.

Matching Grants

By the 1960s, jet travel had made the world a smaller place. More Rotarians met one another at international meetings and explored ways in which clubs and districts in different countries could work together on projects.

CHILDREN IN KENYA PUMP CLEAN WATER FROM A WELL FUNDED BY A FOUNDATION GRANT.

120

The Foundation established Special Grants (later called Matching Grants) in 1965 as a way of leveraging the Foundation's funds while simultaneously increasing participation among Rotarians and clubs. Suddenly, Rotary clubs in two or more countries could partner with one another in a World Community Service project and apply to The Rotary Foundation for funds to match what they raised locally.

Foundation Matching Grants have been given for as much as US$150,000 for groups of Rotarians from different backgrounds and cultures to come together and drill irrigation wells, establish "revolving loans" that lead to the self-development of people in impoverished villages, purchase agricultural equipment, and fund teacher training and ambulances.

Matching Grants are not blank checks sent out to good causes. They require the active involvement and oversight of Rotarians from a club where the project is located and by an international partner.

Dr. David Buckley is an Irishman who spent two years as a medical volunteer in the Turkana Desert, a remote region of northern Kenya. He knew firsthand how the villagers suffered and often died for lack of modern medical facilities. Pregnant women were especially at risk and often lost their babies and their own lives during childbirth. When Buckley's term ended, he returned to Ireland and shortly thereafter joined the Rotary Club of Tralee. When he learned about The Rotary Foundation's Matching Grant program, Buckley's club and a partner club in Kenya put together a proposal to obtain and equip an all-terrain vehicle that could serve as a mobile medical clinic and ambulance. His club members contributed $942 toward the project and their fundraising event brought in another $8,684. District 1160, the Tralee club's home district, added $1,500 from its District Designated Fund (DDF). This all totaled $11,126, and the club then successfully applied to The Rotary Foundation for a Matching Grant of $11,126. Thus a small Irish Rotary club leveraged its own relatively modest contribution into a $22,252 project that is providing modern health care to 40,000 women in remote African villages.[8]

In Korea, clubs in District 3640 teamed up with District 2810 in Japan, and each raised $10,000 for a project to provide free meals to 546 primary school pupils in a poor district of Seoul. The Foundation then matched their contributions with another $20,000, and the two countries—though for centuries bitter enemies—together fed needy children for seven months.[9]

7   THE ROTARIAN, November 2000, 40.
8   THE ROTARIAN, November 2000, 38.
9   The Rotary Korea, No. 16, 2000, 21.

Health, Hunger and Humanity (3-H) Grants

The Health, Hunger and Humanity (3-H) Grants program was the brainchild of 1978-79 RI President Clem (now Sir Clem) Renouf of Australia, though he credits the program's early success to his immediate predecessor, W. Jack Davis of Bermuda. While president in 1977-78, Davis wanted to involve more Rotarians in humanitarian work and to involve RI in the mass immunization of children; he was an early and influential advocate for getting 3-H on the Rotary agenda. In 1978, the Trustees launched 3-H Grants with the objective "To improve health, hunger, and enhance human, cultural, and social development among peoples of the world."[10] 3-H Grants cover a broad spectrum of projects that are integrated and provide sustainable development. 3-H Grants generally range in size from US$100,000 to $300,000. The funding for the 3-H program initially came from the 75th Anniversary Fund, in support of which Rotarians were asked to contribute $15 per capita.

The first 3-H Grant in 1978 helped immunize 6.3 million children in the Philippines against polio—the project that evolved into PolioPlus, which is discussed in chapter 20.

Another health grant in the Philippines provided medical equipment for three hospitals, along with 75 biomedical technicians who trained local personnel how to use and repair the equipment. This project had a nationwide impact on health-care education and patient diagnosis and treatment.

> In 2002, The Rotary Foundation achieved a major milestone when the number of Major Donors reached 5,000. A Major Donor is an individual or couple who contributes US$10,000 to the Foundation's Annual Programs Fund or Permanent Fund. The largest gift to date has been from Paul Elder of Turtle Creek, Pennsylvania, USA, in the amount of $7 million.

A third 3-H project improved the income and quality of life in an entire community. The Rotary club in the poor region of Arusha, Tanzania, partnered with the Rotary Club of Guelph, Ontario, Canada, and obtained a 3-H Grant to equip a health center, provide vocational training for leprosy victims and street children, improve farming methods, and install a hydrogenerator to produce potable water.

In Costa Rica, the Rotary Club of San Jose used a 3-H Grant to create a buffer zone around a protected rain forest. It provided training for alternative farming methods for residents of four communities located near the rain forest, along with a community credit fund for revolving loan funds.

Bangladesh is one of the poorest countries on earth and has one of the lowest literacy rates. Rotarians in Bangladesh and Australia saw a perfect

ROTARY VOLUNTEER DR. JARL MAGNUSSON FROM SWEDEN ON A
MEDICAL MISSION IN KENYA

opportunity for aid from The Rotary Foundation. Their $500,000 Health,
Hunger and Humanity Grant helped them introduce a literacy and numeracy
program that their fellow Rotarians, led by Australian Past District Governor
Dr. Dick Walker, had successfully implemented in Thailand a few years earlier.[11] After a two-year test in 33 schools, the program was expanded nationwide as a five-year program. In the first three years, literacy rates rose from 26
percent to 55 percent.[12]

Individual Grants (formerly Rotary Volunteers Grants) cover the travel
costs for a Rotarian to work on a World Community Service project in another
country. Thus, a British educator could teach students in Madagascar how to
use solar-powered radios, an Indian engineer could assist flood victims in Mozambique, and a Rotarian physician from Spain could teach physical thera-
pists in Paraguay.

The *SHARE* System

The Rotary Foundation currently raises more than US$65 million in
its annual fundraising for educational, humanitarian, and cultural exchange
programs. This money comes from the Rotary clubs and districts around the
world. The *SHARE* system was devised in the early 1990s to allocate a portion
of the funds raised to the Foundation's World Fund.

The balance is credited to the District Designated Fund. Districts that
contribute to The Rotary Foundation have discretion over how some of those
funds are spent. Thus, districts whose clubs give large amounts to the Foundation are allotted more Ambassadorial Scholarships than those that give less.
Through District Designated Fund allocations, the district receives credits for
a percentage of its donations to the Foundation.

---

10 Clifford L. Dochterman, *The ABCs of Rotary* (Evanston, Illinois: Rotary International, 2000), 33.
11 Clem Renouf, *The Health, Hunger and Humanity Program of Rotary International* (Parramatta, NSW:
    RDU Books, 2000), 3.
12 THE ROTARIAN, November 2000, 30.

"Let there be peace on earth…"

When the New Horizons Committee met in 1982 to chart a strategic long-term plan for Rotary, it adopted an idea suggested by the World Understanding and Peace Committee to initiate Rotary Peace Forums. These conclaves began convening twice annually in various world cities under the auspices of the Foundation.[13] The Trustees soon changed the name to the Rotary Peace Program, and so began the series of educational seminars focused on such issues as the environment, economic development, conflict resolution, and peacemaking.

As the 21st century dawned, Rotarians realized that their commitment to aid the cause of peace was needed more than ever. Looking ahead, The Rotary Foundation launched a significant and proactive peace initiative: the Rotary Centers for International Studies in peace and conflict resolution. The Rotary Centers offer individuals who are committed to peace and cooperation the opportunity to pursue a fully funded, two-year master's-level degree or certificate in a field such as international studies, peace studies, or conflict resolution.

124

To implement the academic programs, Rotary has partnered with the Universidad del Salvador (Buenos Aires, Argentina), University of Queensland (Brisbane, Australia), University of Bradford (West Yorkshire, England), Sciences Po (Paris, France), International Christian University (Tokyo, Japan), University of California, Berkeley (California, USA), and University of North Carolina at Chapel Hill and Duke University (North Carolina, USA).

The first class in 2002 included 70 scholars from 35 countries, most of whom spoke at least three languages. Starting in 2004 and every year thereafter, 70 young men and women will graduate with the philosophy, education, and practical tools needed to effectively influence future international relations, working for organizations such as the United Nations, European Union, and World Bank, their government's diplomatic corps, and nongovernmental organizations and multinational corporations. In a decade, 700 people will be working in positions of influence, each trained and committed to reduce conflict and resolve disputes peacefully.

The Rotary Foundation's accomplishments are impressive. Nearly 36,000 scholars from 110 countries have received Ambassadorial Scholarships valued at US$429 million. More than 46,000 people have participated in 10,600 Group Study Exchange teams at a cost of more than $82 million, and 18,000 Matching Grant projects in 166 countries have been funded at a cost

---

13 Dochterman, 36.

of more than $182 million. Through PolioPlus, Rotary has committed more than $500 million to global polio eradication efforts.

Since 1947, Rotarians have contributed more than $1.4 billion to the Foundation, with total contributions averaging more than $85 million annually. There are more than 800,000 Paul Harris Fellows, and new fellows are being added at a rate of 45,000 per year. The Rotary Foundation spends about $100 million annually on its programs and since 1917 has funded $1.4 billion in program awards and expenses—yet still maintains net assets of almost $500 million.

The endowment dreamed up by Arch Klumph has become a reality. The Permanent Fund Initiative (PFI) was created in 1992 with the purpose of providing an ever-increasing stream of revenue to secure the future of the Foundation's programs. An organized structure of PFI advisers and district leaders identified hundreds of generous major donors who brought the fund to $250 million by 2003, well on its way to its initial target of $1 billion.

ORPHANS OF CIUDAD LOS NIÑOS IN LIMA, PERU, DISPLAY EGGS FROM THEIR CHICKEN FARM, A VOCATIONAL TRAINING PROJECT FUNDED BY A MATCHING GRANT.

But statistics tell only a part of The Rotary Foundation story. Like Rotary itself, The Rotary Foundation is not about money; it is about people.

It is about the people who donate to their Foundation, and the joy they feel from the act of giving. Some donate because they seek the honor of becoming a Paul Harris Fellow. Others give but request that the recognition be conferred on someone else: a parent, mentor, local volunteer, or worthy citizen. Mother Teresa, Nelson Mandela, Kofi Annan, King Baudouin of Belgium, President Habib Bourguiba of Tunisia, President Vaclav Havel of the Czech Republic, Prince Charles of England, Indira Gandhi, Israel's Yitzhak Rabin, Luciano Pavarotti, King Hussein of Jordan, the Aga Khan, Pope John Paul II, and hundreds of other celebrated personalities were named Paul Harris Fellows. But so have thousands whose names few of us would recognize: the woman who feeds the homeless, the beloved local teacher, the counselor at the AIDS clinic. To donor and recipient alike, the presentation of Paul Harris Fellow Recognition is an honor and a privilege.

The Foundation is also a story about the people who benefit from these gifts. When a Rotarian in Turkey is named a Paul Harris Fellow, the $1,000 he gives to The Rotary Foundation funds enough textbooks to educate 2,000 children in a school in Papua New Guinea. When the Rotarian in Finland makes a gift to the Foundation in honor of the doctor who saved her daughter's life, she is providing a better life for women in Nicaragua, who receive $50 microloans enabling them to start a craft business to support their families.

A $1,000 gift will provide enough money to help with the travel costs for Texas Rotarians who sacrifice a month of their lives as volunteers in Poland to teach ethical commercial practices to business students. It buys the polio vaccine for 2,000 babies in Nigeria, while prompting tens of thousands of Rotarians to mobilize the immunization campaign. The Foundation is the story of those mothers who can now see their children for the first time. It is the story of the land-mine victim who can now wheel himself to a table and work in a job that restores his dignity.

The Rotary Foundation has been so effective because it matches money with people. In the words of Arch Klumph:

NELSON MANDELA, FORMER PRESIDENT OF SOUTH AFRICA, 1993 NOBEL PEACE PRIZE WINNER, AND 1997 ROTARY AWARD FOR WORLD UNDERSTANDING AND PEACE RECIPIENT

RI President Edward F. Cadman greets Pope John Paul II, 1982 recipient of the Rotary Award for World Understanding and Peace.

"Money alone does little good.

Individual service is helpless without money.

The two together can be a Godsend to civilization."[14]

Writing to Klumph in 1934, Paul Harris mused: "I have a feeling that we shall some day suddenly, and perhaps without any particular effort on our part other than the effort which you have been giving the movement for years, find ourselves with something of real importance."[15]

The words, penned at a time when support for The Rotary Foundation was scarce, were prescient indeed. Klumph died in 1951, when The Rotary Foundation was already becoming a significant force for good. But could even Arch Klumph have imagined the immense reach and scope of the idea he considered "a little inspiration"?

---

14 Arch Klumph to Paul Harris, 12 December 1934.
15 Paul Harris to Arch Klumph, 21 November 1934.

Chapter 11 ~ Rotarians in Their Clubs

In many ways, Rotarians represent a contradiction. To qualify for club membership, one must command a leadership position, by definition, a busy person. Yet Rotarians gladly find the time to serve. As business and industry leaders, Rotarians are focused on the bottom line, to quantify return on investment in both effort and money expended—yet they collectively contribute hundreds of millions of dollars in tangible gifts and volunteer time willingly. Rotarians are stereotypically "the boss," all business at work—yet at Rotary club meetings, they become disciples of fellowship.

These seeming contradictions have existed since the first days of the movement. The concept of Rotary grew from Paul Harris's yearning for the trustworthy, friendly companionship he loved as a boy in his Vermont village. "To the members of the small group which came together in the big city of Chicago, Rotary was like an oasis in the desert," he wrote in *My Road to Rotary*.[1] Long before the term "Club Service" was adopted in Rotary, its members practiced it. Indeed, Club Service existed before any of the other three Avenues of Service. Rotarians broke bread together, told jokes, sang songs, and went on outings. As the young men married, they included their families in many of these social events.

Paul Harris and other early members of the Rotary Club of Chicago, at Comely Bank in December 1942

Overleaf: President-elect S. Kendrick Guernsey (center) and other Rotarians practice archery at the 1947 International Assembly in Sun Valley before the San Francisco convention.

The one millionth Rotarian was Jean-Paul Moroval, a 40-year-old industrial engineer from Thionville, France. Jean-Paul and his wife, Danielle, were honored at the 1986 RI Convention in Las Vegas, Nevada, USA, by RI President Ed Cadman. Moroval was sponsored by Jean Bertrand, a longtime Rotarian from Thionville.

The Fun of Rotary

Paul Harris was himself a contradiction. At first glance, he was an austere man not given to loudness or laughter, a staunch defender of the law and of high moral and ethical conduct. He looked and acted as the very model of propriety. Yet just below that stern exterior lay a boy wanting to have fun with his friends. Rotary was the mechanism to release the amiable boy inside.

In the early days of the first Rotary club, practical jokes proliferated, with Paul Harris often the ringleader. On one club excursion to Michigan, Monty Bear—one of the club's most handsome bachelors—flirted with a pretty waitress named Lib. This became a matter of great discussion within the club. A few weeks later, Paul arranged for a telegram to be sent to Monty in Lib's name stating she was coming to Chicago to visit him and was shipping her trunk in advance to his office address, and asking him to take very good care of it. Just before her train arrived, the trunk was delivered, but Monty's Rotary "friends" hid it while he was out. At the appointed hour of her arrival, Monty was so distraught he could not bring himself to go to the station and meet Lib for fear of what she would say when he confessed to the lost trunk.

Entertainment parks, retail stores, airlines—even places of worship—know that fun brings people back for more. So it is with Rotary. Club presidents over the years knew that their members were busy people with competing demands on their time. Astute presidents always appointed Club Service directors who created a convivial atmosphere in the club, so that attending the weekly meeting felt like a refreshing oasis after the often-dry desert of the workaday world.

In a world where the nightly news increasingly has led off with scenes of violence, corruption, scandal, and disaster, it is little wonder that Rotarians value the fellowship of Rotary.

In the earliest meetings of the Rotary Club of Chicago, members met for dinner at the Sherman Hotel, then held their meeting in a hotel room. Here were some of the civic and business leaders of Chicago, sitting on the bed, on the floor, chairs, atop the radiators, even perched on windowsills, recalled Rufe Chapin in 1925. It was hard not to feel close to one another when all the organizing and planning for the new club was conducted in such a casual environment.

1   Paul Harris, *My Road to Rotary: The Story of a Boy, a Vermont Community, and Rotary* (Chicago, Illinois: A. Kroch and Son, 1948), 232.

> "I believe Rotary is basically a simple thing, and that we may be in danger of losing sight of the real Object of Rotary because we become engrossed in exterior forms and procedures. We must try to free ourselves from unnecessary overstructures, reclaiming the fundamentals.... Let us be simple, for the simple way is often the best."
>
> *Gian Paolo Lang, Livorno, Italy*
> *RI president, 1956-57*

Chapin revealed that the practice of calling members by their first names became a habit, rather than a written rule, from the very beginning. "It became a valuable discovery of Rotary," he wrote, "the first step that breaks down the individual who suffers from an overplus of dignity." Many countries have followed the hundred-year tradition of North American Rotarians: When the doctor, car mechanic, senior diplomat, and small shop owner meet through Rotary, they leave their titles at the door and call one another by their first names. This simple gesture bridges gaps that divide humankind and instead emphasizes what they have in common.

In some cultures where tradition dictates that formal titles and surnames be used, this Rotary way seems uncomfortable at first. Chapin reminded members in 1925 that it was a specific objective of the 1905 Rotarians—and those who followed—to "penetrate the shells of pity, ego, and pomposity and reveal the real man inside."[2]

A long tradition among Rotary clubs in many countries is the levying of monetary fines. Most of the income for the Rotary Club of Chicago in the early years was derived from fines. The sergeant-at-arms is the club officer charged with exacting fines from the members, and he or she is usually a person with a sense of humor—and an eagle eye. Infractions such as having one's photograph in the newspaper, being late to a meeting, or inadvertently calling another member "Mister," will invariably cost the miscreant a dollar or so. Some sergeants-at-arms fine members when they forget to wear their Rotary pin or when their birthday falls on a club meeting date. Sometimes, it seems as if there is no end to the devious creativity of this club enforcement officer—to the great delight of all members, even the poor Rotarian who is penalized.

"WELCOME TO OUR ROTARY CLUB!" A NEW MEMBER IS INDUCTED.

The fellowship that comes from sharing the ideal of service with men and women of different religions, customs, and occupations is so powerful, that it extends far beyond one's local club. Rotary clubs encourage their members to maintain regular attendance; if Rotarians miss their own club meeting, they can make up at any club in the world within two weeks before or after the missed meeting. Many clubs award pins denoting the years of perfect attendance members have attained, and districts publish statistics showing the attendance percentage of each club.

Clearly, Rotarians make up because they enjoy the fellowship at other clubs, just as they do in their home club. It is a wonderful thing to be visiting a town halfway around the world and know that wherever there is a Rotary club meeting, those members will throw open their doors in a friendly welcome. There are numerous anecdotes of Rotarians who made up at a club far from home and were invited home for dinner, or given a tour of the area, by fellow Rotarians they met at a make-up meeting.

In 1924, several districts contributed toward the expense of a "great lounge" as the meeting place for members attending the Toronto convention. It was the beginning of an unbroken tradition at Rotary International conferences and conventions. The House of Friendship is the international version of what happens each week at the local clubs. People exchange greetings and club banners, show family photographs, and swap stories on Rotary activities. Many of these encounters lead to exchanges of letters, home visits, and cooperation on international service projects. At such Rotary gatherings, people of every conceivable ethnic background, language, and vocation meet to share friendly moments where, for a few days, the world seems united in peace and goodwill.

"I am one of the optimists who believe that the world is growing better," wrote Chicago Rotarian Frank Jennings in 1913. "The universal brotherhood of man may be a dream, and from a commercial standpoint impracticable, but the movement is surely under way and Rotarianism is giving it a tremendous boost."[3]

2   Rufe Chapin, "An Outline of Rotary's Beginnings," RC Chicago, Historical Club Files, RI Archives.
3   THE ROTARIAN III, no. 7 (March 1913): 34.

ROTARIANS RAISE A TOAST WITH THEIR COFFEE CUPS DURING
A MORNING CLUB MEETING.

Membership in Rotary Clubs

Originally, there was only one category of membership, but before long Rotary clubs accepted honorary members. Over the past century, many heads of state, royalty, politicians, luminaries in the arts and sciences, and other notables have accepted honorary membership in Rotary clubs. (See appendix 4, "100 Prominent Rotarians.")

As circumstances changed, Rotary added new categories of membership, such as senior active, past service, and additional active. The 2001 Council on Legislation simplified the membership process, saying, in effect: You are either a Rotarian or not. They also relaxed some of the old, restrictive rules for admission, so that the organization is no longer limited to one member per classification. Rotary club membership, deemed the Council and Convention, should be available to persons of good character who occupy a leadership position in their vocation and are dedicated to the ideal of service.

There is a discernable difference in the makeup of clubs, generally depending on location. Clubs in big cities tend to attract executives from large organizations, whereas small-town clubs often include local civic leaders, small-business owners, and farmers and ranchers. In some countries—Germany, Switzerland, and Japan, to name but three—

ROTARIANS FROM THE NETHERLANDS
(LEFT) AND THE PHILIPPINES EXCHANGE
CLUB BANNERS.

Membership retention has been a concern of Rotary clubs from the beginning. Two of the first four Rotarians dropped out shortly after the organizational meeting. Gus Loehr, the mining engineer whose office was used as the first meeting place, resigned after the second meeting. Merchant tailor Hiram Shorey quit after a few weeks and moved to his home state of Maine. He returned to Chicago, rejoined Rotary, then resigned again. About 10 percent of members leave Rotary annually for a variety of reasons.

only the highest-echelon executives are invited to join Rotary clubs, and membership is considered a great honor. In other countries, such as Italy, the Rotary club is considered an enclave for intellectuals, the leaders in academia. In the vast majority of places, Rotary is a solidly middle-class institution.

Two of the first four Rotarians dropped out of the club within a year of its formation, and membership retention has remained a vital objective ever since. Many clubs hold "fireside chats" every few months for their new members. In a social setting, perhaps at the president's home, club board members describe Rotary's history and the local club's work, while answering questions from the new member and exchanging ideas and opinions.

The reasons for accepting an invitation to join a Rotary club are many: the desire to serve one's community, prestige, the perceived business potential, the opportunity to network with influential people and develop friends. Once in the club, some come to the meeting, eat, and run off to their next appointment. The probability is that those people do not get much from their membership. But the vast majority of Rotarians are those who enjoy their meetings, who count their fellow Rotarians among their closest friends and feel that by being a part of such a group, they can contribute something worthwhile to their community and to the world.

ROTARY FELLOWSHIP WARMS UP A CLUB MEETING IN AN IGLOO.

CHAPTER 12
COMMUNITY SERVICE

Chapter 12 — Community Service

F
ellowship and mutual business boosting, not community service, attracted the first members to Rotary. It was not that those first Rotarians were opposed to volunteerism; it was simply not a common concept in the early 20th century. Rotarians today can consider Donald M. Carter to be the father of Rotary's community service consciousness.

Frederick H. Tweed, a glass ornament manufacturer, joined the Rotary Club of Chicago in December 1905. He quickly became an enthusiastic member who introduced many others to the club. In April 1906, he invited his patent attorney, Don Carter, to join the Chicago club. Carter was both flattered and interested and asked to see the objectives and membership requirements of this new organization. Tweed proudly produced the newly printed brochure explaining what Rotary stood for—but Carter was not impressed. The document stated that Rotary had two objectives:

First. The promotion of the business interests of its members.

Second. The promotion of good fellowship and other desiderata ordinarily incident to social clubs.

"Desiderata?" Carter sneered, slowly pronouncing each syllable. "That's a word right out of a lawyer's dictionary." He told Tweed that he was not interested in joining a club with such insular motives, but added: "Such a club has great possibilities if it could do something of some benefit to people besides its own members. I believe it should do civic service of some kind."

RI President Glen W. Kinross (right) helps inaugurate a low-cost housing project in the Philippines.

Overleaf: Vicky Jackson (center), 2001-02 president of the Rotary Club of Salt Lake City, Utah, USA, leads a ground-breaking ceremony for a barrier-free playground, a community service project of District 5420.

Tweed suggested that Carter join the club and then draft and propose such an amendment. Within the month, Carter was a Rotarian, and the next time Fred Tweed visited him, the attorney showed him the handwritten draft of his proposed change to the Rotary Club Constitution. Tweed liked it and had his own secretary type it up. At a club meeting shortly thereafter, the members overwhelmingly adopted the simple but profound addition:

Third. The advancement of the best interests of Chicago and the spreading of the spirit of civic pride and loyalty among its citizens.

Carter's idea, added to the club constitution in 1906, was adopted by all future Rotary clubs and changed forever the focus of the movement.

For several months after the Third Object was added, there were no deeds to support the words. Then in 1907, Rotarian Dr. Clark W. Hawley spoke at a club meeting about a preacher who lived near Joliet, Illinois, 30 miles (48 km) from Chicago. The man's horse had died, and because he was too poor to buy another one, he was unable to make the rounds of his country churches and parishioners. The club responded quickly and within two weeks had bought the preacher a new horse. This simple, spontaneous act of generosity was Rotary's first community service. Club leaders took note of how motivated the members were to help and began looking for other such opportunities.

A few weeks later, while attending the Association of Commerce meeting, Paul Harris heard a discussion concerning the need for public restrooms— "comfort stations" was the term used then—in downtown Chicago. In those days, the only places women could find toilet facilities were inside department stores; men had to use the restrooms inside the many taverns. There was an implicit obligation to spend money with the merchant in exchange for using his facilities.

Chicago was building a new City Hall at the corner of La Salle and Washington streets, and Paul Harris proposed that the Rotary club construct comfort stations for men and women outside the new edifice. The club endorsed the idea, but it soon ran into formidable opposition. The Chicago Association of Brewers argued that its 6,000 tavern-owning members already provided sufficient men's rooms;

WEBSTER UNIVERSITY PRESIDENT RICHARD MEYERS AND FACULTY MEMBER JOE TUTTLE, BOTH ROTARIANS, VOLUNTEER ON A JOINT PROJECT WITH HABITAT FOR HUMANITY IN MISSOURI, USA.

> "In industrialized countries ... the availability of community service projects is diminishing in direct relation to the fact that governments and other institutions are taking over. ... But despite this ... you and I know there is much to do. ... In many areas of service, Rotarians can provide the 'personal touch' that no welfare program can meet."
>
> *Ernst Breitholtz, Kalmar, Sweden*
> *RI president, 1971-72*
> *1972 RI Convention in Houston, Texas, USA*

the Association of Department Stores supported the bar owners' position and claimed that women need only visit their stores to use the toilets.

But by 1907, the Rotary Club of Chicago boasted some influential members. They enlisted the support of other organizations in a two-year battle against their formidable opponents. One such member, Fred Bussey, president of the County Commissioners, helped win the club a $20,000 grant to complete the project. "I stretched my authority [as club president] to its utmost tension and even went so far as to steam ahead on my own initiative and without reference to a board of directors who lacked faith in my project," admitted Paul Harris later.

The comfort stations remained in place for several decades, and the community service idea became the very soul of Rotary. The head of the Chicago YMCA voiced the sentiment of both Rotarian and non-Rotarian Chicagoans of the day when he said, "The Rotary Club of Chicago has now shown reason for its existence."[1]

As San Francisco, Oakland, and soon dozens—and then thousands—of other cities formed their own Rotary clubs, community service became the jewel in their crown. It was the hallmark of Rotary in those towns and cities, although for many years it was the unwritten rule for Rotary clubs to perform their acts of service quietly—almost anonymously—eschewing publicity or any claim for credit for their work.

On 18 January 1909—just weeks after he had started the Rotary Club of San Francisco—Homer Wood wrote to Paul Harris:

"The Rotary Club here is going on record as the first organization to start promotion of a big celebration in San Francisco to take place on the third anniversary of the San Francisco Fire. It will be called the Home Coming Celebration and Carnival."

That month, San Francisco Rotarians formed a committee to help rebuild the City Hall that had been destroyed in the great earthquake and fire of 1906.

In 1911, the Rotary Club of Boston took the initiative to launch a transcontinental highway project, an enormously ambitious scheme for a local Rotary club.[2] But through articles in *The National Rotarian* magazine and presentations made at national conventions, other clubs soon joined the campaign. The *Boston Post* later published a story that credited Boston Rotarians with creating a national highway that ran for 2,800 miles (4,500 km), from Boston to San Francisco.[3] It became known as the Lincoln Highway; and when it opened in time for the San Francisco Exposition in 1915, traffic increased between 300 and 500 percent over the previous year, opening the West to tourism and commercial growth.[4]

A spirit of voluntary service swept across America, initiated by the influential business and professional men in Rotary clubs. Rotarian E.L. Skeel of the Seattle club headed the Civic Committee of the National Association of Rotary Clubs, and his report to the 1912 Rotary Convention, along with the stirring speeches advocating the ideal of service, sent delegates back to their home clubs motivated to launch community service projects of their own. The exchange of business was no longer considered the primary objective of Rotarians.

In 1913, tornadoes wrought death and destruction in Nebraska, as did floods in Ohio and Indiana. Rotary clubs in those states leapt into action, coordinating rescue squads, feeding people and farm animals, and launching a rebuilding campaign. International Association President Glenn Mead of Philadelphia sent a telegram to every Rotary club, and soon help poured in from around the nation. For the first time, Rotary had shown that in a time of crisis it could muster its resources from within—and far beyond—the local community.

In 1918, the Rotary Club of Los Angeles founded Settlement House as a community service project. For seven years, it provided the management and funding—between $10,000 and $50,000 annually—to this outreach for immigrants in one of the city's poorest neighborhoods.

As the movement spread around the world, new clubs were quick to act on their slogan, Service Above Self. In 1916, the Rotary Club of Havana, Cuba, established the traffic laws for their city, maintained the tourist information bureau, and launched a plan for safe bathing beaches and Rotary parks—all within a year of the club's formation.[5]

Rotarians in Britain and Ireland undertook countless acts of civic service during World War I. Once the returning troops were demobilized, Rotary clubs launched job training schemes and other economic programs. Many of these efforts were small acts of kindness to destitute families whose breadwinners had died in the war. Other programs provided mentoring and training for youth and the handicapped.

In 1928, King George V had just recovered from a near-fatal illness thanks to a new electrotherapeutic "sun ray" treatment. When a Dr. Beaumont spoke about this revolutionary treatment to the Inner London Rotary Club of St. Pancras, Rotarian George Kimber was so moved by its lifesaving potential that he asked to address the club's board of directors. He asked them

1   Paul P. Harris, *This Rotarian Age* (Chicago: Rotary International, 1935), 76.
2   *The National Rotarian* II, no. 2 (January 1912): 29.
3   *The National Rotarian* II, no. 5 (May 1912): 17.
4   THE ROTARIAN VII, no. 6 (December 1915): 513.
5   THE ROTARIAN X, no. 4 (April 1917): 334.

to think about how they could become a beacon of hope in their community; if such specialized care could save a king's life, why not make it available to save the life of "the neediest child in St. Pancras."

The St. Pancras club was already active in community service, having initiated prison visitations, youth sponsorships, and projects to aid the unemployed. Kimber challenged the club to do something to help the sick, and to kick off the project he made a gift on the spot of £10,000.[6] The result was the Institute of Ray Therapy and Electro Therapy Clinic (known popularly as the Camden Town Clinic), which was later renamed the Medical Rehabilitation Centre.[7] For many decades—until the late 1980s—the clinic was a testimony to local Rotarians' contributions to the most needy people in their community.

Today, Rotary has evolved into a global organization that partners in multimillion-dollar projects with influential organizations such as the World Health Organization and UNICEF. Yet the vast majority of Rotarians—and non-Rotarians—will identify the organization's work with something in the local community. Rotarians the world over are proud of the role they play in peacemaking, international scholarships, and the Rotary PolioPlus program to eradicate this dread disease worldwide. But when they think of Rotary, most Rotarians still think of the fellowship they enjoy at their local club and the community service projects they work on together. Much of the attention has gone to major club initiatives, such as building hospitals. Yet the true heart of Rotary's service to the community has been in the small projects—the wheelchair ramp at the library, the mentoring program for at-risk children, the senior citizens' Christmas party.

DISTRICT 5010 GOVERNOR CAROLYN JONES READS A DR. SEUSS BOOK TO A CHILD IN A TOMSK, RUSSIA, ORPHANAGE SUPPORTED BY THE DISTRICT.

"In our families, we must act with integrity to preserve the values we treasure. Let us build an atmosphere of trust and encourage the teaching and living of high moral principles. When we Rotarians care for the world's children, we care for the world's families.... We build our local communities and ultimately the world community."

Herbert G. Brown, Clearwater, Florida, USA
RI president, 1995-96

Rotary's commitment to community service is part of the organization's fabric. When a smallpox epidemic struck Veracruz, Mexico, in 1925, local Rotarians immunized 36,000 people. One wonders how many of the sons and grandsons of those Mexican Rotarians helped to immunize their neighbors against polio in the PolioPlus program 60 years later.

In 1931, the wife of E.J. Johnson, past president of London's West Ham Rotary club, suggested the club present the borough's 450 blind residents with white sticks so they could navigate the streets more safely, especially at night. The club enthusiastically endorsed the idea, and the entire London district adopted it. By 1935, 116 Rotary clubs across Britain and Ireland had "white stick" community service projects, and the idea soon spread around the world.

When Rotary clubs turned the program over to the National Institute for the Blind, that organization wrote: "It is impossible to estimate the number of accidents that have been circumvented and the amount of suffering that has been avoided by the scheme."[8] Yet the same can be said today of the Rotary clubs in India and Latin America whose avoidable blindness programs are restoring sight to thousands of people in their communities through routine cataract surgery.

In 1981, Ian Scott of the Rotary Club of Mornington, Victoria, Australia, initiated a program that became known as the Australian Rotary Health Research Fund (ARHRF). The fund had its own board of directors and raised an initial $2 million with the objective of funding long-term research in health problems within the community. It quickly grew and adopted cot death, or sudden infant death syndrome (SIDS), as an early project. ARHRF has evolved into a much-praised autonomous body within Rotary in Australia, now raising more than $2 million annually for medical and mental-health research.[9]

By 1990, local community-service activity (supplemented by World Community Service assistance) took on a new dimension. Rapid growth, especially in Asia, and the increased visibility from massive PolioPlus immunization efforts gave Rotary a larger presence in the community.

6   Rotary International, *Rotary: Fifty Years of Service* (Evanston, Illinois, 1954), 36.

7   Malcolm J. Holmes, "Camden Town Clinic," 15 September 2001, personal e-mail (15 September 2001).

8   Vivian Carter, *The Romance of Rotary in London* (London: Rotary International in Britain and Ireland, 1947), 167.

9   Paul Henningham, *Seventy-Five Years of Service: Rotary in Australia, Papua New Guinea and Solomon Islands 1921-1996* (Parramatta, NSW: Rotary Down Under for the Australian Rotary Institute, 1996), 72.

ROTARIANS PLANT TREES IN A PARKWAY AS PART OF A
PRESERVE PLANET EARTH ACTIVITY DURING THE 1998 RI
CONVENTION IN INDIANAPOLIS.

In India, Pakistan, Indonesia, Thailand, and neighboring countries, Rotary clubs developed thousands of community service projects each year, including eye camps and hospitals, rehabilitation facilities for disabled children, food and water projects, and literacy programs. The Rotary Village Corps (now Rotary Community Corps) program brought the Rotary gearwheel emblem into even the smallest, most remote communities.

Especially where communication or transportation was difficult, Rotary clubs found themselves working with local governments to meet local needs. Sometimes Rotary filled gaps governments could not serve. "In such localities," noted Past RI Director M.K. Panduranga Setty of India, "the influence of Rotarians in the community reached very high levels."

When Turkey was devastated by a deadly earthquake on 17 April 1999, Rotarians immediately sprang into action, building a tent city for 1,300 in Izmit—with Rotarian architects, engineers, electricians, and health-care professionals designing the service buildings, including a 24-hour-a-day infirmary. Other Rotarians planned for the long-term welfare of the thousands of homeless citizens, taking charge of their education, health, and welfare, even providing psychological counseling.

In his autobiography, *My Road to Rotary*, Paul Harris wrote: "Deeds preceded the written word and after service had been rendered in manifold forms, the word 'service' was written into the Rotary plan. ... Those who could not contribute money contributed labor. Anyone who could drive a nail became a carpenter, while druggists and grocers became bricklayers and plumbers when occasion demanded."[10]

That sounds a bit like Habitat for Humanity, a Georgia, USA-based housing and shelter program in which thousands of Rotarians and clubs participate today, or the ongoing initiative by 1997-98 RI President Glen W. Kinross of Australia to provide low-cost housing in poor communities.

Rotary's century of community service has not been for personal gain or even for public recognition; few of the projects even have the word Rotary ascribed to them. Rather, it was in response to the needs of the communities where Rotarians live, raise their families, and earn their living. When the earthquake, flood, or hurricane strikes, the elderly are ignored, the poor need shelter, the young and old need food; it is then that Rotarians make service to their community their most visible acts of kindness.

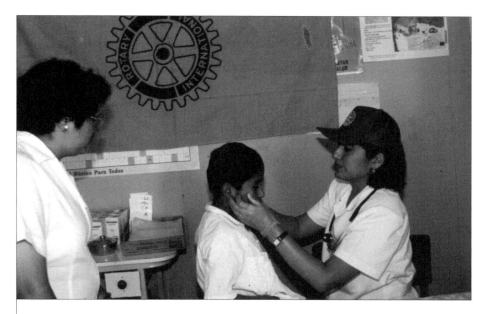

AS PART OF OPERATION CONDOR, FUNDED BY A MATCHING GRANT, A ROTARIAN PHYSICIAN EXAMINES A BOY IN A CLINIC IN HUANUCO, PERU.

10 Paul Harris, *My Road to Rotary: The Story of a Boy, a Vermont Community, and Rotary* (Chicago, Illinois: A. Kroch and Son, 1948), 240.

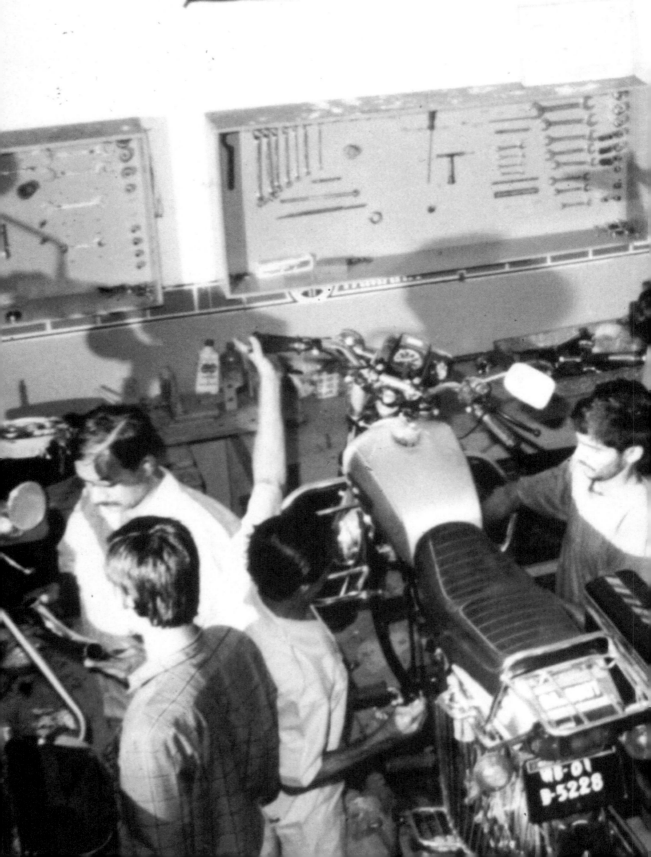

RATION, CALCUTTA
30 DEC '92

CHAPTER 13

VOCATIONAL SERVICE

Chapter 13 ~ Vocational Service

B usiness! Mankind was my business. The common welfare was my business; charity, mercy, forbearance, and benevolence were all my business. The dealings of my trade were but a drop of water in the comprehensive ocean of my business!"

So declares the ghost in Charles Dickens's "A Christmas Carol," a sentiment echoed in the RI theme for 2001-02. Business and professional life are the bedrock of the Rotary movement, and Vocational Service has always been a significant force in promoting honor, integrity, and trustworthiness in the business world.

Over the years, Rotarians have often struggled to succinctly define Vocational Service. They enjoyed the camaraderie of Club Service, the satisfaction in serving the needs of their communities, and the hope that their International Service promotes world peace. But Vocational Service is difficult to define. And so it is sometimes referred to as the "Forgotten Avenue of Service." One reason is Club, Community, and International Service activities usually involve groups of Rotarians; Vocational Service—the second Avenue of Service—is generally conducted by individual members.

The foundation of Rotary is its classification system of membership. The fact that originally only one representative from each business or profession was invited to join a club distinguished Rotary from other organizations. Paul Harris suspected that if, for example, six insurance agents joined the club, they would either sit together and "talk shop" or compete against one another for other members' business.

A participant learns sewing as part of a vocational training project in Soweto, South Africa.

Overleaf: Unemployed men learn motorcycle maintenance in a Rotary Club of Calcutta vocational service project.

"Rotary has reinforced this concept [of the Golden Rule], terming it Vocational Service; but long before Paul Harris founded our organization in 1905, most businessmen both large and small were trying to operate on the principle of 'he profits most who serves best.' They knew that the fly-by-night, chiseling, fraudulent operators were unfair both to legitimate business and to the public. That is why they organized into trade groups and why they have taken the lead in creating protective legislation."

J.C. Penney, Rotarian and U.S. businessman

One day in 1908, Ches Perry noticed a member, Charlie Newton, checking off names on the club roster. "As a Rotarian," Charlie explained, "I have been trying to find some way to be helpful to every member of our club, but Barney Arntzen the undertaker has me stymied." He later found a way to fulfill his personal mission. On his way to Rotary, he stopped to say hello to Barney and noticed a new ambulance parked outside. "The finest of its kind in Chicago," said Barney of his new vehicle. Charlie then visited another member, Doc Baxter, and asked if he ever needed an ambulance. "Certainly do. Why?" Then Charlie told him about Barney's new ambulance and suggested the two men talk about doing business together.[1]

Chambers of commerce, networking clubs, and trade associations have long operated on the basis of business exchange. Even after Rotary eliminated trade-boosting activities, a University of Chicago study found:

"The inhibitions of Rotarians about profits reflect no credit on Rotary. If the search for profits is 'selfish' and unworthy, then all of American civilization and the entire social and economic order of the western world are selfish and unworthy, for they have been created by business profits, developed by profits, and preserved by profits."[2]

By the time the National Association of Rotary Clubs held its first convention in 1910, the networking emphasis had begun shifting. The majority of clubs told the new Civic Committee that Rotary should move from being a booster club to improving their communities. In 1910, Arthur Frederick

WOMEN LEARN SEWING SKILLS AT A VOCATIONAL SCHOOL SPONSORED BY THE ROTARY CLUB OF CELAYA, MEXICO, AND FUNDED BY A 3-H GRANT.

---

1   Chesley Perry to Hiram Smith, Fullerton, California, 15 February 1960.
2   University of Chicago, Social Science Committee, *Rotary? A University Group Looks at the Rotary Club of Chicago* (Chicago, IL: The University of Chicago Press, 1934), 209.

Sheldon introduced "profit" in a new light when he told the first convention in Chicago: "He profits most who serves his fellows best." A year later, he modified the statement to He Profits Most Who Serves Best. The delegates immediately adopted the phrase as Rotary's slogan. After Minneapolis Rotarian Ben Collins introduced the phrase "Service, not Self," Rotary slightly modified it to Service Above Self and added it to the Sheldon slogan. In 1912, Paul Harris struck "statistician" from the list of Rotary club officers, and Rotarians were no longer required to exchange business with one another.

150

"Business should be a pleasure, and God pity the man who doesn't love his business enough to get pleasure out of it," said Cleveland Rotarian J.J. Wemple at the 1913 convention in Buffalo, New York. "The manufacturer's first business is the making of men. Rotary's business is to polish them after they are made."[3]

Rotarians, who occupied positions of influence in their profession, were ideally placed to use their stature to make things happen. In 1909, the fledgling aviation industry turned to the Rotary Club of Los Angeles for help in promoting the new form of transportation. Predicted club president Dick Ferris: "A few years ago people said, 'You couldn't pay me to ride in one of those things' when an automobile was mentioned, but now everybody wants a ride. That will be the case with flying. Inside of 10 years you will see equipment like Pullman trains going east through the air."[4] Los Angeles members spontaneously pledged their influence—and $1,000 of their own money—to sponsor the Gordon Bennett Coupe Internationale d'Avion, America's first aviation rally.

In 1940, Rotary International defined the Object of Vocational Service this way:

"To encourage and foster:
High ethical standards in business and professions;
The recognition of the worthiness of all useful occupations;
The dignifying by each Rotarian of his occupation as an
opportunity to serve society."[5]

Rotarians in Buffalo, New York, USA, sponsored weekly 15-minute radio broadcasts called "Choosing Your Career" and distributed thousands of career counseling pamphlets to young people. Members in Portland, Oregon, exposed and publicized local graft schemes. In St. Paul, Minnesota, the Rotary

> "I am encouraged by the current awakening of business firms and the professions to their social responsibilities. Rotarians . . . in business and industry have been leaders in helping train the unskilled, providing employment for the so-called unemployables, creating opportunities for recent graduates . . . developing markets, and generally helping to lift the standard of living. This is Rotary action in the finest sense."
>
> *Kiyoshi Togasaki, Tokyo, Japan*
> *RI president, 1968-69*

club staged Home Products Week, which urged townspeople to buy locally made products. The new Rotary Club of Singapore helped form the Singapore Manufacturers Association to promote the city as a Southeast Asian commercial center, and that association is still doing business today.

In Ghana, Rotary clubs from the Netherlands and United States helped local Rotarians establish a 52-acre (21-hectare) model farm on which 120 students were taught the latest techniques in food production and preservation. The Rotary Club of Semarang Kunthi, Indonesia, trained villagers on Atauro, a tiny island in Timor, to improve their productivity and increase their income through fish marketing and preservation training. Clubs in Buenaventura, Colombia, and Salvadore, Brazil, encouraged their members to bring employees to their Rotary meetings to introduce them to the organization's ideals of service and integrity.[6] In 1989, after communism collapsed in Eastern Europe, Texas Rotarians sent business leaders to Hungary and Poland to teach those emerging democracies free enterprise business concepts.

The Code of Ethics

When Philadelphia's Glenn Mead succeeded Paul Harris as president of the International Association of Rotary Clubs in 1912, he continued to push the organization in its new direction. "Rotary is a solid and substantial bridge from the old order of the business world to the new," he said. He recommended that Rotary contribute to "the advancement of business morality" by formulating a code of business ethics.[7]

Fraudulent and deceptive business practices were so ubiquitous then that both Mead and his successor, Russell Greiner of Kansas City, urged Rotary to help restore the public trust in business. There were no consumer protection laws, no truth-in-advertising statutes—the unwritten law was caveat emptor, "Let the buyer beware." Rotary's early leaders often cited the Golden Rule—"Do unto others as you would have them do unto you"—as the guiding principle of Rotary's Vocational Service.

THE ROTARY CODE OF ETHICS,
AS ADOPTED BY THE 1915
CONVENTION IN SAN FRANCISCO

---

3   THE ROTARIAN IV, no. 1 (September 1913): 37.

4   Rotary Club of Los Angeles, *History of the Rotary Club of Los Angeles,* Vol. II (Los Angeles: RC Los Angeles, 1989), 9.

5   Guy Gundaker, *Vocational Service 'The Corner Stone of Rotary'* (Evanston, Illinois: Rotary International, October 1940), 2.

6   THE ROTARIAN, June 1974, 22.

7   THE ROTARIAN IV, no. 1 (September 1913): 20.

A young man learns tractor maintenance at City
of Youth, a home and school for street children in
Campinas, Brazil.

In September 1913, Greiner appointed a committee headed by Rotarian Robert Hunt of Sioux City, Iowa, USA, to draft a code of ethics for presentation to the 1914 Rotary Convention in Houston. Months passed and the committee had completed nothing. Two weeks before the convention, Hunt admitted that the draft wasn't ready and persuaded fellow club member Jacob R. Perkins to compose the code. As the train left Iowa for Texas, Perkins and six of his club mates put pen to paper. Throughout the night as the train rumbled across America's heartland, they tried to condense Hunt's 5,000-word research notes into a concise document. As they pulled into the Houston station, they finished their job: a 100-word preamble followed by 11 simple articles. Not one member of the committee appointed to draft the code was present. The delegates at the convention unanimously approved it, as did the delegates to the 1915 San Francisco convention.

With the adoption of the Rotary Code of Ethics, Rotarians became ambassadors of improved business conduct from the clubs to their trades and professions. Philadelphia's Guy Gundaker, who became Rotary's 13th president in 1923, used it as the blueprint for the National Restaurant Association's ethical business code. "At least 145 national industrial codes of correct practice which have been adopted since 1922 [were] directly a result of the influence of Rotarians," reported the University of Chicago researchers in the book *Rotary?*[8]

E.M. Statler, a Chicago Rotarian and owner of the Statler Hotel, was moved to compose the Statler Service Codes, which he instructed all employ-

8   University of Chicago, 204.
9   THE ROTARIAN III, no. 7 (March 1913): 29.

ees to adopt. One excerpt read: "Life is service. The one who progresses is the one who gives his fellow a little more—a little better SERVICE."[9]

Beginning with the 1916 Cincinnati convention, "vocational sections" convened wherein Rotarians engaged in the same business or profession met to discuss how they could raise the ethical standards of their chosen trade. Delegates to that same convention also became the first U.S. organization to adopt a resolution calling for truth-in-advertising laws.

Rotarians practiced what they preached. The new Employer-Employee Relations Committee reported to the 1919 Salt Lake City convention how employers could practice the Golden Rule of fairness and efficacy toward employees. The association urged clubs to form local employer-employee relations committees. Starting in 1917, THE ROTARIAN published numerous articles, such as "Conflict between the Employer and Employee," "The Welfare of the Worker," and "The Employer's Service to Employees."

The Four-Way Test

When the Great Depression hit in 1930, many Rotarians faced the greatest challenge of their lives. There was no better time to test for ethical conduct than during such a dire economic crisis and the scramble to survive.

Herbert J. Taylor, a member of the Rotary Club of Chicago, was asked to take over the near-bankrupt Club Aluminum Company in 1932. It was a last-ditch effort to save the company, which had no money, low employee morale,

RI PRESIDENT HERBERT J. TAYLOR DISPLAYS A COPY OF THE FOUR-WAY TEST TO ROTARIANS AND A WOMAN IN ETHNIC DRESS DURING A 1955 VISIT TO ST. PAUL, MINNESOTA, USA.

PAST GOVERNOR JOHN FEROS OF DISTRICT 9600 LOOKS ON AS
TEACHERS AND STUDENTS IN PAPUA NEW GUINEA RECEIVE SEWING
MACHINES AND TYPEWRITERS.

and ruthless competition from other firms in similar straits. Taylor used his Rotary background to draft a 24-word code of conduct that he used to guide all his daily decisions. He found this ethical compass so helpful that he called all the department heads together and asked them to do the same. The code had four points, so Taylor called it The Four-Way Test:

"Of all the things we think, say or do:

1. Is it the TRUTH?

2. Is it FAIR to all concerned?

3. Will it build GOODWILL and BETTER FRIENDSHIPS?

4. Will it be BENEFICIAL to all concerned?"

Club Aluminum applied The Four-Way Test to its dealings with employees, customers, dealers, and suppliers. It deliberately walked away from business that, while profitable, would have failed one or more of its standards.

The company's fortunes turned around; it eliminated its debt, and over the next 15 years paid out $1 million in dividends while building a net worth of $2 million. Herb Taylor credited The Four-Way Test. The RI Board voted to officially adopt The Four-Way Test in 1943; and when Herb Taylor became RI president in 1954, he donated the copyright of the test to the organization. The test has been translated into the languages of more than 100 countries.

A Japanese Rotary club printed The Four-Way Test on umbrellas for passengers at railway stations. The Rotary Club of Bayswater, Victoria, Australia,

> "In 1915, Rotary adopted a code of ethics and began printing it on pocket-sized cards. As members began to carry and read this code, they began to believe it. Thus a Rotary trend developed which, I think, played a major part in changing 'Let the buyer beware' to 'The customer is always right.'"
>
> *H.J. Brunnier*
> *San Francisco, California, USA*
> *RI president, 1952-53*

sponsored an essay and poster contest among the town's 11- to 14-year-olds using as its theme "A man's struggle with his conscience." NASA astronaut Buzz Aldrin planted a Four-Way Test pin on the Moon's surface. In Meerut, India, the Rotary club erected a stone pillar next to the highway, inscribed with The Four-Way Test, and similar monuments were built in public parks by Rotary clubs in Brazil, Japan, and the Philippines. It has appeared in gymnasiums, courtrooms, and labor contracts. Today, the test appears on highway billboards, in schoolrooms and halls of government, and on the walls of businesses the world over.

Vocational Service remains at the heart of Rotary. In 1987-88, RI President Charles C. Keller reinvigorated the Avenue by appointing the first Vocational Service Committee in 50 years, chaired by William Sergeant of Tennessee, USA. The committee redefined how clubs could more effectively participate in Vocational Service and drafted the new Declaration of Rotarians in Businesses and Professions.

Chapter 14 ~ Serving the World Community

O n the drought-stricken plains of East Africa, Swedish pediatrician
Hakan Simonson sends a dust trail high into the sky as the pickup
truck speeds him toward waiting patients in remote Masai villages. In other

158

communities, Ulmka Lidén restores sight to a blind mother who now sees her

child for the first time. Dentist Ingvar Persson examines 3,500 children during

the three weeks he spends at a Kenyan orphanage, and Gunnar Isabsson

teaches Zambian health-care workers how to treat and care for AIDS

patients. These volunteers for the Rotarian-supported Doctor Bank, founded

in Sweden, represent scores of Scandinavian health-care professionals who

devote countless hours each year to fighting disease in developing nations.

On the other side of the world, a group of Australians are laying down
their tools after a day of backbreaking work building a school in Indonesia.
At the same time, a larger group of their countrymen are constructing and
equipping a health clinic in a mountain village of Papua New Guinea. Meanwhile, in San Francisco, California, USA, plastic surgeons are boarding their
flight for Santiago, Chile, where for the next 10 days they will perform surgery
on children with facial deformities.

RI President Clifford L. Dochterman and
Ramon Tamames of the University of Madrid
at the 1992 President's Conference of Goodwill
and Development in Barcelona

Overleaf: In Kenya, RI President Robert Barth
(left) greets a local man at a project sponsored
by districts 5950 and 5960 (Minnesota, USA)
and the Rotary Club of Mombasa.

On the surface, these people have nothing in common. Yet they are Rotarians, joined together by the bonds of international service, giving a week or more of their time for a vacation with a purpose. Many Rotarians hear the call to service in their home communities; others feel drawn to programs for which they have a special interest, such as The Rotary Foundation's Ambassadorial Scholarships. Others seek projects beyond their own national borders.

"Never has greater need existed for cooperation and goodwill. If selfishness, distrust, and fear prevail, disaster is the inevitable result. The welfare of the world demands that the facilities for better conditions of living and health...be shared by all peoples in a spirit of mutual helpfulness." Those are stirring words as Rotary celebrates its centennial, yet General Secretary Ches Perry first wrote them more than 70 years ago, shortly after International Service became a part of Rotary's Object.

Early Rotary activities focused on club and community service. Then, in 1914, eight Rotary clubs in Britain and Ireland helped house refugees who had fled from the impending war in their native Belgium. In 1919, a hurricane and tidal wave struck Texas, USA, causing widespread death and destruction. Rotary clubs in other countries responded with donations to the Rotary International Relief Fund. When an earthquake in Japan destroyed vast sections of Tokyo and Yokohama in 1923, Rotarians from other countries quickly collected US$40,000 to help. It was a gesture that the Rotary Club of Tokyo willingly reciprocated when two years later it sent $25,000 to help U.S. tornado survivors.

When World War I ended and Rotary began its global expansion, this informal international fellowship exchange spread further; and some clubs even arranged exchange visits. When the conflict ended, it was only natural that RI President Estes Snedecor and delegates at the 1921 convention in Edinburgh, Scotland, wanted to further emphasize this trend. They adopted International Service as the sixth Object of Rotary—although it was later changed to the fourth Avenue of Service in the Object of Rotary. International Service thus became the last plank to be added to the platform of the programs of Rotary International.

Danish Rotarian and educator Dr. Sven Knudsen launched a youth exchange project in 1927 between Danish and American teenagers. The idea spread quickly across the borders of many other nations to become one of Rotary International's most cherished and enduring programs: Youth Exchange. Clubs

ACTOR AND C.A.R.E. SPOKESMAN
DOUGLAS FAIRBANKS JR. WITH PAST RI
PRESIDENT HARRY ROGERS IN 1947

in Nice, France, inaugurated Youth Exchange the same year. Today, more than 7,000 young people annually exchange visits for up to a year, studying in another country while living with Rotarian families. The program is a powerful lesson in cross-cultural understanding—part of Rotary's objective of bringing about world peace.

In 1927, two Rotarians each from Denmark, Finland, Iceland, Norway, and Sweden formed the first Rotary intercountry committee to promote fellowship on an international scale. Rotarians in France and Germany—enemy countries during the Great War—formed *petits comités* to exchange club visits, home stays, and promote better understanding between their citizens.

These exchanges spread beyond Rotary, and the idea blossomed around the world. In Rotary's first century, hundreds of thousands of Rotarians, students, and community leaders have participated in exchanges. Some of these are formal programs of The Rotary Foundation; others happened due to chance meetings at an RI Convention or when traveling Rotarians made up at club meetings.

The two elements that drew Rotarians into international service were warm fellowship and compassion for the needy. Rotarians tend to be gregarious, inquisitive, and interested in things beyond their own daily routine. Small wonder that they responded enthusiastically to the opportunity to learn about and socialize with Rotarians from other nations. To some, these were little more than opportunities for fun, to share sports or hobbies such as golf

"The space age has brought mankind closer together, and Rotary should attempt to take advantage of this great force in welding us together into a compact human race with the idea of belonging to one another. The moment we try to minimize the importance of internationalism of Rotary, that moment will spell the death of Rotary."

Nitish C. Laharry, Calcutta, India
RI president, 1962-63

or sailing with Rotarians from another country. The Rotary Fellowships were formed to bring together Rotarians from around the world who share such diverse interests as golf, skiing, and stamp collecting, and many get together throughout the year in regional and international gatherings.

Over the years, some have questioned Rotary's emphasis on international service, especially between citizens of hostile nations. Rotary has answered by pointing out that the goal of all Rotarians is to advance world peace and understanding between all people, and the work of individual Rotarians in international service is the fuel that powers that engine.

There have been many occasions during wars or border skirmishes when Rotarians of both sides of the conflict have worked for resolution of the dispute. Rotarians from Argentina and Chile helped broker an end to the longstanding border dispute between their countries in 1936. The Rotary Club of Buenos Aires took the cannons that had been facing one another and melted them down, ordering that the iron be recast into a statue of Jesus. When they erected the enormous image on the border, high in the Andes, their friends from the Chilean Rotary clubs placed a plaque on it that reads, "May these mountains crumble into dust before Argentineans and Chileans shall break this peace."[1]

"The Fourth Object of Rotary neither states nor implies any direct connection of Rotary with the relations between the governments of two or more countries," Ches Perry wrote in 1938. "It has rather to do with friendly relations between individual persons or small groups of persons."[2] Frequently, while governments of nations such as Britain and Argentina, India and Pakistan, and Bolivia and Paraguay were lobbing shells at each other, Rotarians from those countries met to celebrate what they had in common, using that as the starting point in their quest for peace.

As the 20th century progressed, Rotarians were at the forefront of those who suggested that environmental, business, and public health actions should have a global outlook. "A world-minded Rotarian looks beyond national patriotism and considers himself as sharing responsibility for the advancement of international understanding, goodwill, and peace," advised one Rotary International leader in the 1950s.[3] This led, in 1957, to a new approach to international service. Rotary convened a series of Into Their Shoes conferences at which speakers from other countries would discuss topics of international interest at community gatherings, often introducing a perspective that the local citizens had not previously considered. The RI Board even designated each February as World Understanding Month and 23 February—Rotary's anniversary—as World Understanding and Peace Day. During this time RI encourages clubs to arrange activities that can bring about better understanding among

SERVING THE WORLD COMMUNITY

1   Rotary International, *Rotary: Fifty Years of Service* (Evanston, Illinois, 1954), 91.
2   THE ROTARIAN, February 1938, 7.
3   Clifford L. Dochterman, *The ABCs of Rotary* (Evanston, Illinois: Rotary International, 2000), 6.

people of differing political, religious, or cultural viewpoints.

The 1961 Rotary Institute for present and past RI officers recommended to the incumbent RI Board a "world community service" program. The original proposal was for teams of Rotarians with expertise in education, public health, agriculture, and industry to travel to developing countries to share knowledge. The Board adopted the proposal at its January 1962 meeting. The World Community Service (WCS) program began that year and probably did more to bring international service to local clubs than anything in the 57 years that preceded it. Suddenly, here was a vehicle through which single clubs—even individual Rotarians within a club—could become actively involved in serving mankind in a distant community. WCS helped clubs in developing countries launch service projects in their local communities and paired them with other clubs in the developed world that had the desire and the resources to help.

One of the earliest examples of international harmony between Rotarians of the United States and Canada was in 1917 when a bridge was built between the cities of Fort William and Port Arthur, Ontario, and Duluth, Minnesota. Rotarians in each community raised funds for a bridge across the Pigeon River, an international boundary. A Canadian Rotarian volunteered his engineering skills.

To facilitate exchanges between clubs, Rotary International established a project library. Those clubs and districts with a WCS project would file a report with RI, describing the idea and outlining their needs. Meanwhile, Rotarians or clubs in other countries would offer their talents, financial gifts, or supplies. Most projects were planned well in advance, but World Community Service also helped clubs respond to natural disasters, such as the devastating 1970-71 floods in Bangladesh, the 1973 Nicaraguan earthquake, the 1975 cyclone in Darwin, Northern Territory, Australia, and the aftermath

VILLAGERS OF MAKAIBAN, PHILIPPINES, ADMIRE THEIR NEW WELL, A WORLD COMMUNITY SERVICE PROJECT OF THE ROTARY CLUB OF SANTA MARIA, PHILIPPINES, AND THE ROTARY CLUB OF YAO, JAPAN.

of Hurricane Mitch in Central America in 1999.

Through International Service programs such as WCS, Rotarians became citizens of the world. This concept was considered progressive when the RI Board of Directors first adopted it in 1949 with the statement "Attributes of a World-Minded Rotarian." World War II was over, and Rotary had played an important role in the formation of the United Nations and UNESCO. Rotary International realized that its worldwide membership—then in excess of 300,000 Rotarians in 80 countries—could be a powerful force for peace. The Board urged all Rotarians to influence their own governments to adopt policies that would lead to "international understanding and goodwill toward all peoples."

YOUTH EXCHANGE STUDENTS NOBUYO OKAJIMA OF JAPAN AND CHRISTIAN JENSEN OF DENMARK DISTRIBUTE HOLIDAY GIFTS TO CHILDREN IN A SYDNEY, NEW SOUTH WALES, AUSTRALIA, HOSPITAL AS PART OF A PROJECT BY THE ROTARY CLUB OF WEST SYDNEY.

Successive RI presidents and officers helped show Rotarians that poverty, hunger, polluted drinking water, illiteracy, injustice, and disease were not just problems of a faraway land. The world is small, and here were opportunities to improve the lives of people everywhere. As Rotary volunteers returned from Africa, Asia, and South America to their local clubs and districts, they told spellbound audiences: "I thought I was going to give and that the local people would be the recipients. But I have received so much more from this powerful experience than I ever gave."

The 13 years from 1956 to 1969 marked the coming of age for international service. During that time, The Rotary Foundation (which is profiled in chapter 10) underwent tremendous growth and took in the funds to launch many humanitarian projects. Within a few years, the vast majority of Rotary's international service projects were made possible by funding from The Rotary Foundation.

Rotary International President Carl Miller introduced the Matched Districts and Matched Clubs program in 1963-64, urging Rotarians to participate in WCS and to communicate across international borders. Correspondence often led to exchange visits; and with the strengthening world economy and the advent of low-cost air travel, Rotarians criss-crossed the globe in search of cross-cultural exchanges and service opportunities.

Since 1921, Rotary International has held several international meetings each year "to stimulate, inform, and inspire officers and members, so that they will be motivated to make Rotary thrive at the international, district, and club levels."[4] The annual convention is the largest such event and meets in a different city around the world each year, attracting between 17,000 and

4   Rotary International, *Rotary Basic Library: International Service Vol. Five* (Evanston, Illinois, 1995), 69.

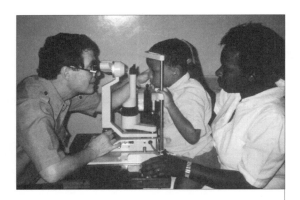

DR. GEORGE SPOERL CONDUCTS AN EYE EXAM ON A CHILD IN ARUSHA, TANZANIA, AT A FREE EYE CLINIC SPONSORED BY THE ROTARY CLUB OF LAKE FOREST, ILLINOIS, USA, AND THE ROTARY CLUB OF ARUSHA.

40,000 Rotarians and guests. The RI president often convenes regional conferences, presidential summits, peace conferences, conferences of goodwill and development, and other gatherings. These meetings are a microcosm of the Rotary world, serious in purpose but bubbling with international fellowship. They usually include training sessions for incoming officers, inspiring addresses from speakers describing Rotary programs, and an evening of home hospitality as guests of Rotarians in the host community. A project exchange forum is often held, during which clubs and districts needing help with their local service projects will meet fellow Rotarians from other countries wishing to adopt a new WCS project or work out a Matching Grant with The Rotary Foundation.

Walking through the House of Friendship at any RI meeting, one sees and meets men and women of every ethnic background greeting one another, engaged in the common language of service to mankind.

In 1980, three RI presidents—W. Jack Davis (1977-78), Clem Renouf (1978-79), and James L. Bomar Jr. (1979-80)—appointed a committee to decide an appropriate way to celebrate Rotary's 75th anniversary. The result was the Health, Hunger and Humanity program, which RI officially launched in

VOLUNTEERS BUILD A DOMINICAN REPUBLIC CHILDREN'S HOSPITAL, A WORLD COMMUNITY SERVICE PROJECT.

1978 and which became known informally as "3-H." It began as a seven-year program, during which funds would be collected and projects launched. It was different from WCS in that it was a "corporate" program, centrally managed from the RI Secretariat, which urged every club in the world to participate. For the first time since the Boys Work and "crippled children's work" of the early 1920s, Rotary encouraged every club to get involved in a coordinated program. This was controversial with some clubs—and even some RI past presidents—yet 3-H caught the imagination of Rotarians the world over. (For more on 3-H, see chapter 10.)

> Rotarians are often the first to respond with emergency relief to distant disasters. Following Turkey's devastating 1999 earthquake, which took 3,000 lives, Rotarians in District 3640 (Korea) quickly raised US$22,000 to provide food, supplies, and set-up tents for the homeless. By year's end, they had donated $146,000 for earthquake relief in Turkey and Taiwan. Rotarians in Germany also provided extensive aid.

WCS had long been involved in projects that addressed health, hunger, and humanity, but 3-H brought a sharp new focus. The 3-H Committee named three co-chairmen—Dr. Ben N. Saltzman, Webster Pendergrass, and Clifford L. Dochterman (later RI president)—who were responsible for health, hunger, and humanity projects, respectively. The program was a resounding success. It also raised the consciousness of Rotarians to opportunities for international service. It raised millions of dollars, which made possible numerous new projects. And as the organization's gift to the world on its 75th anniversary, it was Rotary's raison d'être. Best of all, 3-H became the spark that ignited the brightest candle in Rotary's history: PolioPlus.

It is impossible to tell in one chapter, or even in one book, the whole story of Rotary's international service. It is not a story best told from the headquarters level but rather from a personal perspective. A member of the Rotary Club of Marlton, New Jersey, USA, took relief supplies to Beirut, Lebanon, during that country's civil war. "I hated Americans because I always considered them to be responsible for supplying our enemy with the bombs he drops on us every night," admitted a Beirut Rotarian as he and the American brought medicine to an orphanage. "But now I realize that I can disagree with a government's policy, but that I should not hate its people. Thank you for helping our children."

Group Study Exchange (GSE) began as an exchange between districts in California, USA, and Japan in 1965. Rotary International adopted GSE as a major program of The Rotary Foundation and has since had more than 40,000 business and professional men and women participate. The Australian FAIM (Fourth Avenue in Motion) program, which was founded by Keith Hopper of the Rotary Club of Inverell in 1963,[5] is a model for launching international service projects. Following the civil war in East Timor (now Timor-Leste), Rotarians from Australia and New Zealand helped rebuild schools, provided employment opportunities, and even built a factory that produced corrugated tin roofs.[6]

In 1995, Rotarians down under built Kokoda Memorial Hospital in Papua New Guinea, and hundreds of Rotarians and their volunteer friends have since visited the hospital on work missions. In its first five years, doctors of Kokoda treated more than 100,000 patients and delivered more than 500 babies.[7] Over the next 40 years, FAIM—with its all-volunteer staff—organized almost 1,000 work teams like the one that served in Timor-Leste, bringing relief and hope to needy communities around the world.

Past General Secretary Herbert Pigman went to Korea in 1961 as a staff member of THE ROTARIAN to report on the state of Rotary in the war-ravaged country. He recalls being escorted by Rotarians to the outskirts of Pusan—city of a million refugees—along 19 miles (30 km) of muddy roads to a farmer who was able to support his nine children thanks to a cow that the Rotary Club of Pusan had given him. The animal pulled his plow and provided milk for his family; the only condition the club made was that the farmer donate back to the club his cow's first calf so that it could be passed on to another needy family. But less than two decades later, Korean Rotarians were among the greatest contributors in the world to WCS projects. They sent US$10,000 worth of computers and medical equipment to China, $15,000 worth of powdered milk to children in North Korea, rushed $20,000 in disaster relief to victims of earthquakes in Turkey and Taiwan, and donated $6,000 worth of

166

A FAMILY IN ZARSZYN, POLAND, PROUDLY DISPLAY A COW PROVIDED BY HEIFER PROJECT INTERNATIONAL THROUGH A PROJECT FUNDED BY DISTRICT 5690.

The Canadian International Development Agency (CIDA) started offering matching grants to Rotary clubs and districts to expand World Community Service projects in 1975. This unique partnership started with the Rotary Club of Guelph, Ontario, Canada, under Past District Governor David Kennedy. More than 600 projects and US$30 million have provided self-help aid to developing nations in Africa, Asia, the Caribbean, and Central and South America. In 1998, CIDA pledged $35.5 million to fund immunizations against childhood diseases, including polio.

medical equipment to orphanages in Ukraine.

International Service is not just about giving money—although tens of millions of dollars are given each year in the name of Rotary's fourth Avenue. The act of giving money alone can be satisfying but can also feel impersonal; there is rarely a sense of connection between the donor and the recipient. To Rotarians, the greatest reward of international service is the personal satisfaction of being bridge-builders to another culture—the joy of compassion in using one's time and talents to help the downtrodden and disadvantaged residents of the global village.

More than 80 years after Rotary adopted International Service as its fourth Avenue of Service, it is a thriving, bustling avenue indeed. It brings together students, young adults, and Rotarians from disparate cultures and is the glue that cements countless projects in almost every country on earth. To some it may seem a contradiction: it delivers tens of millions of dollars in aid—yet it is not about money. It encourages citizens of hostile nations to talk with one another—yet Rotary International remains nonpolitical and refuses to act as a corporate entity in resolving such conflicts. It espouses the attributes of every major world religion—yet Rotary has no religious message or affiliation.

Just as with the other important tenets of life—truth, integrity, loyalty—international service comes down to the individual Rotarian. Others may despair at the daily media reports of famine, disease, and bloody disputes in distant countries with the dismissive "What difference can one person make?" But Rotarians of every race, color, and creed in 166 countries and geographic regions sing a well-known song: "Let there be peace on earth, and let it begin with me."

5   Paul Henningham, *Seventy-Five Years of Service: Rotary in Australia, Papua New Guinea, and Solomon Islands 1921-1996* (Parramatta, NSW: Rotary Down Under for the Australian Rotary Institute, 1996), 123.

6   *Rotary Down Under*, April 2001, 24.

7   *Rotary Down Under*, October 2001, 18.

CHAPTER 15

ROTARY'S COMMITMENT TO YOUTH

Chapter 15 ~ Rotary's Commitment to Youth

Rotarians have felt drawn to serve the needs of children and young people from the earliest days of the International Association of Rotary Clubs. In December 1913, the Rotary Club of Syracuse, New York, USA, appointed a crippled children's committee. Their interest was sparked by the plight of a disabled girl whose parents couldn't afford the surgery and rehabilitation that was needed to restore her mobility. The *Syracuse Herald* endorsed the club's project and in two weeks collected $2,728.74 from its readers.

The club then conducted a citywide survey of similarly needy children and found 200 of them. This opportunity motivated the new Rotarians to make "crippled children's work" their primary community service, and they mobilized social workers, medical caregivers, and rehabilitation specialists to their cause. Club members provided food baskets to the poorest families and clothes, toys, and books to physically disabled children. In 1914, the club added 40 blind children to the program, and every surgeon and hospital donated their services.[1]

Inspiring stories such as these appeared in THE ROTARIAN magazine just at the time when both the association and its clubs were trying to shed Rotary's image as a self-serving business-boosting organization. Other clubs picked up the idea and looked for similar needs in their own communities.

Participants, some in medieval costume, attend a RYLA event in Italy.

Overleaf: Rotaractors pull an airplane for charity at the 1993 Rotaract Preconvention Meeting in Melbourne, Victoria, Australia.

In 1915, a Toledo, Ohio, USA, Rotarian learned of a 16-year-old quadriplegic boy named Alva Bunker who was unable to read or write. The club discovered a unique school in Michigan that specialized in educating such children, so it raised enough money to pay for the boy to be fitted with artificial limbs and to complete his education. The Toledo Rotarians wanted to continue their work with other handicapped children, so they formed the Toledo Society for Crippled Children.[2] When automobile magnate Henry Ford donated a large sum of money to help disabled children, the press credited the Rotary Club of Toledo's work for drawing Ford's interest.[3]

GEORGE WRIGHT OF THE MADISON SQUARE BOYS' CLUB PRESENTS RI PRESIDENT A.Z. BAKER WITH THE BOYS' CLUBS OF AMERICA GOLDEN ANNIVERSARY AWARD IN 1956.

Not far from Toledo was Elyria, Ohio, home of Edgar F. "Daddy" Allen. Allen owned a successful lumber company that supplied railroad ties and telephone poles throughout the East and Midwest, but his wealth and business accomplishments meant nothing when his beloved son Homer, 18, and other people were killed in a streetcar accident in Elyria. The loss seemed even worse when officials told Allen that had there been a hospital in the town, Homer probably would have survived. Allen dedicated the rest of his life to helping children, especially those with physical disabilities. When an eight-year-old orphan boy insisted on calling him "Daddy" for all the help he gave him, the name stuck.[4]

Daddy Allen sold his business and within two weeks had raised $100,000 to start work on the Elyria Memorial Hospital, so named in honor of the victims of the streetcar accident. After it was completed, the doctors approached him to build an extension especially equipped for crippled children. Allen not only raised the money to finish that building; he became so aware of the need for such treatment centers that, dividing Ohio into eight districts, he persuaded hospitals in each area to erect their own crippled children's wings.[5]

To nobody's surprise, Daddy Allen, a member of the Rotary Club of Elyria, convinced his club—and other Rotary clubs across the country—to make crippled children's work a major focus of their own community service outreach.

Rotary clubs outside the United States initiated similar projects. When the English industrialist Lord Nuffield visited New Zealand, he was so impressed with the work undertaken by local Rotarians that he donated £50,000

ROTARY'S COMMITMENT TO YOUTH

---

1   THE ROTARIAN V, no. 3 (September 1914): 31.
2   Rotary International, *Rotary: Fifty Years of Service* (Evanston, Illinois, 1954), 60.
3   THE ROTARIAN X, no. 1 (January 1917): 42.
4   Pat Boone, *The Human Touch: The Story of Easter Seals* (New York: Wieser & Wieser, Inc., 1991), 18.
5   THE ROTARIAN, October 1922, 180.

to their cause. Aucklanders Mr. and Mrs. W.R. Wilson donated a house to Rotary and 13 acres of land to be used for a crippled children's home, at which point Lord Nuffield added another £10,000 to his original gift.

Many Rotary clubs formed city and then state societies for crippled children. This led to the formation of the National Society and then the International Society for Crippled Children in 1921, of which Paul Harris was chairman and Daddy Allen was president. This worthy organization added "and Adults" to its name in 1944, and in 1979 dropped the term "crippled" to become the Easter Seals Society.

Boys Work

While Rotary was actively supporting projects for disabled children, it also invested in something called "Boys Work." Boys comprised the vast majority of juvenile delinquents, truants, and youth prison inmates at that time. Rotarians saw the opportunity to act as mentors who could be positive role models with the resources and desire to steer the boys in the right direction.

RI President Clifford L. Dochterman receives a Boy Scout neckerchief during a 1992 visit to District 9110 in Nigeria.

So many clubs launched Boys Work projects that the 1916 Cincinnati convention authorized a standing committee to promote and coordinate such programs throughout the Rotary world. Each convention for many years thereafter voted to continue this committee, and in 1920 delegates to the Atlantic City convention even voted to amend the Rotary bylaws to include Boys Work. In January 1924, RI established the National Boys Work Committee and U.S. President Calvin Coolidge became its honorary chairman.

It is easy to see why Boys Work appealed to Rotarians. The objectives— "to develop boys into good citizens and honorable businessmen, to afford every boy the opportunity to attain his full potential, [and] to encourage vocational training"—were congruent with their own beliefs. Every issue of THE ROTARIAN contained stories of clubs actively involved in Boys Work.

"It is essential to our future preservation that the youth of nations become men and women of high moral character.... Every great world movement concentrates on youth as the necessary foundation for success. Let us in Rotary carry on a crusade among our youth for justice, for truth, and for liberty. I hope The Four-Way Test plan can help us do the job."

Herbert J. Taylor, Chicago, Illinois, USA
RI president, 1954-55 and originator of The Four-Way Test

Ed Smallwood of the Rotary Club of Raleigh, North Carolina, USA, tutors a student as part of a District 7710 mentoring project.

Clubs frequently organized Boys Weeks, during which parades, conferences, and newspaper articles were dedicated to the project. Many clubs sponsored Boy Scout troops, citizenship training and character-building and vocational-training classes. Others created summer camps, orphans homes, and boys clubs. Many Rotarians volunteered their time in juvenile courts, reform schools, and prisons as counselors for boys already in trouble.

When fathers left home to serve their countries in two world wars, Rotarians stepped in to be the positive male role models. When wars and the Great Depression caused rampant unemployment and family despair, Rotarians provided jobs, playgrounds, and a sense of hope to boys everywhere. The Rotary Club of Atlanta, Georgia, USA, formed an educational foundation in 1920 and in its very first year provided enough funds to put six boys through college. By 1940, the number had grown to 900 students, 700 of whom had graduated. Two California districts emulated the Atlanta model and provided college scholarships for 200 students from 40 countries.[6]

Rotary's work with youth cuts across all Avenues of Service. When a club organizes a Boy Scout troop or takes disabled children on an outing, that is Community Service. When it mentors teenagers with job skills or teaches a physically challenged youth how to work with his hands, that is Vocational Service. When Rotarians in one country provide assistance to children in another or host a Youth Exchange student, they are performing International Service.

RYLA

In 1959, Rotarians from Queensland, Australia, selected outstanding young people from their communities to attend a weeklong conference hosted by the Rotary Club of Brisbane. The teenagers participated in an agenda filled with social, cultural, and educational activities. The club was so impressed with

the students, and the students were so effusive in their praise of how it had helped them with their personal growth, that they continued and expanded the program each year. Soon, other clubs in Australia heard about Brisbane's Rotary Youth Leadership Awards (RYLA) and began similar programs.

RYLA spread across the Rotary world, and in 1971 the RI Board officially adopted RYLA as a Rotary youth program. Today, teenagers in many countries attend RYLA conferences to learn about leadership, decision making, goal setting, good citizenship, conflict resolution, and other life skills from accomplished business, community, and political leaders.

Interact

In the early 1960s, a committee of five Rotarians—one each from Asia, Europe, Latin America, North America, and the Southwest Pacific—developed Interact, a service club modeled along the lines of a Rotary club, but for boys and girls ages 14-18 who were in secondary school. Interact (a contraction of the words *international* and *action*) usually meets in the high school and has a teacher and local Rotarian as advisers, and members often work together with their sponsoring local Rotary club. The first Interact club was launched in 1962 at a high school in Melbourne, Florida, USA. Due in large part to its early champion Bill Robbins, who became RI president in 1974, it quickly spread around the world. In 1999, the RI Board designated one week in November as World Interact Week. By Interact's 40th anniversary in 2002, the program had grown to almost 200,000 members in 7,700 clubs in 107 countries and geographic regions.

> "Hundreds of thousands of boys playing baseball today owe their start to the impetus of the efforts of Rotary clubs, Legion posts, and other organizations, which got together in the drive to reduce juvenile delinquency by the common-sense plan of making sport more attractive than crime."
>
> *Tris Speaker*
> *Hall of Fame baseball player and Rotarian, 1939*

Rotaract

As Interact grew in popularity, Rotarians noticed a gap in the chain of service. Interact covered high school students and Rotary club membership was available to business leaders, but what about the young adults in between? Rotary's answer was Rotaract, which began in 1968 in Charlotte, North Carolina, USA. Rotaract is not a youth program. It is designed for young adults ages 18-30 who want to serve the community and the needy, are committed to high ethical standards, and seek fellowship with those of like mind, but do not yet qualify for membership in a Rotary club. Most of Rotaract's growth occurred outside North America in community-based clubs; today, more than 170,000 Rotaractors meet and serve their communities in 7,500 clubs in more than 155 countries and geographic regions.

ROTARACTORS SPORT GIANT-SIZED WOODEN SHOES AT THE 1989 EEMA ROTARACT CONFERENCE IN THE NETHERLANDS.

While Rotary inspired the birth of Interact and Rotaract, young people themselves inspired their Rotarian sponsors. Members of the Interact Club of Trelew, Argentina, organized a milk bank, where orphaned and abandoned children received bread and milk each afternoon—often their only meal of the day. Thai Interactors acted as tutors at an elementary school; their peers in Brazil vaccinated stray dogs against rabies; Kenyan Interactors donated blood and helped maintain a home for disabled children; and the Interact Club of Hakodate, Hokkaido, Japan, raised money to support international service projects in Africa and India. Rotaractors helped rebuild homes for the elderly in Britain and worked with the disabled in Australia. In Italy, Rotaractors collected enough money to purchase polio vaccine for tens of thousands of children in the Philippines.

Youth Exchange

Youth Exchange has been one of Rotary's most successful and popular programs and is stronger today than at any time in its history. But the Youth Exchange journey should be told through the words of each individual participant. It begins with the exciting news that a young person has been accepted into the program and matched with a host family in another country. Letters are exchanged and the culture and language studied. Then the day arrives when the youth bids farewell to his or her parents and hours later greets a host at an airport halfway around the world.

The cultural adjustments are often difficult, but there is always the host Rotary club to guide them as their "adopted" guest. By the time the visit is over, tears often mark their departure, for this teenager has genuinely become a part of the host family.

It is impossible to calculate the contribution to world peace and understanding that these leaders of tomorrow will make by being exposed to another culture at such an important stage in their development. "Thanks to Rotary, my heart has grown older and bigger every day," admitted Lilia Hernandez from Via Hermosa, Mexico, after her exchange visit to Ontario, Canada.[7] "My experiences have touched the lives of all I have come to know and call my friends," said Christian Otto, a German exchange student who lived with a U.S. host family. "Now multiply that by thousands of exchanges all over the planet, and you will realize that through Rotary this world is coming together—one friendship, one exchange at a time."[8]

Rotary has organized Youth Exchange visits since 1927, when the Rotary Club of Copenhagen, Denmark, arranged to host several American boys. A year later, the program grew to 61 Youth Exchanges. In 1927, the

176

BEDECKED WITH BADGES, BUTTONS, AND PINS, YOUTH EXCHANGE STUDENTS BRIGHTEN A ROTARY CONVENTION.

U.S. YOUTH EXCHANGE STUDENT WILLIAM MAY (RIGHT) RIDES AN ELEPHANT DURING HIS YEAR IN THAILAND.

Rotary Club of Nice, France, initiated Youth Exchanges with other European clubs. And in 1928, some 300 American boys spent five weeks visiting families in Scandinavia as "Youthful Pilgrims of World Peace."[9] Today, Rotary annually places about 7,000 students ages 15-19 with Rotarian families in another country for periods ranging from a few weeks to a year. This has been an excellent starting point for teaching them cross-cultural sensitivity at an age when they are just becoming truly aware of the world beyond their home communities.

It is easy to see why Rotary has made such a commitment to youth for most of its first 100 years. It reaches out to care for children who are sick, disabled, hungry, or forgotten. It provides encouragement through mentoring and scholarships to tens of thousands of teenagers and young adults. And it walks hand in hand along the pathway of service with youth in Interact and Youth Exchange and young adults in Rotaract. Rotarians have lived out their slogan of more than 50 years: Every Rotarian an Example to Youth. They have demonstrated that the best investment of their time and resources is in the generation that will lead the world tomorrow.

7   THE ROTARIAN, March 1985, 38.
8   THE ROTARIAN, March 1985, 27.
9   THE ROTARIAN, September 1999, 24.

Chapter 16 ~ The Women of Rotary

The role of women in Rotary has been discussed since the formation of the National Association of Rotary Clubs. At the first convention in 1910, Chairman Ches Perry asked Irwin Muma, president of the Rotary Club of Los Angeles, about the rumor that his club had a ladies' auxiliary. "There is no ladies' auxiliary in connection with the Los Angeles club, never has been, and probably will not be," replied Muma. Added Kansas City Rotarian Lee Mettler, "I think it is a hard enough job to handle two or three hundred men without having anything to do with ladies."[1] The topic was grist, of course, for newspapers nationwide.

"Women Peril is Seen," proclaimed the *Chicago Daily News* headline the next day.

"Can't Manage a Woman? Men Are Alarmed," trumpeted the *Chicago American.*

The *Chicago Journal*'s headline declared "Rotaries Afraid of Women," while the usually more conservative *Chicago Tribune*'s banner read "Rotarians Ban Fair Sex: 'Unmanageable.'"

Since Rotary's inception, women have played an important role in its work. During the first five years of the Chicago club, however, the only men-

Rotarian Fary Moini takes the blood pressure of a woman wearing a burka at an Afghan refugee camp in Pakistan.

Overleaf: Rotarians Lily Berrish and Connard Hogan of Santa Barbara, California, USA, stain a redwood fence at Camp Whittier United Boys & Girls Club.

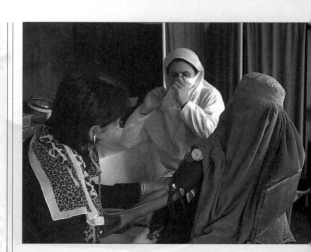

tion of women was the occasional social events to which the Rotarians' wives were invited.

There is no record of a romance in Paul Harris's life until 1904 when his dearest friend, George Clark, from Jacksonville, Florida, introduced him to Grace Irene Mann. For a little over a year the couple exchanged letters twice a week. The correspondence evolved from Victorian formality in the early days to passionate love letters by the winter of 1905.

Grace showed great interest in Paul's idea for a club, and he often sent her drafts of ideas to which she promptly responded. Paul proposed marriage to Grace and she accepted, but as was the custom of the day, he had to obtain her father's permission. There is no record of that conversation, but it seems his answer was no; and although the passion was still present in Grace's letters, it is clear from Paul's side that he did not wish to continue the relationship. There is no mention of any other woman in Paul's life throughout the first five years of Rotary.

Jean Harris, whom Paul affectionately called "my bonnie Scottish lassie,"
played a quiet but supportive role in her husband's work for Rotary. They had no children, but Jean enjoyed helping young people. "Jean throws herself with perfect abandon into every breach to which love or duty calls," wrote Paul. "Her militant spirit was always ready to jump into a cause and defend the needy. This quality of mind and heart was made painfully manifest one day to the driver of a team of horses, which he was brutally belaboring with his whip. He will not soon forget the dressing down he received from the excited and belligerent little girl who appeared upon the scene in an unexpected manner."

Two years after they were married in 1910, Jean and Paul bought their dream house on a wooded hill on Longwood Drive in Morgan Park, the same neighborhood south of Chicago where they had first met. They named their home Comely Bank after the Edinburgh neighborhood where Jean had grown up, and it became their oasis of peace for the rest of their lives together. Across the long, sloping lawn sat the home of Silvester Schiele, Paul's best friend and fellow Chicago Rotarian. When not engaged in his law practice or

> "Not only should we let women share fully in our social functions—we must do this if we want to get to know them, be with them, and educate them in the true Rotary spirit—but we might even give them an organization of their own... and let them be Rotarians in the true sense of the word—Rotarianettes (if you like the term) pledged to work as an auxiliary branch of our clubs, sharing our ideals (and either working separately in their own departments of 'service' or in direct cooperation with the men)."
>
> *Bulletin of the Rotary Club of Edinburgh, Scotland, 1920*

---

1   Rotary Clubs of America, *First National Convention* (Chicago, 1910), 24.

> "To our joy, many friends we had met in far places and near came to us at Comely Bank. There was Angus Mitchell of Australia, Fernando Carbajal of Peru, Armando Pereira of Brazil, Cesar Andrade of Ecuador, and Sir Charles Mander of England [to whom Paul Harris wrote his last letter]. Sometimes men and women from eight or 10 countries would be with us for tea.... Only weeks before Paul passed away, J.C. Penney called."
>
> *Jean Harris, 1950*

Rotary business, Paul would join Jean in tending their prized garden or hosting special Rotary visitors for quiet fellowship.

Paul was already 42 when he met Jean, and within a couple of years a series of serious health setbacks began, including heart attacks, breakdowns, and possibly a stroke. Throughout their 37-year marriage, Jean played the role of nurse, companion, and gatekeeper—fiercely protecting him from those who continually sought his time for Rotary functions. When Paul died in 1947, Jean sold Comely Bank and for awhile rented a room in a Chicago residential hotel, volunteering each day at a skid row homeless mission. In September 1947, she returned to her native Scotland and moved in with her brother, the Rev. John Thomson, in Ayrshire. Other than an occasional letter to friends, she dropped out of sight. In November 1963, RI General Secretary George Means received a letter from Jean's sister in Scotland. "In October, she entered a nursing home and grew weaker and weaker," her sister reported, "finally passing away on 9 November 1963. She slipped away quietly to be with Jesus." Jean was buried in Edinburgh, with a gravestone that reads "She hath done what she could."

Women's Auxiliaries

Despite the opposition of the National Association of Rotary Clubs, women formed clubs based on the Rotary club idea. The *Minneapolis Journal* in 1911 reported:

"Dr. Gertrude Stanton was elected president of the Minneapolis Women's Rotary Club at the meeting of the club yesterday at the West Hotel....The club is composed of business women, one woman from each line of business, making up the membership. The club was organized last spring and has continued to meet during the summer. The object of the club is to promote sociability among the business women and to work for business advantages."[2]

A year later, Ida Buell of Duluth, Minnesota, was granted permission to address the 1912 Rotary Convention. She told the delegates about the Women's Rotary Club of Duluth and asked Rotarians for support in establishing similar clubs in other cities. Although THE ROTARIAN described Buell as "an interesting and entertaining speaker," the delegates took no action on her request.[3]

Despite the reality of several "women's Rotary clubs" and some highly placed support for them within the International Association, the opponents won the day every time the matter came to the RI Board of Directors. In his *Weekly Letter* to club officers, General Secretary Perry reported: "In December 1918, the Board agreed it did not favor the establishment of organizations of women similar to Rotary and that Rotarians should discourage such organizations from using the name Rotary or Rotarians."[4]

In 1921, a contingent of four wives of Chicago Rotarians appeared before the International Association Board requesting permission to organize their group, the Chicago Ladies of Rotary. The Board noted it "appreciates the very worthy purpose underlying the organization" but refused to let them use the name "Rotary." They did so anyway—and right under Ches's nose in his own club.

On 24 May 1921, Women of the Rotary Club of Chicago established themselves as an Illinois nonprofit corporation. Membership was restricted to wives, daughters, sisters, and mothers of Rotarians, and the club grew to 250 members.[5] In 1935, the *Japan Times* published a story on the club and others like it, following an interview with Jean Harris, whom it described as "the mother of Women's Rotary."[6]

Rotary Anns

Wives of Rotarians around the world originally were—and sometimes still are—called "Rotary Anns," as in, "Meet my Rotary Ann, Christine." With the spread of feminism and an increasingly negative attitude against the all-male movement, some considered "Rotary Ann" a demeaning term. But it had an interesting genesis and when coined was a term of endearment.

ANN BRUNNIER (LEFT) AND ANN GUNDAKER, THE FIRST TWO "ROTARY ANNS"

2   *The National Rotarian* II, no. 1 (November 1911): 23.
3   THE ROTARIAN III, no. 1 (September 1912): 11.
4   Chesley R. Perry, "Women's Clubs Similar to Rotary," *The Weekly Letter*, 20 January 1919, 2.
5   University of Chicago, Social Science Committee, *Rotary? A University Group Looks at the Rotary Club of Chicago* (Chicago, IL: The University of Chicago Press, 1934), 122.
6   *Japan Times,* 9 February 1935.

In 1914, California, USA, Rotarians chartered a train to the international convention in Houston, Texas. It had not yet become customary for wives to accompany their husbands to Rotary conventions, and among the large contingent of Rotarians from 13 West Coast clubs there was but one woman: the wife of San Francisco club president Henry J. "Bru" Brunnier. As the train left the station and the Rotarians—who were used to greeting one another by their first names—met her on board, one of them said, "I don't want to call you Mrs. Brunnier; what is your first name?" She replied, "Ann." The festive group immediately nicknamed her "Our Rotary Ann," and she became so popular during the long train journey that Bru joked he never had to buy her a meal because she was always a guest at another group's table.

PRESIDENT-ELECT HERBERT G. BROWN AND THE FIRST GROUP OF WOMEN DISTRICT GOVERNORS, WHO SERVED ON HIS LEADERSHIP TEAM IN 1995-96, POSE FOR A "CLASS PICTURE" AT THE 1995 INTERNATIONAL ASSEMBLY.

184

Rotary publicized the special West Coast train in advance; so when it arrived in Houston, a large crowd was waiting to welcome it. Some passengers had passed the time by composing a song about "Rotary Ann," and the carnival atmosphere on the platform was heightened when the West Coast group lifted Ann Brunnier on their shoulders and marched around the station, singing their ditty. Guy Gundaker from Philadelphia and his wife were among the reception group, and he mentioned that his wife was also named Ann. The Rotarians lifted her into the air and as they continued their march proclaimed, "From now on, all ladies shall be known as Rotary Anns."

During Rotary's first 84 years, the wives and daughters of Rotarians played a vital role in the organization's success—regardless of whether they belonged to a formal auxiliary. Wives of club members worked alongside them in projects, were equal partners in their financial support, and were often the driving force in urging their spouses to take an active role in the organization's leadership and humanitarian projects.

Women's Service Clubs

The Board objected not so much to the idea of women's auxiliaries as to their use of the word "Rotary," which had become a brand name they wanted to protect and preserve. The wives of British Rotarians achieved the same objectives as their U.S. counterparts but with far greater results, simply by using a noncompeting name—Inner Wheel.

For as long as there had been Rotary clubs in Britain, there had been ladies' committees, usually headed by the club president's wife that were active in the club's charity work. In Liverpool, during World War I, wives had staffed an information kiosk for traveling soldiers and sailors and had undertaken many good works for children. In 1923, wives were invited to a dinner hosted by the Rotary Club of Manchester and heard an address by the vice president of Rotary International – Association for Great Britain and Ireland, who suggested they form a women's club.

The club president's wife sent an invitation to other spouses, and 27 women attended a meeting to discuss how it might be done in, of all places, Herriot's Turkish Baths, on 15 November 1923. The venue, she explained, was the only one she could find that would not charge for the room. Margarette Golding, a nurse and successful businesswoman and the wife of Manchester Rotarian Oliver Golding, was elected chairwoman. On 10 January 1924, she and a group of Rotarians' wives held the official organizational meeting of the Inner Wheel Club of Manchester. The name "Inner Wheel" derived from the inner circle of the Rotary wheel emblem. Their colors were the same as Rotary's: royal blue and gold. Membership was initially open to "the wives or womenfolk of Rotarians or of past Rotarians."

Between the gathering at the Turkish bath and the organizational meeting, the women had been busy raising funds and knitting garments for the children's ward at a local hospital. That first Inner Wheel service project set the stage for what continues to this day as Baby Bundles, which the group sends to children at risk all over the world.

Inner Wheel quickly spread across Britain, and by 1929 there were so many clubs that they organized into districts, like Rotary. Margarette Golding, president of the first club, became Inner Wheel's first district chairwoman. Soon, Inner Wheel expanded to other countries, especially to nations with close ties to Britain. Australia was first, in 1931, followed in 1935 by Norway, and South Africa in 1938. Despite the danger of operating a club affiliated

ROTARIAN HELEN LIEBERMAN OF CAPE TOWN, SOUTH AFRICA, WITH TWO PARTICIPANTS IN THE IKAMVA SCHOOL READINESS PROGRAMME

A NEW CLUB MEMBER RECEIVES HER
ROTARY LAPEL PIN.

with Rotary during the German occupation of their country, Norwegian Inner Wheel members continued meeting throughout the war, under the guise of being a bridge club. After the war, clubs sprang up in Singapore, the Netherlands, Malaya, the Philippines, and India. Several years later, Latin American clubs developed very effective support groups among the wives of Rotarians; today, that region is famous within the Rotary world for the contributions they make to local clubs.

In 1919, Zonta International was founded, closely following the Rotary model. Eventually, Sonia Renfer, a veteran senior staff member in Rotary's Zurich regional office, served Zonta as president. In 1996, Janet Long Halstead, longtime manager of The Rotary Foundation, became Zonta's executive director. Like Zonta, Soroptimists and other women's service clubs were organized to serve hundreds of thousands of business and professional women members worldwide.

Inner Wheel never caught on in the United States. Ches Perry reported a visit in 1935 from the president of Women of the Rotary Club of Chicago, who noted the group was "alarmed and going to want to do something to repel or render ineffective the invasion from another country," a reference to Inner Wheel's international expansion.

Inner Wheel is one of the largest women's organizations in the world, with well over 98,000 members in 98 countries; approximately 28,000 members in more than 1,000 clubs in Great Britain and Ireland alone. Anne Koh, the secretary administrator of the Association of Inner Wheel Clubs in Great Britain and Ireland, said, "We hold our conferences back-to-back with Rotary's

ROTARIAN KATHRIN HOYOS AND A
LOCAL HEALTH VOLUNTEER AT AN AIDS
AWARENESS PROJECTS FAIR IN CAPE
TOWN, SOUTH AFRICA

and have club exchange visits, but we also do our own service projects, including the provision of a £700,000 (US$1.1 million) medical ship and the ongoing SightSavers program in Africa."

Changing Attitudes

"The admission of women members to the Rotary Club of Chicago would appear to be unthinkable," concluded a 1934 University of Chicago study. "Rotarians are family men whose wives are home-makers and mothers."[7]

The reasons Rotary remained a male bastion for 84 years are varied. Habit, with the passage of time, becomes tradition, and traditions, to some, are worth fighting for. Some men didn't want women in the club because they had joined a men's club. Many stood on the principle that an organization should have the right to pick its own members.

The fact that some tried to force women on Rotarians through court battles made some members even more entrenched in their stance. To others, change of any sort was a threat. Some used preposterous arguments, such as "We won't be able to tell jokes around the table if women join Rotary" and "My wife would never let me attend Rotary if women were there." Long-standing cultural or religious standards in some countries prohibited commingling men and women in public. "Would it not cause a crisis should a female Rotarian from one country insist on attending a Rotary meeting in a strict Islamic nation?" was, and remains, a valid question.

MEMBERS OF THE ROTARY CLUB OF SAINT-QUENTIN, FRANCE, STAFF A BOOTH AT A NEIGHBORHOOD FLEA MARKET TO RAISE MONEY FOR A LOCAL CHARITY.

In 1978, in direct contravention of their constitution, the Rotary Club of Duarte, California, USA, admitted three women as members. Rotary International revoked the club's charter, prompting a lawsuit by the club and the three women. The suit was based on the Unruh law that California and 39 other U.S. states had incorporated into their civil rights acts. Simply stated, it precludes business

---

7   University of Chicago, 122.

PAST DISTRICT GOVERNOR REKHA SHETTY OF INDIA AND PAST CLUB PRESIDENT
RUSTY BROUGHTON OF THE UNITED STATES ENJOY FELLOWSHIP AT THE PRESIDENTIAL
CONFERENCE OF PEACE AND DEVELOPMENT IN MALAYSIA IN 2002.

establishments from discriminating or refusing to provide service on the basis
of sex, race, color, religion, or national origin. The plaintiffs claimed Rotary
clubs were in the same category as business establishments, based on another
case that broadly defined business establishments as "those generally open to
the public."

Prior to the Duarte case, many Rotary clubs had sent proposals to the
Council on Legislation, Rotary's parliamentary body, petitioning for a constitutional change permitting women to join. The Council on Legislation is the
truest form of democracy in action, meeting every three years and composed
of one voting delegate from each district in the world, those delegates having
been elected by their clubs. With each convening of the Council throughout
the 1970s and 1980s, the vote moved closer to passing such an amendment.

In 1980, the RI Board under President James L. Bomar supported the
proposal, but it narrowly failed. "I have no doubt that the 1989 Council on
Legislation in Singapore would have passed the resolutions to admit women,"
said Past RI President Charles C. Keller, a distinguished attorney and chairman of the 1980 and 1983 Councils.

But the decision was taken out of Rotary's hands.

The case went from one side to the other in the courts, like a game of
legal ping-pong. Each time, the losing party appealed to a higher court. Other

service organizations, including women's clubs, filed amicus briefs supporting Rotary's stand.

On 4 May 1987, in a 7-0 decision, the United States Supreme Court ruled against Rotary International. It agreed with Duarte that Rotary clubs do have a business purpose under the public accommodations legal test and ruled that Rotary International in the United States could not revoke a club's charter merely for admitting women. The RI Board took action that it would not enforce male-only membership provisions in any country whose law clearly required the equal treatment of men and women. At the 1989 Council on Legislation, the Board presented an enactment to eliminate the word *male* from the constitutional documents of RI. It was adopted.

The Supreme Court decision made headlines worldwide. But despite the predictions of the end of Rotary, the organization moved on. Some clubs still have no women. In some countries—Argentina and Taiwan, for example—there are all-women Rotary clubs. Women quickly assimilated into clubs in North America and then in other countries. Contrary to the dire claims of the naysayers, the women who joined were not husband-stealing temptresses, but bankers, shopkeepers, computer executives, school principals, and lawyers. They worked hard, contributing significantly to both the finances and fellowship of Rotary. In due course, women became club presidents and district governors; and in much the same way that years before people of different races and ethnic backgrounds became absorbed into the oneness of Rotary, today's women members are referred to simply as "Rotarians."

Looking back, Rotary has reflected the attitudes of the age in its relationship with women. That was not wrong but rather just a sign of the times. The women themselves inevitably referred to themselves as extensions of their husbands, introducing themselves as "Mrs. Paul P. Harris" or "Mrs. John Nelson of Quebec, Canada." Rotary welcomed them as partners, both individually and in organized auxiliaries; and in its rich history, the organization is quick to credit the women of Rotary for much of its success. As the democratic process moved Rotary closer to accepting female members, the organization battled in the courts against what it considered one club's violation of the constitution to which that club—and 27,000 others—had promised to adhere.

Rotarians have found that the new wave of women members has brought vitality and creativity to their clubs. Today, more than 10 percent of all Rotarians in the world are women. They have accounted for much of the organization's membership growth and have added vigor, dedication, and compassion that will propel Rotary into its second century of service.

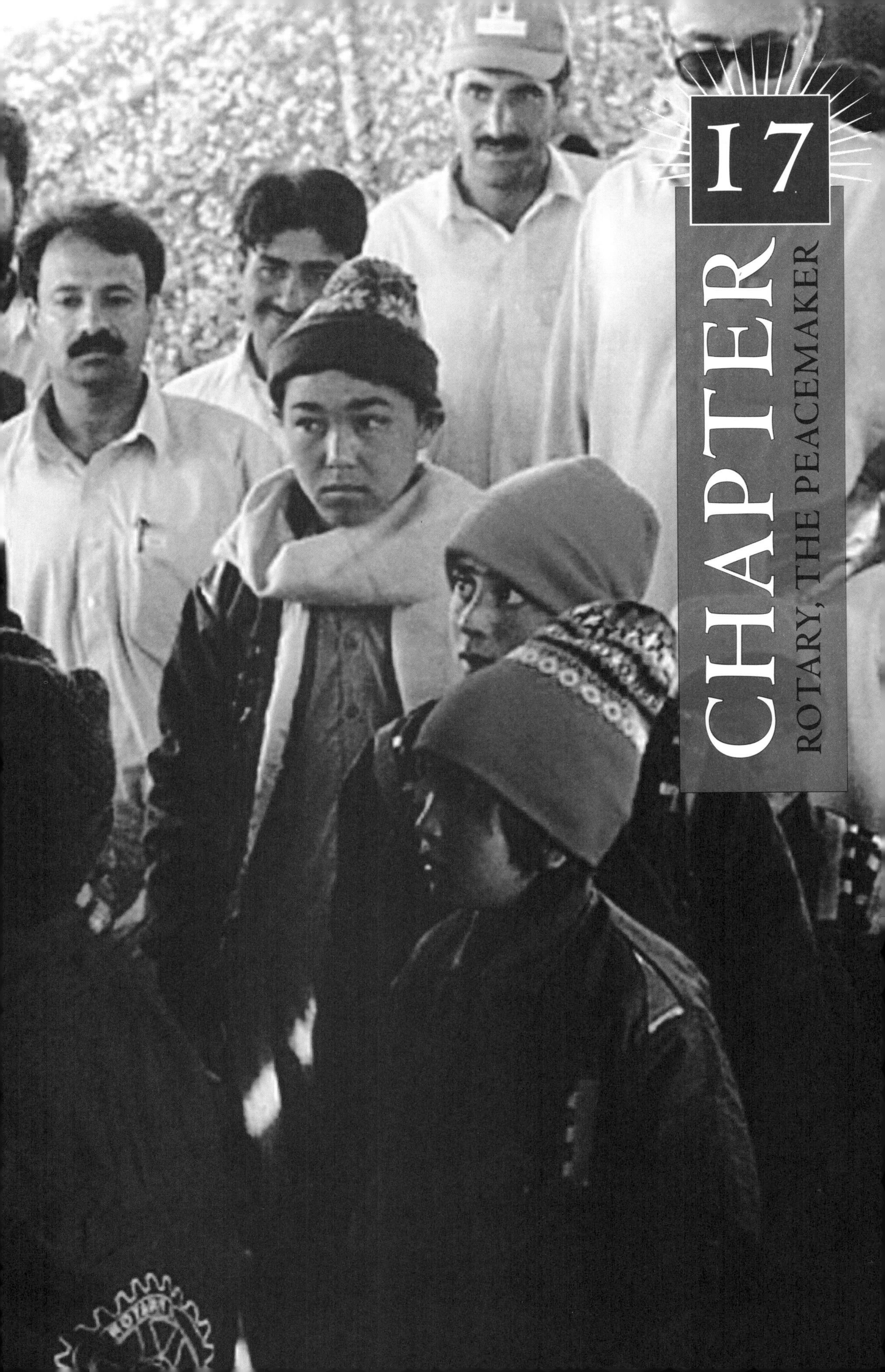

CHAPTER 17

ROTARY, THE PEACEMAKER

Chapter 17 – Rotary, the Peacemaker

Peacemaking was not considered to be a role for Rotary in the organization's early days. The club was conceived as a meeting place for business acquaintances who wanted fun and the fellowship of trustworthy friends and business associates. Still, one of Paul Harris's mantras was the need for tolerance.

"During the period 1912 to 1920, the idea that Rotary was or might be a medium for the promotion of international peace and goodwill was voiced many times," recalled RI Secretary Ches Perry. As World War I began, delegates to the 1914 Houston convention adopted a resolution calling for an international peace conference and for Rotarians to support the international peace movement.[1]

In September 1914, the Rotary Club of Minneapolis sent a peace proposal to the International Association of Rotary Clubs, suggesting that all Rotary clubs become peace advocates in their communities. When U.S. President Woodrow Wilson, an honorary Rotarian, called on all Americans to pray for peace on Sunday, 4 October 1914, International Association President Frank L. Mulholland of Toledo, Ohio, asked every Rotary club to designate its programs that week as "a club conference on ways and means for accomplishing international peace."

After the war ended, Past RI President Arch C. Klumph of Cleveland, Ohio, and incoming president Estes "Pete" Snedecor of Portland, Oregon, paid a visit to the 25 Rotary clubs in Britain. Both men were impressed with the growth of Rotary in that nation, despite Britain's five-year involvement in the war. Klumph told British Rotarians that he envisioned "the splendid part

Trustee Chairman and Past RI President Robert Barth presents Paul Harris Fellow Recognition to United Nations Secretary-General Kofi Annan in 1998.

Overleaf: Past RI Director Lynmar Brock with local Rotarians and Afghan children at Mohammad Khail Refugee Camp in Pakistan

> "I believe mankind is now on a new brink, not the brink of war but the brink of peace.... Now is the time for our generation to build from the multitude of conflicting desire and persistent national and economic rivalries a new relationship among peoples, one that frees the energies of nations and their people for the constructive endeavors that will create a better life for all."
>
> *W. Jack Davis, Hamilton, Bermuda*
> *RI president, 1977-78*

Rotary can play [in creating] a mighty team to preserve Peace, Justice, and Honor among the nations of the world."[2] It was already clear that Rotary's most senior leaders saw peacemaking becoming part of the very definition of the organization.

Delegates to the 1920 Atlantic City convention appointed Rotarian MacRae of Halifax, Nova Scotia, Canada, to chair a committee on including peace as an Object of Rotary. Over the ensuing year, MacRae's team drafted a proposal to incorporate peacemaking into Rotary's constitution and bylaws. The delegates to the 1921 convention in Edinburgh, Scotland, overwhelmingly approved these changes.

Many of the 2,523 attendees at Edinburgh had lost friends and family in the conflict, and the economies of many European countries were in ruin. They were weary witnesses to the need for world peace. Just 16 years after Rotary began as a single Chicago club, it had become an international organization with the worthy objective to "aid in the advancement of international peace and goodwill through a fellowship of business and professional men of all nations united in the Rotary ideal of service."[3]

The resolutions passed in Edinburgh—the peace Object and the name change to Rotary International—were ratified a year later by the 1922 Los Angeles convention. The constitution and bylaws were thus rewritten and became mandatory for all new clubs.

A skeptic might ask: "How can Rotary be a real force for peace? It has no jurisdictional power. It is not a religion. It has no army or tanks, and it insists on being nonpolitical." Such a viewpoint looks at peace as something that can be ordered or militarily enforced, as if it is only the responsibility of governments. Rotary has always approached peacemaking systemically—it has sought to break down the barriers that cause people to point fingers at one another. By trying to understand peoples' points of view and reaching across lines of race, religion, and culture to become partners in service to all mankind, tensions are reduced and friendships are increased. Humanitarian aid has been Rotary's answer to hunger, sickness, illiteracy, and economic disaster, the seeds of conflict.

193

ROTARY, THE PEACEMAKER

---

1   THE ROTARIAN V, no. 2 (August 1914): 58.
2   David Shelley Nicholl, *The Golden Wheel: The Story of Rotary 1905 to the Present* (Estover, Plymouth, England: MacDonald and Evans, 1984), 178.
3   International Association of Rotary Clubs, *Proceedings Twelfth Annual Convention* (Chicago, 1921), 73.

RI PRESIDENT CHARLES L. WHEELER; BRIGADIER GENERAL
CARLOS P. ROMULO OF THE PHILIPPINES, A FORMER RI VICE
PRESIDENT; AND CONVENTION CHAIRMAN STANLEY LONG AT
THE 1944 CONVENTION IN CHICAGO

Over the years, RI Boards of Directors have laid out guidelines and policies that define how individual Rotarians and clubs can contribute to this
peacemaking role, and the RI Secretariat staff has provided suggestions and
support.

In 1939, less than two decades after adopting its commitment to peace,
Rotarians once again found themselves in the midst of a world at war. They
could have thrown their hands in despair and declared their goal to be un-
reachable. But instead, they redoubled their efforts, for there is no time like
war to think about the need for peace.

One American ambassador, speaking to a Rotary club in England, said
this: "I went to the last war as many of you here did, and I really believed I
was fighting a war to end all wars…and that our children would reap some
of the benefits of the sacrifice made by our generation. We did not really care
enough in the intervening years. If we cared enough, we did not do enough
or get enough done. It is rarely in the world's history that men get a second
chance, and we have got a second chance."[4]

Rotarians, of course, had worked hard to improve international peace
and understanding between the world wars. In 1932, acting on the initiative
of local Rotary clubs in Montana, USA, and Alberta, Canada, the U.S. Con-

Japan's Dr. Noboru Iwamura was awarded the first Rotary Award for World Understanding and Peace for his work with the sick and poor throughout Asia, especially Nepal. Dr. Iwamura, honored at the 1981 RI Convention in São Paulo, Brazil, urged Rotarians: "Go to the people; live among the people; work with the people. Start with what they know; build on what they have."

gress and Canadian Parliament created the Waterton-Glacier International Peace Park in a magnificent setting high in the mountains along the U.S.-Canadian border.

In Europe, Rotary clubs in Germany and France organized *petits comités* between communities. These groups exchanged visits, paired people of similar vocations, and convened discussion groups and sporting events. Within five years of the first *petit comité* in 1930, there were 30 such intercountry groups in countries across Europe.

Meanwhile, Rotary's leaders made speeches and wrote articles in THE ROTARIAN that urged members to look beyond the derisive labels so often used for people from other cultures. "If I could plant Rotary in every community throughout the world, I would do it, and then I would guarantee the tranquility and the forward march of the world," U.S. President Warren G. Harding—an active Rotarian prior to his election to the White House—told delegates to the 1923 St. Louis convention.[5]

In 1932, Bolivia attacked Paraguay and the Chaco War began. The bitter conflict killed more than 100,000 soldiers over the next two years, and no amount of pleading from neighboring governments or the struggling League of Nations could stop the fighting. In October 1934, nine Rotarians (three each from La Paz, Bolivia, and Asunción, Paraguay; two from Buenos Aires, Argentina, and one from Montevideo, Uruguay) took peacemaking into their own hands. Their first step was to help repatriate injured prisoners of war. They established a "post office" to facilitate the exchange of mail between prisoners and their loved ones, and they distributed clothing, food, medicine, and relief supplies to POWs on both sides. While the rest of the world ignored the conflict, local Rotarians helped bring humanity to its senses in the jungles of South America. "Rotary cannot prevent or stop a war, but it can smooth the sad consequences of war through the service of individual Rotarians," RI First Vice President Donato Gaminara of Montevideo reported to the 1934 Detroit convention.[6]

Less than a month after World War II began, THE ROTARIAN began publishing a series of features on the need for reconciliation among all nations. One of those commentaries covered the 1940 RI Convention in Havana, Cuba. Long before there was a United Nations, before "human rights" was a term most people even understood, the Rotarians meeting in Havana adopted a resolution calling for "freedom, justice, truth, sanctity of the pledged word,

4   Rotary International, *Seven Paths to Peace* (Evanston, Illinois, 1959), 67.
5   Rotary International, *Proceedings Fourteenth Annual Convention* (Chicago, 1923), 231.
6   Rotary International, *Proceedings Twenty-Fifth Annual Convention* (Chicago, 1934), 175.

and respect for human rights." Indeed, the delegates concluded, where those basic human rights do not exist, Rotary cannot live nor its ideals prevail. It was a major milestone in Rotary history. It threw down the gauntlet and said, in effect, "Rotary has no interest in the religious or political affairs of your country, but if you do not treat your people with the rights any human being deserves, then Rotary cannot operate there."

When the newly chartered United Nations wrote the Universal Declaration of Human Rights in 1948, it used the resolution from the Rotary Havana convention as its framework—and Rotary provided copies of the UN's document for its local clubs to debate and distribute in their communities.[7]

In fact, Rotary as an organization—and Rotarians individually—played an important role in the formation of the United Nations in 1945, and UNESCO even before that.

As bombs rained down on Britain in the darkest days of World War II, Rotarians set about planning for a workable peace once the fighting had stopped. By 1942, London had one of the strongest clubs and most active districts—District 13—in the Rotary world. It was also the temporary home for thousands of other Rotarians whom the winds of war had deposited in the British capital. Some were military officers or diplomats stationed there by their governments; others were refugees from continental Europe.

These Rotarians convened a conference to plan a world at peace; so compelling was their vision that ministers, diplomats, and representatives from 21 governments attended. The outcome was a world body that would serve as a forum for the exchange of ideas in culture, education, and science, and in the months ahead they held several follow-up meetings to bring their dream to reality. This group evolved into UNESCO (the United Nations Educational, Scientific, and Cultural Organization).

196

Bridges of friendship could be built

Where in war men's blood was spilt

Bridges built in Rotary's way

Bridges built to speed the day

When peace and concord will hold sway

That man may reach his long-sought goal

Neighbours all from pole to pole

One human race with ties that bind

One humane world, one humankind.

From After All *by Harold T. Thomas*

Auckland, New Zealand

RI president, 1959-60

UNESCO's formation showed that Rotarians and Rotary could make an impact in a world yearning for peace. World War II had sounded the death knell for the League of Nations; but even before the last gun had fallen silent, politicians began working to create a more effective global organization that could prevent such horrors from occurring again. Beginning in 1943, conferences were convened to address specific issues. The most famous of these meetings were those covering food and agriculture in Hot Springs, Virginia; relief and rehabilitation in Atlantic City; the monetary and financial conference in Bretton Woods, New Hampshire;

7   RI, *Seven Paths*, 33.
8   THE ROTARIAN, April 1945, 11.
9   THE ROTARIAN, August 1945, 8.

civil aviation, in Chicago; and the Dumbarton Oaks (Washington, D.C.) conference on international security.[8] Rotarians participated as working observers in these meetings and duly reported their progress in THE ROTARIAN.

In April 1945, Rotary was in the forefront of arguably one of the most important meetings of the 20th century: the finalizing of the charter of the United Nations in San Francisco.

The UN Charter Conference was the ultimate meeting of world leaders. They gathered to establish how future international disputes would be resolved; governments sent only their highest-ranking ministers, their very brightest minds to San Francisco.

Rotary was invited to attend as one of the observer organizations. There being few UN staff at that time, these 23 Rotarian observers guided agendas, performed translations, suggested wording for resolutions, and helped resolve disputes between delegates. Rotary provided 11 official observers to the U.S. delegation alone—only one other organization had more than three.

"The invitation to Rotary International [as a consultant] was not merely a gesture of goodwill and respect toward a great organization," declared Edward R. Stettinius Jr., the U.S. secretary of state. "It was a simple recognition of the practical part Rotary's members have played and will continue to play in the development of understanding among nations."[9] More than half a century later, Rotary International continues to support representatives to a number of UN and other international organizations, including UNESCO, the World Bank, the United Nations Environmental Programme, Council of Europe, and other agencies. Rotary International currently holds the highest level of consultative status a nongovernmental

UNICEF EXECUTIVE DIRECTOR CAROL BELLAMY ACCEPTS THE 1995 ROTARY AWARD FOR WORLD UNDERSTANDING AND PEACE FROM RI PRESIDENT BILL HUNTLEY ON BEHALF OF THE LATE JAMES GRANT AT THE RI CONVENTION IN NICE, FRANCE.

organization can have with ECOSOC (the UN's Economic and Social Council).

Of the 50 nations that sent official delegations in 1945, Rotary clubs were still active in 32, and 27 of the delegates or technical advisers were Rotarians. Five of them were heads of their delegation. Paul-Henri Spaak of the Rotary Club of Brussels was elected president of the General Assembly (in the first 12 years of the UN, five Rotarians served in that office). Faris El-Khouri, founder of the Rotary Club of Damascus and Syria's prime minister, signed the UN charter for his country. Warren R. Austin, head of the U.S. delegation, was the first president of the Rotary Club of Burlington, Vermont. Rotarian

---

Despite tense Arab-Israeli relations, the 35-member Rotary Club of Nazareth, Israel, hosted both Jewish and Arab Rotarians from 13 clubs in Israel. The group included the mayor of Nazareth, who is a Christian Arab, and the mayor of Haifa, Israel, who is Jewish. The Nazareth club sponsors a US$20,000 Matching Grant that helps teach entrepreneurial skills to young Arabs in Nazareth.

Ricardo J. Alfaro was a former president of Panama and his country's ambassador to the United States.[10]

At first, the speeches were sluggish and dismally formal. Then the diminutive chief of the Philippines delegation arose. He was Brigadier General Carlos P. Romulo, a member of the Rotary Club of Manila and former vice president of Rotary International. Romulo was no stranger to Rotarians, who had long appreciated his eloquence and wit in his many speaking engagements. "The next morning headline readers around the world knew the great conclave at San Francisco had a keynote," reported Leland D. Case in THE ROTARIAN.[11] Romulo went on to become president of the UN General Assembly, and Rotary International set about fertilizing the seeds of peace that he and his fellow delegates had sown.

The Secretariat published a series of booklets promoting the UN and UNESCO and sent them to clubs around the world with instructions that local Rotarians should themselves become better informed and then disseminate the facts as peace advocates in their communities. *From Here On!*, a 124-page booklet on the UN charter, had a circulation of almost a quarter-million, while *In the Minds of Men* (the UNESCO story) and *Report on the UN* by Rotary International were published monthly from 1947 to 1952.

There were wars before Rotary existed and wars after; the senseless slaughter of human life did not stop with the signing of the UN charter in 1945. But whereas the United Nations acts as a corporate body to try to resolve conflict, Rotarians have always tried to help peace percolate up from the grassroots. Peacemaking is first a local matter.

When serious riots erupted between Hindus and Muslims in Bombay, India, in 1947, hundreds were killed and thousands more injured. Members of the Rotary Club of Bombay went into the streets as peacemakers. Some bravely went into ethnic neighborhoods and held meetings that reduced tensions. Others patrolled areas considered flashpoints; still others volunteered as special magistrates.

Rotary peacemakers in Latin America also took a stand. "Between Peru and Colombia, a misunderstanding arose which threatened war. But the friendship of two men—men who understood Rotary and to whom the principles of international understanding were not alien—enabled our two countries to reach an understanding without the shedding of a single drop of blood," reported Past RI President Fernando Carbajal of Lima, Peru, in 1947.[12]

Rotary International President James L. Bomar of Shelbyville, Tennessee, USA, personally intervened after a border dispute erupted between Argentina and Chile. In 1980, he convened a President's Conference of Goodwill and invited 45 couples from each country. After some early uneasiness, by the end of the conference the attendees were mingling, chatting, and discussing ways to reconcile the people of their two nations. Argentina and

"People everywhere—each of them our cousins by blood—want peace.... But people draw distinctions about nations and races different from their own, which give rise to suspicion and distrust. I urge each of you as a Rotarian to bring to a club meeting a non-Rotarian who is of a different race, a different generation, or social background."

Hiroji Mukasa, Nakatsu, Japan
RI president, 1982-83

10 THE ROTARIAN, July 1945, 9.
11 THE ROTARIAN, April 1980, 48.
12 Rotary International, *Proceedings Thirty-Eighth Annual Convention* (Chicago, 1947), 102.

Japanese Rotarians contribute generously to both The Rotary Foundation and the Yoneyama Memorial Foundation, named for the man who introduced Rotary to Japan in 1920. The memorial foundation awards scholarships to students wishing to study in Japan.

Chile have never had bad relations since, and the intercountry committee established by his conference conferred on him the prestigious Condor of the Andes award.[13]

After the Berlin Wall came down in 1989, RI President Hugh Archer of Dearborn, Michigan, USA, spearheaded Rotary's effort to open the organization's first-ever club in Soviet Russia. "The entire Eastern Bloc opened up for the return of freedom, democracy, and Rotary," he said. "It was an exciting period for the Soviet satellite states. For the first time since the iron curtain fell and the cold war iced the planet, peace was given a real chance."[14]

On the other side of the world, the Rotary Club of Oslo-Skayen, Norway, launched the Shalom-Salaam peace project following the Oslo Peace Accords in 1994. Perhaps they drew their inspiration from former Canadian Foreign Minister and honorary Rotarian Lester Pearson, who said on accepting the Nobel Peace Prize in Oslo in 1957, "How can there be peace in the world when people do not know each other, and how can they know each other when they have never met?"

Through their Shalom-Salaam project, Norwegian Rotarians invite groups of university students—half of them Israeli, half Palestinian—to an all-expenses-paid summer study program in Oslo. They work together, eat together, learn together, play together—and return home with a new perspective for those they once thought of as enemies.

Such a commitment to acquaintance, fellowship, and cross-cultural harmony has been woven into the fabric of Rotary's tapestry from its founder to its present-day members. It was Paul Harris who called for "Toleration!" as the nations of Europe went to war in 1914. It was Glenn Mead of Philadelphia, the second international president, who charged Rotarian MacRae with the responsibility of making Rotary a force for peace, and as early as 1917, THE ROTARIAN was calling for a league to enforce peace.[15]

Between the world wars, RI President Will R. Manier of Nashville, Tennessee, USA, fathered the Rotary Institutes of International Understanding. These public forums featured acclaimed speakers booked by local Rotary clubs to advocate peace in high schools, colleges, and community centers. Ultimately, 1.5 million people heard those speeches.

Arch Klumph called Rotary "a world force that has taken on an impetus that cannot be diminished."[16] Klumph made that speech to the Atlanta con-

RI Treasurer-Director Luis Giay, Past District Governor Roberto
F.A. Migliaro, Past RI President James L. Bomar Jr., and Past RI
Director Fernando Friedmann hold the Condor of the Andes
award, presented to Bomar at the 1988 RI Convention in
Philadelphia, Pennsylvania, USA.

vention the year he was RI president in 1917. His words were to assume pro-
phetic significance in Rotary's quest for peace, for it was his vision that led to
the creation of The Rotary Foundation. From the beginning, the single guiding principle of the Foundation has been to bring peace to the world through
education and the relief of suffering and by helping people to better understand one another—particularly in cross-cultural settings.

If grown men are today responsible for the senseless acts of inhumanity to their fellow man, then Rotary pledged to deliver its message of peace to
the world's young people. Youth Exchange has long been one of the organization's most active and enduring programs. Hundreds of thousands of teens
and young adults have now lived in the homes, befriended the citizens, and
learned the culture of people in another country. Those exchanges do not
make headlines or stop wars, but they develop a mutual understanding across
national borders—they build friendships.

That is what those Norwegian Rotarians are doing with the next generation of community leaders from Israel and Palestine. That is why education is
stressed so highly by both Rotarians and The Rotary Foundation. "Why did we
get war?" asked English educator T.A. Warren, who served as RI president in
1945-46. "We got war because our leaders, who wanted peace as much as you
or I, lacked the backing of an informed public opinion that would support
them in bold and maybe self-sacrificing efforts to keep the peace."[17]

13 Rotary International, *1988 Proceedings Seventy-Ninth Annual Convention* (Evanston, Illinois, 1988), 36.

14 Willmon White, Oral History Interview with Hugh Archer, 11 April 2002.

15 THE ROTARIAN X, no. 3 (March 1917): 205.

16 International Association of Rotary Clubs, *Proceedings Eighth Annual Convention* (Chicago, 1917), 4.

17 THE ROTARIAN, October 1945, 11.

> "Keep three central truths in mind: First, service to others is the essence of Rotary, the very foundation of our unity. Second, this unity is stronger than the enormous diversity which surrounds us. And third, peace is the single greatest imperative of our time."
>
> *Charles C. Keller, California, Pennsylvania, USA*
> *RI president, 1987-88*

By the closing years of the 20th century, Rotary wanted to establish a new program where peacemaking was not just a backdrop but was the main focus. This would be the program with which future leaders could be equipped with the professional skills to resolve conflict in the new millennium. Einstein once said, "A new type of thinking is essential if mankind is to survive and move to higher levels."[18]

RI's 1981-82 President Stanley E. McCaffrey, a California university president, dreamed of a University of Peace in the early 1980s, but the time was not right. In 1996, Past RI President Rajendra K. Saboo of Chandigarh, India, was pondering an appropriate way to commemorate the 50th anniversary of Paul Harris's death. While gazing out of the window of his hotel room in Evanston, he noticed Northwestern University. "I thought, 'They have the Kellogg School of Management, so why not a Rotary school of international peace studies?' It would be a place where we could develop people who might later go on to become civil servants, prime ministers, foreign secretaries, and presidents."

RI PRESIDENT BHICHAI RATTAKUL CONGRATULATES ROTARY WORLD PEACE SCHOLAR MARGARET SOO OF MALAYSIA.

After several years of planning, The Rotary Foundation launched the Rotary Centers for International Studies in peace and conflict resolution. A center was established at seven renowned universities in Argentina, Australia, England, France, Japan, and the United States. Each year, starting in 2002, 70 scholars began a two-year master's-level degree program in conflict resolution, peace studies, and international relations. Some will go on to careers with international agencies such as the UN; others will join the private sector, a nongovernmental organization, or the diplomatic corps.

"The establishment of Rotary Centers for International Studies will be one of the most meaningful and innovative initiatives of The Rotary Foundation in the new millennium," said Elise Fiber Smith, president of Women's Edge and a Rotary Ambassadorial Scholar in 1954-55. "I am convinced that preparing new leadership for global peace and problem solving is one of the most critical needs of the 21st century."

Removing land mines planted during the 1990s Balkan wars was a major service project of Croatia's 16 Rotary clubs. The clubs raised about US$500,000, enough to clear 380,000 square meters, with the help of Austrian Rotarians.

One hundred years after Paul Harris founded Rotary, there is, of course, still conflict in the world. No man, no organization in history, has been able to stop war and likely never will. But Paul Harris's idea was more personal. He believed the path to peace was walked one step at a time, one person at a time.

In the never-ending quest for lasting peace, Rotarians often hear the question "What can one person do?" When we look back at Rotary's first century of service, the best answer is, "Look at what one man did."

18

CHAPTER

ROTARY'S ADMINISTRATIVE GEARWORKS

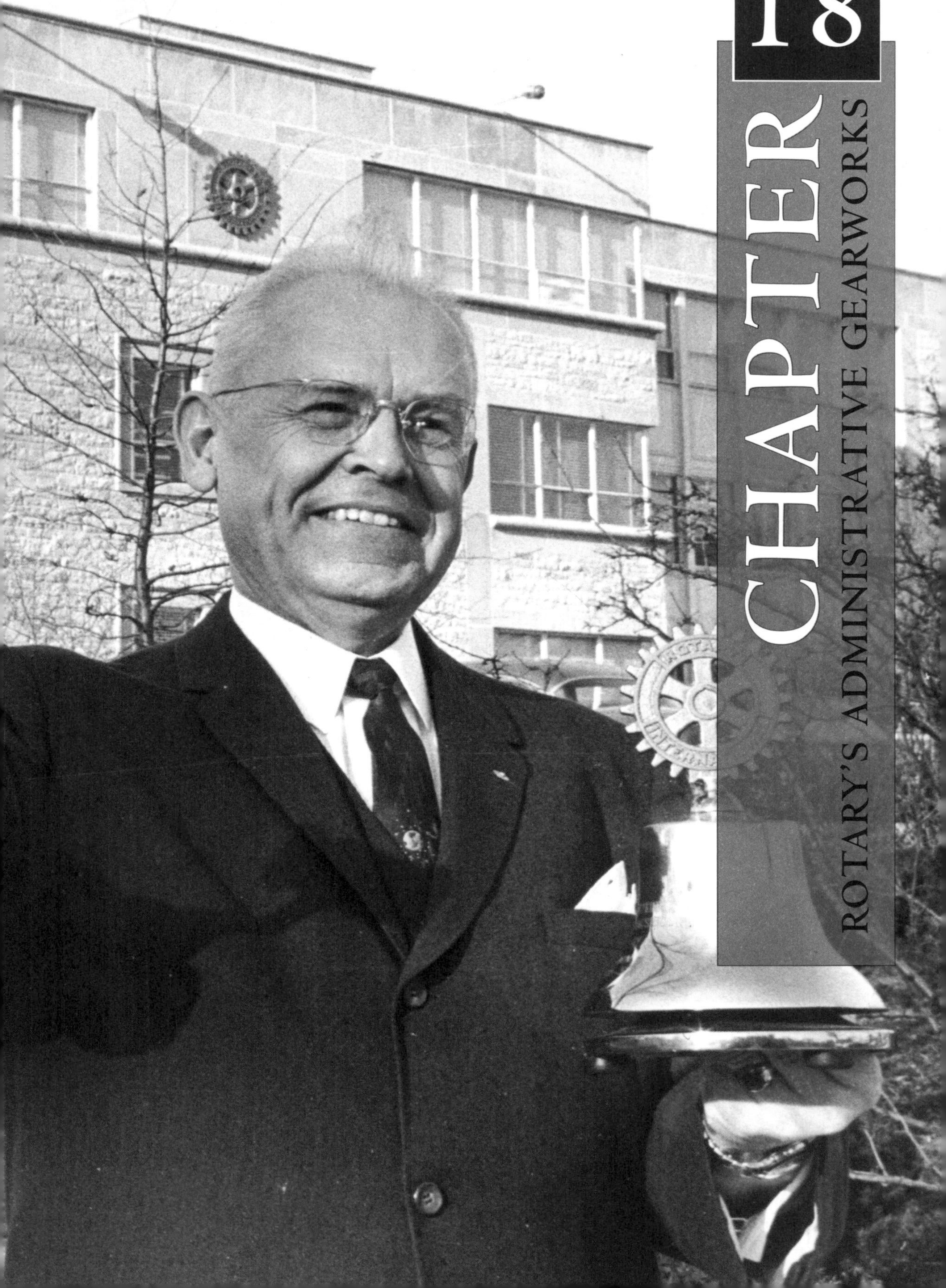

Chapter 18 – Rotary's Administrative Gearworks

Independent and autonomous, the first Rotary clubs were bound together by philosophy rather than bureaucracy. Each club decided who qualified for membership, how often it met, and even designed its own Rotary club emblem. No central administration existed, nor was it required. The formation of the National Association of Rotary Clubs at the first convention in 1910 did little to immediately change that.

But with Chesley R. Perry at the helm as the association's secretary, the organization began to evolve as an information resource and clearinghouse for Rotary clubs and their members. At a borrowed desk in a borrowed Chicago office, Ches Perry became the sole—and unpaid—worker who started to build a behind-the-scenes Secretariat.

Mildred Trosin was Rotary's first paid employee. Perry hired her in January 1912 because his own abilities and time were almost exhausted. Speaking to the Secretariat staff in 1931, Trosin told of the cramped working conditions and how she helped prepare Perry's *Weekly Letter* to clubs. In April 1912, Sarah Malley joined the staff and they moved to larger offices. Mildred recalled the procedure Perry devised when he wanted one of them to come into his office: he would whistle once for her, twice for Malley.

One Rotary Center in Evanston

Overleaf: RI General Secretary George R. Means welcomes Rotarians and staff to the new headquarters building in Evanston in 1955.

There are about 150 licensed vendors of RI merchandise in 31 countries. Any company or individual wishing to manufacture or sell items containing the Rotary name, the Rotary emblem, or any of the other Rotary designs or logos must be authorized by RI. By licensing vendors or makers of Rotary-related goods, RI maintains control over its name and insignia. Years ago, when the Wankel Rotary automobile engine was introduced, an advertisement urged: "Join the Rotary club." The ad was stopped by legal action.

Rotary's Headquarters

In those early years, the association frequently moved between rented offices within the Loop area of downtown Chicago. By 1918, Paul Harris was convinced that Rotary should move its headquarters to the Chicago suburbs to save money, but he couldn't convince Perry and others. By the early 1950s, the Secretariat staff had grown so large that a downtown building was simply too expensive to rent or buy. The RI Board commissioned a search for a permanent headquarters building. Several cities across the country—especially Denver, Colorado—made impassioned proposals for the honor of hosting the home office of Rotary, but in the end, the Board chose Evanston, Illinois, a charming university town on Lake Michigan, just north of Chicago.

Delegates to the 1953 Mexico City convention approved the Board's choice and Rotary soon broke ground on a US$1.3 million, 50,000-square foot (16,660 sq. m) office building on the corner of Evanston's Ridge Avenue and Davis Street. For more than 30 years, this was the hub of the Rotary wheel. But the building that had been home to the 130 Secretariat employees in 1955 was a crowded and unproductive work environment for 300 workers by 1985. When Rotary applied for planning permission to build an extension, the city imposed such heavy restrictions that the project seemed unlikely. So the Board and staff considered other alternatives. In the end, the confluence of incredible luck and good timing helped Rotary.

The American Hospital Supply Company operated its international headquarters in a modern 18-story building at 1560 Sherman Avenue, in the heart of Evanston—and they needed to sell it, following a merger with Baxter International. American Hospital Supply offered to sell its former headquarters for $24 million—or even less if Rotary paid in cash. The 400,000 square feet (37,160 sq. m) of offices—along with its own parking garage and cafeteria—was more than Rotary needed, so the excess space became an income-generating investment that soon paid off the mortgage, full and clear. Today, the Rotary flag flies high atop One Rotary Center, a building that affords spectacular views east to Lake Michigan, south to Chicago's skyscrapers, and north to the wooded campus of Northwestern University.

Secretariat Staff

If Mildred Trosin could see the Secretariat's staff today, she would be astonished. Roughly 500 people work in Evanston for Rotary International and The Rotary Foundation and a little over 100 are in the international offices in Zurich, Switzerland; São Paulo, Brazil; Tokyo, Japan; Seoul, Korea; New Delhi, India; Buenos Aires, Argentina; and Parramatta, New South Wales, Australia. (Eighteen people are on staff at RIBI headquarters in Alcester, England.)

The general secretary, responsible for the Secretariat, is the chief administrative officer of Rotary International, responsible to the RI Board of Directors for the implementation of the policies of RI, the Board, and The Rotary Foundation Trustees. He is chief financial officer of The Rotary Foundation and secretary of all RI committees, the Council on Legislation, and the international conventions. Ten general secretaries have served during Rotary's first 100 years, with just three of them serving for the first 64 years. Those three—Ches Perry (1910-42), Phil Lovejoy (1942-52), and George Means (1953-72)—played an enormous role in shaping the policies and traditions Rotarians today take for granted. Another, Herbert A. Pigman, served twice as general secretary—1979-86 and 1993-95—and returned to the Secretariat as a senior staff member for PolioPlus between and following those assignments.

With a much lower profile than the RI president, the general secretary still occupies an influential position. Presidents, boards, and committees change from year to year, but the general secretary, with the Secretariat staff, is able to consider important matters from a long-term perspective and thus brings a sense of continuity to Rotary's policies and procedures. Ches Perry's contributions to Rotary have been well documented in earlier chapters, but they can be summarized thus: Ches Perry was the rudder that guided Rotary through the early shallow waters, through times of rough sailing, and onto the broad waterway with a sense of vision, consistency, determination, and organizational skill demonstrated by no other Rotarian.

George Means showed that successive general secretaries could make their own profound impressions on the organization. Under his leadership, each employee was held strictly accountable for a high standard of office

ABOUT 500 STAFF MEMBERS WORK AT RI WORLD HEADQUARTERS IN EVANSTON, ILLINOIS, USA.

ROTARY STAFF MEMBERS HOLD A MEETING AT THE RIDGE AVENUE
HEADQUARTERS BUILDING IN EVANSTON IN THE 1970s.

procedures and the completion of their work assignments. A former U.S. Navy officer, he had a commanding voice and insisted on punctuality and a dress code. Before Means became general secretary, the RI Board dispatched him to India after World War II to close an unproductive branch office. Just as he was about to embark for home, they instructed him to stop in Japan to see if he could help restart that country's Rotary clubs.

Means landed in Yokohama harbor and, true to his can-do character, went immediately to see General Douglas MacArthur. The general, who headed up the U.S. occupation forces and was responsible for restoring stability to Japan following the war, was so impressed that he gave Means free reign to travel throughout the country, reestablishing the Japanese Rotary clubs as soon as possible. Within weeks, he had reorganized clubs in Fukuoka, Kobe, Kyoto, Nagoya, Osaka, Tokyo, and Sapporo.

HERBERT A. PIGMAN HAS SERVED AS RI GENERAL SECRETARY TWICE, DURING 1979-86 AND 1993-95.

Today, the latest thinking in the world's most service-oriented companies teaches employees that all shareholders are really "internal customers." Yet this was an approach Ches Perry imbued in the Secretariat staff 65 years ago. Thousands of times each day, cheerful staff answer the telephone with, "Good morning! Rotary International," with no idea how the caller on the other end will start the conversation.

But whatever the language, whatever the topic, they know someone in the Secretariat will have the answer.

The staff receive phone calls, letters, faxes, and e-mails from Rotarians wanting to know the club meeting days in a city they are visiting, from Rotary International officers looking for historical anecdotes for a speech they are writing, or from a club seeking a grant for a humanitarian project. The Secretariat staff provide information on Rotary policy and procedures and act as a clearinghouse for idea sharing. They provide Rotarians and clubs with publications, manuals, directories, videotapes, and information over the RI Web site (www.rotary.org). Other staff members promote some 30 Rotary programs, including those of The Rotary Foundation, while yet others help arrange international meetings and conventions.

Mirroring the internationality of the organization itself, headquarters staff in Evanston represent 41 countries and speak 56 languages or dialects. Nearly 100 employees were born outside the United States, and 222 employees in Evanston speak at least one language other than English. The 37 employees of the RI Europe and Africa Office in Zurich, Switzerland, speak 24 languages among them. World Headquarters in Evanston has translators on staff who produce official documents into and from French, German, Italian, Japanese, Korean, Portuguese, and Spanish. Translations into Swedish and other languages are handled through freelance translators.

Democracy in Action

Rotary may be the first personal experience with democracy for the citizens of some nations. The Rotary year runs from 1 July until 30 June, and by the end of the calendar year, elections have been held to determine the officers who will lead the club, district, and Rotary International for the next Rotary year. Typically, a Rotary club elects a president, vice president, secretary, treasurer, and four directors—one for each of the four Avenues of Service (Club, Vocational, Community, and International).

In 1912, delegates to the Duluth convention saw the need to create geographic groupings of clubs, and they organized the Rotary world into eight "divisions," each headed by a vice president. In 1915, Rotary changed the word *division* to *district* and whereas it had given the divisions geographic names—such as the Western Canada

Attendance at Rotary conventions has varied greatly over 100 years. The two smallest conventions were in Chicago in 1910 (the first, with 60 delegates) and 1945, near the end of World War II (with 141 participants). The largest RI conventions were in 1978 in Tokyo, Japan (39,834 participants), and Seoul, Korea, in 1989 (38,878 attendees). The 2005 convention in Chicago holds promise of setting a new record during Rotary's centennial year.

Division—numbers were used to differentiate the districts. Each district had 45-60 clubs, a number that on average remains today. Just as in 1915, some districts are compacted into a very small geographic area: London, England, is a district in itself—with some 80 clubs. At the other extreme, some districts extend through many countries or across multiple time zones. District 2450, for example, extends from Bahrain to Sudan and also includes Cyprus, Egypt, Jordan, Lebanon, and the United Arab Emirates. District 5010 encompasses Canada's Yukon Territory, the USA's Alaska, and Russia's Siberian territory, east of the Ural Mountains. "My district is 6.5 million square miles," said 2001-02 District Governor Wanda J. Cooksey, of Douglas, Alaska. "It takes me three days just to get to my clubs in Russia."

The district governor is an officer of Rotary International who is chosen for a one-year term by the clubs in the district. The governor must conduct an annual district conference and training seminar for club presidents and visit every club in the district and evaluate their activities—no small task when one's district crosses 12 time zones and three countries.

As early as 1919, Rotary headquarters recognized the need to train district governors to be effective leaders. In that year, it convened the first official meeting of district governors, an opportunity for them to share ideas, learn about new programs and procedures, and increase Rotary fellowship and growth. This International Council was later renamed the International Assembly and is clearly one of the most important meetings of the Rotary year. (See "International Assembly," chapter 19.)

After completing a term as district governor, Rotarians are eligible to stand for election to the Board of Directors of Rotary International. Over the years, the RI Board, currently numbering 18, has varied in number; but it has always represented the geographic distribution of clubs, with directors hailing from 10 to 12 countries. Not a U.S. organization, Rotary is an international organization that just happens to have been founded in the United States and has its headquarters there.

Rotary International groups 12-18 districts into a zone. There is no zone officer or administrative staff, although there is always a Rotary zone institute meeting every year for current, past, and incoming RI officers. Rotary International seeks candidates for director from each geographic zone on a rotating basis; it is impossible for one country to dominate the RI Board, and theoretically, a tiny country with only one or two Rotary clubs could have one of its members elected as a Rotary International director.

212

The highest elected office in Rotary, that of RI president, requires completion of a term as RI director. Candidates must be nominated by their home clubs for the office and then selected by an international nominating committee composed of past RI directors. The president-elect and president both dedicate at least two full years to represent Rotary around the world. When they are not participating in a Board meeting, they are likely traveling to attend a Rotary conference, meet heads of state, visit a Rotary service project, or speak at a Foundation dinner.

In 1949, RI President Percy C. Hodgson of Pawtucket, Rhode Island, USA, distributed his "Objectives for Our Team," launching a tradition for RI presidents to establish a theme for their year in office. Early on, the presidents penned complex multipoint objectives that were difficult for most people to remember. But 1953-54 President Joaquin Serratosa Cibils of Montevideo, Uruguay, chose Rotary Is Hope in Action. It was simple, easy to recall, and effective. Every president from 1957 on has followed that pattern. (See appendix 2 for a list of the RI presidents and themes.)

International Convention

The annual Rotary International Convention combines work and fellowship. All Rotarians are eligible to attend, and every club has a vote or votes based on size. Confirmation of the election of the president and all district governors, the report of the general secretary, and other business are regularly conducted.

But the broader purpose of the convention is to provide a common meeting place for Rotarians of the world. With all their diversity of language, dress, custom, and culture, they meet to celebrate the fellowship of Rotary and enjoy social and entertainment features. A special focus is to stimulate, inspire, and inform incoming club presidents. The convention moves around the world and may not be held in any one country for more than two consecutive years.

Other gatherings also occur at the time of the convention, including an International Institute for past RI officers and meetings of Youth Exchange officers, Rotaractors, and RYLA delegates.

Council on Legislation

Starting in 1910, all matters of significance were debated and decided by delegates to the annual convention. That worked when the organization was small but was a cumbersome undertaking by 1930, when 11,000 people attended the 25th anniversary convention in Chicago. So many proposals were made and debated that the RI Board knew it had to change this tradition.

The result was the Council on Legislation. The 1933 Boston convention adopted the idea, and the first Council on Legislation was created in 1934. The Council on Legislation has been described as Rotary's parliament. Each district in the world elects one delegate, who must have completed a term as district governor, to represent its clubs at the council. These grassroots Rotarians, along with a few ex officio members, have the power to change the face of Rotary by amending its constitutional documents. The Council may also by resolution make recommendations to the RI Board of Directors on policy matters. The Council on Legislation was originally conceived as an advisory board, debating and analyzing proposals before they were submitted to the annual convention for a vote.

In 1970, delegates to the Atlanta convention changed the Council on Legislation from an advisory to a legislative body. Since 1974, it has convened every three years to debate and vote on hundreds of proposals that range from minor alterations in procedure and programs to radical changes in Rotary's objectives. The RI Board, as well as the smallest Rotary club in the world, can each submit a proposal to the Council. All actions taken by the Council on Legislation must be presented to every Rotary club for ratification. To date, no action by the Council has been overturned.

RIBI

Rotary International in Great Britain and Ireland, known as RIBI, is a unique group within the worldwide body of Rotary. Often misunderstood, its status has been hotly debated over the years.

After Stuart Morrow introduced Rotary to Dublin in 1911, he quickly moved on to form clubs in Belfast and then crossed the Irish Sea to do the same in Scotland and northern England. As Morrow was prolifically forming these clubs, others were starting the Rotary Club of London, which also set about planting sister clubs.

In October 1913, representatives of the Rotary clubs in London, Manchester, Glasgow, Edinburgh, Liverpool, Dublin, Belfast, and Birmingham

THE SIGN OF THE RIBI OFFICE IN ALCESTER, WARWICKSHIRE, ENGLAND

met to discuss how they could work together to develop the movement. On 4 May 1914, those self-proclaimed "Founder Clubs" formed the British Association of Rotary Clubs (BARC) "to standardize Rotary principles and practices by all Rotary clubs in the United Kingdom" (which included the whole of Ireland at the time). BARC was not affiliated with the International Association of Rotary Clubs; it was autonomous and self-governing, with its officers elected by its member clubs. "It is a far cry from Chicago," wrote BARC's Honorary Secretary Thomas Stephenson. "British Rotary requires British methods, and if we may say it without offence, British government."

Within two months of BARC's formation, Europe was at war. Communications with the United States had been difficult from the beginning, but during wartime it was almost impossible to maintain timely correspondence between Rotary's Chicago headquarters and clubs and members in Britain. Rotary grew in Britain despite the war, and the infrequent contact with Chicago strengthened the British clubs' reliance on BARC—and their acceptance of it as their Rotary resource and governing body. The British association urged all member clubs to also join the International Association of Rotary Clubs, and most of them did so. But because of the war, most U.S. Rotarians had no mechanism to make their British colleagues feel included in the international movement.

When the war ended, many U.S. Rotarians expected clubs in Britain to embrace the Chicago-based International Association of Rotary Clubs. Yet those clubs felt they already had an efficient association; by 1918 BARC included 30 clubs, arranged into six districts. Over the next several years, some insisted that BARC be banned so that every Rotary club in the world would fall under a single administrative body: Rotary International.

The situation was initially resolved at the 1921 convention in Edinburgh. Delegates decided that when 25 or more clubs existed in one country, they could apply to the International Convention for authority to become an administrative unit. British and Irish clubs immediately applied for recognition as a territorial unit. They submitted their proposed constitution and bylaws to the 1922 Los Angeles convention—choosing the name, "Rotary International – Association for Britain and Ireland"—and it was adopted. But in 1927, the Ostend convention in Belgium eliminated the provision for further territorial or administrative units, leaving RIBI as the sole example of an organization within the larger body. RIBI might be an anomaly, but it continues.

In 1964, strong objection was again raised to RIBI's administrative territorial unit status. The matter was vigorously debated in the Council on Legislation in Toronto, Canada. The primary concern was the precedent that allowed RIBI different officers and financial arrangements—and the threat that other regions might also demand administrative unit status. In 1966, at the next Council meeting, the matter was resolved in a display of Rotary friendliness. RIBI adopted RI titles for district governors and other administrative arrangements. A sharing of RI dues compensated for administrative duties performed for RI by RIBI.

A club council, rather than a board of directors, governs British Rotary clubs, and a district council helps the governor administer the district. Each district governor, along with an elected treasurer, vice president, and president, comprise the General Council, RIBI's governing body. RIBI is divided into two RI zones, which, as with the rest of the Rotary world, are eligible to elect a director to sit on the RI Board. Four past presidents of RIBI have been elected RI president.

The organization has seen many changes in the world over its century of service. Yet just as the power in Rotary resided in the local club back in 1905, so it does today. "Rotary International is not something separate and apart from the clubs, but is the clubs, collectively," wrote Ches Perry in 1957.[1] "And in a still more inclusive sense, [Rotary International] is the Rotarians who constitute the clubs." As Perry recognized, the individual Rotarian and club propel and ride the strongest currents of the Rotary River.

ROTARY'S ADMINISTRATIVE GEARWORKS

1   Chesley R. Perry, "Thinking Out-Aloud #103: Rotary and Democracy" (November 1957), 1.

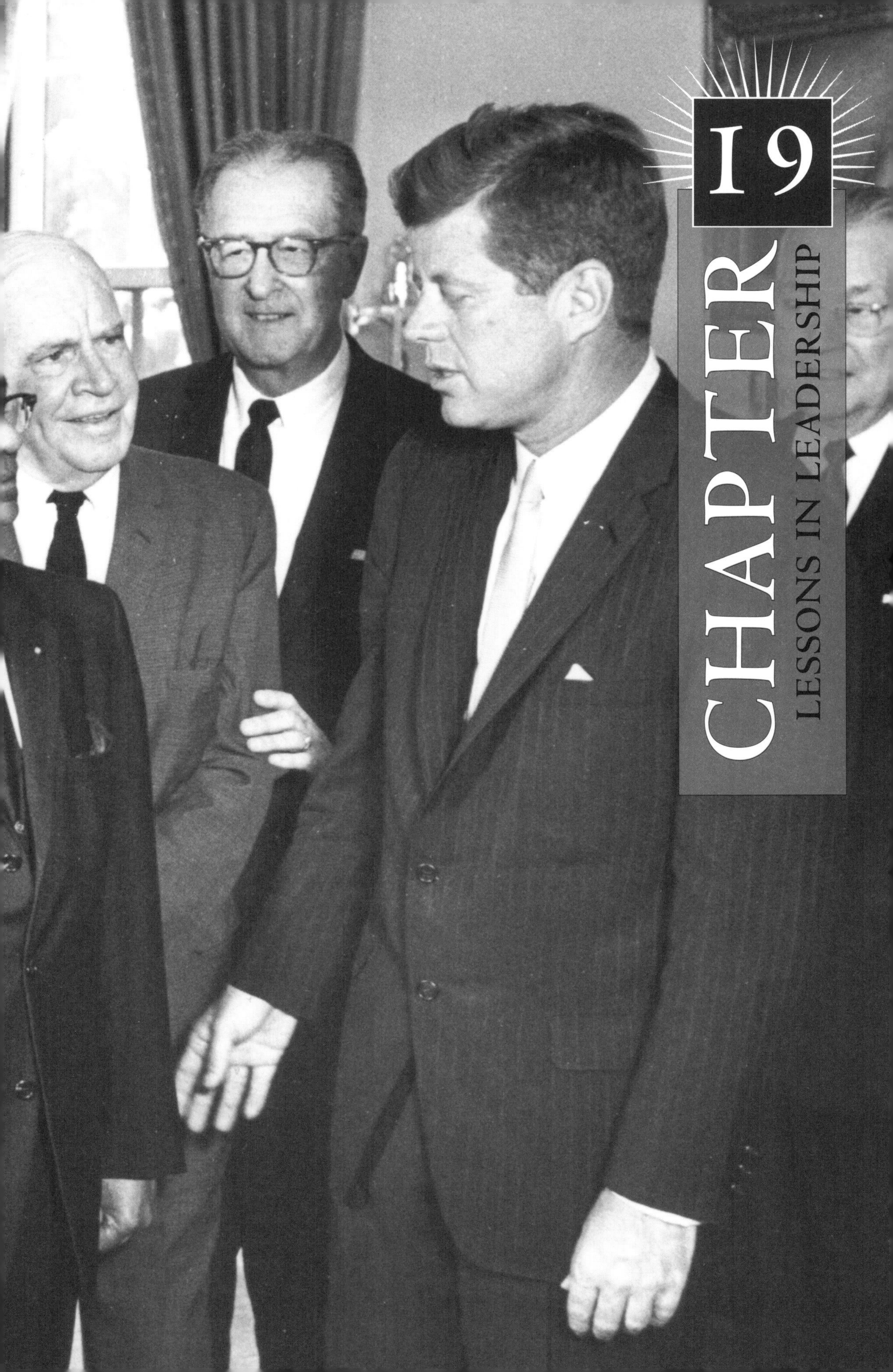

Chapter 19

Lessons in Leadership

Chapter 19 — Lessons in Leadership

O ne of Rotary's distinctive characteristics is that, with the exception of RI directors, who serve two-year terms, and Rotary Foundation trustees with four-year terms, the entire leadership in the organization changes every 1 July. It happens with officers in the smallest club all the way to the Rotary International president. Imagine how a multinational business with 31,000 branches and 1.2 million associates could function if each executive, each branch manager, were to turn over every year. Yet it works effectively in Rotary—and has done so for 100 years. Indeed, this annual change demands that Rotary have a continual supply of good leaders to keep the Rotary wheel rolling; otherwise the entire machine would fail. The continuity called for in long-term strategic planning is maintained, the counsel of past officers is there when advice is needed, but the new crop of leaders brings vitality, fresh ideas, and enthusiasm to the organization and its service mission.

Delegates study proposed enactments and resolutions at a Council on Legislation.

Overleaf: U.S. President John F. Kennedy greets 1962-63 RI President Nitish Laharry at the White House. Also pictured: RI General Secretary George Means (second from left), future RI President Luther Hodges (fifth from left), Past RI President Clinton Anderson (third from left), and Past RI President A.Z. Baker (far right).

Jean Sibelius, Finnish composer and an honorary member of the Rotary Club of Helsinki, was a guiding spirit of the nation's peaceful independence movement away from Czarist Russia. His composition *Finlandia* stirred his countrymen to seek freedom and and earned him the title "the uncrowned king of Finland." Rolf J. Klärich became the first RI president from Finland in 1980-81.

"Our strength is in our continuity, the chain of service that links past governor to current governor…past president to present president…Rotary veterans to newest inductees," wrote Paulo V.C. Costa of Santos, Brazil, when he was RI president in 1991. "It is the melding of experience and innovation that makes Rotary strong yet flexible."[1]

Articles on leadership dominated the pages of THE ROTARIAN throughout the first few decades. They were a collection of how-to features on business methods, ethical practices, salesmanship, employee relations, and character development. When the Rotary Code of Ethics was adopted in 1915, many additional stories and convention workshops focused on the importance of incorporating those qualities as everyday practices within Rotarians' trades and professions.

In the early years, senior officers advanced in much the same way as political candidates. Clubs or districts wanting to see their man as governor, director, or RI president would announce his candidacy and then launch a campaign for his election. Over time, certain Rotarians became known as "king makers," and some clubs and districts were considered powerhouses of votes. Early Rotary conventions resembled the political rallies of today, with banners, badges, and backroom deals all designed to promote the standing of one candidate over another.

Between 1913 and 1916, a system began to evolve whereby candidates for elective office were chosen by nominating committees. By 1970, this became the universal method of selecting leaders in Rotary, and campaigning or politicking in any form was forbidden. The change seemed appropriate for a volunteer organization built on fellowship and the ideal of service to others.

Rotary has been an excellent breeding ground for leaders. RI's 1946-47 President Richard C. Hedke of Detroit wrote: "Rotary conceives of the individual Rotary club as a training ground for leaders for the long crusade to raise business standards, improve community well-being, and enlarge total world understanding. It is as simple as that."[2]

As the first service club in the modern age, and the first such organization that admitted members using the classification system, there was a high-perceived value in belonging to Rotary. In most cases, the Rotary club was the place to associate with the leaders of business, the professions, and the community.

1   THE ROTARIAN, January 1991, 54.
2   THE ROTARIAN, July 1946, 7.

"My first Rotarian involvement at the district level as 'youth delegate' gave me the opportunity to successfully work expanding Rotaract and Youth Exchange," recalls Dr. Carlo Monticelli, 1998-2000 RI director from Milano, Italy, whose profession is international marketing. "My experiences as I rose to positions of leadership in my club, district, and then RI led me to meet great leaders and to learn by actually doing. I often realize how many of the skills and techniques I use in my company and trade association are those I picked up as a Rotarian."

Rotarians are exposed to leadership training almost from the moment they join a club. As a committee chair, then a club officer, people who once may have dreaded public speaking find themselves compelled to present their ideas for new service projects to clubs with a mix of young and old members, men and women, progressive thinkers and die-hard traditionalists. Regional Rotary leadership seminars provide valuable help in personal and professional growth. As new Rotarians progress up the leadership ladder, they become more persuasive, able to listen and evaluate other viewpoints, and then present their plans and ideas in ways that convince even the skeptics. The leadership skills developed in Rotary also prove helpful in their business and professional careers.

Club presidents-elect are required to attend a PETS, or presidents-elect training seminar, convened by their Rotary district. It is here that they meet as many as 250 other incoming presidents, along with dozens of current and past district governors, and often RI directors and perhaps a past RI president. They practice public speaking, planning, goal setting, and budgeting and learn how to motivate club members to become more active and involved.

Rotarians in a New Jersey, USA, district initiated a particularly effective Leadership Institute in 1992. Designed to develop leadership skills by careful training among potential Rotarian leaders, the institute had been extended into 40 districts with international outreach. Rotary clubs recognize the essential need for an unending supply of motivated, trained leaders.

District governors-elect often ask past club presidents who have demonstrated their leadership ability to become assistant governors. This Rotarian is the liaison between the governor and about six clubs, and during the year the assistant governor sits in on many district planning meetings and is the governor's ambassador to clubs. The assistant governor now needs diplomacy, tact, persuasiveness, eloquence, and excellent interpersonal skills to promote the district governor's programs to these clubs—each of which, by Rotary charter, is autonomous.

International Assembly

The district governor is the chief RI representative for 45-60 clubs having a membership of 500 to 5,000 Rotarians. Before taking office, district governors-elect are required to spend a week at the International Assembly—Rotary's ultimate training program and school of leadership. The International

PARTICIPANTS AT THE 2001 INTERNATIONAL ASSEMBLY GATHER FOR THE INTERNATIONAL FELLOWSHIP DINNER.

Assembly dates back to 1919; at that first conclave of governors-elect, senior RI officers provided a thorough education in 11 general topics and 23 specific leadership areas. For 25 years, the assembly had its home in Lake Placid, New York, USA, and after that Boca Raton, Florida, and Nashville, Tennessee. As Rotary grew, so did the space requirements for the International Assembly; it was briefly convened in a few other U.S. cities before settling in its current home of Anaheim, California.

Until the 1980s, governors-elect would receive their International Assembly training just before the international convention, barely a month before their year began. Today, it is held in February or March, which gives the governors several months to prepare for their year of responsibility.

The International Assembly is where, perhaps for the first time, the leaders feel they are part of a global village. The incoming governors and their spouses see the whole world of Rotary—literally—because every incoming district governor, every sitting RI director and

THE INTERNATIONAL ASSEMBLY OFFERS DISTRICT GOVERNORS-ELECT AN OPPORTUNITY TO NETWORK AND SEARCH FOR POTENTIAL SERVICE PARTNERS.

Rotary Foundation trustee, the RI president and president-elect, and most past presidents are brought together for a week of intensive leadership training. The week is marked by plenary sessions, inspiring speeches, and intense workshops—with homework assignments, idea exchanges, and group discussion sessions led by some of the most successful past district governors from around the world, who share their knowledge and skills with the next "class" of governors. Incoming governors leave with a new understanding of the International Assembly motto: Enter to Learn...Go Forth to Serve.

222

Council on Legislation

The triennial Council on Legislation is a fascinating laboratory where past district governors learn parliamentary procedure, cross-cultural understanding, and the best aspects of politics: how to build coalitions and negotiate compromise in order to achieve mutually desired objectives. Delegates typically study more than 400 proposed pieces of legislation and often leave home with a firm opinion on how they will vote on them. But when the Council

James L. Bomar Jr. (far right) confers on a parliamentary point with George Arceneaux Jr. (center), Charles C. Keller (second from right), and other Rotarians at the 1977 Council on Legislation.

convenes and participants hear the impassioned positions of fellow delegates from other races, cultures, and countries, they sometimes modify their views. "Another important lesson for the workplace and life itself," one delegate to the 2001 Council observed. "Always try to understand the other person's point of view." (See "Council on Legislation," chapter 18.)

Rotary Builds Leaders

When elected to the RI Board, Rotarians undergo more training, some formal, some as the protégés of past directors who act as mentors. RI directors travel the world addressing large audiences of Rotarians at institutes, conferences, conventions, training seminars, and club anniversary events.

That rarest of all opportunities comes when a Rotarian is chosen by the nominating committee to be the RI president. Everything learned as committee chair and as club president is still important, but to a much higher degree. As Rotary's ambassador to the world, the RI president will meet royalty, national presidents, cabinet ministers, ambassadors, and UN officials. The president's ability to communicate, inspire, and lead affects 1.2 million Rotarians and many millions more who are served by Rotary's programs.

The traits that a Rotary club instills in its members—planning, volunteerism, organizational abilities, motivation, leadership, tolerance, communication skills—are all invaluable assets to any organization, whether they are demonstrated by an employee, the business owner, or a volunteer.

Membership in Rotary clubs helps volunteers grow as community leaders and in their chosen career. In 1909, Angelo Rossi, who owned a small florist's shop, joined the Rotary Club of San Francisco. He served on several committees and became a club director. "His leadership qualities were brought out through his club membership," reported club historian and past president Paul Rieger. Rossi went on to become San Francisco's mayor. Rieger added, "William J. Quinn joined the club in 1929 and Rotary brought out further his leadership"; Quinn subsequently became chief of police. "In 1930, Charles J. Brennan joined the club and largely through his [leadership skills] being brought out in Rotary, he became chief of the San Francisco Fire Department and the National Chief of Fire Chiefs. Rotary over and over again everywhere brings out the leadership."

Konstantin Päts, recognized as the father of democratic Estonia, shared the same birthday as Rotary—23 February—and was a charter member of the Baltic country's first Rotary club in the capital city of Tallinn. He governed Estonia from 1921 to 1924 and again from 1934 to 1940. Estonia rejoined the ranks of Rotary nations after the dissolution of the Soviet Union in 1991.

Many other Rotarians have gone on to significant leadership positions within their professions or governments. Luther Hodges of Chapel Hill, North Carolina, became governor of North Carolina and U.S. secretary of commerce before rising to RI president in 1967-68. After serving first as a Rotary Foundation Ambassadorial Scholar and then a Rotarian for 20 years in Munster, Indiana, Dr. Young Woo Kang became assistant secretary of special education in the United States. "My years in Rotary have been a training ground for the leadership skills I needed both as a university professor and throughout my career," he said. "More than anything else, Rotary membership taught me to live that maxim, 'Think globally, act locally.'" Ásgeir Ásgeirsson of the Rotary Club of Reykjavik, Iceland, became his nation's president, as did Konstantin Päts of the Rotary Club of Tallinn, Estonia, and Chucri Kouatly of the Rotary Club of Damascus, Syria.

Jonathan Majiyagbe served as chancellor of the Anglican Diocese of Kano (Nigeria) and vice president of the Nigerian Bar Association before becoming RI's first African president in 2003-04. Past RI Director In Sang Song was Korea's finance minister. Bhichai Rattakul, a charter member of the Rotary Club of Dhonburi, Bangkok, Thailand, went on to serve his country for nine terms as a member of Parliament, rising to foreign minister, deputy prime minister, and speaker of the House of Representatives. He served as RI president for 2002-03.

Those leaders are elected democratically, a tenet that goes back to the very beginnings of Rotary. "We must guard the democracy of Rotary beyond all things," Paul Harris urged in 1916. "The democratic spirit is essential to…all worthwhile organizations, but it is the very life spark of Rotary."[3]

In Rotary, the ultimate power always reverts to the grassroots members of the local Rotary clubs. They can veto a decision by the Council on Legislation. They can either ratify or override the choice of the nominating committee for every elective office from district governor to worldwide president. To some Rotarians, particularly those in newly established clubs in countries formerly having totalitarian regimes, Rotary is the first experience in democracy they have ever known.

At least four Rotarians—all from the Rotary Club of Hanyang, Seoul, Korea—have served as prime minister for their nation: Chung Yul Kim, Duck Wo Nam, Choong Hoon Park, and Chang Soon Yoo. Other prominent Rotarians from the same club include In Sang Song, minister of finance, and Chae Kyon Oh, minister of culture and information (both were RI directors), and Young Hui Kim, president of the Korean Development Bank.

District Governors-elect Susan Cook of Canada, Dr. Varinder Singh of Kenya, and fellow incoming governors take notes at the 2002 International Assembly.

If democracy can be defined as "the peoples' decision," then that same word applies to most of Rotary's ideals and programs. Rotary is not an authoritarian, top-down organization but rather one where every leader and almost every program in the past 100 years has originated in a local Rotary club and percolated upward to the national, regional, and global level.

Increasingly through the years, Rotarians have extended leadership training to others. Rotarians in Australia developed Rotary Youth Leadership Awards (RYLA) as early as 1959. This program extends leadership skills and motivation to teenagers in a retreat setting. One of Rotary's most successful youth programs, RYLA is now conducted each year in some 400 Rotary districts worldwide.

High credit is due those who become actively involved in Rotary as leaders. Club presidents spend at least as much time preparing for their weekly meeting as they do running it. In addition, they attend district assemblies and conferences, training events, and club board meetings—a significant contribution of their time.

District governors give thousands of hours of their time to Rotary as they plan and host district events, assemblies, conferences, service projects, training sessions, and fundraising activities—in addition to the traditional club visits. It is not unusual for district governors to be away from home for weeks at a time—from before dawn until late at night—as they visit far-flung clubs whose meetings might just as likely be held over breakfast as at dinnertime.

Diversity is one of Rotary's greatest assets, and it has increasingly capitalized on that strength to develop leaders at the district level. In 1994, a three-year experiment—launched at the district level—began to improve the effectiveness of district structure, administration, and leadership. The result was the District Leadership Plan (DLP), which started in July 1993 as a pilot project within 12 districts across 14 countries.

Past RI Director Genshitsu Sen of Kyoto, Japan, is a 15th-generation Grand Tea Master of the Urasenke Tradition of Tea. Sen, related to the imperial family of Japan, is one of the few invited to serve tea in the Imperial Palace and heads a tea-ceremony organization with four million members in chapters around the world.

After reviewing the results, the RI Board created a new district structure wherein governors could delegate many of the duties to assistant governors, who themselves would be trained for future leadership roles. They reinforced the value of standing committees to bring stability to district projects and continuity to strategic objectives such as membership retention. Each year, the DLP gained even wider acceptance, and the RI Board subsequently ruled that effective 1 July 2002, every Rotary district should follow the plan.

"It's like building a building for which you now have a blueprint," said 1983-84 RI President William E. Skelton of Christiansburg-Blacksburg, Virginia, USA, who spearheaded the change. "You can't send down mandates from the RI Board and make volunteers work for you. This helps the clubs and the districts set direction and then develops the leaders to take them in that direction. This plan has so many implications for the future of Rotary."

By the time a Rotarian becomes a Rotary International director, he or she has probably become an accomplished speaker, problem solver, and a capable spokesperson for the RI Board and president. At the president's request, directors represent the president at district conferences, zone institutes, and other important events all over the world. Directors are also obliged to attend Board meetings and international assemblies and conventions, and serve as liaison members of international committees.

Rotary leaders all have commitments to their families, businesses, religious institutions, and other organizations, yet they gladly and voluntarily give countless hours of their lives to turn the Rotary wheel. What motivates them? It is not money, for they are all unpaid volunteers. It is not for acclaim, for institutional fame is fleeting and the unwritten tradition for most of Rotary's history was for Rotarians to perform their good deeds quietly, without great publicity.

"Commitment is...the language of service," said 1988-89 RI President Royce Abbey of Essendon, Victoria, Australia. "We are made to be committed to an ideal, whether [it] be excellence in competition, business, or service to mankind....Achievement rests on the determination and effort of individuals."[4]

Yet it is a basic truism of human nature that few people will perform without some type of recognition. To Rotarians, the rewards are fun, fellowship, and self-actualization. But the overriding reward is the knowledge that through their service, they—and the Rotarians they lead—are making the world a better place through effective leadership in their workplace, in their Rotary clubs, in their communities, and in the world beyond.

4   Rotary International, *Paul Harris and His Successors: Profiles in Leadership* (Evanston, Illinois, 1997), 318.

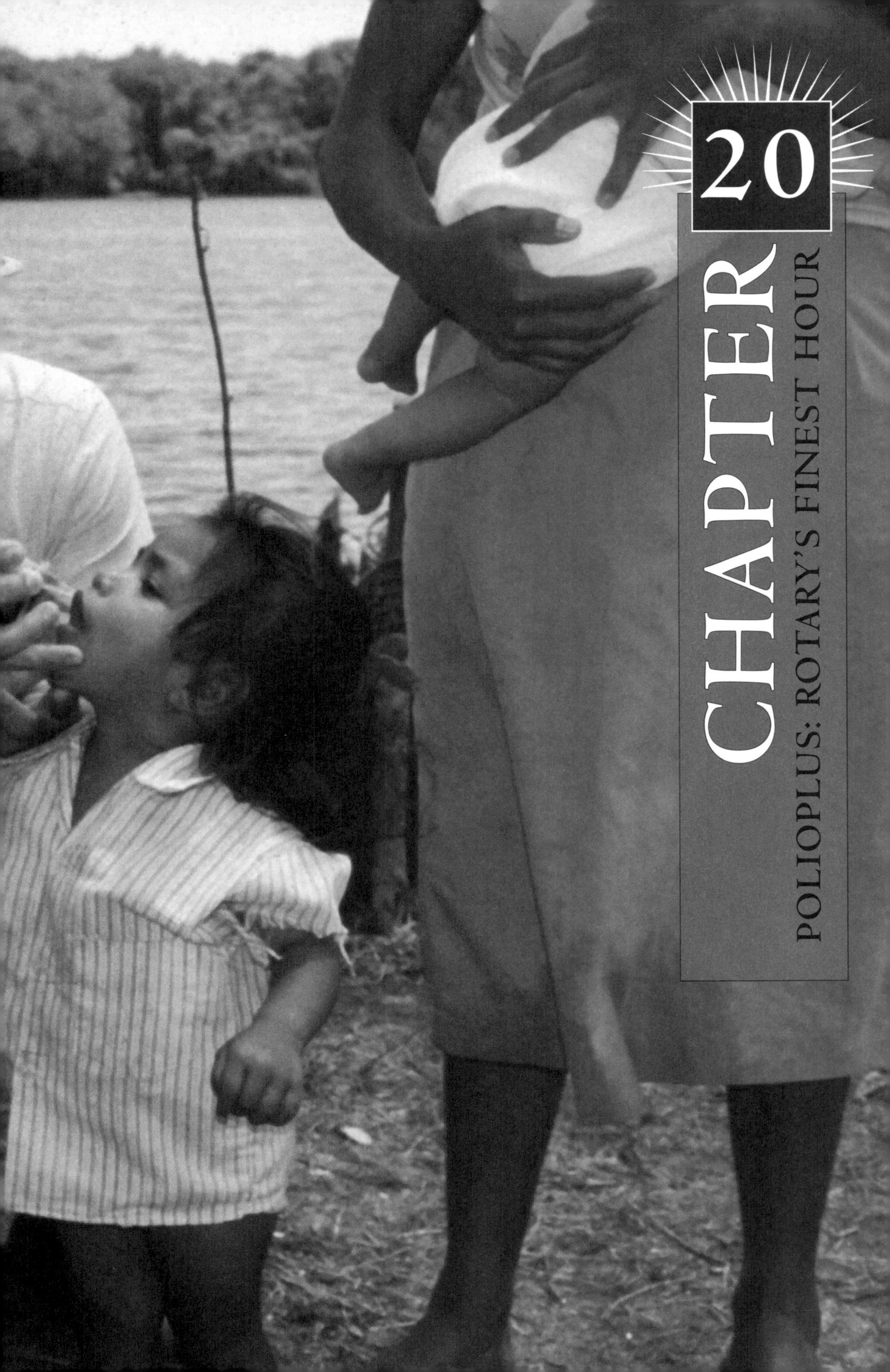

CHAPTER 20

POLIOPLUS: ROTARY'S FINEST HOUR

Chapter 20 – PolioPlus: Rotary's Finest Hour

P olio. For most of the 20th century, few single words could evoke more fear. In the late 19th century, before poliomyelitis had ever been clinically diagnosed, epidemics of "infantile paralysis" hit communities in Europe and North America.

The crippling disease strikes without warning, usually choosing for its victims children who will be forever robbed of the simple gift of walking to school or playing with friends. By 1916, when a polio epidemic that started in New York City paralyzed 27,000 people and killed 7,000 nationwide, the disease had become a dreaded scourge.

Some of Rotary's earliest programs involved "crippled children's work," and for a while it seemed that the organization might adopt the cause as its main service objective. Resolution 23-34 at the 1923 St. Louis convention, which enacted the rule that Rotary clubs were autonomous and that RI could not enforce Rotary-wide programs on them, defeated that proposal. But throughout the years many Rotary clubs continued to provide wheelchairs, vocational training, family assistance, Handicamps (summer camps for disabled youth), and other benevolent acts for disabled children and young people.

But Rotary's emphasis was traditionally on the aftereffects of polio, not on the cause. Perhaps that was because for half a century polio confounded even the experts. Some blamed it on the stable fly; others claimed minute water droplets carried the airborne virus.

Life in an iron lung was the fate of many polio patients in the 1950s.

Overleaf: Dr. Federico Diaz Hawing, then president of the Rotary Club of Alvarado, Mexico, immunizes a child on the banks of the Rio Blanco in 1993.

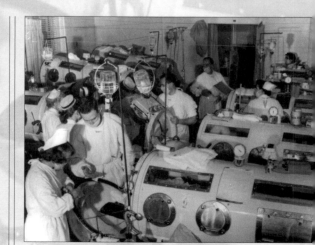

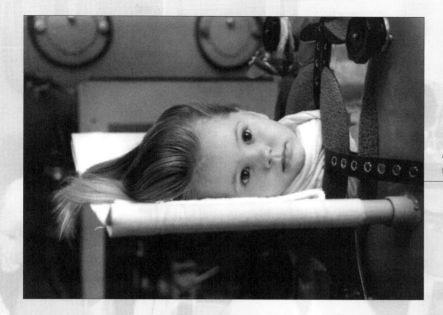

A YOUNG POLIO PATIENT
IN AN IRON LUNG

One fact was clear: polio did not discriminate. It inflicted its devastating effects on children and adults, black and white, urban dwellers and remote villagers, rich and poor. It crippled babies in the ghettoes; it did the same to Franklin Delano Roosevelt, scion of one of America's wealthiest families and a future president of the United States.

Physicians finally discovered that poliomyelitis was a virus, not a bacterium. It enters the body through the mouth and multiplies in the throat and intestines, attacking the nerves in the spinal cord. When the flow of impulses from the brain to the spine is interrupted, the affected muscle fibers shrivel and die.

In an ordinary week on an ordinary street, most children would wake up normally and rush outside to play while two or three might awaken with a slight fever, unable to move their limbs. Polio had struck again. The paralysis would quickly spread through their body. Arms and legs would flop aimlessly, muscles would wither, and for some, breathing became impossible. Three of every 10 such victims would spend months or years in wheelchairs and on crutches; the worst cases spent night and day in iron lungs or died. Swimming pools, cinemas, and schools were closed and terrified parents kept their children away from large gatherings of people.

In April 1955, the U.S. Public Health Service held a ceremony at the White House licensing the polio vaccine developed by Dr. Jonas Salk. Hundreds of thousands of children were vaccinated in countries that could afford the vaccine throughout the industrialized world, and new polio cases almost disappeared.

Dr. Salk had developed an injectable "killed" virus vaccine. Yet other researchers believed a live, attenuated virus, which would be given orally, would be more effective, longer lasting, and certainly more economical. A team led by Dr. Albert Sabin successfully produced the oral polio vaccine and in 1960,

> "Two dear children—Luis Fermin of Peru and Mum Chanty of
> Cambodia—represent the last cases of polio in their regions of the
> world. They symbolize our historic victories over polio. One of my
> fondest memories of Rotary was giving precious polio vaccine to small
> children....In my mind, the good old days are today, thanks to the
> incredible achievements of PolioPlus."
>
> *William T. Sergeant, chairman*
> *International PolioPlus Committee*

in the largest field trials in history, administered it to every person between
the ages of 2 and 20 in the Soviet Union. Seventy-seven million patients were
immunized, followed shortly thereafter by another 23 million in other East
European Soviet Bloc nations. New cases of polio disappeared throughout
the countries where Sabin's vaccine had been administered.

Almost overnight, polio was eliminated from the industrialized world,
whose governments had the resources to launch massive immunization drives.
Soon, a mother's panic over her child's fever and the shocking sight of a human being encased in an iron lung were but tragic memories of the past.

But polio had not disappeared.

It continued to fester in less-developed countries, lurking where health
infrastructures reached few newborns. In 1969, the same time as the first person walked on the Moon, 60 million children were born without protection
from polio. Each hour of the day and night, polio struck 30 more children,
condemning three of them to death while most of the remainder would suffer
lifelong disability and disfigurement.

Rotary's involvement in polio immunization was an evolutionary, rather
than a revolutionary, process.

In the spring of 1972, Charles Rowlands, governor of Pennsylvania's District 730, and his successor, Niles Norman, attended the Rotary Club of Oakland, a section of Pittsburgh. Vocational Service talks have long been a tradition in Rotary, and on that day, it was the turn of the incoming club president,
Dr. Robert Hingson, to tell the club about his career.

Hingson had invented a "peace gun," and he told the club how it could
be loaded with multiple doses of a vaccine and then used to immunize large
numbers of people infinitely faster than the traditional syringe method. The
World Health Organization had successfully used his gun in its mass immunization against smallpox, the only disease ever to be eradicated worldwide.

Norman was so impressed with Hingson's device that he and Rowlands
discussed how the district could partner with Hingson in some meaningful
project during Norman's gubernatorial term. Less than a year later, THE
ROTARIAN reported: "The Rotarians of District 730, in partnership with
Guatemalan Rotarians and their health ministry, plan to inoculate one million
children in May and June 1973 and February 1974."[1] Pennsylvania Rotarians
had raised the money; Guatemala Rotarians had mobilized the communities

232

---

1 THE ROTARIAN, March 1973, 43.
2 Rotary International, *Proceedings Seventy-First Annual Convention* (Chicago, 1980), 108.
3 Rotary International, Board minutes, February 1978, 1.

in which the vaccine was administered. Long before anyone ever used the term "PolioPlus," here was the prototype of a PolioPlus National Immunization Day (NID).

Dr. Albert Sabin was a strong proponent of mass immunization against polio. He saw its effectiveness in the Soviet Union, Eastern Europe, and Cuba. Yet most public health leaders preferred a more gradual approach that addressed several vaccine-preventable diseases simultaneously through routine immunization programs that could be sustained. They did not readily accept "vertical programs," such as mass immunization against polio.

Sabin lived in Cincinnati, Ohio, USA, where he was an honorary member of the Rotary club. He often spoke to clubs and district conferences and in 1980 was invited to address the Rotary International Convention in Chicago. He ended his speech with the challenge for Rotary to become involved in mass immunization against polio.[2]

The Chicago convention—indeed, the entire 1979-80 year—was a special occasion. It was Rotary's 75th anniversary, and the RI Board had for several years been discussing how they could launch an extraordinary mission to commemorate this milestone.

The efforts of three consecutive RI presidents led to the creation of the 3-H program, which eventually grew into PolioPlus. W. Jack Davis of Bermuda, who assumed the presidency in July 1977, suggested that the 75th anniversary planning committee consider a program linked to the United Nations International Year of the Child, in 1979. Davis had spoken at the District 730 Conference in Pennsylvania in 1973, immediately following the Guatemala NID, and vividly remembered Dr. Hingson. Davis invited Hingson to an RI Board meeting, during which the doctor demonstrated his peace gun and challenged RI to hold an NID on each continent during the International Year of the Child.[3]

Davis sent his executive assistant, Herbert A. Pigman, to WHO's headquarters in Geneva, Switzerland, to discuss how Rotary could follow through on

Hingson's proposal. WHO was not encouraging. They painted a bleak picture of the cost—both in manpower and economic terms—of inoculating the world's children against polio. And they dismissed Rotary's one-time immunization project in Guatemala as nothing more

RI PRESIDENT CARLOS CANSECO (LEFT) PRESENTS THE 1985 ROTARY AWARD FOR WORLD UNDERSTANDING AND PEACE TO DR. ALBERT SABIN, DEVELOPER OF THE ORAL POLIO VACCINE, AT THE 1985 RI CONVENTION IN KANSAS CITY.

than a well-intentioned effort that would hinder, rather than help, WHO's ultimate goals. By the time Pigman reported to the RI Board at its next meeting, Davis's year was almost over. The Board deferred action until the new president took office on 1 July 1978.

That president was Clem Renouf of Nambour, Queensland, Australia. When the Board first considered Hingson's global immunization idea, it realized that clubs might object to the "corporate" nature of such a project, and resolution 23-34 still discouraged RI from suggesting collective campaigns or projects for individual clubs.

Renouf created a committee named Health, Hunger and Humanity (3-H), which would act as a clearinghouse to link clubs with World Community Service needs and those with the resources and desire to help meet them. Participation by clubs and Rotarians was voluntary. The Board directed that if there was to be a polio immunization program, it should fall under the auspices of the 3-H Committee.

234

A VOLUNTEER LOADS VACCINE CARRIERS BEARING THE KICK POLIO OUT OF AFRICA LOGO FOR DELIVERY TO GHANA. DISTRICT 6440 (ILLINOIS, USA) PURCHASED 3,400 CARRIERS THROUGH POLIOPLUS PARTNERS.

Renouf had made another proposal to the Board in his closing weeks as president-elect. It led to the creation of a 75th Anniversary Fund composed entirely of voluntary contributions that would be collected over a two-year period beginning in 1978. The funds would be spent on "major international service programs, for example, a worldwide effort for the immunization of children and adults" over no more than five years.[4]

At the 1978 RI Convention in Tokyo, Rotarians were enthralled by Dr. Robert Hingson's keynote address, his peace gun demonstration, and his vision for an international Rotary immunization campaign. As if in a one-two punch, incoming RI President Clem Renouf told the 39,834 attendees how the new Health, Hunger and Humanity Grants program and immunization projects might be linked and paid for from contributions to the 75th Anniversary Fund. The response was immediate. Contributions poured in before the convention was over.

4   Rotary International, Board minutes, Decision 360, April-May 1978.
5   THE ROTARIAN, October 1979, 45.
6   M.A.T. Caparas to Willmon White, 7 May 2000.

Rotary International asked WHO for advice on where to begin. The reply suggested Indonesia, Papua New Guinea, or the Philippines. In early 1979, Dr. Sabino "Benny" Santos of the Rotary Club of Malolos, Philippines, submitted a proposal to 3-H asking that it undertake a polio immunization project.[5] He made a compelling case. Of the 32 nations in WHO's Western Pacific region, the Philippines accounted for 45 percent of all polio cases and 74 percent of all polio deaths. Furthermore, Rotary had a very strong presence in that country—an enormous benefit to the necessary mobilization of volunteers. A former secretary of health was in Benny Santos's club, and the incumbent secretary of health was a member of the Rotary Club of Manila.

Renouf visited the Philippines in March 1979 and met with leading Rotarians, government officials, and WHO representatives to finalize an action plan. Coincidentally, while these meetings were taking place, he received word from RI headquarters that Connaught Laboratories of Canada had discovered a cache of 700,000 doses of tetanus vaccine that was about to expire. Could Rotary use the donation? Elpi Valencia, former Philippine minister of health and a member of the Rotary Club of Malolos, was present and immediately accepted the offer.[6] Within hours, arrangements had been made to fly the vaccine—free of charge—from Toronto to Manila, and Clem Renouf was able to see the very first project of his beloved 3-H program come to fruition.

There were still many hurdles to overcome before the Philippine polio project would be launched. Some were legal, others governmental and logistical. Renouf left office having moved the ball much closer to the goal line, but it would be left to his successor to actually kick it into the net.

James L. Bomar Jr. of Shelbyville, Tennessee, USA, took office as RI president on 1 July 1979. Rotary approved US$760,000 for oral polio vaccine for the very first 3-H project, which would immunize one million children in the Philippines. In September, Bomar

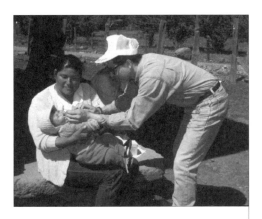

ROBERTO CHÁVEZ GARCIA OF THE ROTARY CLUB OF
MADERA, MEXICO, HELPS IMMUNIZE CHILDREN AT A
REMOTE PIMA INDIAN VILLAGE.

flew to Manila to witness the 3-H kickoff, but first Rotary needed Philippine government permission. Bomar, his aide, Past RI Director (and future president) Charles Keller, and Rotary's new director from the Philippines, M.A.T. Caparas (also to become an RI president), were greeted in the presidential palace by head of state Ferdinand Marcos. It was a very cordial meeting; but when the subject turned to his permission for the immunization project, Marcos said: "I have nothing to do with that sort of thing. You'll have to deal with my wife. She's the interior minister."

Luckily, they were able to get an appointment with Imelda Marcos, but at the appointed hour, she did not show up. Finally, the First Lady appeared—and she was livid. "Look what you Americans are saying about my husband and me," she said bitterly, waving a critical article in *Time* magazine. "Why should I do anything to help you when you spread such lies?"

Bomar and his party were taken aback. But then they quietly assured Mrs. Marcos that in the United States, where there is freedom of the press, the government cannot control what a magazine prints and that, in any case,

Rotary was not an American organization. They told how her signature on the authorization would mean the difference between life and death for thousands of the children in her country. She hesitated momentarily, then gave the project her approval.

The Rotarians immediately drove to a poor neighborhood in North Makati City where hundreds of mothers were already lined up with their children. Many other youngsters were crawling around in the filth and mud, their limbs withered by polio. For them, the vaccine came too late.

ROTARIANS USE ALL METHODS OF TRANSPORT, INCLUDING BOATS, DONKEYS, AND CAMELS (SEEN HERE IN INDIA), TO DELIVER POLIO VACCINE TO REMOTE AREAS.

MARCUS OLENIUK

> "The contribution of Rotary is more than money. It is the commitment of individual Rotarians to polio eradication which has made this initiative a unique collaboration between the public and private sectors."
>
> *Hiroshi Nakajima, director-general*
> *World Health Organization*

Jim Bomar administered the first dose, squeezing two drops of vaccine onto a little girl's tongue. As he did so, he saw tears in her mother's eyes. Then he felt a pull on his trouser leg. Looking down, he saw one of the "crawlers" who had been paralyzed by polio. "Thank you!" the boy said. "Thank you! Thank you!" He paused as if to remember the next word. "Rotary!" Then he lifted his withered arm from the dirt and pointed to the baby to whom Bomar had just given the vaccine. "My sister!" he said, with a proud smile.

Nobody knew it then, but that little girl was to have a most profound effect on the future course of Rotary.

Past RI Director Sabino Santos of the Philippines recalls a sidelight to the immunization story in his country. "Even before we received the first shipment of OPV (oral polio vaccine) with money authorized by the RI Board, we received 500,000 doses in a shipment as a gift from Italian schoolchildren to the schoolchildren of the Philippines. This came through the efforts of Past District Governor Sergio Mulitsch and the newly chartered Rotary Club of Treviglio e della Pianura Bergamasca. The Italian schoolchildren had donated their snack money to purchase the vaccine."

The 75th Anniversary Fund's mandate was to spend all the money it accumulated within five years. But what then?

RI's 1981-82 President Stanley E. McCaffrey established the New Horizons Committee to propose a long-term direction for Rotary. He named Cliff Dochterman as chair. Dochterman, a creative thinker, had been one of the three original co-chairs of the 3-H Committee and would go on to become RI president in 1992-93.

The New Horizons Committee asked Rotarians worldwide for suggestions and then reviewed each of the 2,900 responses. They were intrigued by an idea proposed by Dr. John L. Sever, a past district governor from Potomac, Maryland. By profession, Sever headed the infectious diseases branch of the U.S. National Institutes of Health and was a longtime member of the 3-H Committee. He proposed that Rotary should immunize every child on earth against vaccine-preventable diseases—by the end of the century.

The committee modified his suggestion slightly before recommending it to the full RI Board in 1982, and after a few additional changes the official decision was adopted: to immunize "all of the world's children against polio by the time of the 100th anniversary of Rotary International in the year 2005."[7] They called the program Polio 2005. It would be Rotary's birthday present to the world. The name would later change to PolioPlus in recognition of

---

7   Rotary International, Board minutes, Decision 286, February 1982.

the program's support of a global health effort to combat additional vaccine-preventable childhood diseases.

The 3-H Committee moved Polio 2005 forward with projects in Bolivia, Haiti, Morocco, and Sierra Leone. It was Dr. Carlos Canseco of Monterrey, Mexico, who became RI president in 1984, who lit a spark in the struggling plan. Canseco had been on the front line of his own country's polio eradication efforts in Mexico and was a friend of Sabin. He was a voice of experience, a strong proponent of the mass immunization method.

"If you simply provide money for the country to vaccinate their children in small groups throughout the year, it is a total waste," said Canseco. "It's like whistling into the wind." He argued Sabin's point that if every child in the country is given the polio vaccine on the same day they all become immune simultaneously. If the occasional child is missed, they will likely pick up the immunity just from contacts with those who have received the vaccine virus. Through his personal drive and the work of several friends who were true believers in the program's potential, WHO accepted Rotary as an official non-

238   governmental organization (NGO) partner.

Canseco appointed a Polio 2005 Committee, chaired by Sever and advised by Sabin. By October 1984, the committee had developed a plan:

1. Raise $120 million to provide oral polio vaccine to the world's newborns for five years.

2. Marshal armies of Rotary volunteers to help deliver it.

President Canseco officially announced the Polio 2005 program to the Rotary world on 23 February 1985—Rotary's 80th birthday. Eight months later, at the 40th anniversary of the United Nations, RI General Secretary Herb Pigman announced Rotary's plan to heads of state who had gathered at a meeting to set a goal to raise immunization levels to 80 percent for all children worldwide. Rotary's commitment electrified the global health community. Such an undertaking by an NGO was unprecedented in its financial scope and program potential. Beleaguered public health workers could now call on the business know-how and resources of a million Rotarians to help them overcome obstacles to polio vaccine delivery.

An enormous amount of work loomed ahead. No one organization could successfully undertake such a project single-handedly. Rotary teamed

DURING A NATIONAL
IMMUNIZATION DAY
IN JANUARY 1999,
ROTARIANS HELP
HEALTH OFFICIALS AND
GOVERNMENT LEADERS
IMMUNIZE 125
MILLION CHILDREN IN
INDIA AGAINST POLIO.

up with WHO, UNICEF, and, later, the U.S. Centers for Disease Control and Prevention (CDC); gradually they came to recognize Rotary as a valuable and trustworthy partner. Staff was trained at RI World Headquarters and new committees were formed solely to focus on what was soon renamed the PolioPlus Campaign.

There were two major challenges facing Rotary. The first was to raise $120 million. An International PolioPlus Campaign Committee chaired by Leslie Wright of Birmingham, Alabama, USA, organized the worldwide fundraising. It would be a learning experience at every Rotary level.

Rotary International hired a professional fundraising consultant, Community Counseling Service (CCS), who produced a detailed plan that most of the Rotary world followed like a road map. Rotary realized that all its other programs must continue to operate while the PolioPlus Campaign was being waged, so a new hierarchy of volunteers dedicated to PolioPlus was appointed to operate within the normal club and district structure. Past District Governor Walter Maddocks from Bermuda became campaign director; Past District Governor Jack Blane of Wheeling, Illinois, USA, who was the campaign's international executive coordinator, supported him. Both men worked full-time for two years as unpaid volunteers for the campaign.

They oversaw 44 national/multinational committees, and 11 international coordinators. Those Rotarians in turn provided guidance and direction to 84 national coordinators and were the main contact for the 450 district PolioPlus chairs. Within each district, these chairs assigned seven clubs to each of 3,300 area coordinators who were the liaison to more than 20,000 club PolioPlus chairs. It was a structure to rival many battle plans.

All of the planning reached a climax with the public announcement of the PolioPlus Campaign in New York City on 10 July 1987. RI President Charles Keller and his team of 467 governors worldwide made the campaign their priority. Ingenious campaign activity and normal district activity were somehow integrated.

As the campaign began, senior volunteers were trained to ask for major gifts—something Rotary had never done in its 80-year history. Despite their initial reluctance, they "followed the plan"—a CCS mantra—and Rotarian W. Clement Stone of Chicago made a $1 million gift. Australian Rotarian Les Whitcroft, who led the PolioPlus Campaign in his country, and his wife, Shirley (herself a polio survivor), made a US$250,000 gift. More major donors followed, and even the early skeptics began to realize that there was a purpose in "The Plan."

Other volunteers were trained to obtain government grants, and here came the benefit of Rotary's worldwide network of influential members. Canada, the United Kingdom, the United States, Germany—one by one governments of the world started making large gifts to Rotary's campaign to rid the world of the dreaded scourge of polio. It was a good investment. If it succeeded, the expenditure of polio immunization would no longer be necessary for any nation.

After the major gifts and personal pledges from individual Rotarians came fundraising activities. Rotarians in Argentina's District 488 helped "lick" polio by selling 40,000 commemorative stamps, raising more than $23,000.[8] Verneil Martin, wife of Past District Governor Doug Martin in Calgary, Alberta, Canada, produced a cookbook, *Among Friends*, that became the top-selling cookbook in Canada and raised $2 million. In Holland, the Rotaract clubs of Heemstede and Hillegom-Lisse built an amphibious cycle that could be propelled through the water by 36 people, four across and nine deep. The young adults pedaled their way through Holland, Belgium, France, and across the English Channel to England—raising $210,000 for PolioPlus.[9]

Gradually, Rotarians began to recognize they were engaging in a history-making event. Never before had Rotary embarked on a worldwide project. Never had they undertaken to raise $120 million. Never had they partnered with such visible agencies as WHO, UNICEF, and CDC. Rotary would never be the same again.

The fundraising campaign concluded at the RI Convention in Philadelphia in May 1988. For two years, PolioPlus Campaign Director Walter Maddocks and the thousands of volunteers on his team had set their sights on that date. To some, it seemed to arrive far too soon.

240

THOUSANDS OF ROTARIANS CELEBRATE ROTARY'S "FINEST HOUR"—RAISING MORE THAN US$219 MILLION FOR POLIO ERADICATION EFFORTS—AT THE 1988 RI CONVENTION IN PHILADELPHIA, PENNSYLVANIA, USA.

The second day of the convention, 24 May 1988, is remembered as one of the most exciting moments in Rotary's first century. The Civic Center auditorium was packed to overflowing as Maddocks commenced his roll call of each of the 44 national/multinational committee chairs. Lights had been strung around the auditorium; as each Rotary country announced its fundraising results, one bulb would light for every 800,000 children that could now be immunized. If this long "fuse" could be lit all the way to the end—representing $120 million—it would set off fireworks. As Maddocks moved alphabetically through the list of countries, the illuminated bulbs rounded the corner and began lighting up down the far side of the hall. A large screen reflected the accumulated total—as each region reported in, the applause grew ever louder. The illuminated bulbs represented millions of children who would be protected from polio. The tension became almost unbearable as the last few national committees reported.

Finally, 43 of the 44 committees had conveyed their totals and the screen showed the cumulative total: $100,163,580. Would Number 44 add $20 million to make the goal? With more than a little stage presence, Maddocks introduced Past RI Director Herbert G. Brown (later, RI president for 1995-96) to report the donations from the last region: the United States, Bahamas, Bermuda, and Puerto Rico. Brown reminded the audience that the clubs in the region had set goals totaling $78,406,000...another pause...it was five minutes before noon in the sweltering auditorium, but no one was looking at the clock as he continued. "The USA Committee has exceeded that goal and has actually raised $119,186,869, giving us a grand total for the international campaign of $219,350,449!"

8   THE ROTARIAN, April 1987, 22.
9   THE ROTARIAN, February 1988, 45.

The remaining lights lit up, the fireworks erupted, and a marching band burst onto the convention floor, but even the band was unheard by the 17,000 people clapping and shouting and hugging one another as 15,000 balloons fell from the ceiling and were summarily burst. It was a day when even RI President Keller cried—as did thousands with him. It was, as he declared and the commemorative certificates handed to each attendee read, "Rotary's Finest Hour."

It was during the convention that the World Health Organization ambitiously proposed changing the goal from *control* of polio to *eradication* by the year 2000 (with certification to come later), if Rotary would concur. After hurried consultation with directors, trustees, and campaign and task force leaders, President Keller affirmed Rotary's concurrence and commitment.

By 1993, Rotary's PolioPlus program had reached a critical stage. To coordinate its future involvement, The Rotary Foundation Trustees created the International PolioPlus Committee (IPPC). Past Director and Vice President William Sergeant of Oak Ridge, Tennessee, USA, was named chairman with the charge to manage Rotary's participation in the PolioPlus partnership on an ongoing basis.

For 12 years, Sergeant and the IPPC, with a steady infusion of experienced Rotary and PolioPlus leaders, carefully managed and distributed Rotary funds for vaccines, NIDs, laboratory development and surveillance, and program administration. They developed an efficient and harmonious working relationship with WHO, UNICEF, and CDC. They also created an active advocacy program to encourage participation by world governments.

The $219 million was topped off with late gifts and then was invested wisely while the projects were evaluated and selected. As a way to keep Rotarians involved after the end of the campaign, Rotary International created

WILLIAM SERGEANT, CHAIRMAN OF THE INTERNATIONAL POLIOPLUS COMMITTEE, MEETS WITH HILLARY CLINTON AT THE WHITE HOUSE IN 1997.

NIGERIAN ROTARIANS DELIVER ORAL POLIO VACCINE IN A COOLER
SO THAT IT REMAINS EFFECTIVE.

PolioPlus Partners. Just as clubs had been able to do with World Community Service projects, now individuals, clubs, or districts could choose a specific funding need. It was as easy as picking items off a menu. By the time a last-minute $80 million "top-off" campaign was completed in 2002-03, Rotary had committed more than $500 million to immunize the children of the world against polio. This last effort was led by RI President Bhichai Rattakul; Trustee Chairman Glen Kinross; Foundation Trustees Luis Vicente Giay and James Lacy; Herbert Pigman; Dr. Robert S. Scott of Cobourg, Ontario, Canada; Louis Piconi of Pittsburgh, Pennsylvania, USA; Jack Blane; and the RI polio eradication fundraising campaign staff under Division Manager John Osterlund.

The fundraising effort having exceeded Rotary's fondest dreams, the second challenge Rotary faced was the logistical path that would lead to immunizing every child on earth against polio. No one organization could successfully undertake such a project single-handedly.

Herb Pigman, who since his first exploratory trip to WHO in Geneva had twice served RI as general secretary, was pulled from retirement to direct Rotary's International Immunization Task Force. His task was daunting. He needed diplomacy and persuasiveness to even earn a seat at global health conferences next to health ministers and such venerable institutions as WHO and UNICEF—each of whom had reason to be skeptical of well-intentioned NGOs who had promised much but delivered little.

When word spread that Rotary had more than $200 million to spend on vaccine, it was swamped with requests from all over the world. Rotary's original pledge—to provide oral polio vaccine for five years—was fulfilled. But it soon became clear that a rigorous selection and verification process was required to deploy remaining PolioPlus funds.

What distinguished the PolioPlus eradication effort from past projects by governmental agencies was its vastness. The only *effective* polio immunization program is one where there is blanket coverage of every child under five. Rotary has 1.2 million members, and when those Rotarians' spouses, family members, friends, and associates were included, it was a potential volunteer force of many millions. The brilliance of the partnership between Rotary and organizations such as WHO, UNICEF, and CDC was that each party brought its strengths to the program. WHO has expertise without which Rotary could never have completed a single year of its eradication plan. But Rotary had the infrastructure—clubs and Rotarian volunteers in more than 165 countries and geographic regions around the world—and financial resources that its partners so desperately needed.

The Global Polio Eradication Initiative, as it came to be called by WHO, has three prongs to support a country's routine immunization program: mass immunization, surveillance, and "mop-up."

Once a country agreed to conduct a National Immunization Day, it worked with the global partner organizations to coordinate when it should be held and how many doses must be ordered. Before the NID, Rotary conducted social mobilization activities—spreading the word by working with the local government, TV and radio stations, and religious and community leaders. Every mother, every child, and every schoolteacher was informed that on the designated day every child under five should be brought to an immunization site. In Turkey, leaflets were dropped from helicopters; in Indonesia, imams used the Koran to support the impending immunization day; in Sudan, volunteers performed informational skits as they traveled from village to village.

In some places wars were interrupted; both sides agreed voluntarily to lay down their arms in Days of Tranquility so that the children could be immunized against polio. In the Democratic Republic of the Congo, torn apart by war for decades, both sides of the conflict put their guns away and helped the 250,000 volunteers and health workers immunize 8.8 million children. The same happened for 600,000 children in Sri Lanka, 5.4 million children in Sudan, and 5.7 million in Afghanistan. Once the NID was over, fighting resumed. Days of Tranquility offered brief moments of hope in a world too full of war and disease. But many volunteer Rotarians risked their lives to immunize the children. One example is Dr. Bill Sprague of Grand Rapids, Michigan, USA. He traveled in dangerous areas of Afghanistan, Cambodia, Somalia, and Sudan to coordinate PolioPlus efforts. Rotarians in Angola and Peru braved danger to deliver the precious vaccine.

In an NID, health workers mapped out the entire country, determined vaccine requirements, refrigeration needs, and how the workers and vaccine equipment would be transported. During an NID in Peru, the Shining Path

244

DURING A NATIONAL IMMUNIZATION DAY IN MARCH 1995, THE ROTARIANS
OF SAN PEDRO IN THE PHILIPPINES SHADE AN INFANT FROM THE INTENSE HEAT
DURING VACCINATIONS IN A DEPRESSED BARANGAY. THE PHILIPPINES WAS THE
FIRST COUNTRY TO RECEIVE A GRANT TO IMMUNIZE CHILDREN AGAINST POLIO.

guerillas temporarily laid down their arms so Rotarians could work at 2,300
vaccination stations, make 28,000 lunches for the health-care workers and
volunteers, and donate the use of more than 800 vehicles to transport the vaccine around the country.[10]

The second prong of the campaign was the surveillance undertaken
by the country's national health authorities. Twice (and sometimes three or
more times) each year, every child under the age of five received two drops of
oral vaccine. From the grassroots to the national level, WHO and CDC moni-
tored every reported outbreak of polio. If a new case was suspected—and
people were sometimes even offered cash rewards for reporting a new case
of polio—a stool sample was collected and rushed to the nearest approved
laboratory for testing. This enabled the partners to know with certainty how
well the program was working and to quickly direct extra resources to a specific area in the event of a sudden outbreak of polio. Only when a country
had no new cases of polio for three consecutive years could it be certified as
polio-free.

Developing this worldwide network of approved laboratories was essential to surveillance and the success of PolioPlus. Rotary provided key funding
for the laboratories. Rotary's partners insisted the long-term benefits from
this laboratory network would provide the world with a priceless by-product
in dealing with other diseases long after polio was eradicated.

The final phase of the program, called "mop-up," targeted children who were missed during an NID, and blanketed an entire area where surveillance had identified a new case of polio. The health-care workers used a variety of methods to identify the children they had inoculated: an ink mark or a chalk sign on their door. After the NID, volunteers went from door to door, village to village, asking who might have been missed. In Cambodia, they used dugout canoes to reach the boat people; in India and Thailand, they rode elephants to find tiny gatherings of people deep inside the jungle; and in Burkina Faso, they used camels.

Brazil averaged 2,330 reported cases of polio each year before the Polio-Plus Campaign began; after the NIDs started in 1980 it reported only 122 cases the next year, 69 in 1982, and 45 in 1983. The entire Western Hemisphere, including all of Latin America, was certified polio-free in 1994. In 2000, the huge and populous nation of China and the entire Western Pacific region were certified polio-free. The Europe region, including nations in the former Soviet Bloc, was certified free of polio in 2002.

As the 21st century dawned, polio had not been eradicated from the entire world, but it had been dramatically reduced—far beyond what most thought possible. The major pockets of the disease remained in Africa and South Asia. Africa had often been an almost impossible venue for NIDs because of ongoing conflicts across the continent and the difficulty of transportation and communication.

India had initially been reluctant to hold NIDs and therefore got a late start, compared to other countries. However, once NIDs began, the statistics were simply staggering. India has more children than any country on earth. When it held its first NID in December 1995, there was only enough money to immunize children under three—but two million health workers and volunteers manned 600,000 immunization posts and inoculated 90 million children in a single day. The next year, with four- and five-year-olds now included, the

LUIS FERMIN OF PERU, LAST POLIO VICTIM IN THE WESTERN HEMISPHERE, AT THE POLIOPLUS STATUE IN FRONT OF ONE ROTARY CENTER IN EVANSTON

number rose to 127 million, and in 2000, 152 million children received the two lifesaving drops of oral polio vaccine during a single PolioPlus NID.

In February 2003, India launched the largest mass immunization campaign ever undertaken against polio to combat the worst polio epidemic in recent history. Sixty-five Rotarians from the United States and Canada joined tens of thousands of Indian Rotarians, health workers, and other volunteers in the six-day effort to administer oral vaccine to 165 million children under age five. They enlisted the support of Indian film and cricket stars, community leaders, and Muslim clerics to publicize the campaign and allay fears of the dangers of the vaccine. Deeply concerned about the epidemic in the state of Uttar Pradesh, a PolioPlus grant of about $5 million was awarded, bringing Rotary's total contributions in India to more than $46 million.

By 1997, two-thirds of the world's children were being immunized against polio at one of the NIDs held in 80 countries. Before PolioPlus, in 1988, there were 350,000 new cases of polio in 125 countries each year. By the end of 2002, only seven countries were polio-infected, and they reported 1,919 cases—*a 99 percent decline.*[11]

"If you had not started PolioPlus in 1985," the late Dr. Albert Sabin once told Rotarians, "there would, at the time of Rotary's 100th birthday in 2005, be eight million more children with polio—and probably 800,000 deaths during that period." He should know; his oral polio vaccine saved millions of defenseless children.

Throughout the fundraising campaign, Walter Maddocks reminded Rotarians: "PolioPlus is not about raising money; it is about saving children." And so it is as PolioPlus nears its glorious conclusion. It is not only about the new respect that Rotary has earned on the global stage. It is not only about how PolioPlus had broadened the horizons of Rotarians who now see service opportunities far beyond their club raffle. It is about the babies whose names we will never know but whose lives were protected and improved. It is about the two billion children saved from iron lungs and early deaths and lifetimes in leg braces. But for every one of them…*every single one of them*…there are mothers, fathers, sisters, and brothers saying in 100 languages just what Jim Bomar heard when he immunized that first child: "Thank you! Thank you! Thank you! Rotary!"

11 Rotary International – PolioPlus Department, "New Polio Eradication Milestones," 1 July 2001.

Chapter 21 — A Day in the Life of Rotary International

"Today, we welcome you into membership of the Rotary Club of Greenwich, England, and with this membership come some significant benefits—but also some serious obligations." The club president pauses to affix a shiny new Rotary pin on the jacket lapel of the new member, a computer programmer who was invited by his bank manager to join Rotary. "You will quickly find new friends here and will enjoy the fellowship both at our weekly meetings and also at the social events. You will not be the first person to say 'I have received so much more from my membership in Rotary than I gave.'

"Speaking of the world, you will discover that membership in our club here in Greenwich joins you in fellowship with 1.2 million other Rotarians in 31,000 clubs in 166 countries and geographic regions. It is your passport to a world of service.

"As you know, the Royal Observatory here in Greenwich is where the line of zero degrees longitude passes. You have probably straddled that line, literally having one foot in the Western Hemisphere and one foot in the eastern. Time itself is measured from this very place—Greenwich Mean Time, or GMT. We are now at noon, or 12:00 GMT, and at this very moment, it is one

Scott Dick (with shovel) of the Rotary Club of Carmel Valley, California, USA, and other volunteers prepare the site for a local high school garden project.

Overleaf: Students in Jalalabad, Afghanistan, welcome Stephen Brown and Fary Moini of the Rotary Club of La Jolla Golden Triangle, California, USA. The club raised US$100,000 in 2002 to build a school for refugee children returning from Pakistan.

hour later approximately every 15 degrees you travel east and one hour earlier for roughly every 15 degrees you travel west.

"At this very moment, Rotarians of every race, religion, and nationality are involved in service to humankind in every time zone on earth. The sun never sets on the service performed by Rotary."

GMT –1 hour

It is a cold, blustery day in Praia, capital of Cape Verde, and the harsh wind howls off the Atlantic, making life miserable for those standing in line at the vaccination post. It is a price they gladly pay. For today, Rotary International and its partners WHO and UNICEF are holding a National Immunization Day in Cape Verde and eight other countries in West Africa, just 312 miles (500 km) to the east.

For two weeks, Rotarians from this scattered island nation's two Rotary clubs have been spreading the word by every possible medium, telling mothers to bring their young children to be protected against polio today. The infant mortality rate here is 10 times greater than that in Portugal, from which Cape Verde gained its independence in 1975.

Today, the 43 members of the Rotary Club of Praia feel truly connected to the global organization whose gearwheel emblem they proudly wear: they have seen the logistical support and assistance from Evanston and Geneva. For four hours, they—and the family members, friends, and co-workers they recruited as volunteers—have been gently placing two drops of oral polio vaccine into each child's mouth, forever saving each from the disease that has crippled and killed so many millions in previous generations.

It's 11 a.m. and they have already immunized more than 1,000 children at this post alone. It is a good day to be a Rotarian in the Cape Verde Islands.

MARIE-IRÈNE RICHMOND-AHOUA, THE FIRST WOMAN CLUB PRESIDENT IN WEST AFRICA, IMMUNIZES A CHILD AGAINST POLIO IN CÔTE D'IVOIRE IN 2001.

GMT –2 hours

"There he is!" As Lou Capozzoli points, a Cessna 182 drops beneath the low cloud that extends almost to the ground and, in a driving blizzard, touches down on the runway. The pilot taxies over and opens his door. "Welcome to Greenland!" says Lou, who has landed his Beech Baron 20 minutes earlier.

It is 10 a.m. in Kangerlussuaq, and the Cessna is the last of five aircraft in the transatlantic aerial convoy to land at the former U.S Air Force base at what was called Søndre Strømfjord. There are Americans, Canadians, and a Belgian in the group; some are pilots, others passengers. The common denominator is that they are all Rotarians, members of a Rotary Fellowship group called the International Fellowship of Flying Rotarians (IFFR). They are flying to Europe to attend an RI Convention and meet with Rotary friends in five countries.

"IFFR is a way for us to combine our two favorite passions," says Marcus Crotts, a North Carolina engineer. "We all love flying, and we love Rotary." Capozzoli adds that he has joined other IFFR members in flying to RI Conventions in the United States, Europe, and Latin America and has hosted Rotarians from nine countries in his aircraft.

Such activities go to the genesis of Rotary—they foster fellowship and goodwill. But these flying Rotarians also use their aircraft for service projects. Many IFFR members have flown critically ill patients from remote areas to hospitals; others have used them to fly in food and other relief supplies following natural disasters. Still others have used their aircraft to deliver PolioPlus workers and vaccine to immunization posts in villages that are inaccessible by road.

GMT −3 hours

In the ramshackle shantytown of Sovaco da Cobra—literally translated as "spine of the snake"—there were hundreds of men, women, and children who neither had a fish, nor knew how to fish, figuratively speaking. Children never fully developed, teenagers became vulnerable to disease, adults died young; everyone lived without hope.

Then the women of Rotary heard about Sovaco da Cobra, on the cluttered outskirts of Recife, Brazil, a community of mostly female-led families left alone by husbands who had abandoned them or died an early death. It is 9 a.m. in Sovaco da Cobra, and three members of the Rotary Club of Recife Treze de Maio have come to help. Moema Marques, Celinha dos Santos, and Lucia Mergulhão are the "wind beneath the wings" of one of Rotary's most worthy community service projects in South America.

They stop at the Dona Teresinha Feeding Center—launched by their Rotary club—which has quickly become the focal point of the neighborhood. One hundred children come in each day for nutritious meals. It also serves as a training ground for the local women, who leave their children at the Dona Teresinha Daycare Center while they learn a skill or work at the feeding center. Then the Rotarians move on to the laundry cooperative.

The Rotary Club of Recife Treze de Maio partnered with the Rotary Club of Whitby, Ontario, Canada, between them raising US$35,000 to build a commercial laundry. It has communal toilets, day care, and a 120-meter deepwater well from which they draw fresh, safe potable water.

Originally, 35 women of the shantytown were trained to operate the laundry cooperative; today, 100 work there. They collect dirty laundry from

THE ROTARY CLUB OF OSAKA HIRANO, JAPAN, SUPPORTS THE RESEARCH AND EDUCATION CENTER FOR DISABLED CHILDREN IN HO CHI MINH CITY, VIETNAM.

Recife's wealthier residents and commercial establishments. Then the all-woman work teams clean the garments, iron and fold them, and return them to the customers.

"It is a miracle to see what is happening here," says Santos. "For our club this is a great community service project. But to the 300 women of Sovaco da Cobra—almost all of whom were unemployed and living in deplorable conditions with no food for their families, not even safe drinking water—for them, this represents hope."

"For the first time in years," adds Marques, "they have their self esteem."

GMT –4 hours

"I have traveled all over the world, both when I was RI director and also on my own account, but there is no greater feeling than seeing Rotary at work in your home community," says Jamil E. Dunia of Caracas, Venezuela.

It is 8 a.m. on a hot, humid morning in the poor Barlovento district of Caracas, and Dunia is showing how a Rotary club with only 39 members can make such a positive impact in their community. The Caño-Negro Development Project includes 13 programs that provide preventive health care, a life skills academy, early learning center, small industry development, library, and community garden that provides fresh fruit and vegetables.

Members of the Rotary Club of Antimano and their families take turns as advisers and teachers in each of the project's programs, and the club has tracked significant improvements in the health and development of the neighborhood.

GMT –5 hours

It is 7 a.m. in Santarém, Para, Brazil, and the heat and humidity already feel like the inside of a Turkish bath. Santarém is where the mighty Amazon and Tapajos rivers meet: the "Wedding of the Waters." It could just as aptly be called the "Wedding of the Watercraft," for it is in Santarém that oceangoing ships and dugout canoes meet to exchange passengers and freight between the Amazon communities and the rest of the world.

Ritje Rihatinah is a Rotarian dentist from Bali, Indonesia, who is spending 30 days in Santarém as a Rotary volunteer. As she walks to work along the bustling waterfront, she reflects on how she has been able, through Rotary, to use her vocation to serve others. She is volunteering at the Fundação Esperança, a multidisciplinary healthcare clinic founded in 1973 by a Franciscan priest who became a medical doctor.

254

Rihatinah has tended to patients from various jungle tribes who traveled to the clinic by canoe. Fundação Esperança is their only hope for relief from suffering, and it is strongly supported by the Rotary Club of Santarém (District 4720) and The Rotary Foundation. The walls of the clinic are lined with more than 100 banners of the home clubs of the volunteers the Rotary Club of Santarém has hosted.

She arrives at the clinic at 7:15 a.m., and already there are patients waiting. She was pleasantly impressed on her first day to find such a modern facility. Rotary dentists and grants from The Rotary Foundation procured the six well-equipped dental units.

Rihatinah greets the two full-time dentists, three dental hygienists, two dental assistants, and two administrators. Then it is time to see her first patient of the day, a very scared little girl named Maria, whose infected tooth is unbearably painful. Maria is just one of the 1,500 patients Rihatinah will see pass through the clinic this month. When she is not providing dental treatments, extractions, root canal work, and restorative surgery, she will conduct preventive dentistry and dental health education seminars and in-service staff lectures on infection control.

"My experience here has been fascinating," she says. "The staff and volunteers—and the patients—have made me feel so welcome, and the teamwork has been unforgettable. My volunteer service will not end on this visit. I will continue to volunteer by offering my helping hands for the needy—in the Amazon or wherever I am needed."

GMT −6 hours

When Derek Evans, a Rotarian from Uxbridge, England, retired six years ago, he could not have imagined he would once again be working as a corporate "turnaround specialist" for a troubled pharmaceutical business. Yet here he is, at 6 a.m., checking in at Guatemala City airport for his flight home to London, where it is already noon. Over his final cup of Guatemalan coffee in the departure lounge, he reflects on the amazing events of the last three years.

On his first visit to Guatemala, Evans was asked to help a struggling local pharmaceutical manufacturer that was virtually bankrupt. The company produced low-cost generic drugs for poor and indigenous people but was losing money, paying 28 percent interest on bank loans, and was now unable to pay its vendors.

"Bankruptcy would have caused 60 job losses in a community already plagued by poverty and soaring unemployment," he recalls. "Alternative jobs were not available for those 60 families that were totally dependent on their continuing employment. Closing down the company was not an option."

Working with members of the Rotary Club of Guatemala City, Evans developed a recovery plan that was accepted by the company's banks and creditors. He showed the management how to focus on more profitable products and make the entire operation more efficient and productive.

Over the next two years, sales increased, cash flow improved, new products were introduced, past-due debts were paid, and the company operated profitably again. Then, Evans received word that the company's president had suffered a heart attack. "Could Derek please come back?" they pleaded. And so he did, this time for six weeks.

Since his last visit, sales had grown 1,000 percent, creating a cash flow crisis. Production capabilities were stretched beyond their limits. Many large orders could not be filled, and customers were refusing to pay their bills for partially filled orders, further exacerbating the cash flow problem.

Evans developed another action plan, bought manufacturing equipment, and subcontracted some packaging work. The company desperately needed larger facilities. He learned of a U.S. pharmaceutical company that had closed and wanted to sell its Guatemala City factory. Evans put together a complex three-way deal to buy the plant. All the pieces of the puzzle came together—the employees had their job security, the community's economy was no longer in dire risk of collapse, and the company had the space to expand production and a business plan to follow for the future. Rotarians find a way.

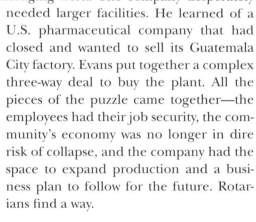

GMT −7 hours

As he pulls out of his driveway in California, he glances at his watch: 5 a.m. A terrible time to have left his warm bed and head out on a damp, foggy morning for the

ORTHOPEDIC SURGEON JOSEPH SERRA

San Francisco Airport. But it is a trip that Dr. Joseph Serra has made countless times before, the first and easiest leg on the long trip to Lilongwe, Malawi.

Joseph B. Serra is an orthopedic surgeon in the Rotary Club of Stockton, California. He has made five trips to Malawi over the past 10 years, during each of which he spends several weeks performing corrective surgery on "crawlers," as the locals call those polio victims with paralyzed legs.

The tragedy is that in many cases, their condition can be remedied by a surgical procedure, followed by a period with braces, then a cane. This time, eight fellow surgeons from Canada and the Netherlands will join Serra.

"It is a long trip, but I know how valuable we will be once we get there, so every hour spent on the journey is worth it," he says. "It's easy to get hung up on statistics. You know, we performed this many operations. But to me, it is the people, not the numbers, that are important. I can remember the names of the crippled little girls who would have never found a husband but who are now married with their own children. I get letters from one boy—Wilborn Chavula—who hitchhiked for 270 miles by truck, boat, and motorcycle to see us. He came in as a crawler; now he is a teacher with a wonderful family of his own. He insists on calling me 'Father' because he says I gave him life again. The fact that I have hundreds of Wilborns—and thousands more waiting— makes this a trip that I take not because I have to but because I want to."

GMT −8 hours

The Rotarians have long since abandoned hope of getting any sleep tonight. As members of the Youth Exchange program for District 5010, which covers Alaska, Yukon Territory, and Russia east of the Ural Mountains, they agreed to someone's idea of a "lockdown" for the students on the district conference weekend during their year in Alaska and Yukon.

Now it is 4 a.m. and the kids are at full strength. They have watched three movies, played countless games, consumed what must be every last pizza in Anchorage, and laughed and hugged and cried.

These young people are the front line in Rotary's campaign for peace and understanding. Some of their parents fought in wars against each other. Now there are 32 teenagers from France and Germany, Japan and Russia—and 18 other countries. While they have shared their cultures with host families in Canada and the United States, 32 students from District 5010 have spent a year abroad—and the Russian part of this vast district has been running its own Youth Exchange program.

As the young people exchange addresses with one another and their hosts, the Rotarians realize they are witnessing the germination of the seeds of peace. Suddenly, they are glad they are not sleeping through it all.

GMT −9 hours

Peter Haertsch blames it on jetlag. Just a few hours earlier, he had fallen into bed, exhausted from a full day of surgery. Now it is 3 a.m. here in Raro-

tonga, capital of the South Pacific's Cook Islands, and he is wide awake. It's been quite a first day, he thinks, and we have a hectic schedule ahead.

Haertsch is part of the visiting Interplast Australia team, a joint venture of volunteer medical practitioners from Rotary and the Royal Australasian College of Surgeons. During the next two weeks, they will operate on at least 50 patients using their vocational skills for corrective surgical procedures for cleft palates, congenital deformities, burns, or other crippling injuries.

"In four days, we performed 18 surgeries in the remote village of Aitu-taki," he notes. "We have an anesthetist with us, but there are no general anesthesia facilities in Aitu-taki, so we did everything we could under local anesthesia and brought those needing major surgery back here to Rarotonga. We will perform about six major surgeries a day here under general anesthesia and twice that many using local."

After the team was featured on Cook Islands Television, word spread quickly, and there has been a nonstop stream of patients. "It is so nice to be so warmly welcomed, with leis and shell necklaces," says Haertsch. "But the real pleasure for us is the knowledge that we are helping people. Many of our patients are considered outcasts because of their deformities. A few hours later, they are ready to be accepted back into their island's mainstream society."

GMT –10 hours

"You cannot quit; you're not even perspiring yet!" Hal Darcey of the Rotary Club of Metropolitan Honolulu, Hawaii, USA, jokingly chastises a fellow Rotarian for sitting down.

"I'm not quitting; it's 2 a.m. and I need some coffee," Dave Livingston shoots back.

The two friends are part of a team of Rotarians who have raised

US$18,000 to purchase 240 wheelchairs for the disabled in Thailand. Now they are racing the clock to stow them all into a shipping container at the Honolulu docks. Shortly after dawn, a giant crane will hoist the container onto a waiting ship that will deliver the cargo to Thailand.

"We partnered with the Wheelchair Foundation on this project, and they matched every dollar we donated, so our $75 bought a wheelchair," Darcey explains. "Imagine that! For $75, we provided a way for a child to attend school, for a father to get to work. Now that is worth missing a night's sleep."

GMT −11 hours

"It's 1 a.m. I have to go to bed!" Bo Hesselmark has just finished sorting the spectacles for tomorrow's patients. Bo and his wife, Helena, from Kvidinge, Sweden, are in Apia, Samoa, on a Rotary volunteer mission to this South Pacific nation. This is the only time they can talk, for during the day they throw themselves into their work. "So many patients, so little time," says Helena. The couple has committed 62 days to this volunteer assignment and has run clinics on four of the islands in Samoa. The Hesselmarks work as a team, testing and evaluating the prevalence of visual defects among the Samoan population. They have brought and dispensed 1,500 pairs of new reading glasses and are taking careful notes of vision status for a report they hope will lead to further eyeglass donations. They have also been training local opticians who are going to make prescription glasses in the new optical lab set up at the National Hospital. This is the first such lab ever in Samoa. All machines and equipment are donated from Sweden; now there is a great need for frames and lenses. Bo and Helena are not surprised to meet other Rotary volunteers in Samoa. They have also met volunteers in Africa during almost every mission and immediately they all speak the same language: of service. "Rotary is in action everywhere," Bo says, turning off the lights.

GMT −12 hours

A church bell nearby interrupts Jose Humberto Mello's thoughts as it peals out 12 slightly off-key rings from an onion-domed steeple. It is midnight in Petropavlovsk.

During the Soviet era, this city, and the entire Kamchatka peninsula, was home to numerous secret military bases. Foreigners—even Russians who did not live here—were forbidden to enter.

LISA MARTIN OF THE ROTARY CLUB OF ROCKPORT, MASSACHUSETTS, USA, WORKS ON THE GROUNDS OF A BILINGUAL PRIMARY SCHOOL IN MEXICO.

"What a difference a decade can make," Mello reflects. Today, Petropavlovsk-Kamchatskiy has two thriving Rotary clubs, and Mello, a member of the Rotary Club of São José do Rio Preto-Sul, Brazil, is 10 days into his 43-day mission as a Rotary volunteer.

He returns to his journal knowing that today's vivid memories will surely fade with the passage of time, and he is determined to capture them all.

Mello tells of the enthusiastic students in his English as a second language class. He writes about Vladimir, whose inquisitive mind wants to know about the world beyond the only city he has ever known. He recounts how young Valentina brought him flowers today and, as always, stayed late to show off her accomplishment: She has vowed to learn one new word of English every day for a year. He notes how, in addition to teaching English for four hours each morning, he has now agreed to teach classes in international business.

Culturally, Petropavlovsk is a world away from the business centers of London, New York, and São Paulo, where Mello studied and worked.

"Some people at home told me I should use this month to tour Europe or America. I suppose a skeptic might even challenge my time here as being too short to make a difference. But I see this as an opportunity to have a lasting impact on everyone I meet. I will forever cherish these times, and I believe my new friends will take to heart the simple message I am bringing them: the message of mutual understanding above winning an argument, of integrity above winning at all costs, of Service Above Self."

But Petropavlovsk is also literally at the end of the earth, 12 time zones east of Greenwich; when it is noon in London it is midnight the night before in Petropavlovsk. At this moment, while the new Rotarian is being inducted into the Rotary Club of Greenwich, it is 1 p.m. in war-ravaged Kosovo.

GMT +1 hour

"Leadership." Ron Brittan pauses to let the word sink in. "Community leadership is crucial to the rehabilitation and advancement of Kosovo." He should know. The acrid smell of tank shells had barely blown away when he and his father first came to Kosovo as Rotary volunteers, committed to the cause of peacemaking. Armed only with the best wishes of Brittan's Rotary club in Monterey Park, California, USA, the two men began a two-pronged campaign for Kosovo.

Brittan takes a few moments away from his work to discuss that word *leadership*. "The people of Kosovo have had little experience in leadership—ever. Over the centuries, they have been put down as inferior by numerous powers. In the past 50 years, first the Communists, then the Serbs, controlled everything. Even now, the international humanitarian relief organizations are telling them what to do.

"I have organized local communities into leadership groups, styled after Rotary clubs. I use a similar model with teenagers and young adults—forming community groups just like Interact and Rotaract clubs. Then, with other volunteers, I teach those community groups about leadership: how to plan, budget, organize, motivate; how to help one another; and all about the rewards of volunteerism.

"The first group we organized soon grew to over 100 members, and many of them were given specific assignments and responsibilities. It is incredible to see the transformation. When they learn to lead, to make their own decisions, to have a vision for their community, their self-worth rises through the roof."

GMT +2 hours

"It becomes a 'must' to volunteer over and over again, so we can help people reach our standard of democracy and standard of living," reasons Oswin Christel of the Rotary Club of Hanau, Germany. He is a veteran of 10 Rotary volunteer missions and is taking a brief lunch break at 2 p.m. in Auce, Latvia, on his latest such trip.

Christel and five Rotarian volunteers from Germany, New Zealand, and the United States have come to Latvia to help build a new hospital. The building they are converting was formerly the Communist Party headquarters, and Christel admits "getting goose pimples every time I walk downstairs past the sound-proofed detention room."

Luckily, Latvia is now enjoying happier times. Rotary is firmly reestablished here, and Rotarians appreciate the volunteer team's work. They work side by side with them on the job and insist on showing off their hospitality and their countryside in the evenings and on Sundays. "The mother of one of them even brought me fresh flowers and fresh-picked strawberries when she discovered it was my birthday," Christel says.

The team came to build a hospital, but they have accomplished so much more. They have built a sense of community and feeling of "belonging" by local Rotarians, who will soon deliver the very first medical center to the people of Auce.

GMT +3 hours

It is 3 p.m. in Musaka, Uganda. Yesterday, Rotarians from Maharashtra, India, and California, USA, arrived in Kampala, and Ugandan Rotarians drove them the four hours to Musaka.

There was little time for relaxation in the African afternoon.

The team of four Rotarian orthopedic surgeons, accompanied by Rajendra K. Saboo, his wife, Usha, and team leader Vittal Rao, spring into action. Rao is a past governor of Rotary District 3130, and Saboo was RI president in 1991-92; but both insist on being treated as rank-and-file Rotarian volunteers on this mission. They will work side by side with local Rotarians who have earned an impressive reputation within their community for caring for the needy.

"Usha and I arrived at the hospital early this morning to prepare the children which the orthopedic medical team had selected for surgery," explains Saboo. "There was no water, no soap, and even no children in the wards: many of them had run away." The team members had brought essential supplies and gradually located their young patients.

The Saboos cleaned the limbs of children who were due for surgery and then carried the children to the operating theater—there are no stretchers or trolleys here. As Saboo carried a beautiful three-year-old girl named Wantago to the operating theater, her smiles turned to terrified cries. A grandfather himself, he decided that the one place in the entire world that he needs to be right now is beside Wantago. As the anesthetist put her to sleep, she wrapped her entire little hand around Saboo's index finger.

Six hours later, she opens her eyes, and the first person she sees is Saboo, still holding her hand. He carries her gently to an anxious mother who speaks no English, but whose eyes speak the language of indescribable gratitude and joy.

But Saboo—and his fellow Rotarians—argue it is they who have been blessed. "I got more satisfaction from helping that one little girl than from anything I did during my entire year as RI president," he admits. "This was the best way I could celebrate my birthday, thanking God once again for this opportunity to serve humankind."

GMT +4:30 hours

While Raja Saboo comforts Wantago in Uganda, it is late afternoon—4:30 p.m.—in Afghanistan as a group of Rotarians from Pakistan, Hong Kong, and the United States arrive at Shalman and Mohammad Khail refugee camps. They are shocked at what they see. For Past RI Director Lynmar Brock Jr. of Philadelphia, Pennsylvania, William Benter of Hong Kong, and Tariq Akhtar Allawala of Karachi, this is the heartbreaking result of man's inhumanity to man.

These camps are home to 48,000 Afghans who have seen their homes, their families, and their livelihoods ripped apart by 20 years of civil war, foreign invaders, and natural disasters. While the rest of the world watched their suffering from the safety of their living rooms, these Rotarians sprang into action.

As individuals, they could have done little to help. But acting through Rotary International, they were able to open important diplomatic doors. Sadako Ogata of Japan, a former Rotary Foundation Ambassadorial Scholar who served as the UN high commissioner for refugees, cleared their mission and arranged a UN transport and security detail for them.

After a harrowing, nearly three-hour drive up the Khyber Pass, the Rotarians find the first tent city. They are deeply moved by the conditions in which several generations of displaced families live, deprived of the most basic human expectations.

They give each family a food package, present ecstatic children with colorful soccer balls, and help install large tanks for storing fresh water. Amputees—some of the victims of the million land mines that litter their homeland—are fitted with prostheses.

After their overland caravan of relief supplies is exhausted, the Rotarians discuss what they should do next. By the time they cross back into Pakistan, they will have a plan: They will spread the word throughout the Rotary world and launch a project—with grants from The Rotary Foundation—to build low-cost shelters, dig deep-water wells for safe drinking water, and provide vocational training programs.[1]

262

GMT +5 hours

It is 5 p.m. in Sri Lanka, and where better to take a tea break than on the very estate that produces some of the world's finest tea leaves.

"The guide books describe Sri Lanka as a tourist's paradise, with sun-bleached beaches kissed by waving palms," Keith Barnard-Jones tells a visitor. "But it is not the impression that I have received having spent the last five weeks here." He has not come to Sri Lanka for a suntan. Rather, the English physician who was president of Rotary International in Great Britain and Ireland (RIBI) in 1996-97 and RI director for 2001-03 has been using his professional expertise to provide oral cancer screening to workers on the tea estates.

"Oral cancer is rare in developed countries," Barnard-Jones explains. "But here, it constitutes up to 40 percent of all malignancies." He attributes this to the habit Sri Lankans have of chewing tobacco and betel and areca nuts, then storing the resultant liquid in their mouths for hours, often overnight.

For five weeks he and other Rotary volunteers, together with local Rotarians, have been traveling over treacherous terrain in the mobile dental ambulance, which was provided through a Matching Grant from The Rotary Foundation. The team includes doctors, nurses, and dental surgeons. When they spot a suspicious lesion, they are able to perform a biopsy right in the ambulance.

"We have found and treated more oral cancer patients in the past five weeks than the government recorded for the entire previous year," Barnard-Jones says. "As I prepare to return home, I realize how valuable this program is. It will save many lives in Sri Lanka, many lives indeed."

---

1 THE ROTARIAN, June 2002, 16.

GMT +5:30 hours

Eight local Rotarians gather for a 5:30 p.m. meeting in Jaipur, India, that will change the lives of people they have never met. Their committee is planning the next expansion of the Jaipur foot program.

Ram Chandra, a local sculptor, was deeply disturbed by the number of amputees and polio victims whose immobility made them outcasts. In 1968, using simple, cheap materials such as rubber and plastic, he created a prosthesis in collaboration with Dr. Pramod Karan Sethi (inventor of the Jaipur foot) that could be prepared and fitted in 45 minutes and was so light and mobile, its users could climb trees and pedal bicycles.

Rotary quickly supported the device's wide distribution. Rotarians have seen "crawlers" in their own city transformed into adults who can hold jobs and provide for their families.

In the next 90 minutes, the Rotarians will plan for an additional limb center in Afghanistan and a new one in Cambodia—both to serve amputee victims of land mines. They agree to ship 500 more prostheses to Bangladesh, send a committee member to Nicaragua on a site visit for a possible limb center, and call a Rotary orthopedic surgeon in Norway to see if he would return to India to perform corrective surgery on several young polio victims.

"It is amazing," muses one Rotarian. "In some of these places, such as Rwanda and Nepal, the people have never heard of Paris or New York, but they have heard of our city—and all because of the Jaipur foot that has given 100,000 of them a chance at living a normal life again."

GMT +6 hours

It is 6 p.m. in Dhaka, Bangladesh, where two Rotarians from the Rotary Club of Indore Uptown, India, are having a very busy day. Ram Avtar Kushwah and ophthalmologist Dr. Kishan B. Verma have come to Bangladesh for 39 days as volunteers on the Rotary Mobile Medical Boat.

The boat is equipped with modern equipment and laboratory facilities to treat patients with medical, dental, and eye problems. For 24 days every month, staffed by Rotary volunteers from around the world along with local paid employees, the boat sails to impoverished, rural river communities that have no other access than by water—and never see a doctor or dentist. To them, the Rotary Mobile Medical Boat is a lifeline, and the 60 or more patients that come aboard for treatment each day are cared for free of charge, thanks to the Rotary Club of Dhaka.

GMT +7 hours

Although it is 7 p.m. in Ho Chi Minh City, Vietnam, to Dr. Ro Chul Myung the heat and humidity feels as oppressive as it did at noon. But the workday is far from over for Myung and his fellow Rotarians from the Rotary Club of Sae Yeongdeungpo, Korea.

ROTARIAN KRISTIN DUCKART OF WISCONSIN, USA, GREETS CHILDREN IN
NIGERIA DURING A NATIONAL IMMUNIZATION DAY IN 2002.

264

Since 1999, he and several other members of his Rotary club have
traveled at their own expense to Vietnam to work in leper colonies. Today,
Myung, a dentist, has been conducting oral hygiene examinations and tooth
extractions for more leprosy victims than he can readily count.

"My club raised W30 million (US$26,000) to purchase and install this en-
tire dental suite," he says, pointing proudly to the modern equipment. "It was
needed so badly that we then raised enough to install complete dental clinics
at two additional leprosy centers in Ho Chi Minh City."[2]

Meanwhile, in northern Thailand, Elsie Choy is thrilled.

The Hawaiian native, a member of the Rotary Club of East Honolulu, is
two weeks into her five-week volunteer mission to teach English to the Lahu
Hill Tribe villagers. One student has lagged far behind the others, so Choy sin-
gled her out for after-school tutoring. Now, at 7 p.m., the teenage girl suddenly
grasps the concept and constructs a sentence in perfect English, pronouncing
each word correctly.

Such moments are precious to Choy. "These people have little formal
education and no English," she explains. "This severely limits their life and
career options. The impact of AIDS and illicit drugs in northern Thailand has
increased the number of wayward children and prostitution.

"By learning English, the Hill Tribe people have opportunities for good
jobs in tourism, the largest industry in northern Thailand. The local Rotary
clubs are very active in community service; and although I am only one person
in the big picture of Rotary's international service, I am very grateful for the
opportunity to raise the education level of the Lahu Hill Tribe people."

GMT +8 hours

"It's 8 p.m., but as long as we still have daylight, I want to keep working."
Kai Holsko, a master builder and Rotarian from Aabybro, Denmark, returns to
the roof he is installing on a low-cost housing unit in Santiago City, Philippines.

2   THE ROTARIAN, June 2002, 40.

Holsko has been here for six weeks, working on a joint project between his own District 1440 and the local District 3770. The mission: to construct 50 low-cost homes for local families who now live in abject poverty in cardboard and tin shanties. "I wanted to work from sunrise to sunset," he says. "But with scorching midday temperatures, we have to take a break and then work into the evening."

Holsko and the local Rotarians are involving the future homeowners in the project, too. They help with construction, and the Rotary Club of Santiago City is already planning programs that will teach them literacy, health education, and vocational training.

"These families have never lived in a house before," he says. "Already, they seem to be regaining their confidence in the future."

GMT +9 hours

The Tokyo meeting should have ended already. But even though it is 9 p.m., everybody knows an important task must be completed before they head for home tonight. The Rotarians are all members of clubs in Japan, and tonight they must select the foreign students to whom they will award scholarships to spend a year at a university in Japan.

They will soon be sending the good news to more than 1,000 young people in countries all over the world, and they will do so under the auspices of the Yoneyama Memorial Foundation. Umekichi Yoneyama, who was the founding president of the Rotary Club of Tokyo and later became managing director of Mitsui Bank, first introduced Rotary to Japan in 1920. He had a passion for peace and committed his life to the furtherance of Rotary's ideals.

In 1952, the Rotary Club of Tokyo initiated the Yoneyama Fund and raised the money with the slogan "Let's make contributions to the fund by giving up smoking for a month." From such a simple idea the fund has provided full scholarships, including travel and living expenses in Japan, to 18,000 students from 95 countries. It is funded by voluntary contributions from Japanese Rotarians. Only non-Japanese students are eligible, and during their year in Japan, scholars are "adopted" by local Rotary families and the club.

Tonight's meeting will last for another hour or more. But the result will be more young people from Cambodia, Vietnam, Malaysia, Nepal, Romania, Chile, and a dozen more countries all coming to Japan to further their education and expand their cross-cultural understanding.

GMT +10 hours

When the six Australian Rotarians finally arrive in Kokoda, Papua New Guinea, it is 10 p.m. They have endured a trip by jet, small plane, and truck—across what team leader Don Durie calls "the worst road in the world"—and are ready for a welcome shower and late dinner. Durie of the Rotary Club of Lindfield and Bob Young of Taree (both in New South Wales), brief the three builders, engineer, and handyman—all members of the Rotary Club of

Corrimal, and a similar team from Eaglehawk—about the project that would keep them busy for the next month.

"Previous Rotary volunteer groups built this 26-bed hospital," they explain. "It's literally a lifesaver to the indigenous people here. But now we need to add to it, and our task is to construct a new 10-bed ward that will have an X-ray room, adjoining darkroom, nurses' station, toilets, and laundry. This will serve as an isolation ward so that seriously sick patients won't be mixed in with the general ward population."

Durie explains that a feature of this and many other Rotary Australia World Community Service projects has been to train local people in the skills the volunteers bring. Some of the locals, who had no building expertise in the past, were trained by previous volunteer teams and became so adept that they have already prepared the roof trusses and dug a trench for the sewer lines.

By the time they retired for the night, much of the fatigue from the journey had disappeared, replaced by enthusiasm for the task ahead and the thought that an empty piece of land would, by the time they headed home, be a hospital ward.

GMT +11 hours

Jesse and Angela Loxton are enjoying their nightcap: a cool drink under the palm trees as a breeze eases the tropical heat. It's 11 p.m. here in the Solomon Islands, a scattered archipelago of almost 1,000 islands in the Southwest Pacific. It is an idyllic setting with pristine beaches, crystalline waters, and a rich culture.

But the Loxtons are not tourists; they are Rotary volunteers from Bardon, Queensland, Australia, who have committed six weeks to work in a unique program for women in the Solomon Islands. Jesse, a family doctor who belongs to the Rotary Club of Indooroopilly, and Angela have been teaching community health at the grassroots level in villages around the island of Malaita.

They start with the village leaders, then conduct seminars for the women on such topics as childbirth, nutrition, sanitation, general health, and disease prevention—with special emphasis on the prevention of malaria, which is prevalent in this region.

"We have 102 groups in nine zones on Malaita alone, and some of them are in such remote areas that the village leaders take up to five hours to reach us by canoe, truck, and foot," says Jesse. "As the program has grown, we cannot teach everyone in every village any more, so now we recruit the community leaders and train them to teach the program. It has evolved into a 'train the trainer' idea, which is also empowering for the indigenous people."

The days are long and the heat is oppressive, but as the Loxtons talk about their work, it is clear they feel they are making a significant difference in the lives of the people they teach each day. They realize that the things they normally take for granted—electricity, hot water for showers, and the ability to easily communicate—are less important than being able to effect meaningful change in the quality of the islanders' health and self-respect.

GMT +12 hours

At exactly midnight—12 hours ahead of those who are gathering in Greenwich—Rob Crabtree, governor of District 9920, walks into a four-room shack in a hillside squat outside of Suva, Fiji. Crabtree's district covers his hometown of Auckland, New Zealand, and then extends to Fiji, Samoa, American Samoa, Tonga, and Cook Islands. This is the district where each day on earth begins; the International Date Line bisects District 9920.

He is in Suva to make his official visit to the Rotary clubs of Fiji, and a local Rotarian is showing him some of the club's community service projects. "Bula!" says a woman with a three-month-old baby at her breast. "Come in!" As Crabtree surveys the tin shack this woman and her five children call home, he realizes that if he extends his arms to both sides, he can just about touch the left and right walls. There are no beds, no electricity, and only one old sofa. All cooking is done on a wood fire.

"What possible future is there for this family, with a husband who's unemployed and has little chance of finding a job?" he asks the local Rotarian. "The children have no books, no toys, and they have to sleep on newspapers on the floor every night."

"That's where we come in," the Rotarian answers as they negotiate the steep hillside on the way back to the road. "The Rotary Club of Suva is partnering with the Salvation Army and has established a food bank for families like this. The next step is to apply for a Matching Grant from The Rotary Foundation for low-cost shelters so the family can have a decent roof over their heads. Then we would like to establish a job-training program that will enable both men and women to use their talents to provide an income for their families. We cannot do it alone. But we can do it with help from the district and Rotary International."

And so it goes in the world of Rotary. From Fiji, you can almost look east across the imaginary date line and see yesterday. From Samoa, look west and you can see tomorrow. And what will tomorrow bring? To Rotarians, it will bring exactly what Rob Crabtree witnessed. He saw people in need being helped by local Rotarians; not just with charity but with programs and training that empower them to help themselves in the long term. He saw one small Rotary club joining together with others in its district and even around the world—and he saw the relatively new concept of Rotary partnering with other organizations and thus leveraging each other's strengths. And he saw people from one relatively affluent society reaching across cultural barriers to better understand and assist their brothers and sisters who were less fortunate. It is a day where the sun never sets on the work of Rotary and where the promise of tomorrow looks bright. It's a good day.

CHAPTER 22

ROTARY'S DREAMS FOR THE FUTURE

Chapter 22 ~ Rotary's Dreams for the Future

M en, my brothers, men the workers, ever reaping something new:

That which they have done but earnest of the things that they shall do:

For I dipt into the future, far as human eye could see,

Saw the Vision of the world, and all the wonder that would be."

So wrote Alfred, Lord Tennyson in "Locksley Hall"; and although he penned the words 75 years before anyone ever heard of a Rotary club, Rotarians could well have used it as the rallying cry in their first century of service. Rotarians are indeed workers—look at them cleaning the local park, building a ramp for wheelchair users, or volunteering at a PolioPlus immunization post. Yet they have never been satisfied with the status quo; they are always reaching forward for "something new." And the single driving force that compels them to offer Service Above Self is the "Vision of the world, and all the wonder that would be."

A world where businesses and individuals share Rotary's commitment to ethics.

A world where communities are safe from hunger, disease, crime, illiteracy, and homelessness.

A world where peace rules over all the people.

A world free of violence, terrorism, and war.

A world where polio is but a topic mentioned in history books.

A Rotarian with schoolchildren at a Subnational Immunization Day in Cameroon in 2003

Overleaf: Rotarian Jim Owens of Seattle, Washington, USA, participates in a National Immunization Day in Ethiopia in October 2002. The effort immunized 14 million children.

> "I believe that Rotary is and must be, above all, a 'Forge of Ideas'—a forge where ideas are born, wrought to be hammered into the shape of new, generous, and useful creations."
>
> *Joaquin Serratosa Cibils, Montevideo, Uruguay*
> *RI president, 1953-54*
> *1954 RI Convention in Seattle, Washington, USA*

Yet visions and dreams are not the exclusive preserve of poets and prophets. For as much energy as Rotary's leaders put into their work in the present tense, they exude an even greater measure of vision for the organization in the future. "I dream of a world where integrity becomes as essential as the air we breathe and the water we drink," said Herbert G. Brown of Clearwater, Florida, USA, upon becoming RI president in 1995. "I dream of a polio-free world. I dream of a world at peace. Ninety years ago, Paul Harris was only one man with a dream. He did not question, 'What can one man do?' He followed his dream and changed the course of history. Love is giving unselfishly to others. In Rotary, we know love by a different name. We call it Service Above Self."[1]

For as long as Rotary has existed, Rotarians have been somewhat reluctant to point to their accomplishments with pride. This has, in part, contributed to the general lack of appreciation or understanding of what Rotary is, and what it does, by the vast majority of the general public. In the future, Rotary—from the local club to the global organization—will be less inclined to hide its light under a bushel.

"Look at most successful companies and a large part of their achievement has come from their advertising and marketing," says Frank J. Devlyn of the Rotary Club of Anáhuac, Mexico, RI president for 2000-01. "Rotarians have always done great things for their communities, yet they kept it a secret, so people had no idea what Rotary did or what Rotarians were. Today that practice—along with many other outdated rules—has changed. In the future, Rotary will need to take its message beyond the confines of its members. We live in a public relations-oriented age. Without being boastful, we need to tell the community what Rotary represents. It's not a bunch of old men eating lunch. It is a force for good, both locally and globally. It stands for peace, education, integrity, the environment, relief from suffering, the development of humankind—and fellowship. Then people will want to join Rotary."

Rotarians have, for 100 years, tended to focus on the future rather than the past. When the Chicago club was still in its infancy, some members were saying, "Let's take this idea to other towns." Even before it had reached the largest cities in America, others were dreaming of expanding the movement overseas. When one club and then another reported in THE ROTARIAN the work they were doing for disabled children, a tidal wave swept

271

ROTARY'S DREAMS FOR THE FUTURE

---

1   THE ROTARIAN, July 1995, 29.

> "For 75 years, Rotarians have been 'torchbearers,' lighting the way to a better life for many people in many countries. Like Olympic runners, we received a torch from those before us—a torch of service that brings light to the shadow areas of mankind: intolerance, ignorance, disease, and hunger. . . . Let people know that Rotary cares—and acts."
>
> *James L. Bomar*
> *Shelbyville, Tennessee, USA*
> *RI president, 1979-80*

across Rotary favoring "crippled children's work" as the major undertaking for the future. It was as if the unofficial motto of Rotarians was "Promise a lot, but do even more."

A club in Florida started Interact—and Rotarians the world over embraced the idea and adopted it in their own communities. A tiny program called RYLA began in Australia—and it quickly spread throughout the Rotary world. Barely had they immunized the first children in the Philippines before Rotarians were dreaming about expanding the project to inoculate every child on earth against polio. And no sooner was PolioPlus a reality than some were thinking about what Rotary's next "finest hour" should be.

So having spent these chapters looking back in history, what will the future of Rotary look like?

"It is unthinkable that we should take any other course except that which keeps the door of the future wide open for great usefulness and service," said Glenn Mead, who succeeded Paul Harris as Rotary International's president in 1912-13.[2] Mead wrote those words 90 years ago, yet few would disagree that his framework for the future of Rotary is just as valid today.

Over the years, several RI presidents and Boards have commissioned task forces to study the future of Rotary. Their findings generally fall into two categories: membership and programs.

Membership has declined in almost every Western service organization, fraternal group, and mainline church over the past 25 years. Rotary suffered membership declines in the Great Depression, World War II, and part of the 1990s but enjoyed a recent net gain in club membership worldwide, primarily as a result of its expansion in emerging democracies and the admission of women.

Much of this membership decline in various organizations was due to changing social trends. In his illuminating book *Bowling Alone*,[3] Harvard University professor Robert D. Putnam points to a "civic malaise" that had overtaken America by 2000. He uses extensive scholarly research to advance his position that since the mid-1960s, 25 percent fewer Americans vote; 30-40 percent fewer serve as officers in clubs or organizations, or attend school or com-

272

munity meetings. Even bowling leagues have declined. He shows that while service clubs such as Rotary, Kiwanis, and Lions were growing in mid-century, fraternal organizations like Masons and women's clubs were already in decline. Most of Putnam's conclusions apply internationally as well.

As the social fabric of society changed—more women went to work, the "9-to-5" workday disappeared, business travel increased, parents felt obliged to attend their children's many sports and cultural activities—there was less time for organizations that demanded weekly attendance. Putnam claims that in the last 25 years, 25 percent fewer Americans attend club meetings, 33 percent fewer get together for family dinners, and 45 percent fewer invite friends over for social gatherings. The same is true in other technology-driven societies.

Rotary was one of the last service clubs to experience this membership loss, and it was felt hardest in large city clubs. Places like London, Sydney, Rome, New York, San Francisco, Chicago, and Philadelphia typically have half the membership and attendance they did a quarter century ago.

Not surprisingly, various presidential committees on the future of Rotary took a hard look at how to turn around the declining membership. Councils on Legislation subsequently approved many of their ideas, and as a result, the rules for admission and continued membership are considerably more flexible today. The old-timers argued that this would lead to "quantity rather than quality" members. But as John Kenny of Grangemouth, Scotland—a past RI vice president—said, "We still need quality, but a quantity of quality."[4] The actions by the committees and Councils must have been correct, for as the

CHILDREN FROM AN IMPOVERISHED AREA OF KUALA LUMPUR, MALAYSIA, ATTEND KINDERGARTEN AT A SCHOOL BUILT AND SUPPORTED BY PETALING JAYA ROTARIANS.

2 THE ROTARIAN VII, no. 3 (September 1915): 243.

3 Robert D. Putnam, *Bowling Alone* (New York, NY: Simon & Schuster, 2000).

4 John Kenny to District 7500 Conference, Williamsburg, Virginia, 27 April 2002.

CHILDREN IN DHAKA,
BANGLADESH, DRINK FROM
A WELL PROVIDED BY LOCAL
ROTARIANS.

274

21st century began, Rotary's membership began climbing again. This came largely through the vigorous leadership of such RI presidents as Frank Devlyn of Mexico, in 2000-01, Richard D. King of California, USA, in 2001-02, and Herbert G. Brown of Florida, USA, who laid the groundwork for a major membership turnaround during his year in 1995-96.

Today's leaders in Rotary are consistent in their views that membership growth and retention is still the highest priority.

"We are not filling young people with the urge to join Rotary," says William C. Carter of London, England. Carter, who was RI president in 1973-74, says the most common objection—"I don't have time"—led to the introduction of breakfast and "twilight" clubs. "Maybe we need to think of new forms of membership," he adds. "Such as corporate membership, where any member of the company could attend."

"As long as we open the doors to the world by having programs that touch human needs, projects they can really get involved with, young people will want to be involved in Rotary," says Robert Barth of Aarau, Switzerland, RI's 1993-94 president. He paints a bleak picture of today's modern workplace: "Sitting behind a computer all day—it's a dead world. These can become very lonesome people. There is no laughter in their day, just cold data on their screens. Now imagine how attractive it would be for them to leave work and sit down for a glass of wine with other people like them, mingling, talking about how they can do something significant in the world."

Several clubs now meet without incurring the cost—or time—of a formal meal. Many clubs in India merely have tea or soft drinks. William E. Skelton of Christiansburg-Blacksburg, Virginia, USA, says clubs have seen enormous changes since he was RI president in 1983-84. "There's a growing sentiment for clubs to meet twice a month, and I predict that in the future we'll see them having that option. It would do two things: free up more time for community projects and lower the cost of membership because there would be only half as many meals to pay for each *month.*"

Rajendra K. Saboo of Chandigarh, Union Territory, India, RI president for 1991-92, agrees. "Business is the top priority for young men and women today. They worry about how they will move up. Husbands and wives both work; they have little time together and have to be very careful about choosing anything that will put more strain on their time. Time is their most valuable commodity. Rotary can only attract them if it gives them something: a public image, emotional satisfaction, spiritual upliftment, or meaningful camaraderie."

One thing is certain: the demographics of the Rotary club of the future will be nothing like the "rich old men" stereotype of the past. Rotarians will be younger and more ethnically diverse, and will have higher percentages of women in their clubs. "I was against the idea of women joining Rotary; I was wrong in taking such a position," admits 1984-85 RI President Carlos Canseco, from Monterrey, Nuevo Leon, Mexico. "Women have brought new life to Rotary. Every club that has female members is more active, more committed, has more vitality than those without. It took us too many years to realize we were wrong. Women will help steer the future of Rotary in a very exciting direction; and with so many women in business and the professions now, we have unlimited opportunities for growth there."

And yet Dr. Canseco is quick to point out that the traditional opportunities for both Rotary clubs and service projects still remain. "There are 16,000 U.S. communities having populations of more than 5,000 that have no service clubs. Asia and South America will charter hundreds of new Rotary clubs in the future. As economic development brings new industries to emerging markets, there will be thousands of new people capable of joining a Rotary club in those communities."

"Where there is…a starving child…a weeping mother—Rotary can be there. Where there is a cataracted eye, a crooked limb—a need for medicine, braces, surgery—Rotary can be there. Where there is the sigh of the lonely, the despair of the isolated—Rotary can be there. Rotary is the sanctity of fellowship, the love of brotherhood, the warmth of trust."

Edward F. Cadman, Wenatchee, Washington, USA

RI president, 1985-86

That point is seconded by In Sang Song of Seoul, Korea, a past director of RI. "Many of our young people have been educated in the West where they experienced the rewards and fellowship of club life. Now they are returning to jobs in Korea, and they want the same thing here. Living standards are increasing, and after so many years when authoritarian governments and politicians dominated our society, now through Rotary the next generation sees how they can contribute to the future of their country."

"I have a different perspective on membership," says 1978-79 RI President Clem Renouf of Australia. "There's this great emphasis on getting younger people into Rotary. But people retire earlier nowadays—some as young as 55. And they live longer. That means most people have at least 30 years post retirement—with none of the problems with work and kids that young people have. What will they do in those 30 years? I think that segment of the population represents a tremendous opportunity for future membership growth. In fact, I can see us sending those people on long-term assignments as Rotary volunteers—like the Peace Corps."

"People today, especially young people, like to work for causes rather than for ideals," explains 1996-97 RI President Luis Vicente Giay of Argentina. "They want immediate results. They want to work today and see the results tomorrow. In the past, Rotary attracted people because of what we stood for: ethics, fellowship, and the ideal of service. The validity of those ideals is not in danger, but today we need to give local Rotarians a sense of participation. If we can't make them believe they are a part of something wonderful, then Rotary will mean nothing."

Giay is positive about Rotary's future. "If the Permanent Fund of The Rotary Foundation grows at its current rate, in 2025 we will have a corpus of US$3 billion. That will generate $300 million annually for us to spend on programs. Can you imagine? That means we could have a PolioPlus-size project every year—all funded internally. Just think how attractive Rotary will be for people to join, for the service we will be able to perform. But above all, in 2025 we will be reaping the fruits of the seeds we are planting today. The child we immunized against polio today will be graduating from college in 2025—and will know that Rotary saved her life. Now multiply that by two billion youngsters. Rotary in 2025 will be stronger than ever before."

"Hope is the expectation of better things—a polio-free world, a world without hunger, universal peace. It is the spark that keeps a man going, whatever his station. Without it, life is nothing more than existence in despair."

M.A.T. Caparas, Manila, Philippines
RI president, 1986-87

Ed Futa of the Rotary Club of East Honolulu, Hawaii, USA, who became RI general secretary in 2000, expects Rotary club membership to grow as the organization achieves its centennial. He points to the new clubs in Eastern Europe and the Middle East as evidence of the worldwide spread of Rotary's spirit of volunteerism. "Rotary is doing well—and will continue to do well—

ROTARIANS IN WHEATON, ILLINOIS, USA, PROVIDE HEALTH CARE TO CHILDREN AT AN ORPHANAGE IN HUANUCO, PERU.

because we focus on concerns that are relevant to the communities we serve, such as hunger, illiteracy, AIDS, and the environment. Rotarians will continue to work to change the lives of ordinary people."

"Humanitarian partners will play a large role in our future," says Carlo Ravizza of Milano Sud-Ovest, Italy, RI president in 1999-2000. "Private-public partnerships have allowed us to leverage our own funds and abilities with organizations like WHO and UNICEF. I met so many heads of state who thanked me for Rotary's work in polio eradication; it was the PolioPlus partnership that put Rotary onto the global stage as the most respected NGO—and it will be more partnerships like that which will keep us there in the future."

The word *partnering* is used over and over by Rotary's leaders. It is a new phenomenon. Until PolioPlus, Rotary International had, for the most part, chosen to "fly solo" in its service projects. But PolioPlus proved to even the skeptics that while some projects are too big for any one organization to undertake by itself, the impossible becomes possible when the right partners work together. The United Nations could not eradicate polio. Rotary certainly could not have. But when UN agencies WHO and UNICEF, Rotary, and CDC joined hands, miracles began to occur. The future of Rotary will almost certainly include more such alliances.

"WHO and UNICEF won't leave us alone when PolioPlus is finished," laughs Jonathan Majiyagbe of Kano, Nigeria. Majiyagbe became the first African to serve as RI president, in 2003-04. "We've started a business we'll be bound to continue. I see us bringing our incredible social mobilization abilities and our international structure to serve public health needs in the future. It might be with measles or malaria, but I definitely see us partnering again in such areas of need."

Majiyagbe believes that as peace and prosperity gradually sweep across the continent, Africa will be fertile soil for many new Rotary clubs to germinate.

"Right now, Africa represents a negligible percentage of Rotarians worldwide," he adds. "But presently, only rich, powerful people belong to Rotary there. To go to a Rotary luncheon at a hotel, you must be literate. My question is, why? Why must you be an educated man to be a member of Rotary? Why must English be the main form of communication? There are millions of farmers and small-town business people who don't speak English; they may not be considered literate, compared to you and me. But they know what pain is, and they have goodwill and compassion in their hearts. There are 120 million men just like that in Africa. Why not let them meet under the auspices of a local Rotary club and help them work to improve their communities, their vocations, and the young people in their towns? It is my dream."

"PolioPlus raised the bar for Rotarians. It allowed them to think in terms they had never dreamed of before," says Herb Pigman, two-time RI general secretary and a leader in PolioPlus from the beginning. "I don't think Rotary's next grand project will be on the same scale as PolioPlus, but it will be one which capitalizes on Rotary's strengths. For instance, we may continue to be involved in public health, but the target of our service might be set by the needs of a particular country. AIDS in Ghana or Chagas' disease in Argentina, for example."

Pigman adds: "One of the most amazing accomplishments is that we have three very large programs—Interact, Rotaract, and Youth Exchange—that require virtually no RI oversight or funding. We send 8,000 to 9,000 students on overseas exchanges each year, and the program is run by half the time of one staff member. Volunteers do all that work. In contrast, American Field Service sends fewer students abroad and has a staff of 450. So our greatest strength is our motivated corps of volunteers. As we've now seen, if their imagination is sparked, the possibilities for the next grand project are boundless. "

"I think we do need another grand project," says 1987-88 RI President Charles C. Keller of California, Pennsylvania, USA. "You can never go back. It took almost 10 years to incubate PolioPlus. We cannot afford a 10-year period without a grand project." But what should it be? "You can't make it a popularity contest," he warns. "Food, water, health, literacy, housing, the environment—each has its own band of zealots. Nobody will ever get them to change their minds that their cause is the greatest. PolioPlus was perfect. It dealt with kids and a terrible illness with which we were familiar. It was affordable and had a specific in-and-out time frame. Whatever our next grand project will be, it must be able to touch people. And it won't be enough for RI to say, 'The Board of Directors adopted this idea.' It has to have a basis in the hearts and feelings of ordinary Rotarians."

Korea's In Sang Song makes the compelling point of both another "grand" project and the "Rotary begins at home" notion: "At the 2002 World Summit in Johannesburg, [South Africa,] the UN reported that 1.2 billion people are starving—living on less than $1 a day. Another 1.2 billion have no sanitation or clean water. Delegates supported putting 0.7 percent of GDP into projects for sustainable development. Rotary should consider this social trend by world leaders, or we will be out of step with the world." Reflecting on the meeting that day at his own Hanyang Rotary club, he says, "Look at me! I'm 88 years old! Today I went to my club luncheon, met other like-minded Rotarians, helped with an emergency relief project for victims of a typhoon, had some wonderful fellowship, and did something good for my community and mankind. What would I have done with my day, what would I have done to help, if I had not been a Rotarian?"

Clifford L. Dochterman of North Stockton, California, USA, RI president in 1992-93, advocates altering the membership requirements to accommodate the changing work models. He has been intimately involved in nearly all of the long-range planning committees at Rotary International for the past 25 years. "We could become the world's most respected agency that develops understanding and peace," he says. "We could become leaders in educating children—especially girls—or in helping with massive redistribution of food supplies around the world. But all of this depends on whether Rotary clubs are alive and interested in achieving that vision. I think there is greater potential for Rotary today than ever before."

"The yearly, daily, hourly, spirit of Rotary should be the spirit of the Renaissance," wrote Paul Harris in *My Road to Rotary*. "We need men of microscopic visions who will explore the molecules, atoms, and electrons, but we also need men of telescopic vision who will explore the stars." One can hardly imagine how pleased he would be today if he could review the men—and women—of vision who have followed along on their road to Rotary.

One who walked that road was the late George Means, whom Ches Perry hired in 1932, initially to work for The Rotary Foundation. Support was not sufficient at that time for a burgeoning Rotary Foundation, and so George went to work with Paul in the preparation of the manuscript for his book *This Rotarian Age*. George became intrigued by a cheap metal galleon—only three inches from stem to stern—that Paul had bought at Woolworth's and kept on his desk, seemingly for the sole purpose of banging nails into the wall whenever he hung a picture frame.

"This is the good ship Rotary," Paul told George while he was admiring it one day. "Notice that it is going someplace; it is in full sail." On Paul Harris's last day in the office, not long before he died, he gave the ship to George, telling him: "Make sure the good ship Rotary is always under full sail and is always going someplace." Means went on to serve RI as general secretary for 1953-72. "From the day I became general secretary until the day I retired, I never went to a Board meeting, a convention, international assembly, or a conference that I didn't carry that ship with me," he said, with nostalgic conviction.

From Paul Harris to George Means to all the presidents, directors, general secretaries, district governors, club presidents, and "ordinary deck hands," the men and women of Rotary have had their hands on the tiller. They have steered their ship well. The good ship Rotary is indeed under full sail. And as it begins its second century, it is really going someplace.

All aboard!

Conclusion

The Rotary River Flows On

"Well done," American statesman Benjamin Franklin remarked, "is better than well said."

The 20th century was a period that historians will likely note made little progress in the battle against discrimination, war, and corruption. When it came to humankind's movement toward a more civil society, many people expressed opinions on how to make the world a better place. They were "well said"—but not enough put action behind their words.

Rotary was a notable exception.

In paying tribute to Paul Harris just after his death in 1947, THE ROTARIAN wrote: "Paul Harris never claimed to have founded a new philosophy; he referred to the spirit of Rotary as an ancient principle of ethics. What he did was to teach men of all nations and of all races to join together in practicing and applying it."[1]

Rotary was misunderstood and therefore ignored by some and criticized by others during its early history. Unquestionably, one of the objectives of those who joined the first Rotary clubs was "boosterism" and the mutual exchange of business. While there is nothing inherently wrong with such practices—indeed, "networking clubs" are very much in vogue today—they provided fodder for a press skeptical that the local businessman could also feel altruistic toward his community. Then came the widely read writers of the 1920s and 1930s—Chesterton, Lewis, Shaw, Mencken—who delighted in lampooning Rotarians as bumbling, hypocritical do-gooders.

From the beginning, some political and religious leaders simply could not fathom Rotary's absolute insistence on spiritual and political neutrality. A Rotarian's duty was—and is—to his or her own country and faith first, and despite the attempts by some to paint Rotary as an American institution, its very internationality has become a proven fact. While Rotarians embraced a code of ethics and did more than any other body to spread those standards to other trades and professions, it caused some in the Roman Catholic Church's hierarchy to claim that this code proved Rotary was promoting a universal religion. Others claimed—without a shred of evidence and despite vehement denials by Paul Harris and other RI leaders—that Rotary had Masonic ties and thus should be banned.

---

1 THE ROTARIAN, March 1947, 8.
2 Clifford L. Dochterman, *The ABCs of Rotary* (Evanston, Illinois: Rotary International, 2000), 39.

It is quite remarkable that Rotary was able to grow in almost an unbroken line for 100 consecutive years and at the turn of the century was adding a new Rotary club every 14 hours of every day.[2]

Past RI General Secretary Herb Pigman once compared the growth and development of Rotary with that of flight. "Early in this century, a fragile machine of wood and wire and fabric lifted from the dunes of Kitty Hawk," he told an audience in Harrisburg, Pennsylvania, USA. "Shortly thereafter, from the commercial canyons of Chicago, there arose an equally fragile idea—that of Rotary. In the [100 years] since, both have thrived. Flight has linked communities, nations, and continents. So has Rotary. Flight has promoted a sense of our global community. So, indeed, has Rotary. Flight brings a wider horizon. Intellectually, so does Rotary. When Orville Wright (he was an active Rotarian, incidentally) took off, he didn't know where his invention would lead. When he was 77 years old in 1948, THE ROTARIAN interviewed him. He was asked whether he ever dreamed that the airplane would become a worldwide movement, that the Wright brothers' brainchild would grow into aviation as we know it today. 'Not at all,' said the great pioneer of flight. 'My brother Wilbur and I did it for fun. We got interested in the problem of whether it was possible to fly, and we kept at it because we wanted to see if we could work it out.'"

Paul Harris started Rotary for fun and fellowship, and like the Wright brothers, he had no idea where it was going. Today, there is no part of the globe that an airplane cannot reach in a day, and there is no part of the globe that has not in some way been touched and improved by Rotary.

As we conclude the first century of Rotary service, it is natural to look back and ask, "Why?" Why has Rotary succeeded? Why is the ideal of service so compelling? And as we turn our glance from the view over our shoulder to the present, we ask, "Is Rotary relevant and necessary today?"

England's Bill Huntley, who was RI president in 1994-95, believes Rotary has succeeded for three reasons:

1. "We cross boundaries. Look at District 1160—there is one district for all of Ireland, where strife has boiled for generations.

2. "We talk at all levels because of the quality of our members—kings, government officials, and business leaders. We have entrée into the U.S. White House Oval Office and the United Nations. Local club presidents can talk to city councilors. Rotary has a say in affairs of the community.

3. "We're trusted. Our history covers 100 years of faithful community service, and our badge has become the emblem of integrity. In Istanbul, Turkey, for example, Rotarians were called in as the arbiters in industrial disputes."

Rotary has also succeeded because it has given men and women the opportunity to enjoy the trust and fellowship of one another while always reaching out. They reach out to their communities. They reach out to help young people and the elderly. They reach out far beyond their own borders to those in need. And they do so in an organization that teaches them to broaden their thoughts and minds culturally, with a desire for world understanding and peace.

To Rotarians, the "development of acquaintance"—to cite the old but still appropriate objective—transcends one's own race or religion. That is why there has never been a schism among Rotarians in Belfast or Beirut or Johannesburg while their cities were embroiled in civil unrest. Their similar interests far outweigh in importance their differences. And those interests can be summarized as the ideal of service.

"The ideal of service is the real tie that binds," states 1987-88 RI President Charles C. Keller. "It's the idea that distinguishes us from everything and everyone else. And service means really helping people, not just doing nice things. In a world where people speak different languages, eat different food, dress in different clothing, worship differently—for those people to bond together requires a powerful adhesive. In Rotary that adhesive is the ideal of Service Above Self."

It is a powerful ideal indeed and one that must seem incomprehensible to the person who has not discovered the joy of service. What makes a retired accountant spend countless hours tutoring at-risk children? Why would a stockbroker leave her desk in the middle of the day to spend time with her club's Interact students? Who can explain why a funeral director—who hires a landscaper to do his own gardening—so thoroughly enjoys planting flowers around the Rotary sign at the entrance to town? And what causes an orthopedic surgeon to forego thousands of dollars in lost fees while he acts as an unpaid Rotary volunteer at a clinic halfway around the world?

All of these, and thousands more, are among the random acts of kindness that Rotarians perform. And here is the critical point: They do not perform them under pressure or obligation; they do so because they derive enjoyment from the act of service. When a parent gives a child the shiny red bicycle he has been yearning for all year, the child cannot hide his excitement and appreciation. Perhaps the parent had to make some sacrifices to afford the bicycle, but the act of giving, seeing someone she cares about so happy, is a reward that far exceeds the sacrifice.

The ideal of service is needed as much in 2005 as on that cold February night a century ago when Rotary began. As Rotarians celebrate their gift to the world with the eradication of polio through the PolioPlus program, they know they dare not rest their heads on the pillows of self-satisfaction. Peace among warring nations, drugs, illiteracy, disease, poverty, hunger, homelessness, the environment—all present Rotarians with opportunities for service in the years ahead. It is hard to imagine Rotary ever not being needed.

Nobel Peace Prize recipient Albert Schweitzer, an honorary Rotarian, once said: "I don't know what your destiny will be. But this I do know: the only ones among you who will ever be truly happy are those who have sought and found how to serve others."[3]

For 100 years, Rotarians have resoundingly affirmed Dr. Schweitzer's point. They have adopted the ideal of service because they felt a sense of obligation to answer the cry of a fellow human being in need; they have advanced ethics and environmental protection and peacemaking and the elimination of suffering and disease because they saw those needs and decided to become a part of the solution rather than stand idly by and, therefore, be a part of the problem.

No one Rotarian could have been effective in addressing those concerns, but when individual Rotarians suggest an idea that is taken up by their club, and then their district, and then joined by other clubs around the world, they have become a mighty force for good. As the result of their voluntary efforts, they have shown that they do not *go* to Rotary—they *are* Rotary.

This book began by comparing Rotary to a river. In 1905, the Rotary River surfaced in the form of a tiny spring in Chicago. Millions of springs percolate up all the time, only to dry up, or stagnate in swampy ground. But this one was different. It trickled along, picking up speed and strength. Soon, other tiny rivulets surfaced and fed into the stream. For a while, it meandered, not quite sure in which direction to head. But as it grew from a stream to a river, its destiny developed purpose and certainty. It personified a century of service.

The Rotary River brought life to those who depended on water. Where once there was hopeless drought, now there is life; where once children suffered in silence, now they frolic in its waters. It became a channel of commerce that connected people of different lands and disparate faiths and cultures—but who met and sailed together on the river.

The Rotary River is a mighty force. Its direction is no longer a question; its value to all is beyond doubt. The only question remaining is not about the river, but about those who sail on it. American jurist Oliver Wendell Holmes once said, "I find the great thing in this world is not so much where we stand, as in what direction we are moving: To reach the port of heaven, we must sail sometimes with the wind and sometimes against it, but we must sail, and not drift, nor lie at anchor."

May the winds of peace and the strong current of service carry those who sail on the Rotary River to far horizons we today can hardly imagine.

Selected Bibliography

The following writings were helpful in the preparation of this book. Just as this publication is not meant to be the complete history of every Rotary club, district, project, or personality, this bibliography does not contain every published work on Rotary. Many countries, districts, clubs, and past RI presidents have produced their own books that compile the history of their particular interest in Rotary's evolution. The Archives Department at RI World Headquarters in Evanston has many of these books.

Anazawa, Yoichi. *Music Everywhere: The Rotary Spirit in Action.* Tokyo: International Publishing Institute, 1990.

Arnold, Oren. *The Golden Strand: An Informal History of the Rotary Club of Chicago.* Chicago: Quadrangle Books, 1966.

Carter, Vivian. *The Romance of Rotary in London.* London: RI in Great Britain and Ireland, 1947.

Charles, Jeffrey A. *Service Clubs in American Society.* Champaign, Illinois: University of Illinois Press, 1993.

Davidson, Lillian Dow. *Making New Friends: From Near to Far East for Rotary.* Chicago: Rotary International, 1934.

Dochterman, Cliff. *The ABCs of Rotary.* Evanston, IL: Rotary International, 1999.

Evans, Richard L., Jr. *Richard L. Evans: The Man and the Message.* Salt Lake City, Utah: Bookcraft Inc., 1973.

French, Jay. *Inner Wheel: A History*. London: Association of Inner Wheel Clubs in Great Britain and Ireland, 1977.

Giay, Luis Vicente. *Homenaje a un hombre de acción y visión*. Rosario, Argentina: Editorial Rotaria Argentina, 2000.

Harris, Paul P. *My Road to Rotary: The Story of a Boy, a Vermont Community, and Rotary*. Chicago: A. Kroch and Son, 1948.

————. *This Rotarian Age*. Chicago: Rotary International, 1935.

————. *Peregrinations, Volume II: We Become Pacific-Ocean Minded*. Chicago: Rotary International, 1935.

————. *Peregrinations, Volume III: Our Neighbors on the South*. Chicago: Rotary International, 1937.

————. *A Visit to Great Britain and South Africa*. Chicago: Rotary International, 1934.

Henningham, Paul. *In Search of Health. Good Health...to All! The Story of the Australian Rotary Health Research Fund*. Parramatta, New South Wales: The Australian Rotary Health Research Fund, RDU Books, 2001.

————. *Seventy-Five Years of Service: Rotary in Australia, Papua New Guinea and Solomon Islands 1921-1996*. Parramatta, New South Wales: Rotary Down Under for the Australian Rotary Institute, 1996.

Hewitt, C.R. *Towards My Neighbour: The Social Influence of the Rotary Club Movement in Great Britain and Ireland*. London: Longmans, Green and Co., 1950.

Hunt, Harold. *The Story of Rotary in Australia 1921-1971*. Australia: The Regional Rotary Institute of Present, Past and Incoming Officers of Rotary International in Australia, 1971.

Joseph, N.T. *The Story of Rotary in India 1919-1972*. Cochin, Kerala, India: Rotary Club of Cochin, 1972.

Kessel, Milton. *Rotarians Make a Difference!: Inspirational Short Stories about Rotarians and What They Do*. Dallas, Texas: Rotary International District 5810, 1999.

Leverton, Stanley. *The Story of the Rotary Club of London 1911-1961*. London: Rotary Club of London, England, 1961.

Levy, Roger. *Rotary International in Great Britain and Ireland: "Very nice gentlemen, really."* Great Britain: Continua Productions, 1978.

Marden, Charles F., Ph.D. *Rotary and Its Brothers: An Analysis and Interpretation of the Men's Service Club.* Princeton, New Jersey: Princeton University Press, 1935.

McCaffrey, Stanley E. *World Understanding and Peace through Rotary: People to People Efforts for Peace.* Fresno, California: Pioneer Publishing Co., 1985.

Mitchell, Angus, et al. *Leaders in Service Down Under.* Paramatta, New South Wales: RDU Books, 2000.

Mountin, William J. *History of the Rotary Club of San Francisco.* San Francisco: Rotary Club of San Francisco, 1940.

Nicholl, David Shelley. *The Golden Wheel: The Story of Rotary 1905 to the Present.* Estover, Plymouth, England: Macdonald and Evans, Ltd., 1984.

Parnaby, Owen. *Angus Mitchell: Rotarian and Peace Maker.* Melbourne, Australia, 1998.

Postel, Mitchell. *Seventy-Five Years in San Francisco: A History of Rotary Club Number 2.* San Francisco: Presidio Press for the Rotary Club of San Francisco, 1983.

Putnam, Robert D. *Bowling Alone.* New York: Simon & Schuster, 2000.

Renouf, Clem. *The Health, Hunger and Humanity Program.* Paramatta, New South Wales: RDU Books, 2000.

Romulo, Carlos P. *I Walked with Heroes.* New York: Holt, Rinehart and Winston, 1961.

Rotary Club of Chicago. "History." Unpublished document, property of RC Chicago.

Rotary International. *Adventure in Service.* Chicago, 1949.

———. *Convention Proceedings.* Chicago and Evanston, 1910-2003.

———. *Fellowship and Service: The Foundation of Rotary's Dreams.* Evanston, 1998.

———. *Historical Review of Rotary*. Evanston, 1990.

———. *Honoring Our Past: The Words and Wisdom of Paul Harris*. Evanston, 1996.

———. *Horizons of Hope: Rotary in Action*. Evanston, 1989.

———. *Images of Rotary: A World Imagined*. Evanston, 1991.

———. *In the Minds of Men: The Constitution of the United Nations Educational, Scientific and Cultural Organization*. Chicago, 1946.

———. *Manual of Procedure*. Chicago and Evanston, 1920-2001.

———. *Paul Harris and His Successors: Profiles in Leadership*. Evanston, 1997.

———. *Peace: A Selection of Winning Entries from Rotary's Letters for Peace Contest*. Evanston, 1987.

———. *Revista Rotaria* (Spanish-language official magazine). 1933-90.

———. *The Right to Read: Literacy around the World*. Evanston, 1985.

———. The Rotarian (official magazine). Chicago and Evanston, 1911-2003.

———. The Rotarian *Reader: A 75-Year Anthology*. Evanston, 1986.

———. *Rotary Basic Library*. 7 vols. Evanston, 1985.

———. *Rotary Basic Library*. 2nd ed. 3 vols. Evanston, 1995.

———. *Rotary: Fifty Years of Service 1905-1955*. Evanston, 1955.

———. *The Rotary Foundation: 75 Years of Service*. Evanston, 1992.

———. *Rotary News Network*. Video magazine series. Evanston, 1988-90.

———. *Rotary Wisdom: Reflections on Service: Why I am a Rotarian*. Evanston, 1991.

———. S*ervice Is My Business*. Evanston, 1967.

———. *Seven Paths to Peace*. Evanston, 1959.

————. *The World of Rotary*. Evanston, 1975.

Taylor, Herbert J. *The Herbert J. Taylor Story*. Downers Grove, Illinois: Intervarsity Press, 1968.

Thomas, Harold T. *It's All in a Lifetime*. New Zealand: Rotary Clubs of New Zealand, 1968.

————. *Rotary Mosaic*. New Zealand: Rotary Clubs of New Zealand, 1974.

University of Chicago, Social Science Committee. *Rotary? A University Group Looks at the Rotary Club of Chicago*. Chicago: The University of Chicago Press, 1934.

Walsh, James P. *The First Rotarian: The Life and Times of Paul Percy Harris Founder of Rotary*. West Sussex, Great Britain: Scan Books, 1979.

Zapffe, Carl A. *Rotary! An historical, sociological and philosophical study based upon the half-century experience of one of the larger Rotary clubs*. Baltimore, Maryland: The Rotary Club of Baltimore, 1963.

288

In addition to THE ROTARIAN, the official magazine of Rotary International, the Rotary World Press includes 31 regional magazines, which are distributed in 129 countries and published in 24 languages. These magazines represent a rich resource of current and past Rotary activities. The following is a list of the Rotary regional magazines, the countries they serve, and the year in which they were first published.

Vida Rotaria (Argentina) — 1955

Rotary Down Under (Australia, New Zealand, Timor-Leste, and 10 Southwest Pacific islands) — 1965

Rotary Contact (Belgium) — 1984

Brasil Rotário (Brazil) — 1924

El Rotario de Chile (Chile) — 1927

Rotarian Monthly (Republic of China) — 1960

Colombia Rotaria (Colombia) — 1970

Rotary Good News (Czech Republic and Slovakia) — 1999

Rotary Norden (Denmark, Faroe Islands, Finland, Greenland, Iceland, Norway, and Sweden) — 1936

Rotary Magazine (Egypt, Bahrain, Cyprus, Jordan, Lebanon, and Sudan) — 1929

Le Rotarien (France and 37 other French-speaking countries) — 1952

Rotary Magazin (Germany and Austria) — 1929

Rotary Magazine (Great Britain and Ireland) — 1915

Rotary News [English] / *Rotary Samachar* [Hindi] (India, Bangladesh, Nepal, and Sri Lanka) — 1952 and 1983

Rotary Israel (Israel) — 1993

Rotary (Italy) — 1924

Rotary-No-Tomo (Japan) — 1953

The Rotary Korea (Korea) — 1967

Salam Rotary (Malaysia, Brunei, Indonesia, and Singapore) — 2003

Rotarismo en México (Mexico) — 1974

De Rotarian (The Netherlands) — 1927

El Rotario Péruano (Peru) — 1933

Philippine Rotary Magazine (Philippines) — 1977

Swiat Rotary (Poland) — 2003

Portugal Rotãrio (Portugal) — 1984

Rotary Africa (South Africa and 17 other African states) — 1927

España Rotaria (Spain) — 1992

Rotary Suisse-Liechtenstein (Switzerland and Liechtenstein) — 1926

Rotary Thailand (Thailand) — 1983

Rotary Dergisi (Turkey) — 1983

Nueva Revista Rotaria (Venezuela and 11 other Latin American countries) — 1992

Landmarks and Turning Points in Rotary's First Century

1905

Rotary founded in Chicago, Illinois, USA, by Paul P. Harris.

1907

First service project —a public comfort station in Chicago.

1908

Second Rotary club organized in San Francisco, California, USA.

1910

National Association of Rotary Clubs formed at the first Rotary Convention.

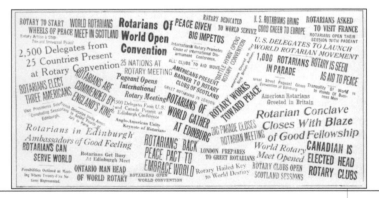

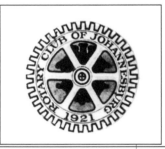

1918

First Rotary club organized in South America (Montevideo, Uruguay).

1919

First Rotary club established in Asia (Manila, Philippines).

1920

Rotary reaches continental Europe (Madrid, Spain).

1921

First Rotary clubs in Australia (Melbourne) and Africa (Johannesburg, South Africa).

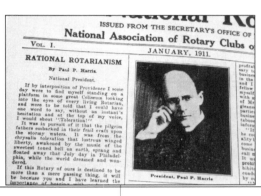

1911

The National Rotarian launched (predecessor to THE ROTARIAN).

1912

Rotary becomes international with admittance of club in Winnipeg, Ontario, Canada, followed later by clubs in Great Britain and Ireland.

1916

Rotary club established in Havana, Cuba— first non-English-speaking club.

1917

Rotary Endowment Fund announced, predecessor to The Rotary Foundation of RI.

1922

Convention approved Rotary International – Association for Great Britain and Ireland (RIBI) as its own territorial unit. (In 1927, new territorial units were disallowed; RIBI remains the only territorial unit in Rotary.)

1923

St. Louis convention rejects single-program focus (crippled children). Resolution 34 adopted, establishing Rotary policy toward club autonomy regarding service projects.

1927

Youth Exchange initiated in Copenhagen, Denmark, and Nice, France.

1928

James W. Davidson begins three-year mission to organize clubs in Asia and the Middle East.

1932

Chicago Rotarian
Herbert J. Taylor
formulates
The Four-Way Test.

1940

At Havana, Cuba,
convention, RI
adopts resolution
"Rotary Amid World
Conflict" to promote
world order and
peace.

1943–46

Rotarians in London,
England, meet pre-
liminary to UNESCO.
Rotarians participate
in preparing and
chartering the United
Nations. Rotary
International fosters
worldwide support
for UN.

1947

Death of Paul Harris.
First program of The
Rotary Foundation
established, called
the Fellowships for
Advanced Study
(today known as
Ambassadorial
Scholarships).

1970

Council on
Legislation
becomes
Rotary's
"parliament."

1971

Rotary Youth
Leadership Awards
(RYLA) officially
adopted, based
on 1959 model in
Queensland,
Australia.

1976

Network of
Rotary regional
magazines
approved.

1978

Health, Hunger
and Humanity
(3-H) Grants
program developed.

1957

Paul Harris Fellow
Recognition
proposed to fund
Foundation programs.

1962

First Interact
club formed in
Melbourne,
Florida, USA.

1963

Matched District and
Club Program provides
impetus for World
Community Service,
Matching Grants,
Group Study Exchange,
Carl P. Miller Discovery
Grants, and World Fel-
lowships (now Rotary
Fellowships).

1968

First Rotaract
club chartered in
Charlotte, North
Carolina, USA.

1980

The Trustees of
The Rotary Founda-
tion establish
the Endowment
for World
Understanding
and Peace
(renamed The
Rotary Foundation
Permanent
Fund in 1994).

1983–88

3-H project leads to
PolioPlus. Rotarians
worldwide raise
US$219 million
for polio eradication.
(By 2005, Rotary's
contributions will
exceed $500 million.)
Partnership created
with WHO, UNICEF,
and CDC.

1985

Rotary membership
reaches one million.

1986

Rotary Community
Corps is initiated
(originally called
Rotary Village Corps
and Rotary Commu-
nity Service Corps).

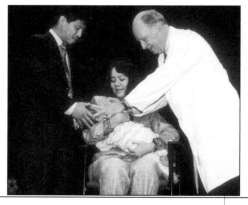

1987

Women admitted
to Rotary member-
ship in United States
by action of RI Board
of Directors.

1989

Council on
Legislation
opens Rotary
membership
to women
worldwide.

1990

Rotary enters
Russia and other
countries in former
Soviet Union.

1993

International
PolioPlus Committee
created to manage
Rotary's continuing
polio eradication
efforts.

2002

The first Rotary
World Peace
Scholarships
awarded for study
at the Rotary
Centers for
International
Studies in peace
and conflict
resolution.

2005

Rotary celebrates
100th anniversary.

Highlights of Rotary's First 100 Years

1905

Rotary is founded on 23 February when Paul Harris, Silvester Schiele, Gustavus Loehr, and Hiram Shorey meet in Room 711 of the Unity Building, 127 Dearborn Street, in Chicago. The name derives from the practice of rotating meetings among members' places of business. Meetings at restaurants for lunch or dinner are later initiated. Rotarian Harry Ruggles begins the tradition of singing at Rotary meetings.

1906

Montague Bear designs a wagon-wheel emblem for the Rotary club. Other early members: Rufus Chapin, William Jensen, Dr. Will Neff, Charles Newton, Frederick Tweed, Al White, and Max Wolff. First constitution and by-laws of the Rotary Club of Chicago are printed.

1907

Rotary Club of Chicago begins plan for two public comfort stations as its first community service project (not built until 1909). Also provides horse for country preacher in need.

1908

Chesley R. Perry, who later served as the association's general secretary for 32 years, is invited to join the Rotary Club of Chicago along with Arthur Frederick Shelton (He Profits Most Who Serves Best). Rotary Club of San Francisco formed. Paul Harris voices hope that Rotary clubs will be organized in every major city in the United States.

1909

Rotary clubs formed in Oakland, California; Seattle, Washington; and Los Angeles, California. By 30 June, Rotary had five clubs with a total of 510 members. Later in the year, clubs were formed in New York City, New York, and Boston, Massachusetts.

1910-11[1]

President: Paul P. Harris, Founder
Chicago, Illinois, USA
Number of clubs:[2] 16; **members:** 1,085; **countries:** 1
New country or geographical region: Canada
Convention of 1910 (15-17 August):[3] Chicago, Illinois, USA
Registration: 60

HIGHLIGHTS: First Rotary Convention held. National Association formed with 16 clubs. Paul Harris elected president and Chesley Perry first secretary. Objects of Rotary formulated. First club outside the United States formed in Winnipeg, Manitoba, Canada (organized November 1910 but not actually admitted until 1912). Paul Harris marries Jean Thomson, a native of Edinburgh, Scotland. In January 1911, *The National Rotarian* (later THE ROTARIAN) is launched.

---

1   From 1910 to 1913, the new presidential year began with the convention. In April 1913, it was decided that the 12-month fiscal "Rotary year" would be from 1 July to 30 June.
2   The number of clubs, members, and country figures are official RI membership statistics and reflect membership as of 30 June, the day before the start of the new Rotary year.

1911-12

President: Paul P. Harris
Number of clubs: 20; **members:** 3,750; **countries:** 2
New countries or geographical regions: England, Ireland, and Northern Ireland
Convention of 1911 (21-23 August): Portland, Oregon, USA
Registration: 149

HIGHLIGHTS: Rotary crosses the Atlantic with new clubs in Dublin, Ireland (organized March 1911); Belfast, Northern Ireland (organized August 1911), and London, England (organized August 1911). The Rotary platform was adopted at the 1911 convention. Service Above Self and He Profits Most Who Serves Best are proposed as Rotary mottoes.

1912-13

President: Glenn C. Mead
Philadelphia, Pennsylvania, USA
Number of clubs: 44; **members:** 5,008; **countries:** 5
New country or geographical region: Scotland
Convention of 1912 (6-9 August): Duluth, Minnesota, USA
Registration: 598

HIGHLIGHTS: Name changed to International Association of Rotary Clubs. First Rotary emblem embodying a gearwheel adopted at convention. Paul Harris "retires" from active leadership and becomes president emeritus.

1913-14

President: Russell F. Greiner
Kansas City, Missouri, USA
Number of clubs: 74; **members:** 10,000; **countries:** 6
Convention of 1913 (18-21 August): Buffalo, New York, USA
Registration: 930
Convention of 1914 (22-26 June): Houston, Texas, USA
Registration: 1,288

HIGHLIGHTS: Rotary clubs contribute US$25,000 for flood relief in Indiana and Ohio, USA, first of many appeals to aid disaster victims. British Association of Rotary Clubs (BARC) formed. 100th Rotary club chartered in Phoenix, Arizona, USA.

1914-15

President: Frank L. Mulholland
Toledo, Ohio, USA
Number of clubs: 123; **members:** 15,000; **countries:** 6

HIGHLIGHTS: Outbreak of war in Europe slows expansion of Rotary in that region. Eight clubs in Great Britain and Ireland support relief efforts, including housing of Belgian refugees. Official Rotary flag adopted.

---

3   The annual conventions during 1910-13 were held in August. In 1914, the convention was held in June. In 1915 and 1916, it was held in July. Although it appears that Frank L. Mulholland didn't have a convention, he was elected at the Houston convention in 1914. It also appears that Russell F. Greiner and Arch C. Klumph each had two conventions, but those were shared with their predecessors and successors. Beginning in 1917, the convention was held in May or June and marked the end of the president's leadership year.

1915-16

President: Allen D. Albert
Minneapolis, Minnesota, USA
Number of clubs: 167; **members:** 20,700; **countries:** 6
New countries or geographical regions: Cuba* and Hawaii
Convention of 1915 (18-23 July): San Francisco, California, USA
Registration: 1,988

HIGHLIGHTS: Rotary clubs grouped into districts for first time. Standard Rotary Club Constitution and model bylaws adopted. Rotary Code of Ethics adopted. First Rotary club chartered in a non-English-speaking country (Rotary Club of Havana, Cuba). First Rotary club formed in the South Pacific (Rotary Club of Honolulu, Hawaii). Boys Work initiated.

1916-17

President: Arch C. Klumph
Cleveland, Ohio, USA
Number of clubs: 230; **members:** 27,000; **countries:** 8
Convention of 1916 (16-20 July): Cincinnati, Ohio, USA
Registration: 3,591
Convention of 1917 (17-21 June): Atlanta, Georgia, USA
Registration: 2,588

HIGHLIGHTS: At the Atlanta convention, Klumph proposes an endowment fund, which was the forerunner of The Rotary Foundation. Crippled children's work started.

1917-18

President: E. Leslie Pidgeon
Winnipeg, Manitoba, Canada
Number of clubs: 321; **members:** 32,600; **countries:** 8
New countries or geographical regions: Puerto Rico and Wales
Convention of 1918 (24-28 June): Kansas City, Missouri, USA
Registration: 4,145

HIGHLIGHTS: Clubs in United States engage in major effort to support war relief. First *Rotary Song Book* published in response to requests by Rotary clubs.

1918-19

President: John Poole
Washington, D.C., USA
Number of clubs: 415; **members:** 38,800; **countries:** 10
New countries or geographical regions: Philippines and Uruguay
Convention of 1919 (16-20 June): Salt Lake City, Utah, USA
Registration: 3,083

HIGHLIGHTS: Rotary enters two continents: South America and Asia. Clubs are established in Montevideo, Uruguay, and Manila, Philippines. The Allied Rotary Club for American Servicemen (forerunner of the Rotary Club of Paris, France) is formed.

Country or geographic region not currently in Rotary

1919-20

President: Albert S. Adams
Atlanta, Georgia, USA
Number of clubs: 516; **members:** 45,000; **countries:** 12
New countries or geographical regions: Argentina, China,* India, and
Panama
Convention of 1920 (21-25 June): Atlantic City, New Jersey, USA
Registration: 7,213

HIGHLIGHTS: End of World War I marks expansion of Rotary with formation of clubs in Buenos Aires, Argentina; Shanghai, China; Calcutta, India;
and Panama City, Panama.

1920-21

President: Estes Snedecor
Portland, Oregon, USA
Number of clubs: 758; **members:** 56,800; **countries:** 16
New countries or geographical regions: Australia, France, Japan,
Mexico, New Zealand, and Spain
Convention of 1921 (13-16 June): Edinburgh, Scotland
Registration: 2,523

HIGHLIGHTS: Rotary enters continental Europe and Australia with the
formation of a club in Madrid, Spain, and in Melbourne, Australia. Edinburgh convention is the first held outside the United States. Convention
delegates adopt international peace and goodwill as one of the Objects
of Rotary.

1921-22

President: Crawford C. McCullough
Fort William, Ontario, Canada
Number of clubs: 975; **members:** 70,000; **countries:** 22
New countries or geographical regions: Newfoundland,
Norway, Peru, and South Africa
Convention of 1922 (5-9 June): Los Angeles, California, USA
Registration: 6,096

HIGHLIGHTS: Name of association changed to Rotary International.
Constitution and bylaws completely revised, and standard club constitu-
tion made mandatory for all new clubs. First club in Africa is chartered in
Johannesburg, South Africa.

1922-23

President: Raymond M. Havens
Kansas City, Missouri, USA
Number of clubs: 1,234; **members:** 83,150; **countries:** 26
New countries or geographical regions: Brazil, Channel Islands,
Denmark, and The Netherlands
Convention of 1923 (18-22 June): St. Louis, Missouri, USA
Registration: 6,779

HIGHLIGHTS: Rotarians encouraged to have business and trade associations adopt "codes" or "standards of practice" based on model code suggested by Rotary. U.S. President Warren G. Harding, a Rotarian, is the
first head of state to address a Rotary convention. Resolution 34 codifies
Community Service principles for all clubs.

1923-24

President: Guy Gundaker
Philadelphia, Pennsylvania, USA
Number of clubs: 1,494; **members:** 92,800; **countries:** 29
New countries or geographical regions: Belgium, Bermuda, Chile,
Isle of Man, Italy, and Switzerland
Convention of 1924 (16-20 June): Toronto, Ontario, Canada.
Registration: 9,173

HIGHLIGHTS: Rotarians worldwide provide relief efforts in response to
major earthquake in Japan, which kills more than 143,000. Board adopts
the current cogwheel emblem with six spokes, 24 cogs, and a keyway.
Rotary membership surpasses 100,000. First House of Friendship instituted
at Toronto convention.

1924-25

President: Everett W. Hill
Shawnee, Oklahoma, USA
Number of clubs: 1,796; **members:** 102,000; **countries:** 34
New countries or geographical regions: Alaska and Guatemala
Convention of 1925 (15-19 June): Cleveland, Ohio, USA
Registration: 10,216

HIGHLIGHTS: A Secretariat branch office is opened in Zurich,
Switzerland, to better serve European Rotarians (later named the RI Europe
and Africa Office). More than 400 men representing 50 organizations meet
in Chicago for the first annual International Boys Work Conference sponsored by Rotary. 2,000th Rotary club formed in Ketchikan, Alaska.

1925-26

President: Donald A. Adams
New Haven, Connecticut, USA
Number of clubs: 2,096; **members:** 108,000; **countries:** 36
New countries or geographical regions: Austria, Czech Republic
(Czechoslovakia), Hungary, Portugal, and Sweden
Convention of 1926 (14-18 June): Denver, Colorado, USA
Registration: 8,886

HIGHLIGHTS: Emphasizing Rotary fundamentals, Adams calls for "the
education of Rotarians as to what Rotary really is." First Pacific Regional
Conference for eight nations meets in Honolulu, Hawaii, for fellowship
and discussion of the region's problems. Admiral Richard E. Byrd carries
Rotary flag to the North Pole.

1926-27

President: Harry H. Rogers
San Antonio, Texas, USA
Number of clubs: 2,396; **members:** 120,000; **countries:** 41
New countries or geographical regions: Colombia, Costa Rica,
El Salvador, Finland, and Venezuela
Convention of 1927 (5-10 June): Ostend, Belgium
Registration: 6,412

HIGHLIGHTS: King Albert I of Belgium officially opens the first RI Convention in continental Europe. Youth Exchange originates in Copenhagen, Denmark, and Nice, France.

1927-28

President: Arthur H. Sapp
Huntington, Indiana, USA
Number of clubs: 2,628; **members:** 129,000; **countries:** 45
New countries or geographical regions: Bolivia, Ecuador, Germany,
Indonesia (Java, Netherlands East Indies), Korea (Chosen, Japan),
Pakistan, and Paraguay
Convention of 1928 (18-22 June): Minneapolis, Minnesota, USA
Registration: 9,428

HIGHLIGHTS: James W. Davidson, the Canadian "Marco Polo" of Rotary,
embarks on three-year round-the-world tour with his wife and young daughter to organize Rotary clubs in Asia and the Middle East. The name of the
Rotary Endowment Fund changed to The Rotary Foundation. Paul and
Jean Harris visit Rotary clubs in England and continental Europe.

1928-29

President: I.B. Tom Sutton
Tampico, Tamaulipas, Mexico
Number of clubs: 2,932; **members:** 137,000; **countries:** 52
New countries or geographical regions: Egypt, Greece, Honduras, Israel
(Palestine), Nicaragua, Romania, and Yugoslavia
Convention of 1929 (27-31 May): Dallas, Texas, USA
Registration: 9,508

HIGHLIGHTS: Second Pacific Regional Conference held in Tokyo, Japan.
Tireless extension work, especially by Honorary General Commissioner
James W. Davidson.

1929-30

President: M. Eugene Newsom
Durham, North Carolina, USA
Number of clubs: 3,177; **members:** 144,500; **countries:** 59
New countries or geographical regions: Algeria, Belize (British Honduras),
Luxembourg, Malaysia (Federated Malay States), Morocco, Myanmar
(Burma),* Sri Lanka (Ceylon), and Zimbabwe (Southern Rhodesia)
Convention of 1930 (23-27 June): Chicago, Illinois, USA
Registration: 11,008

HIGHLIGHTS: Rotary celebrates its 25th anniversary in the city of its birth as
the Great Depression begins to shatter national economies; still, eight new
countries join the family of Rotary nations. Admiral Richard E. Byrd carries
Rotary flag to the South Pole.

1930-31

President: Almon E. Roth
Palo Alto, California, USA
Number of clubs: 3,349; **members:** 153,000; **countries:** 66
New countries or geographical regions: Estonia, Hong Kong, Kenya,
Poland, Singapore (Straits Settlements), Taiwan (Formosa, Japan), and
Thailand (Siam)
Convention of 1931 (22-26 June): Vienna, Austria.
Registration: 4,296

HIGHLIGHTS: Intercountry committees originate with France and Germany.
Despite a weak global economy, seven more nations establish Rotary clubs.
Rotary has small but successful convention in Vienna. For the convention,
the Austrian government releases the first postage stamps honoring Rotary.

*Country or geographic region not currently in Rotary

1931-32

President: Sydney W. Pascall
London, England
Number of clubs: 3,460; **members:** 157,000; **countries:** 72
New countries or geographical regions: Lebanon
Convention of 1932 (20-24 June): Seattle, Washington, USA
Registration: 5,182

HIGHLIGHTS: As Depression deepens, Rotary records membership loss of 27 clubs and an overall decrease of 2,000 members. First European serves as president. Rotarians participate in disarmament conferences in Paris, France, and Geneva, Switzerland. Rotary Club of Los Angeles, California, USA, welcomes Rotarians to 1932 Olympic Games.

1932-33

President: Clinton P. Anderson
Albuquerque, New Mexico, USA
Number of clubs: 3,514; **members:** 155,000; **countries:** 75
New countries or geographical regions: Bulgaria and Latvia
Convention of 1933 (26-30 June): Boston, Massachusetts, USA
Registration: 8,430

HIGHLIGHTS: Chicago Rotarian Herbert J. Taylor formulates The Four-Way Test. A branch office of the Secretariat approved for Southeast Asia (established in Singapore in 1934, moved to Bombay in 1939, and closed in 1948).

1933-34

President: John Nelson
Montreal, Quebec, Canada
Number of clubs: 3,596; **members:** 146,322; **countries:** 76
Convention of 1934 (25-29 June): Detroit, Michigan, USA
Registration: 7,377

HIGHLIGHTS: Membership losses continue. *Revista Rotaria*, Spanish-language counterpart of THE ROTARIAN magazine, launched (discontinued 1990). Emerging from "retirement," Paul Harris travels to England, Scotland, and South Africa as official representative of RI at several district conferences. First Council on Legislation held as integral part of the RI Convention.

1934-35

President: Robert E. Lee Hill
Columbia, Missouri, USA
Number of clubs: 3,692; **members:** 150,000; **countries:** 76
New countries or geographical regions: Iceland and Lithuania
Convention of 1935 (17-21 June): Mexico City, Mexico
Registration: 5,330

HIGHLIGHTS: First Institute of International Relations, sponsored by Rotary Club of Nashville, Tennessee, USA, held to promote international understanding. Rotary gains two new nations, 150 clubs, and 12,406 members, reversing a membership decline. The six Objects of Rotary restated and reduced to four. Founder Paul Harris travels with his wife, Jean, to Asia, Oceania, and the Pacific Islands, then writes *Peregrinations, Volume II: We Become Pacific-Ocean Minded,* describing his travels.

1935-36

President: Ed R. Johnson
Roanoke, Virginia, USA
Number of clubs: 3,842; **members:** 162,406; **countries:** 78
New countries or geographical regions: Fiji and Tunisia
Convention of 1936 (22-26 June): Atlantic City, New Jersey, USA
Registration: 9,907

HIGHLIGHTS: Paul Harris embarks on trip to South America and attends the first South American Regional Conference. He writes *Peregrinations, Volume III: Our Neighbors on the South.*

1936-37

President: Will R. Manier Jr.
Nashville, Tennessee, USA
Number of clubs: 4,004; **members:** 170,000; **countries:** 81
New countries or geographical regions: Monaco and Netherlands Antilles
Convention of 1937 (6-11 June): Nice, France
Registration: 5,790

HIGHLIGHTS: RI adopts a general redistricting plan creating 23 new districts. President Manier predicts there will one day be 15,000 Rotary clubs in the world (mark was reached in 1971-72).

1937-38

President: Maurice Duperrey
Paris, France
Number of clubs: 4,335; **members:** 183,000; **countries:** 83
New countries or geographical regions: Bangladesh, Sudan, and Syria*
Readmitted countries or geographical regions: Venezuela
Convention of 1938 (19-24 June): San Francisco, California, USA
Registration: 10,432

HIGHLIGHTS: With World War II approaching, Germany's 42 clubs forced to discontinue, along with 11 clubs in Austria.

1938-39

President: George C. Hager
Chicago, Illinois, USA
Number of clubs: 4,714; **members:** 200,998; **countries:** 89
New countries or geographical regions: Aruba (Netherlands West Indies) and Cyprus
Convention of 1939 (19-23 June): Cleveland, Ohio, USA
Registration: 9,241

HIGHLIGHTS: Delegates at the convention approve the classification of senior membership (later called senior active membership; eliminated in 2001). Italy withdraws its 34 clubs from RI membership. The 5,000th Rotary club chartered in Rockmart, Georgia, USA.

*Country or geographic region not currently in Rotary

1939-40

President: Walter D. Head
Montclair, New Jersey, USA
Number of clubs: 4,967; **members:** 209,887; **countries:** 87
New countries or geographical regions: Guam and Senegal
(French West Africa)
Convention of 1940 (9-14 June): Havana, Cuba
Registration: 3,713

HIGHLIGHTS: Delegates at the convention adopt a "respect for human rights" resolution (later a model for UN's Universal Declaration of Human Rights): "...where freedom, justice, truth, sanctity of the pledged word, and respect for human rights do not exist, Rotary cannot live nor its ideals prevail." US$50,000 appropriated for war relief through the Red Cross, and Rotary Relief Fund set up to aid Rotarians and their families affected by war. Twenty-eight Rotary clubs in Spain removed from RI membership when disbanded in the wake of 1936 civil war. Rotary clubs in former Czechoslovakia cease to operate. Despite the hardships of World War II, Rotary continues to grow.

1940-41

President: Armando de Arruda Pereira
São Paulo, São Paulo, Brazil
Number of clubs: 5,066; **members:** 213,791; **countries:** 85
Convention of 1941 (15-20 June): Denver, Colorado, USA
Registration: 8,942

HIGHLIGHTS: A series of radio programs featuring talks by prominent Rotarians and others promoting goodwill and understanding are broadcast by 100 U.S. and Canadian radio stations and worldwide by shortwave radio. Due to World War II, Rotary loses 11 more countries. Several of Japan's 44 disbanded clubs continue to meet as Day of the Week clubs.

1941-42

President: Tom J. Davis
Butte, Montana, USA
Number of clubs: 5,058; **members:** 211,416; **countries:** 74
Convention of 1942 (21-25 June): Toronto, Ontario, Canada
Registration: 6,599

HIGHLIGHTS: Thousands of Rotarians and family members affected by the war. Rotarians launch food parcel deliveries to prisoner of war camps in Europe. Clubs in neutral Switzerland organize relief efforts for French and Belgian refugees. RI establishes a committee to study needs for a postwar peaceful world.

---

4   Readmitted countries or geographic regions do not include countries that lost their membership
    due to their own governmental intervention and were reinstated to RI membership after WWII.

1942-43

President: Fernando Carbajal
Lima, Peru
Number of clubs: 5,069; **members:** 208,363; **countries:** 70
New country or geographical region: Dominican Republic
Convention of 1943 (17-20 May): St. Louis, Missouri, USA
Registration: 3,851

HIGHLIGHTS: Rotary conference in London convened for ministers of education and observers of many nations to consider organizing a vast educational and cultural exchange, eventually resulting in UNESCO. Chesley R. Perry retires as RI general secretary; succeeded by Philip C. Lovejoy.

1943-44

President: Charles L. Wheeler
San Francisco, California, USA
Number of clubs: 5,174; **members:** 209,689; **countries:** 69
Convention of 1944 (18-22 May): Chicago, Illinois, USA
Registration: 403

HIGHLIGHTS: 290 clubs in 21 districts sponsor Institutes of International Understanding. In Finland, Rotary clubs initiate projects to aid children orphaned by World War II.

1944-45

President: Richard H. Wells
Pocatello, Idaho, USA
Number of clubs: 5,213; **members:** 227,913; **countries:** 63
Convention of 1945 (31 May, 5, 12, 19 June): Chicago, Illinois, USA
Registration: 141

HIGHLIGHTS: In Sweden, Rotarians play a prominent role in caring for 32,000 Finnish children uprooted by war. United Nations Relief and Rehabilitation Association calls upon clubs in the United States and Canada to spearhead community used-clothing drives for war-torn areas. Reorganization of clubs in liberated areas begins with Guam, Marianas Islands, and Dagupan, Philippines. Forty-nine Rotarians serve as delegates, advisers, or consultants of the original 50 member countries of the United Nations Conference on International Organization in San Francisco, California, USA.

1945-46

President: Thomas A. Warren
Wolverhampton, West Midlands, England
Number of clubs: 5,441; **members:** 247,212; **countries:** 65
Readmitted[4] country or geographical region: China*
Convention of 1946 (2-6 June): Atlantic City, New Jersey, USA
Registration: 10,958

HIGHLIGHTS: Boys Work and Boys Work Committee names changed to Youth Service and Youth Committee, respectively. World War II ends. With the required number of ratifications, the United Nations charter comes into force; during Charter Week every Rotarian encouraged to learn more about the UN. Discontinued clubs in Europe and Asia reinstated in Belgium, Burma, Czechoslovakia, France, Greece, Luxembourg, Norway, The Netherlands, and Straits Settlements.

Country or geographic region not currently in Rotary

1946-47

President: Richard C. Hedke
Detroit, Michigan, USA
Number of clubs: 5,828; **members:** 279,881; **countries:** 75
New country or geographical region: Macau
Convention of 1947 (8-12 June): San Francisco, California, USA
Registration: 14,678

HIGHLIGHTS: Founder Paul Harris dies 27 January 1947. As a memorial, graduate fellowship plan initiated with 18 fellowships granted for the 1947-48 academic year. RI Board issues call to comply with a mandate of the 1938 convention to raise US$2 million for The Rotary Foundation. Rotary returns to Italy, Malaya, Netherlands Indies, Siam, and Trieste.

1947-48

President: S. Kendrick Guernsey
Jacksonville, Florida, USA
Number of clubs: 6,234; **members:** 300,529; **countries:** 78
New country or geographical region: Aland Islands (Finland)
Readmitted country or geographical region: Taiwan (Formosa)
Convention of 1948 (16-20 May): Rio de Janeiro, Brazil
Registration: 7,511

HIGHLIGHTS: Rotary Foundation contributions exceed US$955,000. Fund of $15,000 allocated to continue relief to war-affected Rotarians. First convention held in the Southern Hemisphere. *Service Is My Business*, a 140-page manual for Vocational Service, published. Rotarians who left mainland China restore Rotary in Taiwan.

1948-49

President: Angus S. Mitchell
Melbourne, Victoria, Australia
Number of clubs: 6,540; **members:** 318,259; **countries:** 79
New country or geographical region: Tanzania (Tanganyika)
Readmitted countries or geographical regions: Japan and Korea
Convention of 1949 (12-16 June): New York, New York, USA
Registration: 15,961

HIGHLIGHTS: The last book written by Paul Harris, *My Road to Rotary*, published independently and sold by Kroch's Bookstores in Chicago. Rotary reestablished in Austria, Germany, and Saar Basin.

1949-50

President: Percy Hodgson
Pawtucket, Rhode Island, USA
RI theme: Objectives of Our Team for 1949-50

1. Each new member admitted into a Rotary club to be adequately informed about his duties and obligations before his induction—properly introduced to the club—and effectively assimilated into the work of the club during the first year.

2. A better understanding and application of the principles of Vocational Service as set forth in *Service Is My Business*.

3. A contribution to world understanding and peace through an intensification of our international service program.

4. An outstanding district conference in every district.

Number of clubs: 6,834; **members:** 329,342; **countries:** 82
Convention of 1950 (18-22 June): Detroit, Michigan, USA
Registration: 6,949

HIGHLIGHTS: Four-Way Test plaque distributed to all Rotary clubs. Since the end of World War II, more than 12,000 food and merchandise parcels sent to former Rotarians and their families in war-ravaged regions. The Rotary Foundation grants graduate fellowships to 55 students in 23 countries.

1950-51

President: Arthur Lagueux
Quebec, Quebec, Canada
RI theme: Goals for 1950-51

1. In club service we must beget our heirs.

2. In vocational service honesty is still the best policy.

3. In community service we can plan for the future.

4. In international service we must reexamine our world.

5. And finally we can extend the influence of Rotary.

Number of clubs: 7,113; **members:** 341,716; **countries:** 83
Convention of 1951 (27-31 May): Atlantic City, New Jersey, USA
Registration: 8,453

HIGHLIGHTS: The newly formed People's Republic of China dissolves 23 clubs. The Rotary Foundation's US$2 million goal reached. Convention delegates vote to change Rotary's Objects to one Object with four Avenues of Service—Club, Vocational, Community, and International.

1951-52

President: Frank E. Spain
Birmingham, Alabama, USA
Number of clubs: 7,357; **members:** 349,867; **countries:** 83
Readmitted country or geographical region: Kenya
Convention of 1952 (25-29 May): Mexico City, Mexico
Registration: 6,804

HIGHLIGHTS: Assignment of charter numbers to clubs discontinued. Convention delegates vote to build an RI headquarters building in or near Chicago.

1952-53

President: H.J. Brunnier
San Francisco, California, USA
Number of clubs: 7,574; **members:** 361,641; **countries:** 83
New countries or geographical regions: Namibia (South West Africa), Vietnam,* and Zambia (Northern Rhodesia)
Convention of 1953 (24-28 May): Paris, France
Registration: 10,107

HIGHLIGHTS: Philip Lovejoy retires as general secretary; succeeded by George R. Means. Ground is broken for a new headquarters building in Evanston, a Chicago suburb.

*Country or geographic region not currently in Rotary

1953-54

President: Joaquin Serratosa Cibils
Montevideo, Uruguay
RI theme: Rotary Is Hope in Action
Number of clubs: 7,841; **members:** 374,855; **countries:** 87
New countries or geographical regions: Brunei and Suriname
Convention of 1954 (6-10 June): Seattle, Washington, USA
Registration: 8,015

HIGHLIGHTS: Consultative groups set up to review and make Avenues of Service more effective. Rotary Foundation Fellowships granted to 101 students from 32 countries.

1954-55

President: Herbert J. Taylor
Chicago, Illinois, USA
RI theme: Six Objectives for 1954-55

1. Glean from the past and act

2. Share with others

3. Build with Rotary's Four-Way Test

4. Serving youth

5. International goodwill

6. Good Rotarians are good citizens

Number of clubs: 8,313; **members:** 392,628; **countries:** 89
New countries or geographical regions: Democratic Republic of the Congo (Belgian Congo; Zaire), Ethiopia, Malawi (Nyasaland), and Turkey
Convention of 1955 (29 May-2 June): Chicago, Illinois, USA
Registration: 14,312

HIGHLIGHTS: Rotary celebrates its golden anniversary, publishes a book, *Rotary: Fifty Years of Service*, and releases a motion picture, *The Great Adventure*. Commemorative postage stamps issued by 27 nations.

1955-56

President: A.Z. Baker
Cleveland, Ohio, USA
RI theme: Develop Our Resources
Number of clubs: 8,780; **members:** 418,933; **countries:** 92
New countries or geographical regions: Angola, Burundi (Ruanda-Urundi), Côte d'Ivoire (Ivory Coast), Iran,* Iraq,* Jordan, and Swaziland
Convention of 1956 (3-7 June): Philadelphia, Pennsylvania, USA
Registration: 10,003

HIGHLIGHTS: Rotarians help with flood relief to northeastern United States following hurricanes Connie and Diane. Baker travels 20,000 miles for six weeks to visit clubs in 10 African countries; visits a total of 40 countries and covers more than 60,000 miles during his year. Forty-eight Rotary Information and Extension Counselors appointed. The first biennial meeting of the Council of Legislation held immediately preceding the convention.

Country or geographic region not currently in Rotary

1956-57

President: Gian Paolo Lang
Livorno, Italy
RI theme: Three Targets 1956-57

1. Keep Rotary Simple

2. More Rotary in Rotarians

3. Learn More about Each Other

Number of clubs: 9,140; **members:** 433,798; **countries:** 99
New countries or geographical regions: Cambodia (Khmer Republic), Cameroon, Central African Republic, French West Indies (Guadeloupe), Liechtenstein, and Uganda
Convention of 1957 (19-23 May): Lucerne, Switzerland
Registration: 9,702

HIGHLIGHTS: One-day Rotary Information Institutes made a part of the program for Rotary districts. Paul Harris Fellow Recognition program launched. Rotary Foundation annual contributions top US$500,000. Foundation Week designated for week including November 15.

1957-58

President: Charles G. Tennent
Asheville, North Carolina, USA
RI theme: Enlist-Extend-Explore-Serve
Number of clubs: 9,507; **members:** 449,758; **countries:** 102
New countries or geographical regions: Chad (French Equatorial Africa), Republic of Congo (French Equatorial Africa), Eritrea, French Guiana, Laos,* Papua New Guinea (Papua), Trinidad & Tobago (British West Indies), and Virgin Islands
Readmitted countries or geographical regions: Belize and Indonesia
Convention of 1958 (1-5 June): Dallas, Texas, USA
Registration: 14,035

HIGHLIGHTS: A new International Service approach, Into Their Shoes conferences, initiated in which community groups representing different nations debate international issues.

1958-59

President: Clifford A. Randall
Milwaukee, Wisconsin, USA
RI theme: Help Shape the Future
Number of clubs: 9,878; **members:** 464,245; **countries:** 110
New countries or geographical regions: Ghana, Guyana (British Guiana), Jamaica (West Indies Federation), Madagascar (Malagasy), and Nepal
Convention of 1959 (7-11 June): New York, New York, USA
Registration: 15,475

HIGHLIGHTS: The week including 20 March (later including 23 February) designated World Understanding Week (changed to World Understanding Month in 1983). A new book on International Service, *Seven Paths to Peace,* introduced at the convention.

1959-60

President: Harold T. Thomas
Auckland, New Zealand
RI theme: Vitalize! Personalize! Build Bridges of Friendship!
Number of clubs: 10,226; **members:** 480,569; **countries:** 113
New countries or geographical regions: French Polynesia, San Marino, and Yemen*
Convention of 1960 (29 May-2 June): Miami-Miami Beach, Florida, USA
Registration: 11,354

HIGHLIGHTS: Rotary surpasses 10,000 clubs. Rotary Youth Leadership Awards (RYLA) takes root in Australia and New Zealand. Rotary world photo contest launched.

1960-61

310

President: J. Edd McLaughlin
Ralls, Texas, USA
RI theme: You Are Rotary—Live It! Express It! Expand It!
Number of clubs: 10,701; **members:** 498,616; **countries:** 116
New countries or geographical regions: Gabon, Mali, Nigeria, Reunion, and Somalia*
Convention of 1961 (28 May-1 June): Tokyo, Japan
Registration: 23,366

HIGHLIGHTS: THE ROTARIAN, commemorating its 50th year of publication, inserts a plastic recording of a message from the president. Rotary membership surpasses 500,000 in 122 countries and geographic areas. McLaughlin meets with U.S. President Dwight Eisenhower, honorary Rotarian.

1961-62

President: Joseph A. Abey
Reading, Pennsylvania, USA
RI theme: Act (Aim for Action, Communicate for Understanding, Test for Leadership)
Number of clubs: 11,021; **members:** 513,059; **countries:** 123
New countries or geographical regions: Bahamas, Barbados (British West Indies), Haiti, and New Caledonia
Convention of 1962 (3-7 June): Los Angeles, California, USA
Registration: 22,302

HIGHLIGHTS: The Rotary Foundation provides 134 Fellowships for International Study, bringing the total to 1,452 since 1947. U.S. President John F. Kennedy becomes honorary Rotarian in Hyannis, Massachusetts.

1962-63

President: Nitish C. Laharry
Calcutta, India
RI theme: Kindle the Spark Within
Number of clubs: 11,309; **members:** 528,297; **countries:** 128
New country or geographical region: Sierra Leone
Convention of 1963 (9-13 June): St. Louis, Missouri, USA
Registration: 10,779

HIGHLIGHTS: Small Business Clinics project to assist developing nations begins in five countries. Interact, a Rotary-sponsored service club for secondary school youth, started with first club in Melbourne, Florida, USA.

*Country or geographic region not currently in Rotary

1963-64

President: Carl P. Miller
Los Angeles, California, USA
RI theme: Meeting Rotary's Challenge in the Space Age
Number of clubs: 11,566; **members:** 542,432; **countries:** 129
New countries or geographical regions: Liberia and Mozambique
Convention of 1964 (7-11 June): Toronto, Ontario, Canada
Registration: 14,661

HIGHLIGHTS: Miller launches the Matched District and Club Program, a major international service initiative. Golfing Rotarians initiate World Fellowship (later Rotary Fellowships) activities.

1964-65

President: Charles W. Pettengill
Greenwich, Connecticut, USA
RI theme: Live Rotary
Number of clubs: 11,801; **members:** 558,638; **countries:** 125
New country or geographical region: Mauritius
Readmitted country or geographical region: Brunei
Convention of 1965 (30 May-3 June): Atlantic City, New Jersey, USA
Registration: 9,368

HIGHLIGHTS: During 60th anniversary year, president challenges Rotarians to fill three new classifications in each club and to charter three new clubs in each district. Thousands of Rotarians from around the world attend Rotary meetings at New York World's Fair.

1965-66

President: C.P.H. Teenstra
Hilversum, The Netherlands
RI theme: Action, Consolidation, and Continuity
Number of clubs: 12,114; **members:** 581,436; **countries:** 128
New countries or geographical regions: Bahrain, Benin (Dahomey),
Cayman Islands (British West Indies), Comoro Islands, and Gibraltar
Convention of 1966 (12-16 June): Denver, Colorado, USA
Registration: 12,929

HIGHLIGHTS: Rotarians from Europe, North Africa, and the eastern Mediterranean gather for Rotary conference in Amsterdam. Three new Foundation programs launched: Group Study Exchanges, Awards for Technical Training, and Grants for Activities in Keeping with the Objective of The Rotary Foundation (later called Matching Grants). Annual Foundation contributions exceed US$1 million.

1966-67

President: Richard L. Evans
Salt Lake City, Utah, USA
RI theme: A Better World through Rotary
Number of clubs: 12,460; **members:** 599,945; **countries:** 133
New countries or geographical regions: Rwanda and Saint Lucia (British West Indies)
Convention of 1967 (21-25 May): Nice, France
Registration: 19,362

HIGHLIGHTS: Clubs encouraged to support international service through the Matched District and Club Program, World Community Service, and Small Business Clinics. World Community Service program officially launched.

1967-68

President: Luther H. Hodges
Chapel Hill, North Carolina, USA
RI theme: Make Your Rotary Membership Effective
Number of clubs: 12,906; **members:** 620,827; **countries:** 134
New countries or geographical regions: Afghanistan, British Virgin Islands, Djibouti (French Territory of the Afars and the Issas), Faroe Islands, Malta, Niger, Northern Marianas (Trust Territory of the Pacific), Togo, and Tonga
Convention of 1968 (12-16 May): Mexico City, Mexico
Registration: 11,840

HIGHLIGHTS: Rotaract, a service organization for young men and women (18-30 years old), launched with its first club sponsored by the Rotary Club of North Charlotte, North Carolina, USA. Leadership Training Program formed to develop leadership at the club and district levels. Rotary Volunteers Abroad, in which Rotarians offer technical training and management counsel to developing countries, introduced. The Rotary Foundation celebrates its 50th anniversary.

1968-69

President: Kiyoshi Togasaki
Tokyo, Japan
RI theme: Participate!
Number of clubs: 13,324; **members:** 639,140; **countries:** 143
New countries or geographical regions: Cook Islands, Grenada, Libya,* and Seychelles
Convention of 1969 (25-29 May): Honolulu, Hawaii, USA
Registration: 14,453

HIGHLIGHTS: Significant Achievement Awards for clubs with outstanding international or community service projects presented for the first time. The Rotary Foundation funds 224 scholarships.

1969-70

President: James F. Conway
Rockville Centre, New York, USA
RI theme: Review and Renew
Number of clubs: 13,853; **members:** 660,259; **countries:** 146
New countries or geographical regions: American Samoa, Montserrat (British West Indies), and Saint Kitts-Nevis (West Indies Associated States)
Readmitted country or geographical region: Tunisia
Convention of 1970 (31 May-4 June): Atlanta, Georgia, USA
Registration: 10,803

HIGHLIGHTS: A worldwide poster contest for youth of secondary schools held with the theme World Peace through Understanding. The Rotary Foundation has a record year in contributions, numbers of awards granted, and Paul Harris Fellows. Delegates at Atlanta convention designate the Council on Legislation as the legislative body of RI.

Country or geographic region not currently in Rotary

1970-71

President: William E. Walk Jr.
Ontario, California, USA
RI theme: Bridge the Gaps
Number of clubs: 14,364; **members:** 682,183; **countries:** 148
New country or geographical region: Samoa
Readmitted country or geographical region: Indonesia
Convention of 1971 (16-20 May): Sydney, New South Wales, Australia
Registration: 16,646

HIGHLIGHTS: Foundation establishes new grants for Teachers of the Handicapped. Rotary Youth Leadership Awards (RYLA), a program originating in Australia and New Zealand, adopted as RI program.

1971-72

President: Ernst G. Breitholtz
Kalmar, Sweden
RI theme: Goodwill Begins with You
Number of clubs: 14,890; **members:** 706,372; **countries:** 149
New countries or geographical regions: Botswana, St. Vincent and the Grenadines (British West Indies), and Vanuatu (New Hebrides)
Convention of 1972 (11-15 June): Houston, Texas, USA
Registration: 13,287

HIGHLIGHTS: Rotarians worldwide respond to the plight of East Pakistan (now Bangladesh) refugees fleeing civil strife to India. George R. Means retires as RI general secretary; succeeded by Harry A. Stewart. The Council on Legislation meets for first time as the "parliament" of RI.

1972-73

President: Roy D. Hickman
Birmingham, Alabama, USA
RI theme: Let's Take a New Look—and Act
Number of clubs: 15,375; **members:** 725,271; **countries:** 149
New countries or geographical regions: Antigua and Baruda* (West Indies Associated States) and Norfolk Island
Convention of 1973 (13-17 May): Lausanne, Switzerland
Registration: 17,187

HIGHLIGHTS: Rotary Club of Chicago cedes territory for a second club at O'Hare Airport. New slideset, "The Most Important Man," produced for clubs. Presidents of four service organizations meet—Rotary, Kiwanis, Lions, and Junior Chamber. Rotarians respond to earthquake that kills 12,000 in Nicaragua.

1973-74

President: William C. Carter
Battersea, London, England
RI theme: A Time for Action
Number of clubs: 15,748; **members:** 742,493; **countries:** 150
New country or geographical region: Dominica (British West Indies)
Convention of 1974 (9-13 June): Minneapolis-St. Paul, Minnesota, USA
Registration: 10,015

HIGHLIGHTS: RI sponsors a worldwide photo contest on Rotary in Action; more than 1,000 entries and 3,500 pictures submitted; 50 winners chosen from 23 countries. Rotary membership surpasses 750,000.

1974-75

President: William R. Robbins
Ft. Lauderdale, Florida, USA
RI theme: Renew the Spirit of Rotary
Number of clubs: 16,087; **members:** 761,074; **countries:** 151
Convention of 1975 (8-12 June): Montreal, Quebec, Canada
Registration: 12,975

HIGHLIGHTS: Rotary Foundation scholarships awarded to 699 students. *The World of Rotary*, a 144-page book of photos and text, published in five languages. Rotarians from around the world aid victims of cyclone Tracy that destroys 90 percent of Darwin, Northern Territory, Australia.

1975-76

President: Ernesto Imbassahy de Mello
Niteroi, Rio de Janeiro, Brazil
RI theme: To Dignify the Human Being
Number of clubs: 16,520; **members:** 779,373; **countries:** 151
Convention of 1976 (13-17 June): New Orleans, Louisiana, USA
Registration: 13,935

HIGHLIGHTS: In May 1976, Rotary returns to Spain by organizing a club and being recognized as an association by the minister of the government of Spain. Rotary Foundation scholarships awarded to 794 students.

1976-77

President: Robert A. Manchester II
Youngstown, Ohio, USA
RI theme: I Believe in Rotary
Number of clubs: 16,917; **members:** 796,806; **countries:** 151
New country or geographical region: Lesotho
Readmitted country or geographical region: Spain
Convention of 1977 (5-9 June): San Francisco, California, USA
Registration: 14,168

HIGHLIGHTS: Network of Rotary regional magazines authorized as "official." A nine-year program, divided into three-year segments, matches clubs and districts as partners for international service projects. A world photo contest, Rotary in Action—Focus on Youth, brings in 429 entries and 2,000 photographs from 46 countries. The Rotary Club of Madrid, Spain, readmitted to RI membership in June 1977. First Handicamp in Norway includes able and disabled young people from several countries. Contributions to The Rotary Foundation top US$10 million annually.

1977-78

President: W. Jack Davis
Hamilton, Bermuda
RI theme: Serve to Unite Mankind
Number of clubs: 17,364; **members:** 813,704; **countries:** 152
New countries or geographical regions: Andorra, Anguilla, and United Arab Emirates
Convention of 1978 (14-18 May): Tokyo, Japan
Registration: 39,834

HIGHLIGHTS: Rotary Foundation educational awards granted to 820 students. Largest convention attendance in RI history.

1978-79

President: Clem Renouf
Nambour, Queensland, Australia
RI theme: Reach Out
Number of clubs: 17,814; **members:** 834,092; **countries:** 154
New country or geographical region: Mauritania
Convention of 1979 (10-13 June): Rome, Italy
Registration: 14,429

HIGHLIGHTS: Herbert A. Pigman succeeds Harry Stewart as RI general secretary. In keeping with the UN Year of the Child, RI adopts the slogan Rotary Cares...for the Child. Renouf initiates Health, Hunger and Humanity (3-H) Grants program. Rotary clubs begin to contribute to a two-year 75th Anniversary Fund for the development of the 3-H program. Pope John Paul II holds audience for Rotarians and guests at Rome convention.

1979-80

President: James L. Bomar Jr.
Shelbyville, Tennessee, USA
RI theme: Let Service Light the Way
Number of clubs: 18,252; **members:** 851,547; **countries:** 152
New countries or geographical regions: The Gambia and Greenland
Convention of 1980 (1-5 June): Chicago, Illinois, USA
Registration: 18,309

HIGHLIGHTS: Rotary celebrates its 75th anniversary worldwide. First 3-H polio immunization event (leading to PolioPlus) held in the Philippines. RI branch offices established in Stockholm, Sweden (closed in 1992); Parramatta, New South Wales, Australia; São Paulo, Brazil; and Tokyo, Japan.

1980-81

President: Rolf J. Klärich
Helsinki-Helsingfors, Finland
RI theme: Take Time to Serve
Number of clubs: 18,827; **members:** 875,949; **countries:** 154
Convention of 1981 (31 May-4 June): São Paulo, Brazil
Registration: 15,222

HIGHLIGHTS: Number of educational awards granted by The Rotary Foundation surpasses 1,000. In support of the UN's International Year of Disabled Persons, Klärich emphasizes needs of the disabled. First World Understanding and Peace Award goes to Dr. Noboru Iwamura of Japan.

1981-82

President: Stanley E. McCaffrey
Stockton, California, USA
RI theme: World Understanding and Peace through Rotary
Number of clubs: 19,339; **members:** 895,740; **countries:** 156
Convention of 1982 (6-9 June): Dallas, Texas, USA
Registration: 13,222

HIGHLIGHTS: McCaffrey emphasizes world understanding and peace, especially through eight Goodwill Conferences around the world. Seven-volume *Rotary Basic Library* information resource published in nine languages.

1982-83

President: Hiroji Mukasa
Nakatsu, Oita, Japan
RI theme: Mankind Is One—Build Bridges of Friendship throughout the World
Number of clubs: 19,785; **members:** 907,943; **countries:** 157
Convention of 1983 (5-8 June): Toronto, Ontario, Canada
Registration: 16,250

HIGHLIGHTS: Saint-Hilaire-du-Harcouët (Manche), France, becomes 20,000th Rotary club. Mukasa tours clubs, districts, and Rotary countries not often visited by an RI president. RI Secretariat branch office established in New Delhi, India.

1983-84

President: William E. Skelton
Christiansburg-Blacksburg, Virginia, USA
RI theme: Share Rotary—Serve People
Number of clubs: 20,189; **members:** 925,571; **countries:** 157
New country or geographical region: Burkina Faso
Convention of 1984 (3-7 June): Birmingham, England
Registration: 22,452

HIGHLIGHTS: Through Skelton's Presidential Citation Program and special emphasis on sharing Rotary, 714 new clubs chartered—the most clubs added in any Rotary year. The film *Your Secretariat* produced for clubs worldwide. 100,000th Paul Harris Fellow recognized.

1984-85

President: Carlos Canseco
Monterrey, Nuevo Leon, Mexico
RI theme: Discover a New World of Service
Number of clubs: 20,838; **members:** 961,256; **countries:** 159
Convention of 1985 (26-30 May): Kansas City, Missouri, USA
Registration: 12,920

HIGHLIGHTS: RI Secretariat branch office opens in Buenos Aires, Argentina. Polio 2005 (later PolioPlus) announced to immunize all the world's children as Rotary celebrates its 80th anniversary. In support of Canseco's one-million-member goal, a record 968 new clubs chartered.

1985-86

President: Edward F. Cadman
Wenatchee, Washington, USA
RI theme: You Are the Key
Number of clubs: 21,669; **members:** 991,047; **countries:** 159
New country or geographical region: Guinea
Convention of 1986 (1-4 June): Las Vegas, Nevada, USA
Registration: 18,426

HIGHLIGHTS: Rotary's membership tops one million in February 1986, as Jean-Paul Moroval of Thionville, France, recognized as millionth member. RI Secretariat branch offices authorized for Seoul, Korea, and Manila, Philippines (closed in 2000). New clubs admitted to RI total 824, the second-highest number in Rotary history. Rotary announces three-year fundraising goal of US$120 million for PolioPlus.

1986-87

President: M.A.T. Caparas
Manila, Philippines
RI theme: Rotary Brings Hope
Number of clubs: 22,365; **members:** 1,013,033; **countries:** 160
New country or geographical region: Solomon Islands
Convention of 1987 (7-10 June): Munich, Germany
Registration: 26,909

HIGHLIGHTS: Philip H. Lindsey succeeds Herbert A. Pigman as RI general secretary. Rotary Village Corps pilot program established to improve the quality of life in villages, neighborhoods, and communities. Rotary abides by a U.S. Supreme Court decision admitting qualified women to clubs in the United States.

1987-88

President: Charles C. Keller
California, Pennsylvania, USA
RI theme: Rotarians—United in Service—Dedicated to Peace
Number of clubs: 23,095; **members:** 1,038,747; **countries:** 160
New country or geographical region: Mayotte
Convention of 1988 (22-25 May): Philadelphia, Pennsylvania, USA
Registration: 16,316

HIGHLIGHTS: PolioPlus Campaign nearly doubles its original goal of US$120 million and raises more than $220 million for polio immunization. RI embarks on partnership with the World Health Organization and UNICEF to eradicate polio worldwide. The Rotary Foundation initiates Peace Forums. One Rotary Center, the organization's new World Headquarters in downtown Evanston, Illinois, USA, dedicated. For first time in 50 years, the RI Vocational Service Committee meets and redefines focus on club project opportunities. *Rotary News Network* video magazine debuts as information resource.

1988-89

President: Royce Abbey
Essendon, Victoria, Australia
RI theme: Put Life into Rotary—Your Life
Number of clubs: 23,679; **members:** 1,056,888; **countries:** 162
New country or geographical region: Saint Pierre and Miquelon
Readmitted countries or geographical regions: Hungary and Poland
Convention of 1989 (21-24 May): Seoul, Korea
Registration: 38,878

HIGHLIGHTS: Rotaract restructured to provide members more responsibility. A strategic plan for RI developed that includes district reorganization. Rotary Volunteers in Action launched as a pilot program. The triennial Council on Legislation, meeting in Singapore, votes to allow all clubs to admit qualified women. The Rotary Village Corps (later Rotary Community Corps) granted official program status. The Foundation recognizes the 250,000th Paul Harris Fellow.

1989-90

President: Hugh M. Archer
Dearborn, Michigan, USA
RI theme: Enjoy Rotary!
Number of clubs: 24,419; **members:** 1,091,056; **countries:** 167
New countries or geographical regions: Micronesia, Russia (USSR), and Slovenia
Readmitted countries or geographical regions: Czech Republic and Mozambique
Convention of 1990 (24-27 June): Portland, Oregon, USA
Registration: 21,053

HIGHLIGHTS: The Rotary Club of Moscow, first service club in the (former) Soviet Union, chartered. The 25,000th Rotary club (Torreon-Campestre, Coahuila, Mexico) chartered. Archer promotes Rotary's Recreational and Vocational Fellowships. Spencer Robinson Jr. named RI general secretary.

1990-91

President: Paulo V.C. Costa
Santos, São Paulo, Brazil
RI theme: Honor Rotary with Faith and Enthusiasm
Number of clubs: 25,160; **members:** 1,121,230; **countries:** 172
New countries or geographical regions: Croatia and Slovakia
Readmitted country or geographical region: Estonia
Convention of 1991 (2-5 June): Mexico City, Mexico
Registration: 15,638

HIGHLIGHTS: Costa originates Preserve Planet Earth program; more than 2,000 clubs carry out environmental projects. Audiovisual department wins Television and Video Association Gold Award for environmental video, *We Are the Guardians*. The Rotary Peace Programs (Rotary Peace Forums) of the Foundation granted official status. Limited-edition book, *Rotary Wisdom: Reflections on Service*, published.

1991-92

President: Rajendra K. Saboo
Chandigarh, Union Territory, India
RI theme: Look Beyond Yourself
Number of clubs: 25,583; **members:** 1,143,333; **countries:** 172
New countries or geographical regions: Albania, Cape Verde, and Ukraine
Readmitted countries or geographical regions: Algeria, Bulgaria, Latvia, Romania, and Serbia and Montenegro (Federal Republic of Yugoslavia)
Convention of 1992 (14-17 June): Orlando, Florida, USA
Registration: 19,111

HIGHLIGHTS: The Rotary Foundation celebrates 75th anniversary with annual contributions of US$41 million, PolioPlus contributions of nearly $4.6 million, and an endowment of over $8 million. The Foundation awards 1,060 scholarships. Rotary, together with World Health Organization and UNICEF, marks achievement of 80 percent level of immunization of the world's children against six major diseases, including polio. Saboo convenes four Presidential Conferences for Cooperation and Development and speaks at United Nations celebration of Universal Childhood Immunization. In Hong Kong, Rotary cosponsors Third International Abilympics for the disabled.

1992-93

President: Clifford L. Dochterman
North Stockton, California, USA
RI theme: Real Happiness Is Helping Others
Number of clubs: 25,928; **members:** 1,155,810; **countries:** 184
New countries or geographical regions: Lithuania and Sao Tome & Principe
Convention of 1993 (23-26 May): Melbourne, Victoria, Australia
Registration: 22,083

HIGHLIGHTS: Sixteen Salutes to the Programs of Rotary recognize Rotary service around the world. Dochterman leads Rotary, Rotaract, and Interact clubs worldwide to raise US$3 million in aid to refugees of the former Yugoslavia. RI Presidential Conferences for Goodwill and Cooperation held in Spain and South Africa and at the United Nations in New York, USA. Rotaract celebrates its 25th anniversary. A 10-year drug and alcohol abuse prevention program initiated. At the Melbourne convention, the symbolic 500 millionth child immunized against polio.

1993-94

President: Robert R. Barth
Aarau, Switzerland
RI theme: Believe in What You Do—Do What You Believe In
Number of clubs: 26,525; **members:** 1,173,558; **countries:** 187
New country or geographical region: Belarus
Convention of 1994 (12-15 June): Taipei, Taiwan
Registration: 31,161

HIGHLIGHTS: Eight outstanding Rotary at Its Best service projects are recognized in different regions. Presidential Conference on Goodwill and Development held in Geneva, Switzerland, to celebrate Rotary's partnership with UN. Preserve Planet Earth and Rotary Volunteers adopted as official programs. Herbert Pigman named general secretary a second time.

1994-95

President: Bill Huntley
Alford & Mablethorpe, Lincolnshire, England
RI theme: Be a Friend
Number of clubs: 27,026; **members:** 1,190,102; **countries:** 185
New countries or geographical regions: Former Yugoslav Republic of Macedonia and Mongolia
Readmitted country or geographical region: Cambodia
Convention of 1995 (11-14 June): Nice, France
Registration: 34,077

HIGHLIGHTS: Rotary, PAHO (Pan American Health Organization), WHO, UNICEF, and others celebrate the eradication of polio in the Americas. Council on Legislation, meeting in Caracas, Venezuela, affirms global polio eradication as "a priority of the highest order for all of RI." Six Presidential Friendship Conferences held. Celebrating Rotary's 90th anniversary, World Window Week features public displays of Rotary projects worldwide. *Rotary World* newspaper launched in 10 languages, replacing several newsletters.

1995-96

President: Herbert G. Brown
Clearwater, Florida, USA
RI theme: Act with Integrity, Serve with Love, Work for Peace
Number of clubs: 27,446; **members:** 1,170,936; **countries:** 186
New countries or geographical regions: Kazakhstan, Republic of Palau, and Turks and Caicos Islands
Convention of 1996 (23-26 June): Calgary, Alberta, Canada
Registration: 24,963

HIGHLIGHTS: A Commitment to Family emphasis instituted. RI establishes Web site (www.rotary.org). The PolioPlus Partners program created. The first eight women serve as district governors. Rotary reorganized into 34 zones for the purpose of nominating RI directors. Brown's emphasis on recruiting new members increases Rotary membership by 35,176. Membership opened to qualified retired persons. Past RI Vice President William Sergeant begins tenure as chair of International PolioPlus Committee. Geoffrey S. Large named RI general secretary.

1996-97

President: Luis Vicente Giay
Arrecifes, Buenos Aires, Argentina
RI theme: Build the Future with Action and Vision
Number of clubs: 28,134; **members:** 1,206,112; **countries:** 189
New countries or geographical regions: Antarctica and Armenia
Convention of 1997 (15-18 June): Glasgow, Scotland
Registration: 23,506

HIGHLIGHTS: A New Generations initiative by Giay encourages involvement with youth. District Leadership Plan adopted by 30 districts, giving districts more flexibility in structure and administration. The Rotary Foundation launches three new programs: Helping Grants, New Opportunities Grants, and 3-H Planning Grants. Educational Programs celebrate 50th anniversary. Annual Programs contributions reach US$60.3 million. 1,277 Ambassadorial Scholarships awarded to students from 60 countries to study in 66 countries.

1997-98

President: Glen W. Kinross
Hamilton, Brisbane, Queensland, Australia
RI theme: Show Rotary Cares for your community, for our world, for its people
Number of clubs: 28,736; **members:** 1,213,748; **countries:** 190
New countries or geographical regions: Republic of Georgia and Republic of Moldova
Readmitted country or geographical region: Eritrea
Convention of 1998 (14-17 June): Indianapolis, Indiana, USA
Registration: 19,002

HIGHLIGHTS: Emphasis on "urban peace" initiated as Kinross spotlights the need for improved shelter. Literacy adopted as a pilot program. The first RI President's Conference held in Russia. The Council on Legislation meets in New Delhi, India, and liberalizes rules for attendance. S. Aaron Hyatt becomes RI general secretary.

1998-99

President: James L. Lacy
Cookeville, Tennessee, USA
RI theme: Follow Your Rotary Dream
Number of clubs: 29,113; **members:** 1,201,595; **countries:** 195
New countries or geographical regions: Azerbaijan and Kyrgyzstan
Convention of 1999 (13-16 June): Singapore, Singapore
Registration: 17,903

HIGHLIGHTS: Lacy encourages Rotarians to take on projects addressing children's needs. The RI Board and Rotary Foundation Trustees adopt a one-time US$20 million initiative called Children's Opportunities Grants to fund projects helping children. Special Dreams for the Future Committee formed to evaluate new project ideas from Rotarians. The Foundation agrees to establish a new program, the Rotary Centers for International Studies in peace and conflict resolution.

1999-2000

President: Carlo Ravizza
Milano Sud-Ovest, Italy
RI theme: Rotary 2000: Act with Consistency, Credibility, Continuity
Number of clubs: 29,728; **members:** 1,193,461; **countries:** 195
New countries or geographical regions: Bosnia-Herzegovina
Convention of 2000 (4-7 June): Buenos Aires, Argentina
Registration: 14,301

HIGHLIGHTS: Foundation Trustees approve 10,000th Matching Grant, US$22,633 for medical equipment to Ukraine. Edwin H. Futa named RI general secretary.

2000-01

President: Frank J. Devlyn
Anáhuac, Distrito Federal, Mexico
RI theme: Create Awareness—Take Action
Number of clubs: 29,626; **members:** 1,180,550; **countries:** 197
Convention of 2001 (24-27 June): San Antonio, Texas, USA
Registration: 24,092

HIGHLIGHTS: Western Pacific region, including People's Republic of China, declared polio-free. Devlyn focuses attention and support on treating avoidable blindness and promotes Rotary presence on the World Wide Web and Internet. Rotary surpasses 30,000 clubs.

2001-02

President: Richard D. King
Niles (Fremont), California, USA
RI theme: Mankind Is Our Business
Number of clubs: 30,149; **members:** 1,188,492; **countries:** 197
Readmitted country or geographical region: United Arab Emirates
Convention of 2002 (23-26 June): Barcelona, Spain
Registration: 19,059

HIGHLIGHTS: Emphasis on membership growth adds 54,939 members, a 4.6 percent increase. The European region, including countries of the former Soviet Bloc, declared polio-free. Presidential Peace Forums held in Jordan and Turkey. A supplemental campaign, the polio eradication fundraising campaign (PEFC), initiated to raise US$80 million. Foundation annual giving reaches $81 million. 929 Ambassadorial Scholars from 56 countries study in 59 countries; 35 university teachers from nine countries serve in 24 countries.

2002-03

President: Bhichai Rattakul
Dhonburi, Bangkok, Thailand
RI theme: Sow the Seeds of Love
Number of clubs: 30,256; **members:** 1,243,431; **countries:** 200
New country or geographical region: Democratic Republic of Timor-Leste
Readmitted country or geographical region: Afghanistan
Convention of 2003 (1-4 June): Brisbane, Queensland, Australia
Registration: 14,147

HIGHLIGHTS: First class of 70 Rotary World Peace Scholars begins studies. Rotary and the U.S. Department of State sponsor a meeting in Seattle, Washington, focusing on the global scourge of abandoned land mines. The number of Paul Harris Fellows reaches 850,000. Rotarians worldwide raise US$111,499,350 for the PEFC, the 15-month polio eradication fundraising campaign.

2003-04

President: Jonathan B. Majiyagbe
Kano, Nigeria
RI theme: Lend a Hand
***Number of clubs:** 31,561; **members:** 1,227,545; **countries:** 166
Convention of 2004 (23-26 May): Osaka, Japan

HIGHLIGHTS: Majiyagbe, the first RI president from Africa, places emphasis on poverty alleviation, health concerns, literacy and education, and promoting the family of Rotary. *A Century of Service— The Story of Rotary International* introduced at the International Assembly in Anaheim, California, USA.

*As reported in semiannual report for the period 1 January to 30 June 2003.

2004-05

President: Glenn E. Estess Sr.
Shades Valley, Alabama, USA
Convention of 2005 (19-22 June): Chicago, Illinois, USA

HIGHLIGHTS: Rotary celebrates centennial worldwide. Rotary moves into its second century of Service Above Self as the world's first and most international service club organization.

Rotary Award for World Understanding and Peace

T he Rotary Award for World Understanding and Peace was first presented in 1981 to recognize and honor a non-Rotarian or organization for outstanding achievement consistent with the ideals and objectives of

Rotary International.

Rotarians may nominate individuals or organizations involved in local or international humanitarian efforts. A selection committee reviews the
qualifications of each nominee and chooses a recipient. The RI president and
trustee chairman confirm the selection on behalf of the RI Board of Directors
and The Rotary Foundation Trustees.

Prior to 1993, a cash award was presented in the form of 10 Rotary Foundation scholarships designated by the recipient. Since 1993, a contribution of
US$100,000 has been donated to support a project of the recipient's choice,
with the approval of the RI Board.

1981

Dr. Noboru Iwamura of
Japan, medical volun-
teer and activist.

1982

Pope John
Paul II,
pontiff of
the Roman
Catholic
Church.

1983

Lotta Hitschmanova of Canada, founding director of the Unitarian Service Committee, Canada.

1984

The World Organization of the Scout Movement. Accepted by Laszlo Nagy, then secretary-general of the organization.

1985

Dr. Albert B. Sabin of the United States, developer of the oral polio vaccine.

1986

The International Committee of the Red Cross. Accepted by Harald Schmid de Gruneck, Red Cross delegate to international organizations.

1987

Hermione, Countess of Ranfurly, O.B.E. of Great Britain, founder of Ranfurly Library Service (now International Book Aid).

1988

The Salvation Army. Accepted by Andrew S. Miller, then United States national commander of the organization.

1989

No award given.

1990

Václav Havel, former president of Czechoslovakia and first president of the Czech Republic (1993-2003).

1991

Javier Pérez de Cuéllar of Peru, former secretary-general of the United Nations.

1992

Edward J. Piszek of the United States, philanthropist and developer of Peace Corps Partners in Teaching English.

1993

Dr. Frederick Hollows of Australia, ophthalmologist and medical volunteer. Grant project: Fred Hollows Foundation.

1994

Jimmy Carter, former president of the United States, founder of the Carter Center in Atlanta, Georgia, USA, and 2002 Nobel Peace Prize laureate. Grant project: Council of Freely Elected Heads of Government Program of the Carter Center of Emory University.

1995

James P. Grant, former executive director of UNICEF. Grant project: Polio Eradication in Egypt, program of UNICEF.

1996

Sadako Ogata of Japan, former UN high commissioner for refugees. Grant project: GLOBE—environmental education program of UNHCR. (Ogata is a former Rotary Foundation Scholar.)

1997

Nelson Mandela, former president of South Africa and 1993 Nobel Peace Prize laureate. Grant project: Nelson Mandela Children's Fund.

1998

Dr. Catherine Hamlin of Australia, obstetrician and founding director of the Addis Ababa Fistula Hospital in Ethiopia. Grant project: Addis Ababa Fistula Hospital.

1999

Dr. Muhammad Yunus of Bangladesh, founder of the Grameen Bank (introduced the concept of microcredit or village banking in developing countries). Grant project: Grameen Foundation USA.

2000

No award given.

2001

Dr. Pramod Karan Sethi of India, orthopedic surgeon and inventor of the Jaipur foot. Grant project: Jaipur Limb Training Centers.

2002

Dr. Norman E. Borlaug of the United States, agricultural researcher known as the father of the Green Revolution and 1970 Nobel Peace Prize laureate. Grant project: Educational agricultural projects in Iowa, USA, and Mexico.

2003

Professor Federico Mayor of Spain, founder and chairman of Fundación Cultura de Paz (Culture of Peace Foundation) and former director-general of UNESCO. Grant project: Peace conferences in Europe and democratic media training workshops for young people in Guatemala.

100 Prominent Rotarians

The following list reflects the diversity of intellectual, cultural, military, sports, and government leaders around the world who have been active or honorary members of Rotary clubs. The list is a selective sampling and by no means complete.

1. Neil Armstrong, astronaut and first man to walk on the Moon, USA
   (RC Wapakoneta, Ohio)
2. Ásgeir Ásgeirsson, president, Iceland *(RC Reykjavík)*
3. Eusebio Ayala, president, Paraguay *(RC Asuncion)*
4. King Baudouin I of Belgium *(RC Brussels)*
5. Fernando Belaunde Terry, president, Peru *(RC Lima)*
6. Prince Bernhard of The Netherlands *(RC Amsterdam)*
7. Clarence Birdseye, developer of a process for quick-freezing food, USA
   (RC Gloucester, Massachusetts)
8. Harry A. Blackmun, Supreme Court justice, USA *(RC Rochester, Minnesota)*
9. Frank Borman, astronaut, USA *(RC Space Center, Houston, Texas)*
10. Sir Norman Brearley, aviation pioneer, Australia
    (RC Perth, Western Australia)
11. John Briggs, concert pianist, England *(RC Bingley)*
12. Jose Luis Bustamante y Rivero, president, Peru *(RC Arequipa)*
13. Richard E. Byrd, admiral and Arctic explorer, USA
    (RC Winchester, Virginia)
14. Josep Ma. Vayreda Canadell, painter, Spain *(RC Girona)*
15. Alcino Cardoso, secretary of state, Portugal *(RC Porto-Douro)*
16. Roger Chapelain-Midy, painter, France *(RC Paris)*
17. Sir Winston Churchill, prime minister, England *(RC London; RC Wanstead & Woodford)*
18. Max Cointreau, owner of Cointreau liquor enterprises, France *(RC Paris)*
19. Arthur Holly Compton, Nobel Prize laureate in physics, USA
    (RC St. Louis, Missouri)

20. Sir William Deane, governor general, Australia *(RC Sydney, New South Wales)*

21. Michel Debré, prime minister, France *(RC Amboise)*

22. Maurice Denuzière, writer, France *(RC Vitry-Sud-Est de Paris)*

23. Walt Disney, animation filmmaker, USA *(RC Palm Springs, California)*

24. Jorge Fidel Duron, minister of foreign affairs, Honduras *(RC Tegucigalpa; past RI director)*

25. Thomas A. Edison, inventor, USA *(RC Orange, New Jersey)*

26. Marcelo B. Fernan, Supreme Court chief justice, Philippines *(RC Cebu West)*

27. Prince Frederik of Denmark *(RC Copenhagen)*

28. J. William Fulbright, senator, USA *(RC Fayetteville, Arkansas)*

29. Sir Kenneth Fung Ping-Fan, director of the Bank of East Asia, Ltd., Hong Kong *(RC Hong Kong; past RI district governor)*

30. Sir W. Hudson Fysh, founder of Qantas Airlines, Australia *(RC Sydney)*

31. Hans-Dietrich Genscher, foreign minister, Germany *(RC Bonn Süd-Bad Godesberg)*

32. Edgar A. Guest, poet and journalist, USA *(RC Detroit, Michigan)*

33. King Carl XVI Gustaf of Sweden *(RC Stockholm)*

34. Lorenzo Guerrero Gutierrez, president, Nicaragua *(RC Granada)*

35. Warren G. Harding, president, USA *(RC Washington, D.C.)*

36. Joel Chandler Harris, author, USA *(RC Atlanta, Georgia)*

37. Reijiro "Rei" Hattori, chairman of Seiko, Japan *(RC Tokyo Ginza; past RI director)*

38. Steingrimur Hermannsson, prime minister, Iceland *(RC Reykjavík)*

39. Thor Heyerdahl, explorer and oceanographer, Norway *(RC Larvik)*

40. Sir Edmund Hillary, explorer and mountaineer, New Zealand *(RC Auckland)*

41. Ko Hirasawa, anatomist and president of Kyoto University, Japan *(RC Kyoto East)*

42. John F. Kennedy, president, USA *(RC Hyannis, Massachusetts)*

43. Abdulla Khalil, prime minister, Sudan *(RC Khartoum)*

44. Chung Yul Kim, prime minister, Korea *(RC Hanyang)*
Note: Other prime ministers from this club include Duck Woo Nam, Choong Hoon Park, and Chang Soon Yoo

45. Karl Kobelt, president, Swiss Confederation *(RC St. Gallen)*

46. Chucri Kouatly, president, Syria *(RC Damascus)*

47. Hans Küng, theologian, Germany *(RC Reutlingen-Tübingen)*

48. Sir Harry Lauder, entertainer, Scotland *(RC Glasgow)*

49. Jean Leclant, Egyptologist, France *(RC Paris)*

50. Franz Lehar, composer, Austria *(RC Wien)*

51. Douglas MacArthur, army general, USA *(RC Milwaukee, Wisconsin; RC Melbourne, Australia; RC Tokyo, Japan; RC Manila, Philippines)*

52. Thomas Mann, novelist and Nobel Prize laureate in literature, Germany *(RC Munich)*

53. Robert Manuel, theater director, France *(RC Paris)*

54. Guglielmo Marconi, inventor and Nobel Prize laureate in physics, Italy *(RC Bologna)*

55. George C. Marshall, army general and Nobel Peace Prize laureate, USA *(RC Columbus, Georgia; RC Savannah, Georgia; RC Charleston, South Carolina; RC Uniontown, Pennsylvania)*

56. Jan Masaryk, foreign minister, Czechoslovakia *(RC Prague)*

57. Konosuke Matsushita, president of Matsushita Electric Co., Japan *(RC Osaka)*

58. Dr. Charles H. Mayo, co-founder of the Mayo Clinic, USA *(RC Rochester, Minnesota)*

59. Cornelius "Connie Mack" McGillicuddie, baseball manager and team owner, USA *(RC Philadelphia, Pennsylvania; RC Fort Myers, Florida)*

60. Dr. Karl Menninger, psychiatrist and co-founder of the Menninger Clinic, USA *(RC Topeka, Kansas)*

61. Cesare Merzagora, president of the senate, Italy *(RC Rome)*

62. Toyohiko Mikimoto, president, K. Mikimoto and Co., Ltd., Japan *(RC Tokyo)*

63. Lennart Nilsson, photographer, Sweden *(RC Stockholm)*

64. Georges Octors, orchestra conductor, Belgium *(RC Bruxelles, Brabant)*

65. Raul Sapena Pastor, prime minister, Paraguay *(RC Asunción; past RI district governor)*

66. Norman Vincent Peale, clergyman and author, USA *(RC New York, New York)*

67. Lester Pearson, prime minister, president of UN general assembly and Nobel Peace Prize laureate, Canada *(RC Ottawa, Ontario)*

68. James Cash Penney, founder of J.C. Penney Company, USA *(RC New York, New York)*

69. John J. "Black Jack" Pershing, army general, USA *(RC St. Louis, Missouri; RC Lincoln, Nebraska; RC San Antonio, Texas)*

70. Prince Philip, Duke of Edinburgh *(RC Edinburgh, Scotland; RC King's Lynn and RC Windsor & Eton, England)*

71. Antoine Pinay, prime minister, France *(RC Saint-Etienne)*

72. Leopoldo Pirelli, president of Pirelli Tire Co., Italy *(RC Milano)*

73. Joan Abello Prat, painter, Spain *(RC Barcelona Condal)*

74. Emilio Pucci, couturier, Italy *(RC Florence)*

75. Prince Rainier III of Monaco *(RC Monaco)*

76. James Whitcomb Riley, poet, USA *(RC Indianapolis, Indiana)*

77. Sigmund Romberg, composer, USA *(RC New York, New York)*

78. Carlos P. Romulo, president of UN General Assembly, Philippines
(RC Manila; past RI vice president)

79. Franklin D. Roosevelt, president, USA *(RC Albany, New York)*

80. Wolfgang Schallenberg, secretary general of the ministry of foreign
affairs, Austria *(RC Paris Ouest, Hts-de-Seine, France; RC Madrid, Spain;
RC Wien)*

81. Walter Scheel, president, Germany *(RC Bonn)*

82. Albert Schweitzer, physician, philosopher, and Nobel Peace Prize
laureate, Gabon *(RC Colmar, France; RC Passau, Germany)*

83. Kiyoshi Seike, architect, Japan *(RC Tokyo-Meguro)*

84. Donna Shalala, secretary of health and human services, USA
(RC Madison, Wisconsin; RC Coral Gables, Florida)

85. Kenjiro Shoda, president, Osaka University, Japan *(RC Osaka)*

86. Jean Sibelius, composer, Finland *(RC Helsinki-Helsingfors)*

87. Tris Speaker, baseball player, USA *(RC Cleveland, Ohio)*

88. Sir Sigmund Sternberg, businessman and philanthropist, England
(RC London)

89. Adlai E. Stevenson, ambassador to the United Nations and governor of
Illinois, USA *(RC Springfield, Illinois)*

90. Prince Tsuneyoshi Takeda of Japan *(RC Tokyo-North)*

91. Margaret Thatcher, prime minister, England
(RC Westminster East, Greater London)

92. Claude Vuitton, owner of Vuitton luggage enterprise, France
(RC Paris Nord)

93. Charles R. Walgreen Jr., chairman of Walgreen Drug Co., USA
(RC Chicago, Illinois)

94. Earl Warren, Supreme Court chief justice, USA
(RC Sacramento, California)

95. Jack Williamson, science fiction writer, USA *(RC Portales, New Mexico)*

96. Woodrow Wilson, president and Nobel Peace Prize laureate, USA
(RC Birmingham, Alabama)

97. Orville Wright, aviation pioneer, USA *(RC Dayton, Ohio)*

98. Philip Wylie, author and social commentator, USA
(RC Middletown, Connecticut)

99. Chia-kan "C.K." Yen, president, Republic of China-Taiwan *(RC Taipei)*

100. Willy Zumblick, painter and sculptor, Brazil *(RC Tubarão)*

Index

A

Papua New Guinea and, 154, 158, 161, 166, 265–266
PolioPlus and, 239
Queensland, 124, 173, 266, 315 (*See also* Brisbane)
recruiting in, 80, 82
RI office in, 208
Rotaract and, 168–169, 170, 175
Rotary Centers for International Studies and, 202
Rotary presidents from, 122, 145, 197, 227, 234, 306, 315, 317
RYLA and (*See* Rotary Youth Leadership Awards [RYLA])
Solomon Islands and, 161, 266
Victoria, 120, 154–155, 306, 317 (*See also* Melbourne, Australia, club)
women in, 185
Youth Exchange program of, 163
Australian Rotary Health Research Fund (ARHRF), 143
Austria, 73
first club in, 82
in World War II, 98, 99
Austvik, Asbjorn, 2
Aversano, Vince, 2
Ayala, Eusebio, 327

B

Babbit [Lewis], 108, 109–111
Baby Bundles, 185
Bahia Blanca club, 95
Bahrain, 106
Baker, A.Z., 108, 171, 216–217, 218, 308
Carbajal and, 222
Bali club, 253
Balkan states, 108, 203
Balloon (of Piccard), 72
Baltic states, 108
Baltimore Hotel, 72
Bandoeng club, 86
Bangkok, 86, 224, 322
Bangladesh, 122–123, 263, 274
floods in, 162
Bangour Military Hospital, 91
BARC. *See* British Association of Rotary Clubs (BARC)
Barcelona, 158
Bardon club, 266
Bareuther, Ernie, 3
Barnard-Jones, Keith, 262
Barth, Robert R., 156–157, 158, 192, 274, 319
Batavia club, 86
Batt, Bruno, 42, 43
Battersea club, 313
Baudouin I (Belgium), 126, 327
Baxter, Doc, 149
Bayswater club, 154–155
Bear, Montague M. ("Monty"), 54, 68, 131

Beck, Cynthia M., 2
Beirut, 165, 282
Belaunde Terry, Fernando, 327
Belfast club, 79, 90–91, 213, 282
Belgian World War I relief, 64, 100, 159
Belgium, 72, 215, 252. *See also* Ostend club; Ostend convention
king of, 55, 126, 327
luncheon for king of, 76–77, 78
Bellamy, Carol, 197, 235
Benter, William, 261
Berger, Ernest, 81
Berlet, Jack, 69
Berlin club, 96, 107
Berlin wall, collapse of, 109, 110, 200
Bermuda, 122, 233, 314
Bernhard (Netherlands), 327
Berringer, George, 70
Berrish, Lily, 178–179, 180
Bertrand, Jean, 131
Bilger, Frank W., 38
Birdseye, Clarence, 327
Birmingham, Alabama, club, 91, 107, 307, 313
Birmingham, England, club, 80, 213
Bismarck Beer Garden, 49
Bjorge, Oscar, 70–71
Blackmun, Harry A., 327
Blane, Jack, 239, 243
Blind people, 143
Bloemfontein, 108
Bohemia, 99
Bolivia, 161, 195, 237
Bomar, James L., Jr., 164, 188, 199, 201, 222, 315
in Manila, 235–236, 247
quoted on being "torchbearers," 272
Bombay club, 84, 199
Booth, Jessie, 54
Borch, Otto, 117, 118
Borlaug, Norman, 326
Borman, Frank, 72, 327
Boston club, 41, 79
business ethics training by, 64
highway project of, 140–141
Boston convention, 98, 213
Boston Post, 141
Boulder County club, 120
Bourget, Paul, 25
Bourguiba, Habib, 126
Bowling Alone [Putnam], 272–273
"Boy Orator," 30
Boy Scouts, 115, 172, 173, 325
Boyd, Weston, 69
Boys' Clubs of America, 171
Boys to the Farm committee, 92
Boys Weeks, 173
Boys Work, 165, 172–173, 175
Brazil, 95, 151, 152, 155, 252, 253–254
polio vaccine in, 246
Rotaract and, 175
Rotary presidents from, 219, 304, 314, 318

Russia and, 259
Sào Paulo convention in, 69, 195
Brearley, Norman, 327
Breitholtz, Ernst G., 140, 313
Brennan, Charles J., 223
Brevoort Hotel, 20, 29
Briggs, John, 327
Brisbane, 161, 320
    RYLA and, 173–174
    scholarship program and, 124
British Association of Rotary Clubs (BARC), 214
Brittan, Ron, 259–260
Britten, John, 37
Brock, Lynmar, Jr., 190–191, 192, 261
Brown, Ancil T., 81
Brown, Herbert G., 109, 143, 184, 241, 320
    membership turnaround and, 274
    quoted on his dreams for future, 271
Brown, Stephen, 248–249, 250
Bru, Federico Laredo, 102–103, 104
Brunnier, Ann, 183, 184
Brunnier, Henry J. ("Bru"), 155, 184, 307
Brush, Allison G., 117
Brussels club, 198
Bryan, Cornelia, 11
Buch, Walter, 97
Buckley, David, 121
Buell, Ida, 182–183
Buenaventura club, 151
Buenos Aires, 124, 161, 195, 208, 320
Buffalo club, 65, 150
Buffalo convention, 150
Bulgaria, 108
Bullock, Arthur, 41
Bunker, Alva, 171
Burkina Faso, 246
Burlington club, 198
Burma, 85, 86
Burnett, Richard E., 2
Business, 5, 275
    "booster," 26, 27–28, 64, 149, 280
    in early Rotary meetings, 63
    ethics in (See Ethics)
    and first Rotary club, 4, 26, 27–28, 30, 31
    Golden Rule and, 149, 151, 153
    international service and, 161
    leaders in, 219, 220
    and object(s) of Rotary, 62–63, 141
    Penney quoted on, 149
    Togasaki quoted on, 150
    vocational service and, 148, 149
    Wemple quoted on, 150
    women in, 182, 187–188, 275
Bussey, Fred, 140
Bustamante y Rivero, Jose Luis, 327
Butte club, 304
Bylaws, Rotary, 31, 32, 43, 48, 59–61
    amendments to, 172, 193
    model, 60
Byrd, Richard E., 29, 72, 80, 327

C

Cadman, Edward F., 127, 131, 275, 316
Cady, Daniel L., 41, 42, 49
Cairo club, 84
Calcutta club, 85, 86, 146–147, 148, 310
Calgary club, 83, 240
California, 31, 173, 248–249, 250, 256, 274. *See also* Los Angeles club; San Francisco club
    first club in, 38
    GSE in, 119, 165
    Oakland, 38, 64, 140
    Rotary presidents from, 301, 305, 313, 315, 319, 322
    Santa Barbara, 178–179, 180
    Uganda and, 260
    women in, 187–188
California, Pennsylvania, club, 317
Cambodia, 244, 246, 263
Camden Town Clinic, 142
Cameroon, 268–269, 270
Camp Whittier, 178–179, 180
Campinas, 152
Canada, 82–83
    Alberta, 83, 193, 240
    Brazil and, 252
    CIDA and, 167
    during Great Depression, 95
    in IFFR, 252
    Malawi and, 256
    Manitoba, 78, 298
    Montreal, 302
    Ontario, 162, 167, 172, 176, 252, 299
    opposition to Rotary in, 105
    peacemaking by, 194–195, 200
    PolioPlus and, 235, 240, 243, 247
    Quebec, 302, 307
    Rhodesia and, 6
    3-H project of, 122
    United States cooperating with, 162, 195
    during World War I, 91
    Youth Exchange and, 176
Canadell, Josep Ma. Vayreda, 327
Canadian International Development Agency (CIDA), 167
Caño-Negro Development Project, 253
Canseco, Carlos, 233, 238, 275, 316
Canton club, 86
Caparas, M.A.T., 236, 276, 317
Cape Town club, 185, 186
Cape Verde club, 251
Capozzoli, Lou, 251, 252
Caracas, RI visit to, 105
Caracas club, 253
Carbajal, Fernando, 105, 199, 222, 305
Cardosa, Alcino, 327
C.A.R.E., 159
Caribbean, CIDA and, 167
Carmel Valley club, 250

as president, 31–32, 49, 50, 52, 296–297
as president emeritus, 52, 53
quoted on business, 63, 64
quoted on community service, 31
quoted on democracy, 224
quoted on Freemasonry, 104
quoted on "good ship Rotary," 279
quoted on Loehr, 27
quoted on Perry, 46, 54, 55
quoted on "toleration," 50, 200
quoted on Tweed, 30, 41
reason for starting Rotary, 281
religion and, 21
RI World Headquarters and, 207
ROTARIAN, THE, tribute to, 280
Rotary emblem and, 68
Rotary Foundation and, 116, 127
as Rotary's father, 53
as Rotary's roving ambassador, 53
statisticians and, 63, 150
at Tomb of the Unknowns, 90
trees of friendship and, 53
"trophy" office of, 29
at 25th anniversary convention, 93
vagabond years of, 19, 37, 53
wife of, 46 (*See also* Harris, Jean)
Wood and, 40, 140
World War II and, 101
writing in Rotary magazine by, 50, 51, 53
Hartford, Connecticut, club, 99
Hattori, Reijiro ("Rei"), 328
Havana club, 81, 141
Havana convention, 95, 96, 100
Cuba's president at, 102–103, 104
human rights resolution at, 100, 195–196
Havel, Václav, 126, 325
Havens, Raymond M., 299
Hawaii, 93, 257, 264, 276
Hawing, Federico Diaz, 228–229, 230
Hawley, Clark W. ("Doc"), 30, 93, 139
He Profits Most Who Serves Best, 47, 49, 58, 61, 150
Head, Walter D., 95, 102–103, 104, 304
Health, Hunger and Humanity (3-H) Grants, 122–123, 149, 164–165
PolioPlus and, 233, 234, 235, 237–238
Hedke, Richard C., 219, 306
Heemstede club, 240
Heifer Project International, 166
Helsinki club, 82, 219, 315
Helsinki-Helsingfors club, 315
Henningham, H. Paul, 2
Hermannsson, Steingrimur, 328
Hermione, Countess of Ranfurly, 325
Hernandez, Lilia, 176
Herriot's Turkish Baths, 185
Hesselmark, Bo and Helena, 258
Hester, Harry D., 2
Heyerdahl, Thor, 82, 328
Hickman, Roy D., 313

Hilkert, Robert C., 51
Hill, Everett W., 300
Hill, Robert E. Lee, 302
Hillary, Edmund, 328
Hillegom-Lisse club, 240
Hilversum club, 311
Himmler, Heinrich, 97
Hingson, Robert, 232, 233, 234
Hirasawa, Ko, 328
Hitler, Adolph, 96, 97, 98, 108
Hitschmanova, Lotta, 325
Ho Chi Minh City, 253, 263–264
Hodges, Luther H., 216–217, 218, 224, 312
Hodgson, Percy C., 212, 306–307
Hogan, Connard, 178–179, 180
Holland, 6, 240
Hollenbeck Hotel, 39
Hollows, Frederick, 325
Holman, Arthur S., 5, 37, 38, 39, 40
Holmes, Oliver Wendell, 283
Holsko, Kai, 264–265
Home Coming Celebration and Carnival, 140–141
Home Products Week, 151
Hong Kong, 86, 261
Honolulu, 257, 264, 276
Hoover, Herbert, 93
Hopper, Keith, 165–166
Houghton, Michigan, club, 72
House of Friendship, 133, 164
Housing, 138, 145
Houston club, 71
Houston convention (of 1914), 140, 142, 184
Hoyos, Kathrin, 186
Huanuco, 145, 277
Human rights resolution, 100, 195–196
Hungary, 108, 151
Hunt, Robert, 152
Huntington club, 301
Huntley, Bill, 197, 281, 319
Hussein (Jordan), 126

I

Iceland, 160, 224
Idaho, 305
If Christ Came to Chicago [Stead], 25
IFFR. *See* International Fellowship of Flying Rotarians (IFFR)
Igloo, Rotary meeting in, 135
IIE. *See* Institute of International Education (IIE)
Ikamva School Readiness Programme, 185
Illinois, 234, 239, 251, 257, 277. *See also* Chicago club
Imbassahy de Mello, Ernesto, 314
Immigrants, 141
In the Minds of Men, 198
Independence, Iowa, club, 101
India, 84, 123, 143, 144, 155, 199
Interact in, 175

Rotaract Preconvention Meeting in, 168–169, 170

Melbourne, Florida, club, 174

Mello, Jose Humberto, 258–259

Membership and Extension Month, 71

Mencken, H.L., 7, 109, 111, 280

Menninger, Karl, 329

Mergulhão, Lucia, 252

Merzagora, Cesare, 329

Metropolitan Honolulu club, 257

Mettler, Lee, 180

Mexico, 106, 143, 149, 228–229, 230, 235, 258, 271, 274
    polio vaccine and, 238
    Rotary presidents from, 105, 275, 301, 316, 321
    Youth Exchange and, 176

Mexico City convention, 207

Mexico convention, 106

Meyers, Richard, 139

Michigan, 42, 200, 244, 306, 318

Middle East, 276

Midwest, 42–43

Migliaro, F.A., 201

Mikimoto, Toyohiko, 329

Milan club, 82, 106

Milano Sud-Ovest club, 277, 321

Miller, Carl P., 163, 311

"Million Dollar Meals," 116

Milwaukee club, 309

Minneapolis club, 42, 150, 192, 298

Minneapolis convention, 73, 116

Minneapolis Journal, 182

Minneapolis Women's Rotary Club, 182

Minnesota, 42, 52, 158. *See also* Minneapolis club; St. Paul club

Missouri, 139, 302. *See also* Kansas City club

Mitchell, Angus S., 197, 306

Mitsui Bank, 265

Mohammad Khail Refugee Camp, 190–191, 192, 261–262

Moini, Fary, 180, 248–249, 250

Mombasa club, 158

Montana, 194, 304

Montclair club, 304

Monterey Park club, 259

Monterrey club, 238, 275, 316

Montevideo club, 195, 212, 271, 308

Monticelli, Carlo, 220

Montreal club, 302

Moravia, 99

Mornington, Australia, club, 143

Morocco, 238

Moroval, Danielle, 131

Moroval, Jean-Paul, 131

Morrow, Stuart, 79–80, 213

Moscow club, 106

Mott, Frank Kanning, 38

Moyers, Bill, 124, 125

Mozambique, 123

Mukasa, Hiroji, 199, 316

Mulholland, Frank, 54, 71, 81, 192, 297
    Lewis, Sinclair, and, 110

Mulitsch, Sergio, 237

Muma, Irwin J. ("Jerry"), 39, 180

Muncie club, 95

Muncie Plan, 95

Muñoz, Manuel, 4, 6, 36–39
    Harris and, 33, 37, 43
    Wood and, 37

Munster club, 224

Musaka club, 260–261

Muslims. *See* Islamic/Muslim nations

My Road to Rotary [Harris], 130, 145, 279

Myanmar, 86

Myung, Ro Chul, 263–264

N

Nagoya club, 209

Nairobi, 254

Nakajima, Hiroshi, 237

Nakatsu club, 199, 316

Nall, Spencer, 73

Nam, Duck Wo, 224

Nambour club, 234, 315

Nashville club, 200, 303

National Association of Rotary Clubs of America, 43, 58, 149–150
    Civic Committee of, 141, 149
    early difficulties in, 51–52
    formation of, 49
    name change of, 52, 78
    number of clubs in first year of, 52
    objectives of, 62
    Rotary emblem and, 68
    women and, 180, 182

National Boys Work Committee, 172

National Immunization Day (NID), 233, 242, 244, 245
    in Cameroon (subnational), 268–269, 270
    in Cape Verde, 251
    in Ethiopia, 270
    in Nigeria, 264
    statistics on, 246, 247

National Institute for the Blind, 143

National Restaurant Association, 152

National Rotarian, The, 49, 50–51
    "brag sheets" in, 64
    changed to ROTARIAN, THE, 51
    highway project and, 141

National Rotary Club, 39, 40, 43

National Society for Crippled Children, 172

Nazareth club, 198

Nebraska, 42, 141

Neff, Will R., 93

Nehru, Pandit, 85

Nelson, John, 94, 96–97, 107, 302

Nepal, 195, 263

Netherlands, 134, 151, 311

debate about small-town clubs in, 59
emblem design and, 70
during Great Depression, 94
leadership articles in, 219
Lillian Davidson's travelogues in, 85
name change to, 51
New Delhi club written about in, 85
peacekeeping and, 195, 200
Pigman and, 166
polio vaccine and, 232
Rotary Foundation and, 116
in Spanish, 51
tribute to Harris in, 280
UNESCO and, 197
women and, 183
during World War I, 91
during World War II, 97
"Rotarian Club," 28
Rotarians. *See also specific countries, states, and cities*
    African American, 106
    Catholic, 105
    contradictions represented by, 130
    differences among, 58, 60, 133
    first, 26–28
    as Freemasons, 104
    Jewish, 97
    as kings, princes, etc., 86, 281
    as leaders, 130, 219
    Muslim, 106
    nicknames for, 30, 48, 109, 111
    as Nobel Prize winners, 63, 64, 126, 200, 282
    non-Caucasian, 107
    one millionth one, 131
    prominent/notable, 81, 82, 108, 134, 327–330
    refugee, 100, 196
    at signing of UN charter, 199
    women as, 178–189
Rotary. *See also* National Association of Rotary
        Clubs of America; Rotary International
        (RI); *specific cities for specific clubs*
    after Harris stepped down as president, 52–53
    anniversary date of, 71, 161
    as "booster club," 26, 27–28, 64, 149
    community service as soul of, 140 (*See also*
        Community service)
    constitution and bylaws of (*See* Bylaws, Rotary;
        Constitution, Rotary)
    convention of (*See* Rotary Convention[s])
    critics of, 7, 109–111, 280
    definition of, 60, 72
    differing ethnicities, cultures, faiths of, 5, 133,
        162
    districts created for, 61
    dues for, 29, 51, 79
    early names for, 28
    expansion across United States of, 33, 34–42
    expansion to international organization, 51,
        52, 76–87, 159
    father of, 53
    50th anniversary of, 117

fines by, 29, 132
first board of directors of, 29
first club of, 4, 138 (*See also* Chicago club)
first club to meet weekly, 38
first meeting of, 26
first president of, 11, 29, 49
first project of, 24
first roster printed of, 29
first rules established for, 29
as first service club, 4, 6
formative years of, 58
founder of (*See* Harris, Paul P.)
fun at meetings of, 131–133, 160
global spread of, 5, 6
highlights of first century of, 296–323
idea of national body for, 43, 46, 47
landmarks in first century of, 290–295
magazine of, 1, 2, 49, 50–51 (*See also*
        ROTARIAN, THE)
"Marco Polo" of, 83
membership growth of, 29, 93, 96, 281
membership retention in, 135
membership rules for, 29, 60, 134–135, 148
motto/slogan of, 47, 58, 150
naming of, 28–29, 60
number of clubs at beginning of, 29
objects/objectives of (*See* Object[s] of Rotary)
opposition to expansion of, 40–41, 43
origin of, 4
philosophy of, 58–65
pins for perfect attendance at, 133
platform of, 61
politics and, 60, 63, 167
prediction by Cady about, 49
presidents of (*See* Rotary presidents)
reason for success of, 281–282
registered as trademark, 40
second club of, 37 (*See also* San Francisco
        club)
second meeting of, 28
75th anniversary of, 122, 164, 165, 233, 234,
        237 (*See also* PolioPlus)
shift toward service in, 64–65, 149–150
singing introduced to meetings of, 28, 30
in small towns, 58–59, 134
territorial limits of, 60
third meeting of, 28
treasurer of, 30
25th anniversary of, 56–57, 58, 93
UN and early, 5
in United States and Canada, 75
Western Division of the United States, 59
women and (*See* Women)
"Rotary Anns," 183–184
Rotary Award for World Understanding and
        Peace, 106, 118, 126, 127, 197, 233
    all recipients of, 324–326
    first one, 195
Rotary Awareness Month, 71
Rotary banners, 72, 134, 254

350
S